politicizing the person-centred approach

an agenda for social change

edited by

gillian proctor
mick cooper
pete sanders
beryl malcolm

PCCS BOOKS

Monmouth

First published in 2006 by PCCS Books, Ross-on-Wye

PCCS Books Ltd
Wyastone Business Park
Wyastone Leys
Monmouth
NP25 3SR
UK
Tel +44 (0)1600 891 509
www.pccs-books.co.uk

**Politicizing the Person-Centred Approach:
An agenda for social change**

A CIP catalogue record for this book is available from the British Library

ISBN   978 1 898059 72 1

Cover design by Old Dog Graphics
Printed by Imprint Digital, Exeter, UK

CONTENTS

SOCIO-POLITICAL ISSUES AND THE THERAPY RELATIONSHIP

ACKNOWLEDGEMENTS

The Editors wish to thank Sandy Green for her patient copy-editing and proofreading of this book and Maggie Taylor-Sanders for her behind-the-scenes support.

Authors and the Editors would like to thank the following for permission to reprint words and images.

Poems/Lyrics:
Pages 82 & 83. *Bloody Revolutions*. Crass. Southern Records. <www.southern.com>
Page 242. 'Yes' in *The Way It Is: New and selected poems*. William Stafford. Graywolf Press. <www.graywolfpress.org>

Graphic images:
Page 100. *She's Got Your Eyes*. Concept: Warren Neily; photo: Shannon Mendes. Adbusters Media Foundation. <www.adbusters.org>
Page 107. *Nothing*™ *Billboard*. Fiona Jack. Adbusters Media Foundation. <www.adbusters.org>

Chapter 1

OPENING REMARKS

Gillian Proctor

Is the person-centred approach political? The answer to this question often seems clear when people first discover the person-centred approach (PCA). They frequently speak of how the politics and ethics that it is founded upon attracted them. Rogers' (1978) claim that the approach is 'revolutionary' focuses on how the PCA challenged traditional approaches to therapy and relating based on hierarchies; instead promoting an egalitarian ideal of humans relating as equal persons, whatever their roles, status or position.

Surely an approach based on challenging hierarchies and authorities and advocating trust in oneself is political? Surely an approach that aims to liberate us from internalized messages from others (conditions of worth), to be able to grow as individual unique people, is political? Surely an approach so concerned with avoiding taking power over people, and promoting personal power is political? Surely a theory that suggests that distress is not the result of internal individual dysfunction but a result of dysfunctional relationships is political?

Yet the connection between the person-centred approach and politics is far from clear or straightforward. Politics usually involves acting as a collective and speaking about groups of people. However, speaking as 'we' is unusual in the person-centred world. It could be that an emphasis on the uniqueness of each individual and a phenomenological approach seems to lead to a denial or missing of commonalities among people. It could be that a focus on all persons as equal regardless of role or status, leads to an obscuring of inequalities and the effects of this in society. Recently in person-centred literature, the approach has been criticized for its individualism, and lack of attention to the socio-political context. (For further consideration of how structural positions affect therapy and the importance of the therapist's awareness of this see, for example, Kearney, 1996; Moodley, Lago & Talahite, 2004 and Proctor & Napier, 2004.)

Traditionally, professional bodies representing counsellors or therapists have made a point not to take a political position, suggesting these professions should be 'apolitical'. Samuels (in Pointon, 2006) warns that statutory regulation could make political involvement even more difficult for counsellors and therapists. Many, who are well aware that to be 'apolitical' means supporting the status quo, hoped for a different response from the person-centred community, and this is one of the essential theses of this book (see Sanders, Chapter 11 and Proctor

Chapter 9, this volume). However, it seems to be the experience of many people that politics is ignored or sidelined in the PCA, and those who hoped for a home in the person-centred community with like-minded political people are often left disappointed and frustrated. Barfield (2004, and Chapter 22, this volume) describes her story of putting feminism on the agenda in person-centred circles at the Center for Studies of the Person in La Jolla, California (where Carl Rogers was based), in the 1970s. She describes a range of reactions, ranging from defensiveness and hostility to trying to understand what she was saying about commonalities among women. Wolter-Gustafson (personal communication, see Proctor & Napier, 2004: 2) discussed how over decades of trying to get feminism on the agenda at person-centred conferences in the US, she was met with a similar range of reactions. However, she also expressed hope that the recent increasing acceptance of politics could lead to politics becoming a legitimate topic. Indeed, this hope follows a similar trajectory in the UK—almost becoming a noticeable trend. The British Association for the Person-Centred Approach (BAPCA) conference in 2002 had a theme of 'difference and diversity', setting the tone for discussion of inequalities and politics and allowing them to become a prominent theme of discussion throughout. My experience of the various reactions to these issues ranged from hostility, defensiveness and protesting irrelevance to relief that finally a space had been found to discuss these issues. There did seem to be a growing body of people wanting to find a bigger space to put together politics and the person-centred approach. This was reminiscent of previous person-centred meetings where anything political was brought to the agenda (see Proctor & Napier, 2004: 1–2). In October 2005, a network was formed at a Person-Centred Therapy Scotland conference on 'Politics and the PCA'. The new network, 'Person-Centered Practitioners for Social Change' (PCPSC) agreed the following statement at the first meeting:

We want to voice our opposition to inequalities and oppression in the world.
We celebrate diversity and commit ourselves to working towards social justice.
We aim to raise public awareness about the political, social and economic causes of distress in society.
We aim to promote relationships where people listen to each other and each person has a voice.
We believe in acting with honesty, integrity and transparency, whilst aiming to value and understand all others.

So what do we mean by politics, or political? Politics involves looking at society and groups of people, of speaking about how our world is organized and resources distributed. It involves inequalities between people in this distribution and in opportunities and how this is dealt with. Fundamentally it is rooted in sociology rather than psychology, studying society and groups of people and their relationships rather than individual internal psyches. Major political movements such as feminism focus on commonalities among people as a result of their shared position in society. Of course, a simplistic broad-brush approach to talking as if big groups of people are all in the same position is a strategy that was much criticized in second wave feminism (see Warner, 2004). This critique recognized that other aspects of identity (such as ethnicity, class and sexuality) in addition to gender led to important differences among various groups of women. The later move towards 'identity politics' brought a much more individualized approach to politics, emphasizing again the uniqueness of individuals and the 'right' to this uniqueness. This position prioritized the voice of personal experience and each individual's unique story. However, as with a phenomenological method such as the person-centred approach, using each person's individual experience to campaign for political change fails to analyse the structures of power involved in whose experiences are heard. Warner (2004) discusses the dilemmas inherent in using personal experiences politically and suggests we need to be mindful and clear about what strategies are useful in using personal experience. The challenge for politics today is to incorporate all these perspectives from major political movements such as feminism, to be able to talk about commonalities as a result of oppressed positions and structures in society, whilst not ignoring differences within groups of people. Can the person-centred approach live up to this challenge?

This collection of writings is an attempt to begin to answer the question. In this book, we explore the interface between the person-centred approach and radical political theory and activity. Specifically, it aims to explore the contribution that a critical analysis of social and political factors can make to the theory and practice of person-centred therapy, and to examine the contribution that person-centred theory and practice can make to the wider sphere of socio-political theory and activity. This is a gathering of many different voices; a range of contributions from academic theorizing and critical analysis through personal testimony, and description of radical projects to practical suggestions for change.

We hope this collection will encourage the reader to consider their own political positioning both within the PCA and in the wider world, and perhaps inspire contributions to this continuing agenda, both by debate and action for change.

REFERENCES

Barfield, G (2004) A personal odyssey: Shaping political and feminist principles in the Person-Centred Approach. In G Proctor & MB Napier (eds) *Encountering Feminism: Intersections between feminism and the person-centred approach* (pp. 39–58). Ross-on-Wye: PCCS Books.

Kearney, A (1996) *Counselling, Class and Politics: Undeclared influences in therapy.* Ross-on-Wye: PCCS Books.

Moodley, R, Lago, C & Talahite, A (eds) (2004) *Carl Rogers Counsels a Black Client: Race and culture in person-centred counselling.* Ross-on-Wye: PCCS Books.

Pointon, C (2006) Engaging political gear. *Therapy Today: The magazine for counselling and psychotherapy professionals, 17* (1), 4–7.

Proctor, G & Napier, MB (eds) (2004) *Encountering Feminism: Intersections between feminism and the person-centred approach.* Ross-on-Wye: PCCS Books.

Rogers, CR (1978) *Carl Rogers on Personal Power: Inner strength and its revolutionary impact.* New York: Delacorte Press.

Warner, S (2004) Radical politics from the Women's Liberation Movement to Mad Pride. In C Shaw & G Proctor (eds) Women at the margins: Women and Borderline Personality Disorder. *Asylum: The magazine for democratic psychiatry, 14* (3), 30–4.

Chapter 2

POLITICS AND THERAPY: MAPPING AREAS FOR CONSIDERATION

Pete Sanders

Whenever the issues of politics and therapy come up, they bring with them a myriad of possibilities, from the debates concerning regulation and professionalization through to the advantages of including a psychotherapeutic perspective in all government committees. Yet these possibilities are rarely considered, discussed or elaborated in public amongst person-centred practitioners. This short chapter is an attempt to map out the possible intersections between politics and therapy to help locate debates and issues in the readers' wider experiences in the field of therapy and the helping professions. Although this book specifically addresses the intersections between the person-centred *approach* and politics, this chapter concerns itself with a slightly different set of intersections, namely between *therapy* in general and politics.

It is possible, and indeed necessary, to trace and debate the logical and historical trajectories of the areas for consideration on the metaphorical map, but there is not sufficient space to do that here. Instead, I intend to present these areas for consideration *naïvely*, and invite the reader to debate the issues, contents and boundaries of each area, in detail, themselves. This is a deliberate strategy, since engaging in the debate to develop understanding of what therapists do is something in which all therapists must participate for the sake of their prospective clients and for themselves. In a similar vein, whilst this list was compiled in the hope that it might be complete, it surely cannot be. Again the reader is invited to test, develop and discard elements and improve the material presented—it is offered as a starting point.

When preparing this material, I had, in my mind's eye, a checklist with two columns of boxes—that is, two boxes against each of the numbered points. I mentally ticked the first box if I felt that I had addressed the issue in my own thinking and practice. I ticked the second box if I knew of any *person-centred* contribution on theory or practice related to the issue. If I could not tick the second box, I then tried to imagine what a person-centred contribution might be. I invite readers to do the same. A moment's further thought and I realized that we might usefully have a third checkbox indicating whether the issue is dealt with by this book. There would be many unticked boxes in that column, but I hope that, like the collection of papers in this book, this list proves to be a starting point for person-centred therapists to address some of these issues locally and internationally, from personal practice through to professional institutions. Along the way I share some personal musings on what person-centred therapies might contribute.

THE MAP OF AREAS FOR CONSIDERATION

1 The politics of the *helping professions* and their institutions: ideologies, professionalization, regulation

2 The politics of *helping theories*:
    2.1 The nature of the 'problem' including:
        i images of humanness (including, is the client treated as an infant or responsible adult?)
        ii 'pathology' (is distress an illness?):
            a internal factors
            b external factors:
                • interpersonal, e.g. power and the nature of oppression
                • environmental, e.g. material, social and economic conditions
    2.2 The location of the 'problem' (distress): the individual, or social conditions?
    2.3 The nature of possible 'solutions':
        i emancipation
        ii change
        iii adjustment

3 The place of politics in *helping practice*:
    3.1 Is there a way of behaving in and around helping sessions that acknowledges the political domain, or appears to be oblivious to it, or appears to actively ignore it, etc?
    3.2 The role of the therapist (as a 'helper', as a 'companion', as a 'professional', as an 'expert', as a 'person'—a feature of the environment [part of the client's self-chosen resources, becoming part of the actualizing tendency])

4 The contribution that 'helping' as a group of theories, an activity and a profession, makes to contemporary life and contemporary political life: politicization of everyday life, contribution to consumerism, global capitalism, media, employment, ideologies of what it is to be human, success, happiness, etc.

5 How the above issues are dealt with in the *training* of counsellors and psychotherapists

6 The helper as citizen

1 THE POLITICS OF THE HELPING PROFESSIONS AND THEIR INSTITUTIONS

Many therapists, theorists and writers espouse the view that helping—counselling or psychotherapy—is benign and apolitical. Ironically this view is most often found in the very institutions promoting helping as a profession. Often, when it is reluctantly acknowledged that helping might have a political dimension, spokespersons engage with the topic at the level of content only, i.e. suggesting that the professional body is neutral and must therefore present a balanced picture, rather like the BBC is believed to be, which is expected to demonstrate that it is a 'neutral' commentator on events.

The fallacy of this position is not lost on a significant minority of commentators, including, Bates, 2000; Bates & House, 2003; House, 1999; House & Totton, 1997; Mowbray, 1995; Totton, 1999. Indeed in the first part of the twenty-first century, to maintain that the counselling and psychotherapy 'industry' is apolitical is more than faintly ridiculous in the light of the writings of, e.g. Hillman & Ventura, 1992; Rose, 1996; and Smail, 2005. Others have pointed to the medicalization of distress (Sanders, 2005), government guidelines for 'treatment', and the involvement of 'big pharma' in the 'helping professions' (Mosher, 1998; Healy, 2001, 2004) as equally obvious political intersections. Politics is the elephant sitting in the corner of the room whenever the professions of counselling, psychotherapy and psychology convene.

The issues of professionalization and regulation are not simple. For many qualified counsellors, the slender chances of financially viable employment would disappear altogether if they renounced their membership of their professional body. It is clear that employers want compliant, accredited, (possibly soon-to-be registered) counsellors in post, not anti-regulation mavericks. It is often only those who are, by dint of good fortune, beyond the reach of the system who can continue to point to the problematical politics of professionalization. John Heron (1990/1997) and Denis Postle (2005), amongst others, alert us to the disturbing fact that as government-encouraged regulation of counselling and psychotherapy approaches and we must visit a state-regulated therapist for state-approved therapy, we are close to having a state-regulated mental life.

Person-centred practitioners are caught in a particularly uncomfortable position, since Rogers himself could be counted amongst the ranks of the anti-regulationists. Although he did not directly address the issue of regulation and professionalization of therapy in *On Personal Power* (1978), his chapter 'The politics of administration' is critical of hierarchical, undemocratic systems. A few years earlier in a paper presented in 1972 (Rogers, 1980), he *was* more direct in a section titled 'Dare we do away with professionalism?'

> It is my considered judgment that tight professional standards do not, to more than to a minimal degree, shut out the exploiters and the charlatans ... I have slowly come to the conclusion that if we did away

with 'the expert', 'the certified professional', 'the licensed psychologist', we might open our profession to a breeze of fresh air, a surge of creativity, such as has not been known for years. In every area—medicine, nursing, teaching, bricklaying, or carpentry—certification has tended to freeze and narrow the profession, has tied it to the past, has discouraged innovation. ... The question I am humbly raising, in the face of what I am sure will be great shock and antagonism, is simply this: Can psychology find a new and better way? (Rogers, 1980: 246–7)

Whilst Rogers' question still remains, the world moves further towards defensive practice and tighter professional restrictions. For more questioning voices, read Lazarus (2003), Kearney (1996), Thorne (1995, 2002), Mearns & Thorne (2000).

2 THE POLITICS OF HELPING THEORIES

Theories of helping have implicit politics. Although this is, I believe, self-evident, the 'helping professions' make only token attempts to engage with the issues raised by this fact of life. Most often, this avoidance takes the form of an ideological pragmatism, where 'treatments' are chosen, never on the basis of philosophy, politics, or values, but rather according to a (further ideologically embedded) test of whether they work. Of course, ideas of effectiveness are inseparable from theory since each theory reveals its values: is it for emancipation or adjustment? Is the client expected to change, or will we change the social conditions which lead to distress?

Unsurprisingly, to any except the diehard positivists, we find immediate disagreement on the criteria for measurement of 'success'. Nevertheless, in this volume and here on this map, we ask the reader to put pragmatism at the end of this selection process and first engage with the issues of politics and values. Orienting oneself in this way is likely to attract criticism. It will at least be seen as naïve, romantic and increasingly quirky in today's positivist science-oriented helping milieu. John Shlien, however, was unrestrained in his advocacy of practice based on values and spoke for many when he wrote:

This method, client-centered, seems to be the only *decent* one. (Shlien, 2003: 218, original emphasis)

The question is not 'What is new?' but 'What is good?' (Shlien, 1986: 347)

What works is enough. Symptom relief is enough. The world in general is ready to settle for this. (Shlien, 2003: 91)

> [D]iagnosis is not good, not even neutral, but bad. Let's be straightforward and flat about it. ... It is not only that its [the medical model] predictions are flawed, faulty and detrimental to the relationship and the client's self-determination, they are simply a form of evil. (Shlien, 1989/2002: 400)

Of relevance here is the way the theory is positioned regarding the nature of research, evidence and 'effectiveness'—which are, in turn, dependent upon how the theory understands human nature, the location of the problem and the purpose of therapy. Some positions militate in favour of a positivist, quantitative, experimental methodology; other positions militate in favour of heuristic, qualitative methodologies. At the 2005 British Association for Counselling and Psychotherapy research conference, more than a few speakers called for counselling and psychotherapy to be evidence-based, not based on a belief system(!). Were they deliberately omitting to admit that positivism is a belief system? What is beyond doubt is that when government policy determines what type of research is acceptable, what type of treatment is acceptable—i.e. what shall be funded— the politicization of therapy is no longer a matter of theoretical niceties.

Person-centred practitioners, along with many other dissenting voices, face a constant battle against the dominant ideology of 'evidence', which carries sub-texts originating in the medicalization of distress. In order to fit government models for funding and treatment, counselling/psychotherapy has to continuously present itself under banners which proclaim: 'Psychotherapy is scientific, deals with the facts of the world, is based on evidence and so is responsible. Criticisms of evidence-based practice are unevidenced, subjective, politically motivated, rhetorical, based on belief systems and so are irresponsible, since they appeal to and hold false hope for, impressionable, vulnerable people.' This ideology is pervasive and would be insidious if it were not writ so bold and large on everything coming out of professional bodies.

The heart of every psychotherapy theory is its image of human nature. All else—the nature of distress, the nature of therapeutic change—springs from this. Theories take different first positions: from ideas that human beings are variously analogous to computer-like machines, through biological machines, biological organisms, persons, to incarnated energy, and so on. It follows that computer-like machines go wrong in different ways from persons or energy fields, and so need different methods for putting them right. Some metaphors for the nature of human beings do not contain notions of 'normal' or 'abnormal' functioning. Some metaphors are intrinsically reductionistic and favour analysis as a method of understanding, whilst others are holistic and favour synthesis. Some may consider these to be essentially matters of philosophy, and here I include them for consideration in our understanding of political awareness. Questions concerning what a human being *is* will soon turn to what a human being *needs* and when we experience those needs *compete*, we enter the political domain.

The picture becomes more complicated when we have to apply our metaphors not only to how human beings are put together, but how they fall apart. Do they become distressed to varying degrees because of internal malfunctioning intrinsic to the flawed design of the human? Or do they react quite normally and reasonably to the accumulating insults of the world; the world which conspires to abuse them with oppression, poverty, poor nutrition, poor housing, discrimination, torture, abuse, 24/7 violent and degrading media and other generalized indignities?

In short, does the theory locate the cause of distress inside the person (their psychology, and/or their biology), outside the person (social, material and economic conditions) or some combination of the two? The location of distress is clearly a political moment in therapy theory and practice. It reveals something of the inherent view of destiny and human nature, and strongly indicates the nature of the 'treatments' endorsed. Along the way it can be seen to serve the status quo or offer resistance to it.

> The aim of therapy is often that of helping the person to be better adjusted to existing circumstances, to 'reality' as it is frequently called; mental health is often considered to be nothing but this adjustment … the psychologists, using the right words … become the priests of industrial society, helping to fulfil its aims … (Fromm, 1989: 131-2)

> And so the adult says, 'Well, what can I do about the world? This thing's bigger than me.' … 'All I can do is go into myself, work on my growth, my development, find good parenting, support groups.' This is a disaster for our political world, for our democracy … we're disempowering ourselves through therapy. (Hillman & Ventura, 1992: 6)

Although still cast by many as an essentially individual approach, person-centred theory has vibrant strands which point towards our essential social nature, e.g. Peter Schmid casts anthropological and philosophical lights on person-centred therapy, drawing on the work of Levinas and Buber to establish PCT as a dialogical approach (e.g. Schmid, 2002). Mearns and Thorne (2000) quietly yet forcefully argue for a socially mediated actualizing tendency, and Mearns and Cooper (2005) reinforce the case for person-centred therapy as a relational approach. None of this (yet) amounts to revising person-centred psychology as a psychosocial practice, as tentatively proposed by Sanders (2005, and Chapter 11, this volume), although Barrett-Lennard continues to point in this direction in his recent collections (Barrett-Lennard, 2003, 2005). To date, psychosocial interventions have been the main preserve of other therapeutic approaches, but this need not be so. A genuine reappraisal and revision of person-centred psychology will require concerted effort and such commitment is not yet evident. It surely cannot be so difficult for person-centred practitioners to imagine being a part of a social model connecting personal growth with coping strategy enhancement and social support.

George W. Albee, an advocate of prevention through public health initiatives, is clear in his appraisal of the role of 'professionals':

> Psychologists must join forces with persons who reject racism, sexism, colonialism and exploitation and must find ways to redistribute social power and to increase social justice. Primary prevention research inevitably will make clear the relationship between social pathology and psychopathology and then will work to change social and political structures in the interests of social justice. It is as simple and as difficult as that! (1996: 1131)

I hope by now that readers will be able to read the map and anticipate some of the twists and turns in the road. The nature of the possible 'solutions' to distress is clearly dependent upon aspects of the theory briefly addressed above. Is it the person that should change, mending human flaws and shortcomings in order to best fit in with the world, or should we change our world and its structures in order to best support our striving for fulfilment?

Some of Rogers' writings have been misappropriated to give support for questionable positions, for example, Rogers' 'what is most personal is most universal' statement can be translated into the idea of 'synergy', i.e. that by doing the best for myself, I will be doing the best for others, criticized by Mick Cooper (see Chapter 10, this volume). Similarly, Rogers assertion that an integrated individual 'is necessarily more understanding of others and is more accepting of others as separate individuals' (Rogers, 1951: 520) can be used (a) to elevate personal growth to the status of a 'political' act and (b) as a licence to put personal growth before (and possibly at the expense of) any other form of action.

Furthermore, implicit in the person-centred approach is the idea that it is the person that should change, and person-centred therapists tend to speak of 'growth', without tackling the criticism that growth could be a euphemism for 'adjustment'. Finally for this section I invite readers to consider whether the notion of 'empowerment', in the sense of personal empowerment or in Rogers' terms 'personal power' (Rogers, 1978), does anything to clarify the situation.

3 THE PLACE OF POLITICS IN HELPING PRACTICE

Here we come down to the basics of being a helper in sessions with clients. The key question is: 'Are there ways of behaving in and around helping sessions that acknowledge the political domain?' Or does our practice appear to be oblivious to it, or even appear to actively ignore it?

This question exists on at least three levels in this debate. The first involves how the helper enacts their chosen theory in a manner which takes into account the political expressions of that theory. Is the practitioner, in order to be faithful to the theory, behoven to act in a politically aware way? In this volume we see

Seamus Nash (see Chapter 4) amongst others, arguing that there is an *imperative* in person-centred theory to be political.

The next level—beyond theory—concerns how the therapist as an individual practitioner might incorporate political awareness self-consciously into their practice. This might include, for example, (a) issues of access, (location of the service, provision for multilingual and cross-cultural work, access for people with disabilities, free or fee-based services, etc.) (b) issues of identity, and disclosure (identifying as male, female, transgender; identifying the therapist's sexuality; wearing political or religious insignia, etc.).

Finally we come to the person of the therapist—how they bring their political self to the session and how they inhabit that political space. This circumstance has a parallel in the intersection between spirituality and therapy. Here we follow the argument that a more integrated, more fully functioning, well-rounded therapist will be experienced by the client as more therapeutic, and will be less likely to respond to the client out of the therapist's own needs. Such dimensions are difficult to specify or quantify, but whatever our definition of 'well-rounded' might be, it should include a political dimension as it does a spiritual one. We would expect the spiritually and politically developed therapist to be experienced as safer, more whole, more integrated and more grounded. It should also be clear that there is here a further intersection between the therapist as 'professional' helper and the therapist as citizen.

4 THE CONTRIBUTION THAT HELPING, AS A GROUP OF THEORIES, AN ACTIVITY AND A PROFESSION, MAKES TO CONTEMPORARY LIFE AND CONTEMPORARY POLITICAL LIFE

Psychotherapy, connected as it is to psychology, theology, anthropology and social sciences, has its own role in regard to an everyday life where political awareness ebbs and flows. Some assert that in the late twentieth century the stock-in-trade of psychotherapy, the 'self', became commodified, or was even an essential invention of consumerism (Rose, 1996; Hansen, McHoul & Rapley, 2003). It goes without saying that all over the world, everyday life is controlled or at the very least influenced by political ideology—currently (and increasingly) global capitalism and the telecommunications media that serve it. As well as determining such 'hard' issues as employment, social welfare, healthcare and income levels, our political system produces an ideology with a wide range of messages telling us what it is to be human, and the nature of success, happiness, and fulfilment. Whilst most therapists would accept that the last three of these are also the concern of psychotherapy, an increasing number also demand that psychotherapy makes comment on how the first four determine mental health/distress (see Psychotherapists and Counsellors for Social Responsibility, <www.pcsr.org.uk/whoweare.htm>).

Counsellors and psychotherapists appear to believe it is only appropriate to comment on the way we treat children or each other in our families. Interpersonal relationships appear to mark the beginning and end of the therapist's interests and domain. Economic policy, employment law, housing and education policies, proliferation of junk food, violence in the media, images of women and men and the sexualization of children in popular culture—the list goes on—all apparently have nothing to do with the distress that brings people to the counsellor's door.

5 HOW ARE THE ABOVE, AND OTHER HELPING-RELATED POLITICAL ISSUES DEALT WITH IN THE TRAINING OF COUNSELLORS AND PSYCHOTHERAPISTS?

When some ask questions about the status of *helping* (e.g. in Section 1 on professionalization and regulation above), what then must follow are questions about the status of *training* in helping. Specifically: do we need to be instructed to help heal another person, or is it a natural aptitude, the expression of which has been suppressed in our modern age? Do we need a course of instruction in theory and practice or do we need facilitation to simply express our healing potential? This question is not simply philosophical; it has a political edge in the matter of expertism. Are helpers to be seen as experts instructed in the art and science of counselling and psychotherapy?

Such questions have been tackled by writers representing many therapeutic approaches (see House & Totton, 1997), but person-centred responses have been few, ranging from thoughtful to spirited, e.g. Barrett-Lennard (2005: 127–30); Embleton-Tudor, Keemar et al. (2004: 62–79); Mearns & Thorne (2000).

That counselling and psychotherapy are largely middle-class pursuits must be now be beyond dispute (McLeod, 2003), and it might be considered to be a generic problem. We must ask how the training of therapists engages with this difficulty. Access to training is a political issue in terms of the types of institution which provide the training (gone are the days when the neighbourhood adult education centre provided courses), the level of course (degree-level training is fast becoming the entry level to the profession) and then there are the issues of course fees, course structure, and access to education for people with disabilities. How does the training course from its publicity to its staff group and curriculum *speak* to people of different classes, ages and ethnic groups?

Organizational/institutional ethos, mission, course organization, the extended curriculum, all reflect a political dimension which will in some way impinge upon the training experience. However hard course leaders might try (and over the years, I have tried very hard) they cannot isolate the course and insulate it from the institutional environment. This institutional environment starts with the nature of the institution: statutory, voluntary or private sector; includes staffing policies, course recruitment, course fees, library and classroom resources; and ends with attitudes towards learning and assessment.

For courses wishing to include a political dimension, this chapter provides a checklist of contents for inclusion in the counsellor-education core curriculum. Some courses might include various issues in themed workshops or possibly 'options', but that misses the point. If counselling and psychotherapy training revolves around the development of the self of the therapist, then politics (along with spirituality and ethical practice, etc.) must be an omnipresent curriculum strand through which all theory and practice is viewed and understood. Politics, spirituality, values and ethics are not bolt-on components, but the backbone, the very essence of therapeutic work, indeed of life.

6 THE HELPER AS CITIZEN

When the helper leaves work, they still exist in a political milieu as a member of society, a citizen. Do they travel home on a bike, on public transport, or in a Rolls-Royce? Do they get out of their wheelchair and into a car adapted for disabled access? Where do they do their shopping, at the supermarket or local store? Do they buy fairtrade goods or the products of global corporations with no ethical policies? Do they recycle their waste, use energy-efficient appliances? The list could go on and on. The minutiae of how we live our lives is clearly a catalogue of political acts and it is genuinely difficult to get a grip on how such decisions interface with the 'business' of being a person-centred therapist. Are the different domains of our lives connected, or separate? Do they articulate or are they independent?

The message from the women's movement in the 1970s was that 'the personal is political', yet in such a 'personal' experience as therapy, the politics of citizenship does not figure, even when it is increasingly common to hear person-centred therapists speak of 'connection'. If not connection to each other through matters of consumption of resources in our household, neighbourhood, nation and planet, then connection through what? Therapists are experts in understanding the effects of interpersonal pain, but they must not be immune to reasoned argument and consequential action regarding pain caused by social injustice. Of course the issues are complex, but we must begin at least the *discussion* somewhere, or therapists will become irrelevant bystanders or worse: making profit out of human distress that is avoidable if we act together as citizens.

CONCLUSION

So where does that leave those of us wanting to embrace and develop our political awareness and relate it more to our work as therapists? After sketching this map I am uneasy about coming to a conclusion before the ink is dry. But perhaps the task is now more clearly revealed. The most gentle of introductions and gradual opening to political awareness behoves readers to consider, debate, challenge, criticize, reject or refine this map as a preliminary effort. This *is* the business of therapists, clients and all those living in communities where distress is the responsibility of each resident. In short, everyone.

It is sad enough that when we all suffer an economic system that forces us to compete for basic needs such as housing, food, healthcare and education; a system that perpetuates poverty and powerlessness in many so that a few may be wealthy and powerful. It is profoundly distressing that when the poor and powerless crack under the strain, experts step in to explain that there is something wrong with their brains ... (Read, 2004: 168)

REFERENCES

Albee, GW (1996) Revolutions and counter-revolutions in prevention. *American Psychologist, 51*, 1130–3.

Barrett-Lennard, GT (2003) *Steps on a Mindful Journey: Person-centred expressions.* Ross-on-Wye: PCCS Books.

Barrett-Lennard, GT (2005) *Relationship at the Centre: Healing in a troubled world.* London: Whurr.

Bates, Y (2000) Still Whingeing: The professionalisation of therapy. *Changes: An International Journal of Psychology and Psychotherapy, 18,* (2), 91–9.

Bates, Y & House, R (2003) (eds) *Ethically Challenged Professions: Enabling innovation and diversity in psychotherapy and counselling.* Ross-on-Wye: PCCS Books.

Embleton-Tudor, L, Keemar, K, Tudor, K, Valentine, J & Worrall, M (eds) (2004) *The Person-Centred Approach: A contemporary introduction.* Basingstoke: Palgrave.

Fromm, E (1989) *Beyond the Chains of Illusion.* London: Abacus.

Hansen, S, McHoul, A & Rapley, M (2003) *Beyond Help: A consumers' guide to psychology.* Ross-on-Wye: PCCS Books.

Healy, D (2001) The SSRI Suicides. In C Newnes, G Holmes & C Dunn (eds) *This is Madness Too: A critical look at psychiatry and the future of mental health services* (pp. 59–70). Ross-on-Wye: PCCS Books.

Healy, D (2004) *Let Them Eat Prozac: The unhealthy relationship between the pharmaceutical industry and depression.* New York: New York University Press.

Heron, J (1990/1997) The politics of transference. *Self and Society, 18* (1), 17–23. Reprinted in R House & N Totton (eds) *Implausible Professions: Arguments for pluralism and autonomy in psychotherapy and counselling* (pp. 11–18). Ross-on-Wye: PCCS Books.

Hillman, J & Ventura, M (1992) *We've Had a Hundred Years of Psychotherapy (And the World's Getting Worse).* San Francisco: Harper.

House, R (1999) Limits to counselling and therapy: Deconstructing a professional ideology. *British Journal of Guidance and Counselling, 27* (3), 377–92.

House, R & Totton, N (1997) *Implausible Professions: Arguments for pluralism and autonomy in psychotherapy and counselling.* Ross-on-Wye: PCCS Books.

Kearney, A (1996) Becoming respectable: Regulation, professionalisation and accreditation. In A Kearney *Counselling, Class and Politics: Undeclared influences in therapy* (pp. 93–106). Ross-on-Wye: PCCS Books.

Lazarus, A (2003) Psychologists, licensing boards, ethics committees and dehumanising attitudes: With special reference to dual relationships. In Y Bates & R House (eds) *Ethically Challenged Professions: Enabling innovation and diversity in psychotherapy and counselling* (pp. 151–8). Ross-on-Wye: PCCS Books.

McLeod, J (2003) *An Introduction to Counselling* (3rd edn). Buckingham: Open University Press.

Mearns, D & Thorne, B (2000) *Person-Centred Therapy Today.* London: Sage.

Mearns, D & Cooper, M (2005) *Working at Relational Depth in Counselling and Psychotherapy.* London: Sage.

Mosher, L (1998) Letter of resignation from the American Psychiatric Association, 4 December 1998 <www.moshersoteria.com/resig.htm>.

Mowbray, R (1995) *The Case Against Psychotherapy Registration: A conservation issue for the human potential movement.* London: TransMarginal Press.

Postle, D (2005) <ipnosis.postle.net/pages/ChurchFalsePromises.htm>.

Read, J (2004) Poverty, ethnicity and gender. In J Read, R Bentall & L Mosher, *Models of Madness: Psychological, social and biological approaches to schizophrenia* (pp. 161–94). London: Brunner-Routledge.

Rogers, CR (1951) *Client-Centered Therapy.* Boston: Houghton Mifflin.

Rogers, CR (1978) *Carl Rogers on Personal Power.* London: Constable.

Rogers, CR (1980) *A Way of Being.* Boston: Houghton Mifflin.

Rose, N (1996) *Inventing Ourselves: Psychology, power and personhood.* Cambridge: Cambridge University Press.

Sanders, P (2005) Principled and strategic opposition to the medicalisation of distress and all of its apparatus. In S Joseph & R Worsley (eds) *Person-Centred Psychopathology: A positive psychology of mental health* (pp. 21–42). Ross-on-Wye: PCCS Books.

Schmid, PF (2002) Knowledge or acknowledgement? Psychotherapy as 'the art of not-knowing'—Prospects on further developments of a radical paradigm. *Person-Centered and Experiential Psychotherapies, 1,* 56–70.

Shlien, JM (1986) Roundtable discussion. *Person-Centered Review, (1)* 3, 347–8.

Shlien, JM (1989/2002) Response to Boy's symposium on psychodiagnosis. *Person-Centered Review, 4* (2), 157–62. Reproduced in DJ Cain (ed) (2002) *Classics in the Person-Centered Approach* (pp. 400–2). Ross-on-Wye: PCCS Books.

Shlien, JM (2003) *To Lead an Honorable Life: Invitations to think about client-centered therapy and the person-centered approach.* (P Sanders, ed). Ross-on-Wye: PCCS Books.

Smail, D (2005) *Power, Interest and Psychology: Elements of a social materialist understanding of distress.* Ross-on-Wye: PCCS Books.

Thorne, B (1995) The accountable therapist: Standards, experts and poisoning the well. *Self and Society, 23* (4), 31–8. Reprinted in R House and N Totton (eds) (1997) *Implausible Professions: Arguments for pluralism and autonomy in psychotherapy and counselling* (pp. 141–50). Ross-on-Wye: PCCS Books.

Thorne, B (2002) Regulation: A treacherous path? *Counselling and Psychotherapy Journal, 12,* (2). Reprinted in Y Bates and R House (eds) (2003) *Ethically Challenged Professions: Enabling innovation and diversity in psychotherapy and counselling* (pp. 148–50). Ross-on-Wye: PCCS Books.

Totton, N (1997) Not just a job: Psychotherapy as spiritual and political practice. In R House & N Totton (eds) *Implausible Professions: Arguments for pluralism and autonomy in psychotherapy and counselling* (pp. 129–40). Ross-on-Wye: PCCS Books.

Totton, N (1999) The baby and the bathwater: 'Professionalisation' in psychotherapy and counselling. *British Journal of Guidance and Counselling, 27* (3), 313–24.

Chapter 3

FIRST CHANGE THE WORLD, OR FIRST CHANGE YOURSELF? THE PERSONAL AND THE POLITICAL REVISITED

Clive Perrett

Johnny's in the basement, mixing up the medicine.
I'm on the pavement, thinking about the government.
(Bob Dylan, *Subterranean Homesick Blues*)

There is a fault in the reality, do not adjust your mind. (Sixties slogan)

There may be others like myself who were young at the time of the explosion of Sixties and early Seventies radicalism and hedonism which became known as the 'counter-culture' who dimly recall one of the recurrent debates of the time, from street demonstration to hippie commune, which went something like this: Hippie to Radical: 'You can't change the world without first you change your own head, man.' Radical to Hippie: 'First you have to change the society, man, peoples' consciousness won't change until we have equality, and human rights for all.' [1]

At that time many of us believed that a revolution, either in consciousness (to be helped along by cannabis and other hallucinogens) or of a political kind, to usher in an era of global freedom and equality, was just around the corner. At the time of May 1968 in France, or seeing the USA in a virtual state of civil war at the height of protests against the Vietnam War in 1969, this did not seem so unlikely a scenario. In the pale light of 2006 the hope of global revolution (either political or psychological) may have faded, and the fear of apocalyptic disaster may have grown, but the questions about how change 'for the better' does or does not occur, remain.

Although I was vaguely aware of the name Carl Rogers and of a phenomenon called encounter groups in the Sixties, and although I was a firm believer (for a while) in the virtues of communal living, I did not directly experience person-centredness either in therapy or in groups until the year 2000. Having done so, however, I then could recognize the importance of crucial moments in my life, particularly at times of crisis, when someone related to me and accepted me as a whole person, warts and

---

1. In retrospect I am amazed at how sexist sixties talk and culture was. Hippies called everyone 'man', including women. But then in a different way the Sixties was a female era. My first experience of a kind of feminism was going to a Beatles concert at the age of 14 when suddenly all the girls climbed onto the seats and screamed and didn't stop. We boys were completely at a loss. This was a new and strange phenomenon in relation to which we felt disempowered.

all, strengths and weaknesses, enthusiasms and hatreds, and I experienced the unique power of that process. I also recognized times when I had offered the same degree of what Rogers articulated as his primary 'core conditions' for therapy (empathy, unconditional positive regard, and congruence) to others.

The transformative power of what I experienced within the person-centred 'movement' then led me to reflect on some old Sixties questions to do with the 'personal' and the 'political'. This chapter is a product of those reflections. The two main questions I wish to address are: (1) Does the fact that the person-centred approach (PCA) is concerned with the unique experience of the individual and the self-actualization of the individual mean that any politics based on the PCA must be 'individualistic'? and (2) How might we answer the old Sixties conundrum now: first change the world, or first change yourself?

I intend to approach these questions through a mixture of reminiscence, reflection, and allusion.

In 1968, at the age of 19, I was studying for a degree in history. My tutor had required me to produce an essay about the 'causes of the First World War'. To prepare for this I started reading a book which went into graphic detail about the monstrous trench warfare that was known as the Battle of the Somme. I became lost in the horror, the hopeless, futile, industrial slaughter of that battle. I grasped the massive and unpredictable scale on which this war was fought. I relived the experience in my own imagination. I went into a sort of deep contemplation of the process and realized that I did not know how to write the essay that I was required to produce.

I had, a few years previously, come across the Battle of the Somme in another way. One winter evening, I encountered, on a busy South London street corner, an old man going mad. It being 1965, and he having been at the Battle of the Somme in 1916, he had to have been about 70 years old. What was happening to him on that street corner was that he was back in 1916, and there, before him, not six feet away, floating in a blood-red river, were the body parts, the arms and legs and torso, of his mate, of his best friend.

He had been at the Somme and he had survived. He had survived all those years to tell the tale. Or, perhaps, like many others, he refused to tell the tale because it was too horrifying, and no one would believe it if he told it true. He had survived the Depression, he had survived the second massive war, in the Fifties he had 'never had it so good' and he had lived to become old in the 'swinging Sixties'. And then, suddenly, he was mad. Hallucinating and ranting at anyone, like me, in the intensity of youth, about this vision that he saw. This vision of dismembered limbs in a river of blood; dismembered limbs that had been his friend.

When I tried to write the essay I could do little more than articulate the problem as I saw it, that so massive a catastrophe (which could lead also to massive trauma for surviving individuals like my old man on the street) needed a massive explanation. *Why* had all this suffering taken place? Why had there been such meaningless, mechanical slaughter on a scale never before seen? But no explanation was on offer. My essay was dismissed by my tutor: he told me that I should realize that, as an undergraduate, I could not legitimately ask such questions. He then gave me a list of causes of the First World War: a list of contingent, sensible, causes. I read his comments and my heart sank. I felt stupid. I felt misunderstood. Then I became angry and dismissive of an educational process which seemed so blind, deaf and dumb that it could not perceive the enormity of the Armageddon that was the World Wars of the twentieth century, and that could deny the validity of the questions which twisted in my gut.

What could I then do with that anger and that bewilderment? I went on demonstrations against the Vietnam War, but was frightened by some of the violence I encountered there. I went to poetry readings where I heard Adrian Mitchell ranting his poem 'Tell me lies about Vietnam'. I became interested in the ideas of the French 'Situationists': those inspirers of 'May 68', who talked about 'apocalypse for kicks' and the 'society of the spectacle'. But underneath it all I somehow had to deal with my own sense of disenchantment that in the world of the scholars, a world which I wanted to respect and be a part of, neither big questions nor deep feelings were permitted.

This is one way of trying to explore the issue of the relationship between the personal and the political. If you get to deep feelings, it seems to me, you also get to big questions. If our feeling sense is atrophied so our thinking ability will be atrophied. If we cannot feel deeply neither will we think deeply. [2] If we can neither feel deeply nor think deeply, then we cannot be truly ourselves: if we cannot be truly ourselves then how can we make a global society fit for human beings (for all human beings, not just for some)?

In the radical movements of Western Europe and the USA of the Sixties and early Seventies, the slogan that 'the personal is the political' became popular, originating in the women's liberation movement. The experience of the dispossessed or the marginalized or exploited, their *personal* lived experience, was regarded, in these movements, as itself a political issue. Politics was understood as an activity which concerned itself with the *common good*, the well-being, or not, of the whole human community. If some part of that community did not, and *could* not, 'feel good', then this was a political problem. The awareness which permeated the radical and revolutionary movements of the Sixties and Seventies was also global: the question was one of changing the whole world, not just one part of it, and there was an awareness that the whole was interconnected— that the fate of Africa was bound up with the fate of Europe, the fate of Asia with that of America, the fate of the Black person with that of the White, the fate of the male with that of the female.

---

2. The question is perhaps not just one of deep feeling or deep thinking, but of thinking and feeling which are *personally meaningful*. Rogers and Freiburg (1994: 35) criticized the kind of education which 'becomes the futile attempt to learn material that has no personal meaning. Such learning involves the mind only: it is learning which takes place "from the neck up". It does not involve feelings or personal meanings; it has no relevance for the whole person. In contrast, there is such a thing as significant, meaningful, experiential learning.'

In attempting to research my essay in 1968 I had begun to *personally* experience the horrors of trench warfare, both through my reading and from my memory of the old soldier. I encountered the human cost, the cost in human suffering and misery, of this global event whose causes could, according to my academic tutors, be listed only in abstract inhuman terms to do with inter-imperialist rivalries or arms expenditures. I *felt* something: the reality of the First World War became a personal issue to me, but I found myself, in this depth of feeling, intellectually dumbfounded and unable to produce an essay to satisfy my tutor. I then became disillusioned with intellectual effort, and the institution of the university itself. Both because it could not deal with my *personal* question and because it could not deal with what seemed to me a massively big political, social, economic, question. The inability to respond to a depth of personal feeling and the inability to answer big 'naïve' questions about the modern world seemed to go hand in hand.

I was told that my response, my essay, was 'idiosyncratic': in other words that it was something unique to me, something relating only to *my* being, to *my* temperament. And that it was invalid for those reasons. I remember the term 'idiosyncratic' being used as a term of abuse, and that I took it on as such. [3]

So I encountered, in 1968, a crisis at this interface we can call personal/political. It was not for the first time or the last time, but for me this particular crisis was the beginning of a process of alienation from a reality that I experienced as insane. I became more personally disturbed, and then withdrawn. I thought the rest of the world (or most of it) was mad: this proved, of course, that I must be mad. I remember going to a lecture where a highly respected but entirely 'intellectual' philosopher provided a logical proof that the Second World War had not occurred. He seemed to think this was very funny, as did most of his audience. I became more and more disengaged from the studies I was supposed to be pursuing, at the same time as I was quite literally 'doing my head in' reading books. On one occasion, having weighed myself down with impossible amounts of reading, I got into an argument with some defenders of the logical positivist philosopher whose lecture I had found so absurd. At the height of the argument I suffered a sort of nervous collapse, and ended in a heap on the floor as if my brain had short-circuited. A friend, on that occasion, rescued me and looked after me, an act of kindness which saved me from psychiatric attention, but it was one of several 'breakdowns'.

In the five or so years following, I was led to the brink of suicide, to some very wild and self-destructive behaviour, and to the inside of a psychiatric hospital. Once inside the hospital, strange to relate, as well as feeling that the powers that be were trying to psychically destroy or reconstruct me, I also encountered a deep loving and caring from two ordinary psychiatric nurses, whom to this day I regard

---

3. If we look at the etymology of the word 'idiosyncrasy' we find that *idios* = 'one's own' + *(syn* = 'together' + *krasis* = 'a mixing') *synkrasis* = 'temperament'. Idiosyncrasy therefore refers to an individual's own personal 'mixing'—the mix that makes that person. The person as unique but a *mixture*, so the term contains the sense that we are all mixed, we are all part of each other (*Chambers Dictionary of Etymology*, Edinburgh, 1988).

as my saviours. I bless them and thank them. What they did for me, to all appearances, was not a great deal. It was not some spectacular act of rescue. What they did was relate to me as a human being with real feelings and real needs, rather than to someone with a psychiatric label. They related to me as a 'person', as an idiosyncratic being. They offered Rogers' 'core conditions' to me, though they had probably never heard of these. That was how they helped me. At the time I could barely thank or acknowledge them, but as time has gone on the memory of their humanness has become more and more crucial to me. I now feel that if they had not been there for me at that time, I would not have lived to tell my tale.

For the effective conduct of person-centred therapy, as I discovered much later, whatever the client brings, and whatever direction the client takes, needs to be accepted and valued. Rogers came to believe (because he had experienced this over and over again) that the clients themselves, of their own nature, given the nurturing conditions of the therapeutic relationship, would self-actualize, would, in other words, become 'who they really were'. Attending to whatever the client brings means attending, at least potentially, to the *whole* person, to everything about that person. And it is this concept, or process, which is crucial, because it requires us to think about what the *whole* person is.

Another crucial aspect of Rogerian theory is the idea of 'congruence'. To be congruent the therapist must be *self-aware*, and needs to bring that self-awareness into the relationship with the client. The effectiveness of the process in person-centred therapy depends on the quality of the *relationship between* therapist and client. Once we are talking of relationship we are not just talking of individuals or individual psychology. And when we extend the understanding and experience of person-centred process to groups and communities we are talking of multiple relationships (as in an encounter group) in which each individual person attempts to hold the core conditions in relation to all other persons in that community. And if we were to imagine that model extended indefinitely throughout whole societies and then the whole planet we can imagine something which has a curious affinity with Karl Marx's concepts of a society in which the slogan 'from each according to their ability, to each according to their need' [4] would be the norm, and his concept that this society would be one in which 'the free development of each shall be the condition of the free development of all' [5] also seems to resonate curiously with Rogerian ideas. It was in these terms that Marx and his comrades envisaged what they called 'communism'.

Now, communism is/was a political concept and a movement which is now largely discredited, defunct and unfashionable. Those societies which historically defined themselves as communist were a long way from the realization of the

---

4. This phrase occurs in Karl Marx's 'Critique of the Gotha programme' of 1875. (See Karl Marx & Friedrich Engels, 1848/2002: 169.)

5. 'In place of the old bourgeois society, with its classes and class antagonisms, we shall have an association, in which the free development of each is the condition for the free development of all' (Karl Marx & Friedrich Engels, 1848/2002: 244).

Marxian ideal. This might mean the ideal was wrong; it might mean it has never been adequately realized; or it might mean the 'conditions' for its realization were not present. And this itself raises a very important question. To be able to present the 'core conditions' one to another, persons first need to be fed, clothed, housed and watered in a relative degree of comfort and security. So here we have a 'chicken and egg' type of dilemma which brings us back to our debate between the 'first change yourself' hippies of the counter-culture and the 'first change the world' politicos of the radical left. [6]

But how did 'the world' and 'the self' come to be understood as separate in the first place? In Renaissance psychology and philosophy, in sixteenth-century Europe, there was held to be an intimate relationship between what was called the 'macrocosm'—the cosmos as a whole—and the human being who was a 'microcosm'. Everything in the individual human *corresponded to* some element of the universe as a whole. In Shakespeare's plays this philosophy and psychology is evident, and it is usually the person who is most truly themselves, or most true to themselves, (like Kent in *King Lear*) who is the most truly universal, and therefore best able to act in ways which are for the common good (even if that means self-sacrifice). [7] This understanding, and this sense of relatedness (of one human to another, and of all to Nature), permeates the whole of Shakespeare's plays, as does the depiction (in the tragedies) of what is liable to happen if this sense of relatedness, of belonging within a greater social and natural and cosmic whole, is lost. Too many of us in the modern world have somehow come to experience ourselves as separate, alienated individuals, disconnected from each other and from the rest of the universe. Perhaps coming to 'know ourselves' better is one sort of remedy for that alienation. But the coming to know ourselves better may be only one part of the solution, because we also need a society in which our better-known selves can 'realize' themselves, that is, can live in a way that accords with our own unique natures. [8]

---

6. Maslow's 'hierarchy of needs' is perhaps relevant here: the notion that *basic* needs have to be satisfied before other needs can be realized.

7. The fascination of Shakespeare's *King Lear* lies in the way in which psychological, spiritual, ethical and political considerations are interwoven in the drama. Lear is 'old before he is wise', incapable of controlling his own impulsiveness and anger. Because of these weaknesses he not only damages his own family and destroys relationships that are most precious to him (as with his youngest daughter Cordelia) but he also damages the equilibrium of the nation which then degenerates into civil war. Kent, who is Lear's most faithful lieutenant, challenges his master's stupidity. Kent, in Rogerian terms, is a 'fully functioning' human being, who acts in the interest of the whole person, of the nation, and of the truth, and is prepared to risk his own life in the process.

8. The fourteenth-century Italian poet Dante expressed this well, as follows: 'It cannot be that any nature, found/ At odds with its environment, should thrive;/ no seed does well in uncongenial ground./ If men on earth would bear in mind, and strive/ To build on the foundation laid by nature,/ they'd have fine folk, with virtues all alive./ But you distort the pattern of the creature; you cloister him that's born to wield a sword,/ and crown him king who ought to be a preacher;/

The challenge of Rogerian theory and practice, as I understand it and have experienced it, is the encounter with the *whole person*. The client of the person-centred therapist, for the therapy to be effective, needs to be able to bring his or her whole self, and (at least potentially) the whole of his or her own experience, to the counselling room. The process of person-centred therapy is to begin to rediscover the depths and breadths of human potentialities *from within*, from *personal experience*, and in *relationship*. Why should this not be the basis of a rediscovering of what it means for individuals to constitute communities, and for communities to constitute global society, and for that global society to know itself and its place in the cosmos? Social, and political, and psychological knowledge, would, from this basis, be constructed *from the encounter of persons with each other*.

But, Carl Rogers' core conditions for human growth and development need, as I have said, certain preconditions of a material nature (although what these preconditions might be is open to argument). When Shakespeare's King Lear is reduced to 'nothing' in the course of his madness and of the storm, he suddenly empathizes with the poor and the wretched in his kingdom who would ordinarily be exposed to the elements in ways which he has never previously experienced. 'Oh, I have taken too little care of this' he laments. [9] We, too, in our comfortable (actually, I think the point is that 'comfortable' does not adequately describe us: we may be materially comfortable but our lives are in many ways emotionally and psychologically stressful—if this were not the case who would need therapists?) Western lives 'take too little care' of the chaos and neediness and poverty and desolation which our very 'civilization' generates elsewhere in the globe (or in our cities). [10] And when, in some part of the global body politic, some abscess or boil erupts to remind us of the sickness of the whole, what do we do? We either ignore it and hope it will go away, or we wade in with our horrendously expensive and enormously sophisticated military machine and bomb the problem away

---

thus from the path you wander all abroad.' (the *Divine Comedy, Paradise*, translated by Dorothy L Sayers, 1962, London Penguin Books, Canto 8, lines 139–48).

9. Lear, exposed to the storm, suddenly empathizes with the poor in his kingdom who he has customarily ignored, and laments: 'Poor naked wretches, wheresoe'er you are,/ That bide the pelting of this pitiless storm,/ How shall your houseless heads and unfed sides/ Your looped and windowed raggedness, defend you/ From seasons such as these? O, I have ta'en/ Too little care of this! Take physic, pomp;/ Expose thyself to feel what wretches feel/ That thou mayst shake the superflux to them,/ And show the heavens more just' (Shakespeare, *King Lear*, Act 3, Sc 4).

10. It is perhaps not true to say that the dominant civilisation takes too little care in the sense of ignoring, though that is sometimes true; it is the awareness, or lack of awareness of *interconnectedness* which is the problem. Our riches generate their poverty. Their exploitation generates our riches. It is this aspect of Marxist understanding which we need to rediscover. But the psychological understanding we need might also involve an understanding that in our comforts we are anxious or distressed when we are aware, through the media, of discomforts elsewhere in the globe which we cannot alleviate.

(by so doing also ensuring a good market for our beloved arms industries). [11] There is nothing more *impersonal* than modern military technology. This points up the scale of the problem which confronts us. The protest movements of the Sixties saw the destructive impersonality of the Vietnam War and opposed it and ended it, but not before this war had cost untold lives and done untold ecological damage. I remember watching a documentary [12] about Vietnam War veterans who, after the war, found themselves unable to live in normal society, so they lived wild in the forests and wildernesses of America. One of these recounted how, after the war, he had gone back home to live with his parents. He instructed his mother to never wake him from sleep. On one occasion she forgot, and woke him by the method she had used when he was a child, by twiddling his toe. In an instant he awoke and was at his mother's throat attempting to strangle her. Fortunately he came to his senses, but from that moment he decided to live in the wild: he was unfit for normal human interaction. His training as a US Marine, and his experience of the war, had achieved this. I doubt whether his story is unusual, but it is not convenient for the powers that be to repeat such stories too often. Such stories are indicators of the inhuman, impersonal aspects of modern civilization, but this reality, it seems, is one we are reluctant to face.

The biggest change in the political landscape over the past 50 years has been the collapse of any widespread belief in the possibility of a political alternative to the present capitalist world order. Although for most of my father's generation the revelations about the realities of Stalinism put paid to any belief in the so-called Soviet system as a credible alternative, for my generation, particularly with the discovery and dissemination of the writings of the young Karl Marx, there was a renewed hope that a genuine communism could be created, one which justly shared the world's resources *and* respected individuals and their freedoms. Many of us in the 1960s and 70s believed that it would prove possible to create a global society in which, in Marx's words: 'the free development of each will be the condition for the free development of all'.

When and how did that hope collapse? For myself the elements of disillusion were various. There was firstly the growing awareness that communist theory as it had been developed by Marx and others was lacking in its understanding both of human psychology and of 'spirituality' as a dimension of human experience. But what has happened since? There has been an explosion of interest in psychology and in therapies, and so-called 'fundamentalism' in religion has become increasingly influential. Religion has revived in the postmodern age, but in the form of fanaticisms, which seem likely to achieve nothing except the further oiling of the capitalist war machine. Terrorisms have emerged of extremely dubious provenance, some claiming a spiritual lineage, but often subject to manipulation

---

11. Saying this of course is not to deny the enormous wealth of compassion shown in response to natural disasters like the Christmas 2004 Asian Tsunami.
12. The documentary was called *Missing in America,* CBS, 1987, producers Paul and Holly Fine.

by the dark and secretive forces of global intelligence agencies. US secret services, allied with Pakistani secret services, were actively involved, for instance, in the fostering of militant Islam as a means, from the late 70s onwards, of destabilizing the Soviet Union. [13] The Taliban and then al-Quaeda were indirect offshoots of this policy. To my mind the most serious casualty of machinations of this kind is respect for religion itself. If the spiritual can be abused in this way, if 'God' can be on everyone's side in the most barbaric of conflicts, what hope is there for a revival of authentic spiritual awareness? [14]

The second element of disillusion, for myself, came as a result of experience in various kinds of 'community politics' or grass-roots campaigning. Here my most important learning was about the importance of democracy. Time and again it became clear that, without proper democratic structures for accountability and decision-making in even the most minor grass-roots campaigns, egoism and power-mongering of the ugliest kinds could emerge to disrupt and vitiate whatever achievements could be gained. But genuine participatory democracy is hard work and time consuming, and usually, also, very slow. If people at ground level are in general not prepared to undertake the self-discipline necessary to work in these ways, what hope is there that changes at a global level can be achieved? [15]

There is a third major area of difficulty, as I perceive it, which is to do with our relationship with the world of Nature, or the world of creation. Capitalism and the technologies derived from the modern scientific approach to nature have transformed human life on this planet in material terms. But this has been achieved in so uneven, unjust and catastrophic a way as to threaten the very survival of the human race. The dangers of total self-destruction, either by means of war using weapons of mass destruction or via ecological collapse as a consequence of rampant consumerism is not just science fantasy. It is a very close and dangerous reality.

But the forces of religious fundamentalism, whether Christian, Muslim, Judaic,

---

13. See *War and Globalization* by Michel Chossudovsky (Centre for Research on Globalization, 2002) for an account of this.

14. But see the writings of Brian Thorne (in particular *The Mystical Power of Person-Centred Therapy*) for explorations of the connection between the development of spiritual awareness and the person-centred approach. Perhaps the importance of what he explores is that the spiritual is encountered through 'going within', through the intimate encounter with the person's own inner experiencing, on the part of both client and therapist, which then leads to a mystical experience of union. So spirituality is understood as primarily an experiential process, rather than just a question of belief systems.

15. My experience of person-centred communities or encounter groups in recent years leads me to believe that the community group—at its most basic the sitting in a circle within which everyone is of equal status—could provide the basic consensual/democratic model of any progressive political movement. In some senses this concept is modern, in other respects it goes back to millennia of 'gatherings' from the most primitive hunter-gatherer nomadic groups to those of the pre-modern agricultural settlement. For this to again become the 'norm' perhaps it is a celebration of the *process itself* which we need. The mere act of meeting together needs to be re-understood as a sacred as well as a political process: as both communion and community.

Hindu or of any other persuasion, seem oblivious to these dangers, and appear to actively court them. Equally the forces of marketing and advertising seem to 'carry on regardless' with their generation and regeneration of comforting illusions of limitless material resources and goods on a planet whose resources we know (rationally) to be finite and fragile. And behind both of these forces are to be found the corporate commercial forces of capitalism. Capitalism is using religion and the 'magical' remedies of the advertisers to promote its own ends. Both sets of forces seem blind to any possibilities of real human transformation. [16]

We have seen how capitalism (particularly via its advertisers and its marketing and public relations experts) has learnt a new trick or three since the Sixties, so that everything in the glorious world of commodities is now sold to us as personally designed 'just for you'. This has apparently fatally undermined oppositional movements with global ambitions whose thinking needs to be grand and abstract and systematic, at least to some extent, in order to take on the global forces that maintain the status quo. The irony of the present age is that the capitalist/scientific 'status quo' is inherently *destabilizing* of any possibility of a viable future for humanity. In other words consumerist ideologies and cults of media personality, have *apparently* made everything 'personal', but this has deflected us from any attention to, and understanding of, the 'personal', in a way which develops our understanding of the political and spiritual/ universal *connectedness* of human beings to each other and to the cosmos, which would be required to develop any movement coherent enough to challenge the forces which threaten to destroy us.

Fundamentalisms, like other abstract systems of thought or ideology, do not seem to value the person in his or her *uniqueness*. However the scriptures on which the fundamentalist religionists base themselves (the Bible, the Koran, etc.) all teach that God loves and has mercy on human beings and all creation, and that we are in essence inseparable from God, unless we rebel against 'Him'. Furthermore, we are not enjoined to hate ourselves, but to love ourselves. The PCA in therapy, in education, or wherever, aims to foster this same attitude. To *love your neighbour as you love yourself* is a real challenge to all of us who are products of twentieth-century Western civilization because it is surely the case that we do not love *ourselves* very well. If the PCA in therapy or in education allows as all to learn to love and respect ourselves more, there is a real possibility that we then might learn to love each other. [17]

---

16. The BBC documentary series *The Century of the Self* (produced by Adam Curtis, first shown April–May 2002) showed how Freudian concepts were used from early in the twentieth century by advertisers, marketeers and public relations firms to influence public opinion and consumer choice. Rogerian ideas, being more transparent, are perhaps slightly less co-optable.

17. The biblical teaching is first to love 'the lord your God with all your heart and with all your mind and with all your soul' and then to 'love your neighbour as yourself'. It is worth asking what a modern understanding of loving God with all your heart and mind and soul might mean. I would dare to interpret it thus: use *all* your faculties—i.e. become a whole person—and love— engage with, respect, empathize with—*all* of creation.

John Shlien put forward the view that person-centred group psychotherapy gave the *experience of freedom* to its participants. [18] This concurs with my own experience in person-centred community gatherings. I would add, however, that within the experience of encounter there is not only the sense of freedom but also of responsibility. As an individual within the encounter group I am responsive to, and responsible for, every other individual. [19] Being 'myself' I also am bound to respond to others. In my responses is my responsibility. I am responsible for my responses, and in my responses to others I take 'responsibility' not only for myself but for them. [20] In my self-concern I am also concerned for others. 'Above all else, to thine own self be true. Thou canst not then be false to any man.' [21]

Modernity (the conjunction of capitalism and modern science/technology, with the later addition of democracy for a few) promised 'freedom'. In reality this has meant slavery and exploitation for millions and a phoney freedom for a relative few (phoney in the sense that one person cannot be truly free if another is enslaved). But the ideals still remain: the ideals of personal growth, of personal self-realization in harmonious community. The question remains: how can this be *really* achieved? *Can* it be achieved—or are we doomed? (I do believe that is the nature of the choice which confronts us.)

My own experience of person-centred community groups is that in their (sometimes remarkable, often painful, usually mysterious, sometimes miraculous) 'process' I become more truly 'myself'. I feel real. I am who I am. How does this occur? It seems to me that the process is similar to that experienced by the fictional King Lear. He, through the fire of his rage and madness, is reduced to his own essence. In the person-centred community everyone is, for that moment and that process, equal. Everyone also cannot but experience the reality of the others, whether those others articulate verbally or not. They are there in their being, and are experienced as such. All are in a sense psychologically and spiritually 'naked'. This can be both exhilarating and frightening, but either way it is 'real'. Perhaps our modern/postmodern political and spiritual being needs more of this. More reality, less pretence. (This reality does not, however, have to be deadly serious; in a fully-functioning community people will also laugh a great deal.)

But the other thing we need, I contend, is the 'containment' that the group experience provides. As humans in community we are all a part of each other,

---

18. See Shlien, 2003: 135.

19. This question of responsibility within community is to me crucial. Within traditional communities the care of children, for instance, is the responsibility of all adults (see, for instance, Colin Turnbull's account of the hunter gatherers of the Congo in *The Forest People*, Picador, 1976: 118) whereas a childless modern urban Westerner need have nothing to do with children or any other dependants for the whole of his or her life, if he or she so chooses.

20. There is a question perhaps about how to ensure that not only 'freedom' but also 'responsibility' is present within the group. It seems to me that the Rogerian concept of congruence is crucial in this regard, because it involves accepting the responsibility for monitoring one's own inner state and expressing that awareness as appropriate whilst *also* being empathic and showing respect for the other.

21. Shakespeare's *Hamlet*: Polonius' advice to his son.

whether we like it or not. As individuals, we can only be *realized* socially, in communities. Modern society tends to atomize, to break people apart, to break communities apart, to break families apart. [22]

So, what is the relationship between the personal and the political which we need as a healing force for our postmodern and apocalyptic age? I return to the two primary questions on which I have focused: (1) If the PCA is concerned with the actualization of the individual, does that make it 'individualistic'? My answer is no, (a) if the approach is understood as concerned above all with *relationship* (it is the quality of the client/therapist relationship, or of the relationships between the members of an encounter group, which is the key to a successful therapeutic process); and (b) because the deepening *self*-awareness required for both clients and therapists must make both more aware of their *connectedness* to others, and to the cosmos. If as individuals we learn better how to love ourselves (and the whole of creation, see footnote 16 above), we will be better able to love each other. This understanding might then have the knock-on effect of a revival of a genuine, down-to-earth, non-fundamentalist spirituality. (2) What is the answer to the old Sixties question 'Do we change ourselves first, or must we change the world first?' My conclusion is simply that the processes are inseparable, and that it is *that* understanding that could gradually be achieved by the more widespread application of the totality of the person-centred approach in therapy, in communities, in education, and in political movements.

REFERENCES

Chossudovsky, M (2003) *War and Globalization: The truth behind September 11.* Canada: Global Outlook Publishing.

The Century of the Self (2002) BBC Documentary Series, (Adam Curtis, producer). April–May, 2002.

Chambers Dictionary of Etymology (1988) London: Chambers Harrap Publishers.

Dante, G (1962) *The Divine Comedy; Paradise* (trans Dorothy L Sayers & Barbara Reynolds). London: Penguin.

Debord, G (1992) The Society of the Spectacle. New York: Zone Books.

Marx, K & Engels, F (1848/2002) *The Communist Manifesto.* London: Penguin Classics.

Missing in America (1987) CBS, producers Paul and Holly Fine.

Rogers, CR & Freiburg, HJ (1994) *Freedom to Learn* (3rd edn). London: Prentice Hall.

Shlien, JM (2003) *To Lead an Honorable Life. A collection of the work of John M Shlien* (ed P Sanders). Ross-on-Wye: PCCS Books.

Thorne, B (2002) *The Mystical Power of Person-Centred Therapy.* London: Whurr Publishers.

Turnbull, C (1976) *The Forest People.* London: Picador.

---

22. Although, oddly enough, some aspects of new media technologies, like mobile phones and email, can bring families closer together just as they further fragment the public sphere.

Chapter 4

IS THERE A POLITICAL IMPERATIVE INHERENT WITHIN THE PERSON-CENTRED APPROACH?

Seamus Nash

> Politics is a process of change in a rapidly changing world.
> (Kenneth Clarke interviewed on 5 Live, 28th September 2005)

An immigrant, learning-disabled man is paid 29p an hour stacking shelves in a supermarket in Leicester, the body of a man who died in his home lies undetected for 5 years, the 7/7 bombs, Jewish settlers in Gaza moved out, the Provisional IRA finally put their weapons beyond use …

INTRODUCTION

This chapter argues that there is a political imperative inherent within the person-centred approach (PCA) and that this imperative is built into the very fabric of its philosophy and theory including the image of the person that the approach seeks to hold.

It is recognized that there are a substantial number of people who work and live by the PCA principles who are not psychotherapists or counsellors. This chapter, then, will not dwell purely within the therapy room. For that purpose psychotherapy and counselling will be located within the wider applications of the PCA as suggested by Wood (1995).

First, I propose that the PCA is inherently and fundamentally political—it was developed by Rogers (1942, 1951, 1961, 1978) with his peers and students in response to psychological practices that were prominent at that time (Rogers, 1951: 4–5). Rogers pointed out that psychotherapy was about both the individual's relationship with their environment and their relationship to others.

Second, the image of the human being as a person held by the PCA is fundamentally political. This is discussed in relation to the work of Peter Schmid (1998, 2002). I argue that human beings have a basic right to exist by virtue of their humanity. The concept of 'interconnectedness' is also explored and with this concept the gulf between the 'individual' to the 'communal' is bridged. This may have political implications in terms of working with conflict, difference and diversity.

Third, I suggest that when I espouse the principles and ethics of the PCA and live these principles as a 'way-of-being-in-the-world', this becomes an 'imperative', and is, inherently and importantly, political. A 'way-of-being' encompasses both therapeutic and political dimensions and a 'way-of being' is also a form of action—it is not just the practice of spectators as Pete Sanders (2005) has commented.

In conclusion, the time is ripe for *'reconscientization'*, to adopt a term from Paulo Freire, to take stock of our direction and for each of us to reflect and decide the extent of our commitment, not only to the PCA, but also, importantly, to humanity. It is a time to develop further our critical consciousness as an approach that will enable solid, transformative action to take place both individually and collectively.

MY STORY

I came to the PCA as a sceptic and would have described my practice initially as 'integrative'. I had a fascination with Transactional Analysis (TA) especially as a sound diagnostic tool, it was effective with 'difficult' clients and it was cool—I could be very clever. I did not view person-centred therapy as particularly effective.

The majority of my friends were social workers, mental health nurses or housing workers who worked predominately with marginalized individuals and groups. Carl Rogers and 'person-centred' often came up in conversations with regard to how one worked but not so much about how one lived or acted towards others. What was described to me was often woolly and insubstantial—stereotypical middle class, middle American, apple pie and creamery, evocative of sixties throwbacks or 'new age' hippies. However, I read books and I changed. I felt a deep connection with what Rogers was articulating, particularly trusting in the client and being in relationship without any agenda. As a therapist I could relax as I was not in charge! This version of 'person-centred' was indeed, revolutionary.

What first struck me was just how radical and political this approach was— if I empowered people to take their own power and lives back, they would change and not accept the repeated assaults to their dignity that they had previously endured. The approach was inherently democratic, non-labelling and anti-authoritarian. I also came to realize why Rogers was so maligned and why the theory was discredited by the psychological establishment—because it took away the stranglehold of their power, knowledge and expertise. Rogers and his colleagues made the whole process of psychotherapy completely transparent, concrete and visible. Rogers had the affront to suggest that the client knew the direction to proceed in, the client knew what was hurting, the client was the real expert.

Furthermore, by establishing the practice of psychotherapy research and recorded therapy interviews, Rogers and his associates laid down a fundamental challenge to the psychological establishment—to uncover for the first time the hitherto arcane world of therapy. He and his co-workers drew back the veil, to uncover therapy and its workings to everyone, taking it away from the 'professional' experts. Clients were revealed as aware, hard working, knowledgeable and experts on themselves. Trust in the client and their actualizing tendency was the key.

When I chose this approach, I committed myself to a set of epistemological and philosophical assumptions about the nature of humanity. If you are reading this you may have done likewise. Persons who espouse a person-centred way-of-being-in-the-world view the human being as an inherently constructive, pro-social organism; striving to be and become in whatever circumstances life presents. The PCA is based on a premise that humans at their core are trustworthy organisms (Rogers, 1978: 7). Rogers interpreted 'politics' as having power and control over others and self: at the centre of the PCA is a critique of the locus of decision-making power (1978: 4). Rogers explained that in terms of psychotherapy and counselling it was about a person seeking help being treated not *as a dependent patient but as a responsible client*' (1978: 5).

A POLITICAL IMPERATIVE

This political imperative in the very foundations and philosophy of the PCA is based on seeing the human being as a person, with inalienable rights and choices. The human person is in an interconnected relationship with all others on the planet. This imperative is shown most strongly within one's 'way-of-being'. In other words, espousing a person-centred way-of-being, is by its own virtue, political. The concept of an *imperative* in terms of morals and ethics is derived from the philosopher Immanuel Kant (1724–1804). Kant's system of morality was ultimately based on fairness and centres around the 'categorical imperative', namely to 'act only on that maxim which you can at the same time will to be a universal law'.

Kant argued that we find our moral principles from our human, rational nature thus we generate principles of conduct from our free, autonomous will. It is by virtue of our autonomous wills that persons have dignity or are '*ends in themselves*'. From this, Kant arrived at the idea of people mutually respecting each other's autonomous rational wills, and the concept of a free, autonomous will exercising free choice is a central aspect to Sartre's work (for example Sartre, 1958). An imperative, then, is universal yet personal, it is authentic, it is a principle of conduct to uphold human dignity. As John Shlien wrote 'we are the ultimate source' (2003: xiii). This is the *sine qua non* of the PCA.

LIFE, WORTH AND DIGNITY

In its espousal of a non-judgemental position, the PCA has a clear stance in terms of violence and oppression towards humans (Rogers, 1978: 258). The human being is an organism whose worth and dignity are not arbitrary; these are 'givens'. The human being has the basic right to exist. This is inherent and must be upheld since without persons there is no PCA. Therefore when I, as someone who espouses a person-centred way of being, witness oppression and injustice to others, I cannot ignore this. Action is imperative. Therefore, in terms of working alongside others or living the values of the approach, I act from an attitude of understanding towards what I perceive rather than imposing values of my (or our) own. It is trying to 'see people from the inside—how they talk, the way they think and construct their thought, the nature of their interpersonal relationships' (Rogers, 1978: 106). In making fundamental statements about the importance of relationships, the PCA is concerned with the politics of relationships.

THE IMAGE OF THE HUMAN BEING

It follows from the above that the image we hold of the human being is a powerful catalyst to either act in consideration of others, or not. This image is a unique and distinguishing characteristic of the PCA. Kant, as I have outlined, understood the 'Other' in terms of a moral imperative (Schmid, 1998: 78). The 'philosophy of the Other' has been advanced in terms of theology, existentialism and phenomenology and now the PCA takes its place in this process. Foremost in this has been Peter Schmid (1998, 2002).

Schmid takes his lead from Rogers—he sees the human being as a person and puts this 'person' at the centre of activity—be that psychotherapy or any other. Schmid examines the two main notions, and usages, of the term 'person' within PCA and concludes that they enhance each other rather than being mutually exclusive. A human being is a person both with an individual or 'substantive' nature and also a relational nature—a 'being' in relationship with other beings. The PCA sees the human being both as a unique, free, responsible and independent entity and also as a person characterized by relationship, mutuality, connection, dialogue and interrelatedness with others. It would thus be an error philosophically, theoretically and, importantly, practically, to perceive the PCA as an activity that caters exclusively to the 'individual'.

So, a 'person'-centred relationship is a dialogical relationship. Schmid however expresses a differing opinion on the 'I–Thou' relationship as conceived of by Buber. Using Levinas, Schmid introduces the concept of the 'fundamental We'. Schmid (2002) writes that in the beginning, there is contact—the Other and I form a 'We' from which we all commonly spring. I am called into relationship from the beginning by an Other. We spring from the same clay and indeed only exist as part of a 'We', all born within this 'We'. This concept of a 'We' makes it *impossible* to ignore context, our world, our roots.

A WAY-OF-BEING-IN-THE-WORLD OR 'JUST ANOTHER JOB'?

Many reading this chapter may have chosen this approach as a 'way-of -being-in-the-world', as a lived philosophy and as a set of 'values' or ideals. These values and philosophies, which by espousal inform our ways of living and being, are enfleshed in the very fabric of our humanity. By my humanity I am *homo-ousios*— of one being—with the theory. The theory comes alive inside and through this envelope of flesh.

Importantly, this way of being is also central to and informs our practice for some of us who wish to describe ourselves as psychotherapists or counsellors. For others, this is not so: they believe that it is not their whole life and might say 'It is just a job', 'I don't take it that seriously' or 'It is a means to an end'. Having asserted that a way-of-being-in-the-world is fundamentally and inherently political I now make another, possibly controversial proposal. I suggest that when I espouse, embody and act with the principles of PCA and truly believe in them and live them, this is considerably more potent and 'effective' than perceiving what I do as just another job or 'being in it for the money'. I am clear: from my experience and practice I am psychotherapeutically more effective (if that is the point of my practice) when I truly embody and believe what I do. People are not commodities and therapy is not transaction. This way of being sees one in relation to the all— its essence is interconnectedness—what happens to One impacts on the All. A consciousness of interconnectedness is thus a critical consciousness. It is a consciousness of awareness and of action that impacts upon the very nature of my relationships with my clients.

Wood (1995) suggested that a way of being consists of:

> a reliance on the formative directional tendency
> a will to act constructively
> an intention to be effective in one's objectives
> having compassion for the individual and respect for his or her autonomy
>   and dignity
> a flexibility in thought and action
> an openness to new discoveries
> an ability to intensely concentrate and clearly grasp the linear, piece by
>   piece, appearance of reality as well as perceiving it holistically, all at once
> a tolerance for uncertainty or ambiguity
> a sense of humour, humility and curiosity

A way of being is also:

> unique
> constituted and expanded as we live and interact with Others
> concerned with both self-direction and mutuality
> anti-reductionist in all its aspects
> not object related: it is 'amongst seeing' not object seeing
> concerned with the growth of the 'I' and growth of the 'Other'
> a 'verb-like' existence; it is 'letting be'

it is about celebration and energy
compassionate; it is about waking up our exiled compassion
to live in creativity and with honour and integrity
involves, includes and educates
embodied in action

For this writer this concept of a way of being is central to the PCA.

INTERCONNECTEDNESS

Capitalism has propagated a 'separation myth', which conflicts with the PCA view of human nature and our interconnectedness. It asserts that we are all separate units, in competition and it is necessary to distrust others to advance the position of this disconnected individual. If some people are weak, that is their problem; we have to secure ourselves first. In holding extreme individualism at its core, it could be said that capitalism has at least facilitated human survival and may even have helped human societies to develop. Yet I believe we all have paid a price for this focus on the individual.

The PCA has often been accused of being completely 'for' the individual at the expense of the communal. It is increasingly obvious that this is an essential misunderstanding and misinterpretation of the PCA within the psychotherapy and counselling world. I have explored how Schmid reminds us that the approach has two aspects, neither of which is greater than the other—the individual, and the relational/communal. But years of socialization in Western capitalism have embedded the cultural myth of separateness so deeply in the human psyche that any talk of interconnectedness is often perceived as mad. If this separation myth is not decoupled from popular views of the PCA it will redouble the misinterpretations. Moreover it will cloud our understanding of our actions and misinform our ethics. We must insist that human nature is not the problem, the myth is the problem, and it is the myth that the PCA must engage with.

O'Donohue (1998) writes that 'the hunger to belong is at the heart of our nature' (1998: xv). We are not meant to be isolated. A sense of belonging is necessary and this echoes the ancient and eternal values of human life—truth, unity, goodness, justice, beauty and love (ibid.: xvi). From our beginnings we are all brought forth from the Other—I am from and through my parents, my relations and my community. Relationship is the source and everything is intrinsically connected, irrevocably interdependent, interactive, interwoven. A truly evolved society is one which is measured by how well it treats the least of its members, and as Schmid (2002: slide 44) points out, our essential interconnectedness recognizes that 'each of us is somebody else's other'.

CONCLUSION: THE POLITICAL DIMENSION WITHIN THE PCA

Person-Centred Practitioners for Social Change (see page 2, this volume) is a step in the right direction. Marx (1956: 176) wrote that 'if humanity is shaped by its surroundings, its surroundings must be made human'. This is the task ahead for the PCA. There is no point in calling ourselves person-centred if we think that this means that only the *person* must change. The person is at the centre of a world that has a social and material environment that we must bring within our orbit.

The PCA must actively educate the counselling world, deliberately re-directing its perceived focus from the individual to the communal. In espousing a PCA way-of-being it must then be seen as discordant to focus entirely on the 'individual'. What the PCA can realistically offer is a space for a person or people to be, to encounter, to celebrate and to challenge each Other.

Although the PCA started in the therapy room with Rogers' original work, it must not end there. The political dimension of the approach must grow out of the therapy room, however marginal therapy is to the daily lives of the vast majority of people on the planet. We can learn things from this encounter, to inform ourselves of how to proceed within community. It has limitations as noted, chiefly, if divorced from critical reflection and consciousness, and if it does not comprehend the client's life outside the therapy room.

RECONSCIENTIZATION

The Brazilian educationalist Paulo Freire in his book *The Pedagogy of the Oppressed* (1972) advocated a critical approach to literacy. Freire talked of 'conscientization' which is a process by which humans become fully aware of their role in the world. Freire stressed that it is important to understand that as human beings we exist in and with the world.

Conscientization is thus a process of humanization. Conscientization develops our capacity to conduct a critical analysis of this world's 'reality' and create the conditions for humans to act upon and transform that reality. Finally conscientization is a movement, or action, towards transforming our reality. It is not a static state but a continual process of critical reflection and action.

Reconscientization, therefore, is a revisiting of this process, now, in our individual and collective locations. It is reconsidering our stances on division, oppression, social and political issues. It is reaffirming our commitment to person-centred principles and finding ways to act constructively with them. It is evolving and meeting these serious challenges as they confront us.

I hope that we can be inspired to cultivate a sound political base for our actions as person-centred persons. Maybe it is time to 'reconscientize' ourselves both collectively and individually. Let us remember that we are interconnected intimately and there is an urgency to come together, to pool our resources and to act. We have to be honest and realistic. We can only do what we can do. It is a time to consider individual commitment and collective action.

I have argued for a political imperative inherent in the very fabric of the PCA. This imperative is best understood as a way of being-in-the-world. This is a political, moral and ethical life-stance or 'posture', which compels us to examine the nature of the world and relationships around in that world. It further compels the practitioner to cultivate a political philosophy and action, the basis of which is self-reflection and examination of assumptions: a critical consciousness. This enables a politicized PCA: as individuals and collectively; through lobbying, writing, research, policy, individual and collective mobilization.

It is now up to us to prove the cult comic Bill Hicks wrong: we are not just a virus with shoes.

This chapter is dedicated to the memory of Rosa Parks (1913–2005) whose quiet dignity and conviction in the face of naked oppression is an inspiration and a poignant reminder that injustice to one is a travesty for all. And of course to Lily.

REFERENCES

Freire, P (1972) *The Pedagogy of the Oppressed.* London: Penguin.

Marx, K (1956) *The Holy Family.* Moscow: Foreign Languages Publishing House.

Mearns, D & Thorne, B (2002) *Person-Centred Therapy Today.* London: Sage.

O'Donohue, J (1998) *Eternal Echoes: Exploring our hunger to belong.* New York: Bantam Books.

Proctor, G (2002) *The Dynamics of Power in Counselling and Psychotherapy: Ethics, politics and practice.* Ross-on-Wye: PCCS Books.

Rogers, CR (1942) *Counseling and Psychotherapy.* Boston: Houghton Mifflin.

Rogers, CR (1951) *Client-Centred Therapy.* London: Constable.

Rogers, CR (1961) *On Becoming a Person: A therapist's view of therapy.* London: Constable.

Rogers, CR (1978) *Carl Rogers on Personal Power.* London: Constable.

Sanders, P (2005) Self-examination. *Person-Centred Quarterly, November,* 1–5.

Sartre, J-P (1958) *Being and Nothingness: An essay on phenomenological ontology.* London: Routledge.

Schmid, PF (1998) On being a Person-Centred Approach: A person-centred understanding of the person. In B Thorne & E Lambers (eds) *Person-Centred Therapy: A European perspective* (pp. 38–52). London: Sage.

Schmid, PF (2002) *The Characteristics of a Person-Centered Approach to Therapy and Counseling: Criteria for identity and coherence.* Carl Rogers Symposium at the University of California, San Diego, La Jolla, July 27, 2002.

Shlien, JM (2003) *To Lead an Honorable Life: Invitations to think about client-centered therapy and the person-centered approach.* Ross-on-Wye: PCCS Books.

Wood, JK (1995) The Person-Centered Approach: Towards an understanding of its implications. *Person-Centered Journal, 2* (2), 18–35.

Chapter 5

PERSON-CENTRED THERAPY AND TIME-LIMITED THERAPY

PAULINE MACDONALD

INTRODUCTION

I have had an interest in the impact that limits of time have in therapy since 1999 following a placement as a trainee client-centred counsellor in an Occupational Health Service for a large local authority as part of my initial BA in Counselling and Psychology. I wasn't fully aware of the significance this training had as part of a new wave of professional standards for counselling and I chose this course purely on the basis of availability of training within easy travelling distance from home. As a single parent with a restricted income from early ill-health retirement at the age of 33, I had been through some significant life events, and found myself experiencing the depths of depression. Since completion of my degree in 2001 I have been in continuous employment as a counsellor in primary care for various Trusts. I have seen the growth of provision in this area of modernization of mental health services from 'both sides': as counsellor and client.

As a client-centred counsellor in this field, I work entirely within the restrictions of time, the number of sessions usually being somewhere between 6 and 12, with the rare opportunity to work with an individual for up to between 20 and 24 sessions. However, in contrast to this is my own personal experience as a person in psychological distress, and of having accessed therapy from a person-centred perspective outside of this time-limited medical framework. Over a period of three years throughout my degree, I benefited from the student counselling provision. This gave me the opportunity to personally recover from being 'worried sick', to being 'worried well', and to explore and enjoy the possibility of 'self-growth' from outside the constraints of the medical model.

In 2000 John Eatock stated that the National Health Service had become the largest employer of counsellors in the UK (Keithley et al., 2002). One year later, John Mellor-Clarke (Mellor-Clarke et al., 2001) estimated that over half the GP practices in Britain had counsellors as members of primary care teams. At a time when statutory regulation was also, coincidentally, in the early stages of introduction by the government, this has in itself made counsellors in primary care a powerful body of people. As a counsellor in this field, I have started to question some of the consequences of this trend, particularly in regard to the constraints of time; why this may be happening, and how beneficial this may be to whom?

The idea that speed is all important surrounds us in our daily lives in a world where a technological revolution is happening all around us. It should, therefore, probably come as no surprise that the field of counselling has not escaped this wave of change.

There are various definitions of the terms 'brief' or 'time-limited' counselling. However, the underlying principle is that counselling sessions are effectively rationed, stating at the outset of a counselling contract the number of sessions available to the client. Limiting the number of sessions available to the client usually means more clients can utilize the service, whether this be in a primary care setting, employee assistance programme, or in the voluntary sector. However, whilst this may be an effective way of working for some therapeutic models, the limiting of time restricts the possibility for clients to experience the full potential of client-centred therapy.

Carl Rogers rejected the dominant medical model subscribed to by his colleagues, where treatment was seen as being delivered by the therapist (Rogers, 1951). He developed a way of understanding and helping individuals that had never been considered before, resulting in the advent of client-centred therapy, a therapy that did not seek to 'treat' or 'cure' a person, but provided a relationship that could be used for personal growth. Like many of his counterparts at that time (Laing, 1959; Goffman, 1961), Rogers noted the oppressive nature of interactions, which favoured control of the individual within society. In contrast to these oppressive relationships, client-centred therapy saw the client as a worthy individual as they were, acceptable and understandable, and offered a relationship where basic worth could be experienced. This in itself fostered change within the individual. The approach had the potential to bring about not only short-term change, but empowered the client to feel the freedom to exert choice in a world where previously choice and freedom were experienced as only partially available at best.

TIME-LIMITED COUNSELLING—
POLITICAL IMPLICATIONS FOR PERSON-CENTRED THERAPY

GROWTH AND SOCIAL CONTROL

Lord Richard Layard, professor at the London School of Economics, recently (O'Hara, 2005) compared mental health today with unemployment 10 years ago, declaring it to be Britain's biggest social problem. He proposed that psychotherapy for those who are depressed or anxious could be an effective solution to reducing the soaring payments to claimants of incapacity benefit. As a result, therapy was once again considered a 'technique'—a way by which to encourage individuals experiencing psychological distress to get back onto their feet, but more significantly, a method by which to get individuals back into employment. This is an interesting challenge to the client-centred counsellor.

How can the counsellor retain the essence of Rogers' approach wherein each individual heals themselves from within, given an unconditional non-judgemental relationship fostering client self-worth and resulting in the client able to take responsibility for making their own choices in life? In contrast with some psychotherapies, client-centred therapy is not a 'technique', but an attitude, a way of being that facilitates the actualizing tendency—the positive life force of the organism. Indeed, unlike the medical view of psychotherapy, not only does the client-centred process help to heal, it empowers the individual to realize their full potential, free from control by others (Rogers, 1978). Optimally, therapy would allow the client to become a fully functioning person (Rogers, 1967)—different from a person usually structured by society—able to trust their inner feelings as a competent guide to behaviour, not relying upon the judgement of others or a code of action laid down by a group.

Rogers (1967) suggested that when a human being is functioning freely, they are constructive and trustworthy. Being free from defensiveness opens the individual to a wider range of their own needs as well as the wider range of environmental and social demands, and thus can be trusted to be positive, forward-moving, and constructive, and as such:

> We do not need to ask who will socialize him, for one of his own deepest needs is for affiliation and communication with others. As he becomes more fully aware of himself, he will become more realistically socialized. (Rogers, 1967: 194)

Culture defines the amount of freedom of action and amount of autonomy (Kitchener, 1984), and cultural power is a combination of the use of individual and structural factors. In my experience, British culture defines a society in which citizens have little time to be themselves. Not enough time can be given to anything other than the very system structured by the world of work. Indeed, Lord Layard's report (see O'Hara, 2005) makes an explicit link between health and employment, by pointing out that at present there are more mentally ill people on invalidity benefit than the total number of unemployed people.

His proposition, therefore, that a network of counselling centres could be the solution to helping mental health users to get a job in order to get better, once again supports the dominant thinking of modern society—that an individual can only be 'well' if seen as being able to participate as part of the national workforce. This raises an alarming question: is this current National Health Service modernization intended to meet the needs of those using its services or is it a modernization of the methods by which a national institution helps socialize the person?

In addition, the application of psychotherapy now extends into the world of work itself, where it is accessed by individuals having difficulty in coping with the stresses and strains of what modern society demands of them. Here, in therapy, they meet not a growth-oriented healing opportunity, but a mechanism by which they better learn to understand that *system*, and accept it as it is (Cooper & Payne, 1978). Furthermore, stresses related to changing working conditions, cultural alienation, pressure to succeed, abuse and oppression are resulting in human suffering, and impelling people to seek help through counselling and therapy.

Clients using counselling to explore attitudes, emotions, values and goals may also begin to explore the possibility that there are things wrong with the environment in which they exist, and to question whether they subscribe to beliefs and values seen as 'norms' in society. Self-directed growth, therefore, has consequences for society as a whole and the control of the behaviour of its members. It follows that to limit the amount of time an individual may receive client-centred therapy restricts the amount of growth that may be pursued by that client. The more the commercial sector and the Health Service utilize and provide time-limited counselling services to employees/patients, the more restrictions get placed upon the amount of time available to the client for emancipatory self-directed growth. Thus, the time-limiting of counselling can be used as an effective tool to constrain the full potential of client-centred therapy, and consequently the individual's full potential for emancipation, preventing them from becoming a fully functioning person.

EFFECTIVENESS AND COST

The person-centred approach has the potential to generate sufficient power for personal change to affect all aspects of the individual's life. More than that, it can spill over from the individual to affect the very way in which a community may operate (Rogers, 1980). However, where the goal of personal growth stands face-to-face with the goal of profit-making, conflict will arise. Business organizations offering employee counselling, voluntary organizations and the National Health Service place restrictions on the amount of time that will be available for each client—after all, time is money (Haralambos & Holborn, 2000). We also find that since the NHS is the largest provider of counselling services it wields immense power over individual practitioners and clients, and also in determining the way in which the 'profession' itself operates.

The organizing and delivering of psychological therapies (DOH, 2004) considers factors associated with cost effective and safe services, and makes recommendations regarding how to train and retain staff and deliver services safely. It discusses the implications of, amongst other things, empirically validating 'treatment'. One of its recommendations is participation in a collaborative Practice Research Network at the University of Leeds in part by sharing and utilizing the rich data collated by CORE (Clinical Outcomes in Routine Evaluation). However, in my experience, services where a client-centred framework predominantly operates, money is usually not readily available for such participation, and therefore important data is lost. This loss of data supportive of client-centred effectiveness has wider implications. In December 2004, the National Institute for Clinical Excellence (NICE) issued clinical guidelines on the management of depression in primary and secondary care, revealing a 'Stepped Care' model. A part of this includes psychological intervention, and once again the limits of time reappear, minus any mention of client-centred approaches:

> In mild and moderate depression, consider psychological treatment specifically focused on depression (problem-solving therapy, brief CBT and counselling) of 6–8 sessions over 10–12 weeks. (NICE, 2004: 7)

THE COUNSELLING SESSION

To look at the opposite side of the time-limited coin is to discover the potential of 'open-endedness'. In addition to examining their individual world, the client is able to explore the world we live in and make sense of the constraints imposed by the structure of society without the constraints of time. From such understanding comes re-empowerment, personal power and choice. Forcing time limits on client-centred therapy conspires with the political structure in restricting the amount of change that can occur.

That client-centred therapy is effective can be in no doubt since other therapies have adopted its core conditions to facilitate their processes of therapeutic intervention. Most mainstream approaches now include empathy and the need for the therapist to be real and respectful. Why then limit clients' access to these active ingredients? Those who work within the limits of time usually justify the time-limiting practice in terms of 'fairness', i.e. being able to see more clients, or even offering concentrated beneficial work. Others see it as part of counselling boundaries, imposed by others (service managers, for example) and not by the counsellor, and by informing clients of the limits of sessions, they absolve themselves of any complicity. Since counselling concerns itself with the location of the locus of control, we have to ask where, in fact, that resides in the session involving a disenfranchised client and a disenfranchised counsellor.

CONCLUSION

If time limits did not constrain therapy, perhaps more individuals would question the world they live in, and in doing so challenge the status quo. The person-centred approach does not concern itself with therapy alone, but it is a vision of 'being human'. Carl Rogers (1980: 350–2) wrote about this in detail, suggesting that the 'person of tomorrow' has twelve particular qualities:

openness
a desire for authenticity
scepticism regarding science and technology
a desire for wholeness
the wish for intimacy
being a 'process person'
caring
having a positive attitude towards nature
is anti-institutional
acknowledges the authority within
the unimportance of material things
has a yearning for the spiritual

However, he also noted that such people would be presented with much opposition, as these qualities fly in the face of the way in which individuals are exploited by a minority in the social system required by capitalism. Limiting time for client-centred therapy fails the client in not allowing the freedom to choose how far to grow; whether to opt for a quick fix or lasting change. Limiting time therefore, serves effectively as a discrete opposition to creating more 'people of tomorrow'.

Rogers clearly recognized the potential of widely available counselling:

> ... the individual who has experienced optimal psychological growth— a person functioning freely in all the fullness of his organismic potentialities; a person who is dependable in being realistic, self-enhancing, socialized, and appropriate in his behaviour; a creative person, whose specific formings of behavior are not easily predictable; a person who is ever-changing, ever-developing, always discovering himself and the newness in himself in each succeeding moment of time. (Rogers, 1983: 295)

Although he sought to move his therapy away from the constraints associated with the biomedical world, in the years since his death the counselling profession appears to be sanctioning a new set of constraints.

Rogers' belief in the fostering of better communities (rather than institutions) seems at present unlikely to be realized, with time-limited therapy being a contributing factor, unless client-centred practitioners break away from the current dominant trends.

I have woken up to the realization that I need to take an active interest in person-centred therapy, mental health issues and the politics of therapy before it is too late. If I don't I could find myself helplessly practising a mutated version of therapy for reasons I don't agree with.

REFERENCES

Cooper CL & Payne R (1978) *Stress at Work*. New York: John Wiley & Sons.

Department of Health (2002) Organisational Development <www.doh.gov.uk/PublicationsAndStatistics>, August 2002.

Department of Health (2004) Organising and Delivering Psychological Therapies <www.doh.gov.uk/PublicationsAndStatistics>, July 2004.

Goffman, E (1961) *Asylums: Essays on the social situation of mental patients and other inmates*. Harmondsworth: Penguin.

Haralambos M & Holborn M (2000) *Sociology—Themes and perspectives* (5th edn). London: HarperCollins.

Keithley, J, Bond, T & Marsh, G (2002) *Counselling in Primary Care*. Oxford: Oxford University Press.

Kitchener, KS (1984) Intuition, critical evaluation and ethical principles: The foundation for ethical decision in counseling psychology. *Counseling Psychologist, 12*, 43–55.

Laing, RD (1959) *The Divided Self*. Harmondsworth: Penguin.

Mellor-Clarke, J, Simms-Ellis, R & Burton, M (2001) *National Survey of Counsellors Working in Primary Care: Evidence for growing professionalism?* (Occasional Paper 79) Royal College of General Practitioners, London.

NICE (2004) Depression: Management of depression in Primary and Secondary Care <www.nice.org.uk/CG023NICEguideline>, December 2004.

O'Hara, M (2005) Walking the happy talk. *The Guardian*, Wednesday, 30 November.

Rogers, CR (1951) *Client-Centered Therapy*. Boston: Houghton Mifflin.

Rogers, CR (1967) *On Becoming a Person: A therapist's view of psychotherapy*. London: Constable.

Rogers, CR (1978) *Carl Rogers on Personal Power: Inner strength and its revolutionary impact*. London: Constable.

Rogers, CR (1980) *A Way of Being*. Boston: Houghton Mifflin.

Rogers, CR (1983) *Freedom to learn for the 80's*. Columbus, Ohio: Charles E Merrill.

Rogers, CR & Stevens B (1967) *Person to Person: The problem of being human*. Walnut Creek, CA: Real People Press.

Chapter 6

RETHINKING PERSON-CENTRED THERAPY

Khatidja Chantler

This chapter presents a deconstructive reading of the theory and practice of person-centred therapy, and the theory of personality, outlining their political implications. By this I mean that I will be exploring the taken-for-granted and inbuilt assumptions and values of certain aspects of the theory of person-centred counselling. Inevitably this also has implications for practice. Deconstructive ideas are therefore appropriate for a book about politics and the person-centred approach. I am also speaking/writing as a practising person-centred counsellor. I believe that my practice is enhanced by my engagement with theoretical resources outside of person-centred theory, for example, feminisms and critical race theories. For this book, I was approached to write about the political implications of the person-centred approach (PCA) in relation to 'race', but it is important to highlight at the outset the impossibility and the dangers of using one filter through which to encapsulate matters relating to identity. My concerns about the political implications of the person-centred approach are wider than those attributed solely to 'race'. My aim in this chapter is to discuss key aspects of person-centred theory, its relationships to practice and its implications for marginalized people. Specifically, I discuss the actualizing tendency, non-directivity and Rogers' structure of personality.

Person-centred counselling courses have burgeoned since the 1990s and the most widely sold textbook on counselling and psychotherapy is *Person-centred Counselling in Action* (Mearns & Thorne, 1988). The PCA has been enormously influential in a wide variety of 'helping' settings including education and social work. Person-centred counselling is also widely available in a range of counselling settings, particularly the voluntary sector. Cognitive behaviour therapy is the favoured treatment modality (see for example the National Institute of Clinical Excellence (NICE) guidelines on depression, (NICE, 2004) particularly where other approaches have not worked. However, as Ian Hughes reminds us, this is largely because proponents of CBT have been very active in researching the efficacy of the approach (2005: 9). In the climate of evidence-based practice, it is easy to see why researching the effectiveness of therapeutic modalities becomes necessary. I suspect that this sits uncomfortably for many person-centred practitioners. However the consequences of not participating in research may have serious and negative consequences for person-centred counselling. More fruitful may be to consider how to conduct such research so that it is compatible with the values of the person-centred approach. The current situation is that despite its widespread appeal and application, person-centred therapy is frequently dismissed as reductionist, anti-intellectual, naïve and simplistic (Lowenthal & Snell, 2003: 10; cf. Mearns & Thorne, 2000; Merry, 1990; Thorne, 1992; Wilkins, 2003). The (political) project therefore becomes how to intervene within such debates so that person-centred therapy becomes increasingly recognized as an important way of working therapeutically with people. In this chapter, I attempt to do just this—but this does not mean adopting an unquestioning adherence to the approach. Rather, a more critical eye, which teases out the contradictions and taken-for-granted assumptions, offers fertile ground with which to engage in contemporary debates about therapy.

THE ACTUALIZING TENDENCY

The actualizing tendency is a key foundational belief on which person-centred therapy is based. Given the privileged status in which theory is held, it is not unsurprising that theoretical frameworks in general go unchallenged. Here, I examine the actualizing tendency, as it is an aspect of the theoretical framework that is mostly taken for granted. Rogers (1959) formulated it as an innate biological drive, common to all organisms. It is this biological framing of the actualizing tendency that is widely taken as read and leads person-centred theorists such as Wilkins (2003) and Mearns and Thorne (2000) to assume that it is therefore neutral and value free and independent of the social. Donna Haraway, a biologist and feminist, discusses at some length how the biological is culturally produced knowledge, relying on story and metaphor for its explication (1990, 2001). Relating this conceptualization of biology to Rogers' work, it is clear that Rogers, too, relies on metaphor to describe the workings of the actualizing tendency. He uses the 'potato' analogy to highlight growth (however distorted) in response to environmental conditions. One reading of this is that the actualizing tendency exists in relation to the environment, and that growth is dependent on the environment. There are two points that arise from this.

First, Rogers, through his potato story, clearly recognizes the existence of different (and unequal) environments, and this resonates with much feminist and anti-racist thinking. However, whilst feminisms and racisms challenge the status quo, Rogers appears to be accepting of these different environments rather than engaging or critiquing unequal environmental conditions. If, for environment, one can substitute organizing systems of society such as those based on sexisms, racisms, class, disability and the dominance of hetero-normativity, then Rogers' apparent acceptance of these are problematic. Further, as Spinelli (1994) points out, sometimes environmental conditions are so harsh as to produce rotting potatoes or no growth whatsoever.

Second, although the actualizing tendency is presented as biological and scientific (and therefore difficult to question), Haraway's work allows us instead to consider the representations, histories and social relations which give rise to 'facts'. She is concerned that the objective or neutral hides dominant power relations. Following Haraway, the representation of the actualizing tendency as biological and natural both by Rogers' formulation and more recent person-centred theorists (e.g. Bozarth, 1998; Merry, 2000; Mearns & Thorne, 2000; Wilkins, 2003) becomes open to debate and contest. Rogers (1959) is clear about his belief in 'science' being truth—a belief emanating from the cultural and historical context of his time. This belief has since been questioned by feminists, post-structuralists, social constructionists and other critical approaches in relation to epistemology and methodology. Disappointingly, more recent person-centred theorists do not appear to have engaged with the key currents of thought emerging from critical perspectives and have therefore tended to reproduce the notion of 'science' as truth unproblematically. Returning to the actualizing tendency, it becomes important to interrogate instead what kinds of subjects are envisaged and produced through such representations. Rogers' own description in his definition of the actualizing tendency is 'It [the actualizing tendency] is development toward autonomy and away from heteronomy, or control by external forces' (Rogers, 1959: 196). The first point to note is how what starts out as a biological movement to growth is now plainly imbued with psychological and cultural features. Interestingly, psychological and cultural features such as autonomy align with White, male and dominant positions in society as has been pointed out by feminist writers such as Gilligan (1982) and Hare-Mustin and Merecek (1986). Once this is acknowledged, it becomes possible to move away from a universal reading of the actualizing tendency to a contextual one instead. Further, biology has had profound negative impacts both in relation to women and minoritized peoples. There is now a substantial body of literature, particularly from feminist and post-colonial work, which implicates biology in cultural practices and material effects (Fryer, 1984; Haraway, 1990; Millett, 1972; Spelman, 2001). The role of biology in 'scientific' racism cannot be overlooked either. Linnaeus'[1] system of classification of plants and animals was the first to call us Homo sapiens and simultaneously placed us in a hierarchy based on skin colour, with white-skinned people at the top. Craniology, in the eighteenth century, is another example of the link between biology and racism, where the measurements of skulls were taken to indicate brain size. More recently, Jensen, in 1969, maintained that general intelligence (a characteristic seen as residing in individuals) was genetically determined and that this accounted for the difference in intelligence between Black and White people on IQ tests. These examples alert us to the dangers of viewing biology as neutral. Returning to the actualizing tendency, it is clear that the qualities of self-actualization (autonomy and freedom

---

1. See Peter Fryer's (1984) *Staying Power* (pp. 165–90) for a detailed analysis of biology and racism.

from external forces) are more in line with dominant positionings in society (Chantler, 2004, 2005). Any process (such as the actualizing tendency) which purports to be value free but which in fact privileges White, male and middle-class perspectives is more than likely to be masking the gendered, 'raced' and classed constructions inherent in the process.

My challenge to person-centred counselling is that it needs to move away from the assumption that the biological is neutral and instead engage with the constructions surrounding its assumptions of the biological and its relationship to the social. Instead of separating and compartmentalizing 'biology' as objective and value free, I suggest the actualizing tendency be read as a social construct, and to engage with where and what the process leads towards. This opens up the concept to further debate and contestation. The potentiality of subjects (rather than a deficit model) that the self-actualizing tendency suggests is important, but equally important to grapple with is the way in which potentiality is influenced by, and thwarted by, the wider context. This necessarily involves making explicit the gendered and raced dimensions of 'growth' and ensuring that therapy is fully cognisant of its own theoretical and practice assumptions and the power relations they give rise to.

NON-DIRECTIVITY

A second key value stance and building block of person-centred therapy is non-directivity and this is linked to the actualizing tendency, and to the necessary and sufficient conditions of therapy. The formulation of non-directivity is that the actualizing tendency does not require guidance or encouragement, although a non-directive stance as implied by the necessary and sufficient conditions of therapy (Rogers, 1957) best facilitates the actualizing tendency. This highlights the centrality of a deep respect for the client and a strong belief in clients' potential to work through their material. It positions the client as 'expert' in their own process and this offers much hope for those of us in subjugated positions. In theory, non-directivity allows for those in subordinated positions to be 'expert', without undue interference from the therapist. This positioning of client as expert helps to shift the balance of power in the therapeutic relationship, but as Proctor argues, this relates mainly to personal power or power-from-within (2002: 103). The focus on 'personal' power runs the risk of obscuring the ways in which power relations are implicated in the construction of the personal, and in institutional arrangements. Hence this indicates the necessity to ask, how does non-directivity work in practice?

A common representation of non-directivity is the caricature of a wooden counsellor, nodding her head and repeating the words of the client. This rather unkind representation, particularly by critics of person-centred therapy, positions the counsellor as lacking in expertise. So the positioning of the client as expert has come to be read as the counsellor as 'un-expert'. Here it is important to point out that the client as expert is not the same as saying the counsellor has no expertise. I fear that Rogers (and others) may have added to this representation by focusing so strongly on the necessary and sufficient conditions of therapy. The effect of this has been to separate the rest of Rogers' theoretical framework from the process of therapy. Is this a feasible position to maintain? And what are the effects of this position?

Thinking about my own practice, I am very aware that when a client discusses a situation which includes 'I should/ought', these are utterances that I am particularly alert to as they may well indicate conditions of worth. So my responses in these interactions are to incorporate my understandings of Rogers' theory of personality, particularly conditions of worth. In analysing videotapes of Rogers' work with an African-American man (Whiteley, 1977a and b), some of Rogers' most profound responses to his client arise from Rogers' working with the client's conditions of worth where these have been offered by the client as an area of exploration (Chantler, 2004). His theoretical framing can therefore be seen as influencing what and how he responds to client material, and in this sense opens the debate about whether the conditions specified by Rogers are indeed necessary and sufficient. I would argue that the theoretical underpinnings of a theory cannot be divorced from its practice. After all, what would the point of developing a theoretical framework be if it bore no resemblance to practice?

Here I agree with Warner (1998) who argues that absolute non-directivity is hypothetical. She identifies five levels of interventiveness in therapeutic processes (1998: 6–8). Each progressive level increases the extent to which the therapist uses her theoretical framings, and the authority that this gives rise to in therapeutic relationships. Of course, what is important to person-centred therapists is to avoid using the power derived from being informed by person-centred theory, i.e. to avoid the 'expert' position in such a way that it undermines the client's understanding of herself. I contend that it is possible to use theoretical understandings in the practice of person-centred therapy, and to maintain a stance of deep respect for the client and her process. Further, I argue that a failure to engage with the ways in which theoretical ideas shape person-centred practice leaves it open to accusations of ineffectiveness (particularly from its critics). More seriously, the operations of power inherent in any relationship become obscured by an insistence on non-directivity, something that is only ever a hypothetical possibility. Of course, the idea of power relations is inherent in the idea of non-directivity. However, the democratizing intent of non-directivity cannot be met by a simple declaration that one is being non-directive, or a denial of the ways in which theory and one's personal and contextual perspective inform practice. An engagement (or lack of) with one's social locations also impacts on therapeutic practice in a similar way that one's theoretical framing informs practice (see Proctor, 2004). This suggests a requirement for person-centred therapy to be more open to the ways in which theoretical understandings and social locations influence practice, and therefore to interrogate the notion of non-directivity and the social relations it gives rise to more fully.

Wilkins (2003) in his discussion of non-directivity, drawing on Brodley's work (1997), suggests that it is therapist intention that is crucial. Both agree that the enterprise of psychotherapy (of whatever orientation) has the goal of helping clients towards healing and that influencing this process is a crucial part of the therapeutic process. Both agree that how that process is conducted and the intentions behind it are key to determining (non-) directivity. This is a problematic formulation from my perspective, in that much of the 'equalities' industry around racism, sexism and disability has been concerned not just with intent, but also with effects and outcomes. This can be seen in the Race Relations Act (1976), the Sex Discrimination Act (1975) and the Disability Discrimination Act (1995) which all make it illegal to discriminate on 'indirect' grounds. 'Bad' intention is more clearly associated with direct discrimination; indirect discrimination covers intentions which may have been 'good' or non-racist/sexist, but have the effect of producing racist/sexist/disablist outcomes. My key argument is that it is not sufficient to be well intentioned, but to also consider, in the context of therapy, the key theoretical and practice components of the orientation and the power relations they speak to.

Laungani, from a South Asian perspective, raises an altogether different concern in relation to non-directivity (2004). He argues that the aspiration of equality between counsellor and client in person-centred therapy (even if this were possible) is at odds with the hierarchical relationship that clients from South Asian cultures expect. He bases his argument on the sorts of healing that are available on the Indian subcontinent, including faith healers, shamans, gurus, and astrologers. Intrinsic to these relationships is the respect and high status accorded to the healer as a learned, wise person. It leads him to conclude, 'Often a therapist is imbued with magico-spiritual powers of healing … There is also an expectation that the therapist will be didactic; the therapist leads and the client follows, akin to a guru-student relationship' (Laungani, 2004: 226). Whilst allowing for the possibility of differences across generations through acculturation, Laungani remains convinced of this enduring difference between 'East' and 'West'. If this is the case, it presents particular difficulties for the person-centred approach which values non-directivity and places faith in the client's potential for healing. Some of what Laungani says resonates with my own experience as a counsellor, where a person-centred approach with an older person of South Asian origin who has a traditional outlook, or a younger person recently arrived from the Indian subcontinent, has been difficult and which can be attributed to a difference in expectations as outlined by Laungani. However, it is also my experience that clients who have been in the UK longer, respond well to a person-centred approach that is also attentive to issues of minoritization. My contention is therefore that there is perhaps more fluidity and 'hybridity' than Laungani's conceptualization allows for.

STRUCTURE OF PERSONALITY

Rogers described two components of personality: the organismic self and the self-concept. Rather than offering a detailed explanation here (see Rogers, 1959 for a complete explanation), I draw on key features of both of these components of personality, and critique them to illustrate their importance to theory and practice.

The organismic self is represented in Rogerian writing as pure, largely free of external constraints and therefore the authentic self (1959). Indeed this self is central to person-centred therapy as it is hoped that through the provision and experience of the 'core conditions', the client will be able to recapture or to realign themselves more closely with their organismic self, and thus to be more authentic. It is from here that one experiences 'true' feelings and experiences. It is where 'gut' feelings are located, and is linked to the (internal) locus of evaluation and actualizing tendency. The internal locus of evaluation means that gut feelings are trusted and are instrumental in making decisions. As Rogers said, 'doing what "feels right" proves to be a … trustworthy guide to behaviour' (1961: 190). The aura of authenticity is also closely linked to particular notions of childhood as we can see from Rogers' own work. For example, in the videotapes of Rogers' work referred to earlier, Rogers, in one of his voice-overs states:

> V18: This has been a marvellous picture of the wholeness of a child and its disruption by society. I'm trying, as in all my therapy, to help him get back to the kind of realness he had as a child.

Here we have confirmation of childhood as a time of freedom, autonomy, spontaneity, as burdenless, and uncontaminated by society, together with the desirability of a return to this status. Rogers (1959) also describes the organismic self as being prior to the influences of socialization. The organismic self at this point is largely biologically framed, but very quickly assumes psychological and cultural features. This highlights (as also discussed above) the difficulty of seeing biology as 'science' and therefore as value free, rather than as culturally produced knowledge. There are three arguments against such a notion of childhood.

First, the notion of childhood alluded to here indicates a specific childhood: largely belonging to dominant groups, Western, middle class, free of illness or abuse. In contrast, many of the world's children are required to join the labour force at a young age, and live in poverty. Much of the world still lacks clean water with widespread diseases including malaria, cholera and typhoid, with high infant mortality rates. This is clearly not the image of the child that Rogers invokes in his voice-over. The question remains that if the 'realness' of our beings is based on narratives of childhood which reinforce the values and experiences of dominant groups, of what relevance is it for those in minoritized groups?

Second, it seems hopelessly idealistic to assume that the 'realness' of a child is either achievable or even desirable, particularly as an adult. For a child to be 'free', somebody else (most often a mother) is required to take responsibility for the care of the child. The gendered, 'raced', and classed dimensions of a return to such 'realness' speak to the freedom of dominant groups, frequently enjoyed at the expense of subjugated others. Whilst Rogers postulated that an increasing contact with one's organismic self and the actualizing tendency would lead to an increased sense of social responsibility, this claim seems tenuous.

Third, as Proctor also argues, it is unlikely that the organismic self can ever be totally uncontaminated by or pure from our social contexts (2004). Hence, feelings or experiences are also likely to have a social component to them, which can be generated by and mediated through social locations. As Proctor warns, 'As we strive to be more and more aware of our inner experiencing (congruence), there is a danger in assuming these "organismic experiences" are a pure expression of an inner self unaffected by context' (Proctor, 2004: 137). Such individualization is characteristic of psychological approaches, and is in danger of collapsing a person's socio-economic context to a purely individual framework, with the attendant potential of pathologizing the client, rather than their environment.

The self-concept is counterpoised to the organismic self. The self-concept absorbs injunctions and introjects, and in the Rogerian formulation, it becomes distant from the organismic self. We begin to think and behave in ways to win approval from those (normally caregivers) who have offered us conditions of worth and which we have internalized. Conditions of worth are therefore relational, and as I have argued elsewhere, the concept can be usefully expanded to specifically consider the gender, class or 'race' dimensions of conditions of worth (Chantler, 2004, 2005). The relational aspect thus ensures that the impact of the wider socio-political context is not lost. I have termed these 'racialized and gendered conditions of worth'. These make an important contribution to person-centred theory and practice in the following ways:

- Expands/develops Rogers' ideas of conditions of worth
- Connects individual to society and therefore offers a counterpoint to the individualizing tendencies of psychological approaches
- Contextualizes 'experience' and 'feelings', so that they are seen at least in part as in relation to the wider context
- Opens up possibilities for different understandings which are necessary for contemporary society
- Facilitates an openness about differences based e.g. on class, race, gender
- Improves presence of 'core conditions' by fully acknowledging and situating both counsellor and client

Interestingly, similar ideas are also emerging from within the person-centred world as illustrated in various book publications including this one (see also Kearney, 1996; Moodley, Lago & Talahite, 2004; Proctor & Napier, 2004). This suggests that part of the person-centred world is alive to the challenges posed to person-centred counselling in today's contexts. Whether this new thinking has made its way into counsellor training programmes is debatable.

CONCLUSIONS

In relation to Rogers' theoretical framework I have analysed three key features: the actualizing tendency, non-directiveness, and his thinking on the structure of personality. The challenge of acknowledging the social constructions and the power relations involved in the concepts of the actualizing tendency, rather than relying on the assumption that the biological is neutral creates space to examine its racialized, gendered, and class components and to respond accordingly. A firm belief in the biological as value free closes down such explorations, and at the same time renders invisible the power relations inherent in it.

Whilst the desirability of non-directiveness has been discussed, its limitations have also been highlighted. In particular, attention to the ways in which theoretical frameworks influence practice calls for a reconsideration of whether Rogers' (1957, 1959) necessary and sufficient conditions for therapeutic change still (or ever did) stand. I have argued that whilst they are necessary, they are not sufficient. Indeed as discussed above, Rogers' own examples of practice in the videotapes highlighted above, themselves illustrate how his theoretical formulations have a bearing on how he responds to clients (for a fuller analysis of this, see Chantler, 2004).

Within the person-centred literature, the organismic self appears to enjoy a special place within person-centred thinking and practice. The analysis offered above highlights how the organismic self appears to be fashioned on a romanticized notion of childhood with spontaneity, authenticity, autonomy and freedom as its main characteristics. Whilst a critique of this has been provided above, on a more positive note, one could also interpret the organismic self as a reservoir of agency, acting as a counterpoint to the constructions of self formed by conditions of worth. In this sense, Rogers' theory of personality offers the potential both for the construction of subjects, that is the way in which we are all partly constituted through cultural norms and discourses and its attendant self-regulation, as well as agentic behaviour. In my reading, the tension and contradiction between the two cannot ever be completely resolved, but serve as a useful schema to avoid the pitfall of reducing the political to the personal. However, it seems to me that the more common interpretation of person-centred theory places greater emphasis on the organismic self's capacity for agency, rather than the self-concept's regulative effects, thus skewing it to an individualized approach, rather than an approach that is fully engaged with the social context. Concepts of racialized and gendered conditions of worth, alongside an unpacking of the key assumptions of person-centred theory, and a sharper focus on the person in context, will better enable person-centred therapy to respond to contemporary contexts.

REFERENCES

Bozarth, JD (1998) *Person-Centered Therapy: A revolutionary paradigm.* Ross-on-Wye: PCCS Books.

Brodley, BT (1997) The non-directive attitude in client-centered therapy. *The Person-Centered Journal, 4* (1), 18–30.

Chantler, K (2004) Double-edged sword: Power and person-centred counselling. In R Moodley, C Lago, & A Talahite (eds) *Carl Rogers Counsels a Black Client* (pp. 116–29). Ross-on-Wye: PCCS Books.

Chantler, K (2005) From disconnection to connection: 'Race', Gender and the Politics of Therapy. *British Journal of Guidance and Counselling, 33* (2), 239–56.

Fryer, P (1984) *Staying Power: The history of Black people in Britain.* London: Pluto.

Gilligan, C (1982) *In a Different Voice.* Harvard: Harvard University Press.

Haraway, D (1990) A manifesto for cyborgs: Science, technology, and socialist feminism in the 1980s. In L Nicholson (ed) *Feminism/Postmodernism* (pp. 190–233). New York and London: Routledge.

Haraway, D (2001) The persistence of vision. In KK Bhavnani (ed) *Feminism and 'Race'* (pp. 145–60). Oxford: Oxford University Press.

Hare-Mustin, R & Merecek, J (1986) Autonomy and gender: Some questions for therapists. *Psychotherapy, 2,* 205–12.

Hughes, I (2005) NICE in practice: Some thoughts on delivering the new guideline on depression. *Counselling and Psychotherapy Journal, 16* (3), 8–10.

Jensen, AR (1969) How much can we boost IQ in scholastic achievement? *Harvard Educational Review, 39* (1), 1–23.

Kearney, A (1996) *Counselling, Class and Politics.* Ross-on-Wye: PCCS Books.

Laungani, P (2004) *Asian Perspectives in Counselling and Psychotherapy.* Hove: Brunner-Routledge.

Lowenthal, D & Snell, R (2003) *Post-modernism for Psychotherapists.* Hove and New York: Brunner-Routledge.

Mearns, D & Thorne, B (1988) *Person-Centred Counselling in Action.* London: Sage.

Mearns, D & Thorne, B (2000) *Person-Centred Therapy Today: New frontiers in theory and practice.* London: Sage.

Merry, T (1990) Client-centred therapy: Some trends and some troubles. *Counselling 1* (1), 17–18.

Merry, T (2000) Person-centred counselling and therapy. In C Feltham and I Horton (eds) *Handbook of Counselling and Psychotherapy* (pp. 348–52). London: Sage.

Millett, K (1972) *Sexual Politics.* London: Granada.

Moodley, R, Lago, C & Talahite, A (eds)(2004) *Carl Rogers Counsels a Black Client* (pp. 17–35). Ross-on-Wye: PCCS Books.

NICE (2004) *Depression: Management of depression in primary and secondary care.* NICE Guidelines: NICE.

Proctor, G (2002) *The Dynamics of Power in Counselling and Psychotherapy: Ethics, politics and practice.* Ross-on-Wye: PCCS Books.

Proctor, G (2004) What can person-centred therapy learn from feminism? In G Proctor and MB Napier (eds) *Encountering Feminism: Intersections of feminism and the person-centred approach* (pp. 129–40). Ross-on-Wye: PCCS Books.

Proctor, G & Napier, MB (2004) *Encountering Feminism: Intersections of feminism and the person-centred approach*. Ross-on-Wye: PCCS Books.

Rogers, CR (1957) The necessary and sufficient conditions of therapeutic personality change. *Journal of Consulting Psychology, 21* (2), 95–103.

Rogers, CR (1959) A theory of therapy, personality and interpersonal relationships, as developed in the client-centered framework. In S Koch (ed) *Psychology: A study of a science, Vol. 3. Formulations of the person and the social context* (pp. 184–256). New York: McGraw-Hill.

Rogers, CR (1961) *On Becoming a Person*. Boston: Houghton Mifflin.

Spelman, E (2001) Gender & race: The ampersand problem in feminist thought. In KK Bhavnani (ed) *Feminism and 'Race'* (pp. 74–88). Oxford: Oxford University Press.

Spinelli, E (1994) *Demystifying Therapy*. London: Constable.

Thorne, B (1992) *Carl Rogers*. London: Sage.

Warner, MS (1998) Person-centred psychotherapy: One nation, many tribes. In C Wolter-Gustafson (ed) *A Person-Centered Reader: Personal selection by our members*. Boston: Association for the Development of the Person-Centered Approach.

Whiteley, JM (Producer) (1977a) *Carl Rogers Counsels an Individual, I: The Right to be Desperate*. American Personnel and Guidance Association.

Whiteley, JM (Producer) (1977b) *Carl Rogers Counsels an Individual, II: On Anger and Hurt*. American Personnel and Guidance Association.

Wilkins, P (2003) *Person-Centred Therapy in Focus*. London: Sage.

Chapter 7

THE CULTURAL SITUATEDNESS OF LANGUAGE USE IN PERSON-CENTRED TRAINING

Rundeep Sembi

> Words are limited, like the beings that use them, and can only express the affairs of this limited world. (Tai Gong Diao)

As a British Sikh woman with a long-term illness and committed to avoiding oppressive practice, I am conscious of dominant/subordinate relationships that pervade the socio-political landscape. One measure I have taken to counsel ethically is to identify my cultural location and consider how my normative values and spoken language may impede a clear dialogue and limit the potential for establishing a democratic and accepting relationship with another.

Before continuing any further, it feels necessary to stipulate that I am writing from personal experience, memories and insights rather than hard facts. The focus of this discussion will be to explore some of the contradictions that emerged for me as a bicultural person training in the person-centred approach—a model of therapy that is rooted in Western individualistic psychology. My contention lies with the failure to interrogate the everyday speech of course members and make explicit how spoken English is *not* a neutral medium of communication but is a language imbued with cultural-specific values that reinforce the individuated construction of personhood.

The centrality of the individual as a bounded, independent self is perpetuated by the emphasis on speaking in the first person in order to own one's action. During my person-centred training, it was assumed that using 'I' as a self-referent indicated self-responsibility, maturity and autonomy. It logically followed that individuals who did not communicate in this way were somehow devoid of these qualities and were ultimately limiting their actualizing potential.

Whilst these messages felt relevant within a Western context, they lacked any validity within my Punjabi (home) culture, where the personal pronoun 'we' is given primacy over the 'I'. The transition to adulthood, accompanied by a growing sense of responsibility to the community seems to be marked linguistically by identifying as a 'we'. Although adult Sikhs largely use collective terms to refer to themselves when speaking Punjabi, this does not prevent me from experiencing them as unique, responsible persons. Contrary to my experiences on the diploma course, speaking in the first person within my collectivist home culture can feel rude, demanding and almost childish. In essence, saying 'I' in this setting can feel disempowering for me.

My very specific cultural reading of the 'I' clearly exposes the situatedness of language within a given setting. The meanings and values we attach to words or objects are temporarily fixed and defined by prevailing discourses of knowledge which determine not only what is meaningful in a particular topic (such as medicine or sexuality) but also how it can be talked about and whose voices carry authority (Michel Foucault, 1972, as cited in Hawtin & Moore, 1998: 91). Sarah Hawtin and Judy Moore (1998) describe how:

> All societies have procedures whereby the production of discourses is controlled to preserve the structures and conventions of that society. The process is reinforced by our everyday use of language so that the assumptions embedded in our consciousness are repeated in our most mundane utterances. (Hawtin & Moore, 1998: 91)

For instance, the increasing recognition of how patriarchal bias implicit within the English language functions to silence women's subjectivity is demonstrated by 'the predominant use of the male pronoun to describe universal experience' (Hawtin & Moore, 1998: 91).

In similar vein, I want to expose how cultural discourses of individualism were perpetuated through 'certain established ways of speaking' English (John Shotter, 1989: 140) in my person-centred training. The individuated focus built into English limits the conceptual possibilities for self-understanding, lending itself to articulating some experiences more accurately and favourably than others, if not occluding some experiences altogether. During my counselling training, it became apparent to me that the effect of having to conform to an individualized pattern of speech in order to be acknowledged by my fellow trainees resulted inadvertently in the censorship of my collectivist heritage. In the following section I elaborate further on how this felt.

BECOMING BICULTURALLY LITERATE

As with most counselling training, I was required to attend a personal development (PD) group for the duration of my diploma. It is within this context that I first became aware of how my speech composition could be (mis)understood by other PD members. Amidst the discussions with fellow participants, it was often pointed out that I would speak in the second person, when offering my personal opinions to the group. I would use the person pronoun 'you', rather than the 'I', as a self-referent. In the examples below I have tried to illustrate the type of comments which I refer to:

> '*You'd* feel great having achieved that.'
> '*You* probably would behave in that way under those circumstances.'

Talking thus, in the second person, sent out ambiguous messages to the PD group as to whether I was speaking about them or myself. 'Since "you" may be singular or plural, the person or persons being addressed have to interpret who is included and who is not' (Malone, 1997: 69). In PD, my words were construed to be generalizations about the group, prompting irritated glances and criticisms. Furthermore, my motivation for not saying 'I' was deemed to be a way of distancing myself from my experience and avoiding self-ownership.

Whilst I believed the group's assessment of me was plausible to an extent, it felt unjust at times. Puzzled by this, I stayed with my feelings, having learnt to value my affective responses in my person-centred therapy. I was also aware that despite my concerted efforts to speak as an individualized 'I', I continued to lapse into the second person when offering my subjective point of view. I wondered why I refrained from uttering this personal pronoun because generally, I had no qualms about taking ownership of my statements when challenged to do so. If I realized that I was not speaking as an 'I', I would quickly correct myself.

I started paying attention to how I felt making 'I' statements outside of PD and discovered that I felt rude, self-centred and a little immature, irrespective of my cultural context. I realized that I had inappropriately transferred the values attached to the 'I' in a Punjabi cultural frame to a Western setting and felt uncomfortable speaking in an individuated fashion that clashed with my collectivist values. Instead, by saying 'you' I could avoid these intercultural tensions because the 'you' could reference me (the speaker) as well as represent the collective and operate as a 'we' (Harvey Sacks, 1992, as cited in Malone, 1997).

This indefinite quality of the 'you' seemed to reflect my sense of self, which at the time did not feel sharply bounded and separate. I had unconsciously learnt to speak English in a way that reflected my self-experience and encompassed some of the values from my home culture and the majority culture. However, this led to misunderstandings within the PD sessions, because I failed to comply with the accepted text of Western individualism—the meaning structures and codes to which the group adhered. I had not learnt the established 'architecture of address' (Shotter, 1989: 146) to enable me to access the same 'communicative opportunities' (ibid.) that were afforded to group members that spoke in the correct tongue. In short I had to make a choice: either I persisted with my mode of speech and remained marginalized within the group or I adopted the 'legitimate' code in order to be heard and accorded the status of responsible adult. I conceded to the latter position.

Due to the fractious exchanges that arose in PD, I was alerted to my specific style of speaking English, which to my great surprise was considerably influenced by the value systems entrenched in my Punjabi home culture and language. I had not anticipated this because although I understand spoken Punjabi, my verbal proficiency is rather limited. I speak Punjabi to my parents and to other adults in the community but quickly revert to English due to a lack of confidence.

This insight into my pattern of speech has prompted me to revise how I use personal pronouns in both cultural settings, but for now I attend to the collective 'we' in Punjabi and briefly account for my changing perception of this term since completing my diploma. During my teenage years the 'we' had become synonymous with the collective values of my home culture and represented a threat to my independence and voice. When my parents used this collective reference, I felt I was being included in their address and spoken for without my consent, leaving me feeling unheard and angry.

On reflection, I have come to understand my defensive reading of the 'we' at a conscious level, thus recognizing the fallacy of my adolescent interpretation. First and foremost, I am confident that my parents' choice of language would never be motivated to erase me. Secondly, I have realized that I was comprehending the collective 'we' through a Western lens, inevitably setting it up to be deficient and 'Other' because its meaning was being qualified through 'what it was not' rather than in itself. In essence my internal world had come to mirror my external reality, wherein the hegemony of Western individualism functioned as the invisible yardstick from which other cultures are measured.

My challenge has been to find a way of knowing my collective culture in a language that does not negate it. This is difficult because my conscious thoughts and perceptions are mediated through the English language which incorporates a set of values that do exactly this. Instead of conceptualizing the 'we' cognitively, I am trying to unravel its meaning experientially, through my interactions, feelings and intuition. What is noticeable is that I am now more open to my collective heritage at an intrapersonal and interpersonal level, being less preoccupied with defending the individual and more committed to experiencing the uniqueness of a person through relationship. Moreover, because of my changing perspective, what has been intensely rewarding is that I now feel more intimately connected to my parents and Punjabi culture.

CONCLUSION

The merits of becoming biculturally competent are that I feel heard, empowered and integrated within both cultures, thus illuminating the need for me as a practising counsellor to examine how the use of my language locates me culturally and informs my perceptual awareness. By reflecting on my counselling training I have sought to demonstrate the interface between language and society and illustrate how individuals are subject to various contextual limitations discretely interwoven in the use of language.

For this discussion, I have centred on how cultural discourses of individualism were reproduced in my person-centred training through established ways of speaking English. Tutors and students alike failed to challenge the insistence on referencing the phenomenal self as an individualized 'I', thus maintaining the assumption that (1) the self can only be conceived as a demarcated unit, (2) that the sovereignty of the individual is a desirable outcome, (3) that not saying 'I' was exclusively an expression for avoiding self-responsibility, and (4) that all members of the group were complicit with this viewpoint. My intention is to awaken counsellors and trainers from 'the complacency of "conceptual sedimentation"' (Gergen, 1989: 71) by urging them to recognize how those experiences that stand outside the English language (and thus discourses of individualism), often hold less currency or are rendered cognitively inaccessible. This state of affairs has implications for our process of understanding self and others, which is permeated by the values embedded in idiosyncratic language systems.

'Language … serves as a vehicle for the formation of relations of power and control in relationships between people' (McLeod, 2004: 177). In appreciating how my use of language locates me, I make visible the particularity of my standpoint, leading to greater congruence. By identifying those areas in which my understanding of the Other is limited by my cultural positioning I can attempt to set aside any preconceptions and facilitate a deeper, horizontal therapeutic relationship. In my counselling practice this will help me approach more closely the authentic reality of the Other.

REFERENCES

Gergen, K (1989) Warranting a voice and the elaboration of the self. In J Shotter & K Gergen (eds) *Texts of Identity* (pp. 70–81). London: Sage Publications.

Hawtin, S & Moore, J (1998) Empowerment or collusion? The social context of person-centred therapy. In B Thorne & E Lambers (eds) *Person-Centred Therapy: A European perspective* (pp. 91–105). London: Sage Publications.

Malone, M (1997) *Worlds of Talk: The presentation self in everyday conversation.* Cambridge: Polity Press.

McLeod, J (2004) 'On Anger and Hurt' sessions: A narrative social constructionist perspective. In R Moodley, C Lago & A Talahite (eds) *Carl Rogers Counsels a Black Client: Race and culture in person-centred counselling* (pp. 175–89). Ross-on-Wye: PCCS Books.

Shotter, J (1989) Social accountability and the social construction 'You'. In J Shotter & K Gergen (eds) *Texts of Identity* (pp. 133–51). London: Sage Publications.

Tai Gong Diao (1999) as cited in *Taoist Wisdom: Daily Teachings from Taoist Sages* (p. 13). New Arlesford, Hants, UK: Godsfield Press.

Chapter 8

PERSONAL REFLECTIONS ON TRAINING AS A PERSON-CENTRED COUNSELLOR

Lois Peachey

My experience of the person-centred approach (PCA) to therapy is as student, counsellor and client but this chapter is primarily about my experience as a student. I should emphasize that this is my experience of this particular training course—I have no idea if it is typical or not.

I was 38 in 1999 when I moved back to Essex after 15 years in London and abroad. I had identified as a feminist for years and had a series of unfulfilling relationships with men. For a long time I felt that my London life did not match my 'real self' and I was generally unhappy although did not know what changes to make. However, serious illness in 1995 forced some major changes, culminating in the move out of London. I took the PCA introductory course at my local college just to find out more about the subject. I enjoyed that course and was stimulated by the fairly diverse range of people in the group. However, before committing myself to the diploma course I wanted to know more about the other approaches and took a year to do an A level in psychology. Returning to academic study was an amazing experience as it offered a framework on which to pin all of the stuff I'd been grappling with in my head for years—I was hungry for information and ideas. I also met my first female partner and came out in a blaze of optimism, renewed feminism and political awareness.

Having learnt something of other counselling approaches, the PCA was still the one I felt most suited to: I liked the non-judgemental, non-expert approach and its optimism about people. I was offered a place on the diploma course at the local college where I had done the introductory course. I was looking forward to meeting another diverse group of people and to being challenged. However, on the first day, I felt immediately that things were not going to be as I hoped. Twenty students, all White, mostly middle class, seventeen women, three men, almost all married with children and, bar myself and another lesbian (Sue), all identifying as heterosexual. The tutors were all White, middle-class heterosexuals and only one a qualified and experienced counsellor. I immediately felt my difference and didn't come out to the group on that day. Much to our amazement, Sue and I were allocated to co-counsel each other and this relationship had much to do with my experience of the course. Sue was older than me, had been out for longer and had just finished a Women's Studies course in East London. The contrast for her was enormous—she struggled through the first year but didn't make it into the second. We bonded in our difference but much of our co-counselling was spent being angry about the course, the implicit, unacknowledged homophobia and the lack of political awareness. As someone newly out, and someone who would have identified as liberal, I had no expectation of homophobia, particularly on a counselling course, but I was learning very quickly that I had moved into a different part of society, one that is pretty invisible to the majority. This was a painfully sharp learning curve. Gradually I came to understand the politics of homophobia but still found it very difficult to communicate that understanding to my fellow students. There were no opportunities within the training to get these issues out into the open. There was, to me, a deafening silence. The further the course progressed, the more I realized that there wasn't just silence around the issue of homophobia, there was silence around any area that could be perceived as 'political' e.g. gender, class, race, politics, religion.

Two years on from qualifying, I think that the lack of cultural and political awareness on my training course resulted in two main areas of difficulty, one that impacted on the training and one that impacted on me personally.

Firstly, I felt that our practice and understanding of the core conditions of congruence, empathy and unconditional positive regard (UPR) was hampered. Although sociology was part of the course, it provided only very brief, and for me frustrating, sessions on issues such as gender, race and class but there was no real analysis of our attitudes. I was always left feeling that as a group we kept well inside our comfort zone of political correctness. It was as if things like oppression and discrimination were somehow 'out there', and didn't happen in our town. There was also very little analysis of the history of psychotherapy, psychology and psychiatry and their role in shaping attitudes in today's society, for example in attitudes towards homosexuality. Celia Kitzinger (1987) claims that the notion of homophobia (i.e. an irrational, persistent fear or dread of homosexuals) is an invention of liberal humanistic psychology.

I had expected that one role of the experiential group might be to discuss the learning of the day, and it could have been a safer place than the classroom to examine our own politics, but this never seemed to happen. Politics was a taboo subject. The build up to the invasion of Iraq was happening and I went on some of the anti-war demonstrations—I mentioned this in the group a few times but there was no discussion and I wondered if that was perceived as extreme behaviour.

The issue of prejudice was relevant when it came to looking at the core condition of UPR, which was presented as being non-judgemental and unprejudiced. To me, this is meaningless because we are all judgemental—what is important to understand is how our judgements are formed and what we do with them. Having studied stereotyping and prejudice in psychology, I was surprised that this was not part of the training—perhaps other courses do teach it. Although I had acknowledged my own racism when I moved to London and then my homophobia when I came out, gaining an understanding of the processes (and the politics) of prejudice really helped me to challenge and try to unlearn them. Humanistic approaches to psychology grew out of liberalism and obviously, therefore, appeal to 'liberals' (myself included). However, perhaps the paradox is that to acknowledge inequality in society and prejudice within ourselves is too threatening to our beliefs as it must lead to an acknowledgement of some of the failures of liberalism? The world is not as nice as we would like. In my three years' training, there was not one discussion about sexuality and to this day I am unsure why. Perhaps having two, rather outspoken, lesbians (and thus, possibly fulfilling a stereotype) in the group made it difficult in some way. Perhaps the tutors were just not confident in their own views of sexuality or possibly had not thought about it. On one occasion, a student made a very homophobic comment but instead of challenging them, the tutor looked to Sue and I for a response.

Rogers wrote in 1977 that the word 'politics' was new in such contexts as therapy, sex and experience (Rogers, 1977) and of course, there was little written about them then. However, I was studying counselling 25 years later when the politics of these areas was already widely studied and taught in the UK. He recognized the issues of power and control but admitted that his recognition came quite late in his work:

> This new construct has had a powerful influence on me. It has caused me to take a fresh look at my professional life work. (Rogers, 1977, in Kirschenbaum & Henderson 1990: 377)

I might not agree with all that Rogers wrote on the politics of the helping professions but I know that he was at least aware of the issues. Even before 1977, he felt it was important that counselling trainees should, amongst other things,

> ... have a broad experiential knowledge of the human being in his cultural setting. This may be given, to some extent, by reading or course work in cultural anthropology or sociology. Such knowledge needs to be supplemented by experiences of living with or dealing with individuals who have been the product of cultural influences very different from those which have molded the student. (Rogers, 1951: 437)

Some contemporary writing on the PCA mentions politics less than Rogers did. For example, Mearns and Thorne (2000) devote just one page to gender and race but only in respect of identity and make some huge generalizations and simplifications. Part of this, I think, is due to the prevailing attitude towards difference, i.e. we are all unique individuals but we are all equally valued. We would hope to be equally valued in the counselling room but we are not all equally valued in society. My sense of the PCA during my training was that it exists in a vacuum, somehow immune to politics and not acknowledging the impact of politics on the individuals we are trying to help. I identified that part of the problem about acknowledging difference was that it could lead to generalizations about clients' experience. I accept that is a risk but there are common experiences within groups, as well as differences, otherwise there would have been no Black Power, women's or Gay Pride movements. It is important to differentiate between a common experience and an individual's response to that experience. If a therapist has thoroughly explored their own attitudes and politics, then I believe it could be helpful in understanding another's phenomenology to have some knowledge of how difference and politics impact on everyone in our society.

A question that remains with me is how, within the PCA, to help clients understand their current experiences and emotional distress in the context of their historical and current cultural and political influences i.e. the personal is political. It was suggested to me that clients learn to do this through therapy without it being made explicit but I am sceptical about this, especially as many therapists appear not to have learnt it. I understand it is pretty well accepted that counselling courses have an impact on trainees' personal relationships and certainly, on my course, some of the women seemed to become aware for the first time that the inequalities in their heterosexual relationships mirror the gender inequalities in society. However, this awareness can be painful and disruptive and many choose not to notice. I believe it is the absolute duty of a therapist to introduce clients to ideas about the world they live in as it can be very affirming, something I have experienced in my own therapy. I am not talking about the counsellor imposing their politics on the client but the counsellor engaging in exploration with the client of the world beyond the four walls of the counselling room. By not helping the client to understand the influence of history, society and politics, we are in danger of pathologizing the individuals we are working with and their families. With this approach, there can be another outcome to therapy, that of bringing about change beyond the individual—if we are not happy with the world as it is, it is only we who can do something about it. We can influence history, society and politics. A good example for me of a failure to help a client understand this connection was in the classic video of Carl Rogers (plus Albert Ellis and Frederick Perls) counselling Gloria who, amongst other things, was distressed about her sexual needs. She seemed to me to be a very vulnerable woman who was talking to three very confident and powerful men about her sexuality and not one of them helped her to connect her shame and anxiety with the prevailing attitudes towards women's sexuality in America at that time. Obviously, these were only snapshots, and I don't know what Gloria's overall experience was, but viewing the video clips in the early twenty-first century, there was no discussion or recognition in my training of the power dynamic.

One of my conclusions at the end of training was that the difficulties around the huge issue of unconditional positive regard and being non-judgemental severely hampered our understanding and practice of congruence. The experiential group was offered as a safe place to flex our congruence muscles but by common agreement on the course, it failed to do this, for some more than others and sometimes painfully. Although there were gender and class difference in our group, which might have had some influence on how we used the group, in my view the greatest obstacle to congruence was the fear of being seen as judgemental. One group member asked the group if they perceived her as judgemental because she felt she was and would like to explore it. The immediate reaction was to reassure her she wasn't, thereby blocking further exploration. In respect of client work, I think this also made it difficult to understand the concept of transference and counter-transference, which requires awareness of all feelings evoked in the relationship, including negative ones. The understanding of UPR that I took away from the training was that we should be able to like all our clients and that has meant that I have found it very hard to acknowledge any negative feelings I might experience.

As mentioned, the lack of political awareness on the training had an impact on me personally and I know that my experience is not untypical (Hawtin & Moore, 1998).

I spent much of the two-year diploma course feeling alternately frustrated, resentful, angry, self-conscious, isolated, invisible and confused. I knew some of the political criticisms of therapy—that it is a form of social control and actually disempowers people by pathologizing individuals—but I also knew that I had gained great personal benefit from counselling (although I had carefully chosen a politically aware therapist). During the training, I confess I read mainly material that wasn't on the reading list, including *Against Therapy* by Jeffrey Masson and lots of sociological and feminist criticisms of therapy. I realize now that the PCA that I was being taught on my course was not the full story—there was far, far more to it and there were people out there who were asking the sorts of questions that were constantly buzzing around in my head. I never felt that the PCA was not for me; I was just on the wrong course.

I was not passive in my anger and, as I believe in trying to change things by talking to those in power, at the beginning of the second year took my concerns to my personal tutor. On that occasion, I felt that much of what I said was attributed to my being a lesbian, i.e. I was paranoid about homophobia. There was also an attempt to link my experience of the course to that of gay men, which confirmed my view of their limited understanding of gay issues.

Right at the very end of the course, in some spare tutorial time I asked if we could look at social constructionism. In this one session, much of what I had been dying to explore was suddenly introduced—power, gender, exploitation, oppression, political views of therapy. At last, here it was, BUT where had it been? Some recommended reading was a chapter written by Sarah Hawtin and Judy Moore (1998) on 'Empowerment or Collusion? The Social Context of Person-Centred Therapy'. I cried when I read this chapter—I can't describe just how affirming it was for me to read those few pages that so eloquently said everything that I had been unable (due to my inexperience) to say to my fellow students and tutors. What a pity I had not found it before.

There was a good ending to my story. Apparently, the course moderator had also noted the lack of diversity in our group and felt that awareness of the issues around difference, empowerment and collusion should be 'embedded' into the culture, structure and content of the course. I was pleased to be asked by my personal tutor at the end of the course to discuss ways in which some of these issues might be incorporated into the sociology component of the training. The college was actually practising reflectively!

I didn't do any counselling for a year after qualifying but have now been in a voluntary placement with Mind, doing time-limited work, for over a year. I also work as an advocate in mental health. The PCA is at the heart of my practice in both these roles but I am constantly aware of the politics in individuals' personal distress and, when I sense the client might be receptive, will introduce questions and ideas to facilitate wider exploration.

REFERENCES

Hawtin, S & Moore, J (1998) Empowerment or collusion? The social context of Person-Centred Therapy. In B Thorne & E Lambers (eds) *Person-Centred Therapy: A European Perspective* (pp. 91–105). London: Sage Publications.

Kitzinger, C (1987) *The Social Construction of Lesbianism.* London: Sage.

Masson, J (1988) *Against Therapy.* New York: Atheneum Press.

Mearns, D & Thorne, B (2000) *Person-Centred Therapy Today.* London: Sage Publications.

Rogers, CR (1951) *Client-Centred Therapy.* London: Constable.

Rogers, CR (1977) The politics of the helping professions. In H Kirschenbaum & VL Henderson (eds) (1990) *The Carl Rogers Reader* (pp. 376–95). London: Constable.

Chapter 9

THERAPY: OPIUM OF THE MASSES OR HELP FOR THOSE WHO LEAST NEED IT?

GILLIAN PROCTOR

The rise of therapy serves a very convenient purpose for those in power and who benefit from a capitalist and patriarchal society, keeping a few with a lot of power and money at the top and the many underneath. The more people who identify therapy as the solution to their life problems, which are caused by these inequalities, the more these inequalities are concealed and dealt with individually and internally. Karl Marx argues that religion used to be a way to control the population by their belief in a higher moral order or reason to control their behaviour and to accept hierarchies of power with the ultimate male patriarchal figure of God at the top. However in an increasingly secular society, therapy has come along just in time with a great replacement, similarly perpetuating the hierarchical order of things. In addition, the 'psychologization' of life's problems also provides an answer, a meaning, and a purpose in life in the form of 'self-fulfilment', 'self-awareness' and such goals of therapy, as a substitute for the meaning historically provided by religion. Additionally, as with religion, therapy helps people to believe they have more control or power over their lives than they often have in reality by offering the belief that problems are internal, and we can change our internal feelings and thoughts and therefore feel better. We thus have a justification for why we have suffered—we were thinking or feeling wrongly, and if we try harder we can avoid future distress. This way of thinking is not dissimilar to the 'will of God' arguments that led people to accept hardship in the past, or the belief in prayer to change life. Therapy has become the new Opium of the Masses.

Why when most obvious causes of psychological distress are environmental, do all models of individual therapy treat distress as intrapsychic, in that the individual is the focus of change? Therapy tries to change the individual whilst leaving inequalities in society the same. This is despite the effect of inequalities on those oppressed being one of the main causes of psychological distress. At the same time, the institution of therapy perpetuates the inequalities of society. I argue that therapy mainly helps those who are least oppressed—i.e. those who least need it. So why and how do I continue to be a person-centred therapist?

In this chapter, I shall firstly discuss the relationship of powerlessness and oppression to the experience of psychological distress, and discuss briefly psychiatric responses to this. I shall then turn to psychological responses and present my argument that therapy perpetuates inequalities for four reasons. Finally, given this critique of therapy, I will explain why and how I continue to be a therapist.

POWERLESSNESS AND INEQUALITIES

The experience of powerlessness is one of the most significant causal factors contributing to the experience of psychological distress (see Proctor, 2002a). Power, control and the experience of powerlessness are frequently mentioned in understanding all kinds of psychological distress. Particular manifestations of psychological distress have also been strongly associated with issues of power and control. One of the functions of self-injury, for instance, can be to feel more in control and cope with a feeling of powerlessness (Arnold & Magill, 1998; Spandler, 1996). Eating distress is also often explained as a way to regain a sense of control over one's body and has been related to feeling powerless (e.g. see Troop & Treasure, 1997). With respect to depression, Gilbert (1992) also explains this experience as a response to powerlessness. Byrne and Carr (2000) found that depression in married women was associated with a weaker psychological and financial power base (economic and personal assets enabling her to have control over her partner) and less ability to determine the outcomes in decision making. The experience of psychosis can also be understood as not having control over one's sense of self and identity (see Johnstone, 1999). Similarly, the experience of anxiety can be understood as being a result of fear about uncertainty and lack of control over one's environment; again, clearly related to a subjective feeling of powerlessness. I have not found a manifestation of psychological distress that can not in some way be related to the experience of powerlessness.

SOCIETAL STRUCTURAL POWER

Higher prevalence of members of oppressed groups in psychiatry reflects the positions of power of the groups involved, and there is much evidence to associate the likelihood of suffering from psychological distress with the individual's position in society with respect to societal structural power.

The relationship between poverty and distress has been well documented (e.g. Bruce et al., 1991; Gomm, 1996). Work problems, economic stress and unemployment have been found to be instrumental in precipitating suicide and related to rates of diagnosis of schizophrenia (Ahlburg & Shapiro, 1983; Warner, 1994). Stressful life events are more common amongst people in lower socio-economic groups and have been implicated in raised prevalence of stress-related and physical illness within these groups (e.g. Coates et al., 1969).

The higher rates of diagnosis for women compared with men of many 'disorders', such as depression, anxiety and eating disorders, reflect women's position in society with respect to power (see Baker Miller, 1976; Williams et al., 1993; Williams, 1999; Wenegrat, 1995; Brown & Harris, 1978; Johnstone 2000). Feminists have long argued that women are both driven mad by oppression, abuse and expectations in society and labelled mad by the male-dominated psychiatric profession, particularly those women who deviate from gender role expectations. It can be argued that the diagnosis of Borderline Personality Disorder is the latest in obvious ways to label deviant women mad following a long history through witchcraft and hysteria (see Shaw & Proctor, 2005).

The higher rates of diagnosis of Black and Minority Ethnic groups can be analysed in the same way (see Fanon, 1986; Mercer, 1986; Fernando, 1991). Similarly, particularly young lesbians and gay men are more likely to suffer psychological distress and are still likely to come across homophobia in the mental health system (Proctor, 1994).

RELATIONSHIP OF OPPRESSION TO DISTRESS

There is much more evidence for environmental causes of distress than for example biological or genetic causes (e.g. Bentall, 2004). Common factors associated with distress are poverty, deprivation and abuse (e.g. Pilgrim, 1997). All these factors are associated with being a member of an oppressed group. There are two processes through which being a member of an oppressed group could be related to the experience of psychological distress. These are social causation and social construction.

Social causation
It makes sense that experiencing oppression in society can lead to or cause physical harm and psychological distress. Reduced access to material resources and wealth are usually related to oppression which reduces choices and options in life and can lead to anger or hurt at the injustice of seeing others enjoying so much more privilege. Assumptions and stereotypes can lower expectations and limit peoples' choices. Experiences of oppression are often invalidated making it difficult to form a positive sense of identity and may lead to isolation and silencing resulting in depression and low self-esteem. The real fear of violence, intolerance and rejection can lead to high levels of anxiety.

The experience of oppression is associated with an increased likelihood of being subjected to violence and abuse. The experience of oppression includes being in a relatively powerless position in relation to people in majority groups who can use their power over oppressed people. For example, women are far more vulnerable to physical and sexual abuse, in the form of domestic violence and rape. Black and Minority Ethnic groups are vulnerable to racist attacks; gay men and lesbians to homophobic attacks. The experience of abuse is a significant causal factor in all types of psychological distress, with the numbers of survivors of sexual abuse alone being very high among survivors of the psychiatric system (for example Williams & Watson, (1994) suggest a figure of at least 50 per cent).

Experiencing abuse is a profound experience of powerlessness. Finkelhor (1986) identifies four major dynamics following the experience of childhood sexual abuse, one of which is powerlessness. Surviving experiences of abuse is likely to involve regaining power and control (Kelly, 1988).

As Smail (1987: 398) states, clients of the mental health system are 'people upon who the world has impinged in any of a variety of painful ways. They are less people with whom anything is wrong than people who have suffered wrong.' Yet, psychiatric and psychological understandings of distress position the individual as someone who is disordered, ill or distressed; the problem is located in the individual rather than society.

Social construction

This individualization of distress is reinforced by the social construction of distress or madness. The norms of what is mentally healthy are defined by those with power in society; research has shown that people define norms of mental health with respect to White, middle-class and male norms. The concept of madness is constructed to label those who deviate from 'normal' by society's definition of normal being those with power.

Using the specific example of gender, the argument that discourses of (ways of talking about) madness are used to pathologize women follows feminist critiques of psychiatry. Chesler (1972) used the term 'double-bind' to describe the processes by which women can be pathologized both for conforming to, and for failing to conform to, expectations of feminine passivity.

Also useful here is the anti-psychiatric critique exemplified by Szasz (1972). Tracing the history of the modern concept of madness back to the pre-modern discourse of witchcraft, Szasz describes how women whose behaviour threatened social norms were positioned as outsiders and labelled 'witches'. A woman positioned in this way, he argued, could be contained and punished for her deviancy, and the threat that she posed to social norms could be controlled. In tracing the movement from this pre-modern, religious world-view to the current scientific, rational paradigm of modernism, Foucault (1967) described the emergence of a scientifically determined and controlled concept of insanity. This reflects the shift from 'witchcraft' to label women's deviancy, to the emergence of the concept of 'hysteria' in the nineteenth century.

Hysteria occupies a central position in the history of women's madness as a diagnosis long used to indicate behaviours which are disapproved of, and specifically employed as a male term of abuse for 'difficult' female behaviour. More recently, hysteria has been theorized as a response to powerlessness; a reaction to expectations of passivity and an attempt to establish self-identity (Showalter, 1985). The concepts of both 'witchcraft' and 'hysteria' position 'difficult' or 'deviant' behaviour as symptomatic of a disturbed personality and therefore dismiss these behaviours as individual pathology and obscure the social context of gendered power relations which give rise to these behaviours.

Shaw and Proctor (2005) argue that the modern discourse of Borderline Personality Disorder (BPD) operates in much the same way. According to a social constructionist model, BPD (like witchcraft and hysteria) is constructed as a deviation, in this case from the concepts of rationality and individuality. Feminists have argued that psychiatry—far from being a branch of medicine which categorizes disease—is constructed around concepts and expectations that are fundamentally gendered and which profoundly affect how a patient's behaviour is evaluated and responded to. The gendered consequences of the psychiatric preoccupation with 'rationality' have been well explored in feminist theory: women are 'typically situated on the side of irrationality, silence, nature and the body, while men are situated on the side of reason, discourse, culture and mind' (Showalter, 1985: 3–4).

THERAPY: A RESPONSE TO INEQUALITIES?

It is usually assumed that counselling or therapy is more benign, less coercive and power-based than psychiatry. Indeed, in counselling and psychotherapy, the legal position with respect to power is different from that held by a psychiatrist or psychiatric nurse. There is potentially more choice in how the therapist uses or chooses not to use the power given to them. However, as Sanders and Tudor point out:

> Just as it is dangerous to assume that psychiatry is a benign force in social policy or that Home Secretaries know anything about personality disorder, neither should we accept or assume that therapy is in itself benign, useful or effective. (2001: 157)

Miller and Rose emphasize that 'we should be wary of celebrating psychological approaches as alternatives to psychiatry' (1986: 42). Psychological approaches can also be used as part of the armoury of power and control over the population, as Foucault particularly explains (see Proctor, 2002a).

IGNORING INEQUALITIES

As in medical models of mental illness, models of therapy, including the person-centred model, conceptualize the client's problem as internal to themselves, as intrapsychic, thus ignoring the social causes of distress. Person-centred theory theorizes distress as incongruence or internalized conditions of worth, clearly placing the problem as internal. Thus, therapy tries to change the individual whilst leaving society and the inequalities in society unchanged (see Proctor (2004) for more examples of how person-centred therapy ignores the effects of patriarchy on women). How often does therapy become a process of oppressed people learning to accept their oppressed position and keeping quiet about their powerlessness? When therapists ignore the links between social inequalities and psychological distress, they serve the interests of privileged social groups rather than those of their clients.

PERPETUATING INEQUALITIES

In focusing on the individual, therapy leaves society's inequalities unchanged. Furthermore I contend that the institution of therapy actually *perpetuates* these inequalities. I shall justify this argument by considering how people are defined as in distress, by examining the inequalities and dynamics of power in the therapy relationship, by examining the structural societal inequalities perpetuated by the different identities of therapists and clients, and finally by considering who therapy helps.

How do you become a client?

Even clients who voluntarily seek counselling or therapy do not make the decision that they need therapy by identifying some internal distress. It is not like feeling you have a headache and therefore taking a painkiller. Around us everywhere the media, Internet, and 'information' from mental health services have ever been increasing the remit of what counts as a mental health problem or something needing therapy (see Hansen, McHoul & Rapley, 2003). We are each influenced by all this such that the percentage of the population who would consider going for therapy is much greater than 10 and certainly 20 years ago. The effect of this media publicity of mental health is the increasing medicalization and individualization of life's problems, which diverts attention more and more from conditions in society and separates people from each other as they consult 'experts'. Whereas in the 1970s, women went to consciousness-raising groups and discovered their commonalities in distress due to their treatment as women, now most women go to individual therapists and see all their problems as internal.

The dynamics of power in therapy

I conceptualize three aspects to power in the therapy relationship (Proctor, 2002a). The first is the power inherent in the roles of therapist and client resulting from the authority given to the therapist to define the client's problem and the power the therapist has in the organizations and institutions of their work. I call this *role power*. In our society, all counsellors and therapists are given authority and *role power*. Various micro-environments also affect how much role power a counsellor/therapist has in any one situation or work environment. This aspect of power is also dynamic and relational; different therapists use this role power in different ways and have varying attitudes to the effect of role power on the client. Each client that the counsellor/therapist interacts with will have different views about and reactions to this role power of the therapist and their own role power as a client.

The second aspect of power is the power arising from the structural positions in society of the therapist and client, with respect to gender, age, etc. I call this *societal power*. The final aspect of power in the therapy relationship is the power resulting from the personal histories of the therapist and client and their experiences of power and powerlessness. I will call this *historical power*. The personal histories and experiences will affect, and to some extent determine, how individuals are in relationships and how they think, feel and sometimes behave with respect to the power in the relationship.

Role power. There is a clear political agenda in person-centred therapy (PCT) to eliminate the therapist's power-over the client and it is revolutionary in the extent to which it manages to do this. [1] But however equal the therapist behaves in the therapy relationship, therapy is still an institution and the role of 'therapist' still has power attached to it in society.

Feminist authors also help us to understand the power in the institution of therapy. Chesler (1972) reminds us that the therapeutic encounter needs to be understood as an institution beyond how individual therapists are with individual clients and how this *institution* re-enacts the relationship of girls to their father figure in a patriarchal society. Although individual PC therapists challenge this hierarchical expert-based idea of therapy, therapy itself as an institution remains unnoticed, which is likely to be a major factor in clients not perceiving the therapy relationship as equal however the therapist behaves. There is a clear inequality in the roles of therapist and client which is not removed by any kind of therapist behaviour as a person.

Historical power. Historical power is the power resulting from the personal histories of the therapist and client and their experiences of power and powerlessness. We have all been influenced by society's messages about inequalities and absorbed stereotypes, assumptions and unspoken expectations or messages about how society is ordered. The awareness of our own socialization can help a therapist to understand their own conditions of worth in a social and political context and how their current behaviour and ways of relating are likely to be influenced by gender and other identity role expectations. I am not saying that the differing impacts can be predicted or generalized about. However, our structural identities have a big impact on who we are, how people treat us and how we relate to people, and understanding society's messages about these identities and how these are internalized (although responded to differently) by everyone may help us to understand an individual more accurately as situated within their cultural context (see Proctor, 2004). As society's messages are for the most part implicit and often denied, it is likely to be difficult for clients to be able to explain their impact on their way of viewing the world and themselves.

---

1. See Proctor (2002a) and Proctor (2002b) for a detailed discussion of power in person-centred therapy.

If these messages are not understood as part of the implicit context in each of our lives, we run the risk of taking for granted socialization of inequalities and what is 'normal' as an unquestioned part of our culture.

Who are the therapists and who are the clients?

The evidence is well documented showing the inequality of the social structural positions between therapists and clients (e.g. Garrett & Davis, 1995; Binnett et al., 1995). Therapists are more likely to be white and middle class, whereas clients are generally poorer, more disabled mentally and physically, older, younger, more dependent and less socially supported. In the UK these differences are particularly in evidence for therapists working with clients as part of the NHS. Sadly these differences are unlikely to reduce, given that opportunities for education and thus class migration for working-class people have decreased due to huge reductions in educational grants available. An appreciation of the social and material realities of deprivation may be hard for a therapist from a privileged background to achieve.

Outcome of therapy

The results of 40 years of psychotherapy research have consistently discovered two things. The first is that the most effective consistent factor with regard to the therapist is the importance of the *quality* of the therapy relationship for effective and good therapy. Summaries of the research outcome studies over the last 35 years (e.g. see Bozarth, 1998; Paley & Lawton, 2001; Mearns & Cooper, 2005) demonstrate that the effectiveness of psychotherapy depends primarily on the therapy relationship and the inner and external resources of the client. The most consistent relationship variables related to effectiveness are the therapeutic alliance, goal agreement and empathy (Norcross, 2002).

Secondly, research has consistently demonstrated in effectiveness studies a figure of around two-thirds of clients who 'improve' on scales to measure what is considered mental health, and therapy is thus seen to be effective (Lambert & Ogles, 2004). What I am interested in here is the 33 per cent of people who don't 'improve'. Of course these figures are only based on clients who complete a course of therapy, completely missing those who drop out along the way. These statistics can be criticized by person-centred therapists on the basis of how 'improvement' is measured and that clients could benefit from therapy without showing any difference in 'symptom' ratings. However I worry that this is a defensive response from therapists who do not like to believe that therapy may not help people. What is more worrying is that within this group of people who do not demonstrate any 'improvement' in therapy, there is a smaller group of people who actually demonstrate an increase in 'symptoms', i.e. they get worse during therapy (see Proctor, 2005). Furthermore, research shows that if people start to get worse they usually continue, challenging the usual myth that people do get worse before they get better (e.g. Lambert et al., 2001). This research suggests that therapy can be damaging—it is not always benign, and that even therapists with the best intentions may damage clients. However much person-centred therapists try and intend to convey the attitudes of unconditional positive regard, empathy and congruence to the client, there is no guarantee that this is how the therapist will be perceived by the client. There is still a danger in person-centred therapy as human relationships are so complex and idiosyncratic that it is unlikely we could ever predict the many ways in which relationships can hurt or damage people as well as help or heal people. All we can do is trust the stories of those people who do speak up about the negative effects of therapy on them (e.g. Sands, 2000; Heyward, 1993).

Who does therapy not help? There is little evidence about who the people are who do not show a change in therapy. I suspect therapy is most likely to help those people who are most like their therapists, i.e. the most privileged, in the main. I argue this for three reasons: that the people who are most oppressed are least likely to access therapy, that we are better at understanding people who are most like ourselves, and that the most oppressed people are most likely to say they feel better to please the therapist.

People who are most oppressed are simply least likely to be referred and have access to therapy at primary care level. If you are articulate or educated, experience shows that you are much more likely to ask for and be referred to counselling or therapy. Most therapists work in private or primary care settings (where usually only short-term work is offered) and thus work with the least distressed and most privileged people by definition. Access to therapy at secondary or tertiary levels in mental health services is very poor and often characterized by the most controlling and expert-led types of therapy. From my experience in forensic settings, access to exploratory therapy in those settings is usually again for the most articulate, judged 'psychologically minded'. The voluntary services that provide free counselling services and are often most accessible to those most oppressed often have therapists who are least trained and least valued, usually working voluntarily. How many therapists or therapy services work with interpreters? Most do not, whether due to lack of resources, training, knowledge or a belief that they cannot. Yet one of the most marginalized groups in our society is people who cannot speak the dominant language in our country well. Thus accessing therapy when belonging to an oppressed group is often much harder.

In comparing clients who are like their therapists with clients who are unlike their therapists in terms of life experiences, identities and oppression, which people are therapists likely to find it easiest to understand? With whom will they feel most relaxed, most genuine, honest, and easiest to be themselves? With whom will they feel least judgemental? Most people spend most of their time with people very like themselves, working in similar jobs, living in similar areas. It is likely for most therapists to find that those clients most like themselves are those with whom they can most easily create the relationship characteristics necessary for therapy to be effective. As therapists are more likely to be from privileged groups (e.g. Garrett & Davis, 1995), this means the more privileged clients will on the whole receive the most effective therapy.

Inequalities in society are set up such that those at the bottom have to submit to the authority of those above them. This inequality is always present in the therapy relationship due to the roles of therapist and client but it is exacerbated when the therapist has more power than the client due to other aspects of their identity as well. The more characteristics of authority exhibited by a therapist (e.g. being male, well-spoken, articulate, etc.) the more likely the client is to agree with what the therapist says and the more likely the client is to want to please the therapist. So even for the supposedly 'objective' measures of 'symptom' relief, it will be obvious to many clients how to fill in these questionnaires so they look like they've improved. Most clients will know that their therapist would like to think they have improved as a result of therapy, so it is possible that a large percentage of the two-thirds of people who look, according to these measures, like they have 'got better' as a result of therapy are simply clients who did not want to let their therapists down. The more accustomed a client is to submitting to authority, the more likely they are to not question a therapist's perspective or to question the therapist's misunderstanding. Even when a therapist is trying their best not to take power-over a client, if a client generally relates by submission, the therapy relationship could be based on compliance, submission and acquiescence rather than being a mutual empowering healing relationship of two people who have equal respect for each other.

SO WHY DO I STILL DO IT?

Now it's time to admit that despite everything I have said I still practise as a therapist! How can I justify that? Sometimes I feel I cannot, and have had constant debates with myself and others over the time I have been practising as a therapist. However, each time I decide that therapy is a doomed institution and rife with unsurpassable inequalities, I realize that so is the whole of society, and all relationships. Foucault summarizes this position saying:

> I do not think a society could exist without power relations. If by that one means the strategies by which individuals try to direct and control the conduct of others. The problem, then, is not to try and dissolve them in the utopia of completely transparent communication but to acquire the rules of law, the management techniques, and also the morality, the ethos, the practices of the self, that will allow us to play these games of power with as least domination as possible. (Foucault, 1980: 298, cited in Fish, 1999: 67)

I hope that in individual therapy people will feel understood enough for them to have the confidence to work to change their own situation and that of the world. I have seen this happen enough to help me believe in what I try to do. I believe that our job as therapists is to take responsibility for our position of power and be constantly mindful about how dynamics of power play out in therapy relationships. At the same time, I believe that our responsibility is also to understand the wider society and how inequalities affect all of us. Knowing the limits of therapy due to its focus on individual change, I also work politically to try and change wider society. With these broad aims, I hope responsible person-centred therapists can be aware of the following checklist of ways to think about the political implications of their own practice.

• Work to be increasingly aware of inequalities in society and the realities of the lives of those people most oppressed. At the same time working to become increasingly aware of our own privileges.
• Work to try and make therapy accessible to people who most need it, both in individual practice and in structures within which we work.
• Be aware of and informed about environmental and material causes of distress and work with people to try and change their environments, using our power to help wherever possible, e.g. to advocate for people to get better housing etc., awareness of how to get information about benefits etc.
• Work to be ever aware of dynamics of power in therapy and disempower people in therapy as little as possible.
• Be aware that therapy can be damaging and listen to, trust and believe clients and what they say about our relationships. Be honest that we cannot say whether or not therapy will be helpful for a particular client, and only they can decide whether it helps, whilst having hope that it will help.
• Think about whether it is possible to facilitate the existence of alternatives to therapy, specifically self-help groups or community groups where people with similar experiences can meet and learn from each other in a non-hierarchical way.
• Can you become involved politically with campaigns to change inequalities in a material way and to challenge the way mental health systems work, to perpetuate inequalities and diagnose individuals?

SUMMARY AND CONCLUSION

It is imperative that we do not forget that we are all part of an inherently unequal society, with structures of power and inequalities that damage us all. The therapy industry has mushroomed, taking advantage of the increasing numbers of people who are hurt by this society and looking for meaning in a world increasingly ruled by consumerism. Being part of this industry and institution means we have responsibilities to take account of our part in this and examine ways in which we may contribute to these inequalities and causes of distress, rather than hide behind the naïve hope that we are benign healers. I hope this chapter has begun to take apart ways in which we need to examine this and ways in which we can militate against furthering the harm perpetuated by our sick society.

REFERENCES

Ahlburg, DA & Shapiro, MO (1983) The darker side of unemployment. *Hospital and Community Psychiatry, 34*, 389.

Arnold, L & Magill, A (1998) *The Self-harm Help Book.* Abergavenny: The Basement Project.

Baker Miller, J (1976) *Towards a New Psychology of Women.* New York: Beacon Press.

Bentall, RP (2004) *Madness Explained: Psychosis and human nature.* London: Penguin.

Binnett, E, Dennis, M, Dosanjh, N, Mahtani, A, Miller, A, Nadirshaw, Z & Patel, N (1995) *Race and Culture Resource Pack for Trainers.* Leicester: Training Working Party, Division of Clinical Psychology, British Psychological Society.

Bozarth, J (1998) *Person-Centred Therapy: A revolutionary paradigm.* Ross-on-Wye: PCCS Books.

Brown, SW & Harris, T (1978) *Social Origins of Depression: A study of psychiatric disorders in women.* London: Tavistock.

Bruce, ML, Takeuchi, DT & Leaf, PJ (1991) Poverty and psychiatric status: Longitudinal evidence from the New Haven Epidemiological Catchment Area Study. *Archives of General Psychiatry, 48,* 470–4.

Byrne, M & Carr, A (2000) Depression and power in marriage. *Journal of Family Therapy, 22,* 408–27.

Chesler, P (1972) *Women and Madness.* New York: Doubleday.

Coates, D, Moyer, S & Wellman, B (1969) The Yorklea study of urban mental health: Symptoms, problems and life events. *Canadian Journal of Public Health, 60,* 471–81.

Fanon, F (1986) *Black Skin, White Masks.* London: Pluto Press.

Fernando, S (1991) *Mental Health, Race and Culture.* London: Macmillan/MIND.

Finkelhor, D (1986) *A Sourcebook on Child Sexual Abuse.* London: Sage.

Fish, V (1999) Clementis's Hat: Foucault and the politics of psychotherapy. In I Parker (ed) *Deconstructing Psychotherapy* (pp. 54–70). London: Sage.

Foucault, M (1967) *Madness and Civilisation—A history of insanity in the age of reason.* London: Tavistock.

Garrett, T & Davis, J (1995) So who are we anyway? *Clinical Psychology Forum, 78,* 2–4.

Gilbert, P (1992) *Depression: The evolution of powerlessness.* Hove, Sussex: Lawrence Erlbaum Associates.

Gomm, R (1996) Mental health and inequality. In T Heller, J Reynolds, R Gomm, R Muston & S Pattison (eds) *Mental Health Matters: A reader.* London: Macmillan in association with the Open University.

Hansen, S, McHoul, A & Rapley, M (2003) *Beyond Help: A consumers' guide to psychology.* Ross-on-Wye: PCCS Books.

Heyward, C (1993) *When Boundaries Betray Us: Beyond illusions of what is ethical in therapy and life.* New York: HarperCollins.

Johnstone, L (1999) Do families cause 'schizophrenia'? Revisiting a taboo subject. In C

Newnes, G Holmes & C Dunn (eds) *This is Madness: A critical look at psychiatry and the future of mental health services* (pp. 119–34). Ross-on-Wye: PCCS Books.

Johnstone, L (2000) *Users and Abusers of Psychiatry.* London: Routledge.

Kelly, L (1988) *Surviving Sexual Violence.* Cambridge: Polity.

Lambert, MJ, Hansen, NB & Finch, AE (2001) Patient-focused research: Using patient outcome data to enhance treatment effects. *Journal of Consulting and Clinical Psychology, 69,* 159–72.

Lambert, MJ & Ogles, BM (2004) The efficacy and effectiveness of psychotherapy. In M Lambert (ed) *Handbook of Psychotherapy and Behavioral Change* (5th edn) (pp. 139–93). New York: John Wiley and Sons Ltd.

Lowe, R (1999) Between the 'No longer' and the 'Not yet': Postmodernism as a context for critical therapeutic work. In I Parker (ed) *Deconstructing Psychotherapy* (pp. 71–85). London: Sage.

Mearns, D & Cooper, M (2005) *Working at Relational Depth in Counselling and Psychotherapy.* London: Sage.

Mercer, K (1986) Racism and transcultural psychiatry. In P Miller and N Rose (eds) *The Power of Psychiatry* (pp. 112–42). Cambridge: Polity Press.

Miller, P & Rose, N (1986) Introduction (Miller & Rose) and Chapter 1 (Miller), Critiques of psychiatry and critical sociologies of madness. In P Miller & N Rose (eds) *The Power of Psychiatry.* Cambridge: Polity Press.

Norcross, JC (ed) (2002) *Psychotherapy Relationships that Work: Therapist contributions and responsiveness to patients.* New York: OUP.

Paley, G & Lawton, D (2001) Evidence-based practice: Accounting for the importance of the therapeutic relationship in UK National Health Service therapy provision. *Counselling and Psychotherapy Research, 1* (1), 12–17.

Pilgrim, D (1997) *Psychotherapy and Society.* London: Sage.

Proctor, G (1994) Lesbian clients' experience of clinical psychology: A listener's guide. *Changes, 12,* 290–8.

Proctor, G (2002a) *The Dynamics of Power in Counselling and Psychotherapy: Ethics, politics and practice.* Ross-on-Wye: PCCS Books.

Proctor, G (2002b) Power in person-centred therapy. In J Watson, R Goldman & M Warner (eds) *Client-Centered and Experiential Psychotherapy in the 21st Century: Advances in theory, research and practice* (pp. 79–88). Ross-on-Wye: PCCS Books.

Proctor, G (2004) What can person-centred therapy learn from feminism? In G Proctor & MB Napier (eds) *Encountering Feminism* (pp. 129–40). Ross-on-Wye: PCCS Books.

Proctor, G (2005) Should therapy make you worse? *Clinical Psychology, 45,* 7–9.

Rowe, D (1989) Foreword. In J Masson (ed) *Against Therapy.* London: Fontana.

Sanders, P & Tudor, K (2001) This is therapy: A person-centred critique of the contemporary psychiatric system. In C Newnes, G Holmes and C Dunn (eds) *This is Madness Too: Critical perspectives on mental health services* (pp. 147–60). Ross-on-Wye: PCCS Books.

Sands, A (2000) *Falling for Therapy: Psychotherapy from the client's point of view.* London: Macmillan.

Shaw, C & Proctor, G (2005) Women at the Margins: A critique of the diagnosis of Borderline Personality Disorder. *Feminism and Psychology, 15* (4), 483–90.

Showalter, E (1985) *The Female Malady: Women, madness and English culture, 1830–1890.* London: Virago.

Smail, D (1987) Psychotherapy as subversion in a make-believe world. *Changes, 4* (5), 398–402.

Spandler, H (1996) *Who's Hurting Who? Young people, self-harm and suicide.* Manchester: 42nd Street.

Szasz, T (1972) *The Myth of Mental Illness.* London: Paladin.

Troop, NA & Treasure, JL (1997) Setting the scene for eating disorders, II: Childhood helplessness and mastery. *Psychological Medicine, 27,* 531–8.

Warner, R (1994) *Recovery from Schizophrenia: Psychiatry and political economy.* London: Routledge.

Wenegrat, B (1995) *Illness and Power: Women's mental disorders and the battle between the sexes.* New York: New York University Press.

Williams, J, Watson, G, Smith, H, Copperman, J & Wood, D (1993) *Purchasing Effective Mental Health Services for Women: A framework for action.* London: MIND Publications/ Tizard Centre, University of Kent in Canterbury.

Williams, J (1999) Social inequalities and mental health. In C Newnes, G Holmes, & C Dunn (eds) *This is Madness: A critical look at psychiatry and the future of mental health services* (pp. 29–50). Ross-on-Wye: PCCS Books.

Chapter 10

SOCIALIST HUMANISM:
A PROGRESSIVE POLITICS FOR THE
TWENTY-FIRST CENTURY [1]

Mick Cooper

Massacres … famines … global destruction … Like many people in the person-centred world today, I believe a better society for all of us must surely be possible. And when I see the impact that person-centred ideas and practices can have on improving cooperation and communication between people, I have no doubt that this approach can make a major contribution to the amelioration of some of the world's most pressing problems. In this chapter, I would like to outline a vision of what such a person-centred-informed politic might look like. More specifically, I want to outline a politic that incorporates the essence of person-centred thinking into a broadly socialist framework, forging a 'socialist-humanist' politic that, I believe, has the potential to understand, and meet, human beings' wants and needs at both the social and individual level. The chapter begins with an introduction to the socialist-humanist tradition and then goes on to outline potential limits of both humanism and socialism when advocated in isolation from the other. A socialist-humanist model of human existence is then outlined before a discussion of the ways that such a political standpoint could be carried forward.

SOCIALIST HUMANISM

'Socialist humanism' is not a new term, but one that has been used by a variety of people in a variety of contexts across the course of the twentieth century. *Pravda*, for instance, described Khrushchev's Report to the Twenty-first Congress of the Russian Communist Party as 'the magnificent and noble conception of Marxist-Leninist socialist humanism' (see Dunayevskaya, 1965: 72). More commonly, however, the term has been used to refer to a particular form of Marxist thinking that rejected both the 'state socialism' of twentieth-century Eastern Europe and a mechanistic, structural understanding of Marx's writings. Instead, it advocated a form of socialism that prioritized human agency, subjectivity and individuality.

1. Many thanks to Kitty Cooper, Susan Cooper, Helen Cruthers, Carolyn Dougill, Ewan Gillon, Suzanne Keys, John McLeod, Gillian Proctor and Pete Sanders for their feedback on an earlier draft of this chapter. For my mum, Kitty Cooper, with lots of love.

Probably the best known proponent of this viewpoint was Erich Fromm, a twentieth-century Marxist psychoanalyst, whose edited collection of chapters— *Socialist Humanism* (Fromm, 1965)—remains the most comprehensive and lucid discussion of this perspective (see also *Marx's Concept of Man*, Fromm, 1961).

Socialist humanists like Fromm drew primarily from Marx's earliest writings, in particular his *Economic and Philosophical Manuscripts* (Marx, 1988), which was written almost twenty years before *Das Capital*. Here, Marx explicitly equates communism with humanism, and outlines a model of individual and social existence that displays remarkable commonalities with a contemporary humanistic and person-centred perspective (see Fritzhand, 1965, for an excellent overview of Marx's ideal of humankind; and Nord, 1977). Central to this model is a belief, like Rogers (1951, 1959), that modern human beings are radically alienated from their own nature, needs and potential, as well as from their fellow human beings and the natural world. Here, within a capitalist, commodity-orientated society, human beings are driven into a never-ending frenzy of acquisition and consumption; whilst the workers at the base of the capitalist pyramid are reduced to little more than 'commodities', 'machines' or 'horses': 'crippled monstrosities' that are spiritually and physically dehumanized (Marx, 1988: 86). In this respect, contrary to a more structural or economic reading of Marx, socialist humanists like Fromm have argued that Marx's aim 'is not limited to the emancipation of the working class, but the emancipation of the human being through the restitution of the unalienated and hence free activity of all men [*sic*]' (Fromm, 1961: 41). Here, through liberating themselves from the dominion of money, commodification and class hierarchies, human beings can take back control of their own lives (what Marx termed 'auto-activity', cf. an 'internal locus of control' (Rogers, 1959)), actualize their genuine potential, and meet their authentic human needs, including a need for love and affiliation.

PERSONAL BEGINNINGS

A more extended discussion of the commonalities between Marx's early thinking and contemporary humanistic and person-centred ideas could make a fascinating and original paper in its own right. In this chapter, however, I want to present a more personal journey towards a socialist-humanist standpoint: how I came to see the complimentarity between these two world-views and also the psycho-political model of human being that I have developed to try and integrate them.

I was born into a family that had radical politics at its core. My dad, who was already in his fifties when I was born, had joined the Communist Party in the 1920s, and had been both at Cable Street and in Spain as a young man. He moved to the States just before the Second World War, and was relatively proud of the fact that he had been 'asked' to return to Britain during the McCarthyite period. On his return, he set up a company distributing progressive, mainly foreign-language films to cinemas and film societies in the UK; and he, along with my mum, remained members of the Communist Party right up until its breakdown in the early 1990s. My dad was a very warm man, particularly when I was younger, and I remember visualizing him once in a therapy group as a big, brown, affectionate bear. He played games with my older sister and I, taught us political songs from places like Ireland and the Soviet Union, and cuddled and wrestled with me in equal measure. But he could also be stubborn, defensive and closed-minded. He seemed almost incapable of listening to any criticisms of the Soviet Union or China without rushing to their defence, and rarely acknowledged the possibility that communism could have its flaws.

As a young boy, I simply believed that communism was right. Consequently, throughout my school years, I engaged in numerous political arguments with my fellow pupils: from repression in the Soviet Union ('It might not be perfect, but America is a lot worse') to the viability of a communist utopia ('People can learn to live without money'). One of my strongest memories is of standing up to sing a song during a rainy 'wet break' at infant school when I was about six. After renditions of 'Jesus Loves Me' and 'Twinkle, Twinkle, Little Star' by various other pupils, I burst into 'Our Engines Roaring', a soviet military anthem, which goes:

> Our engines roaring, roaring into battle
> Up in the air, above the clouds we fly
> Our bombs are ready, our machine guns rattle
> The first, red air fleet in the world flies higher
> And higher, and higher
> Our emblem the Soviet star
> And every propeller is roaring
> Defending the USSR.

As I reached my late teens, however, I began to consider the possibility that some chinks might exist in my communist 'armour'. One of the biggest factors here was that I had started to listen to punk music, and became exposed to critiques of Soviet-style communism that were coming from the even-more-radical left, as opposed to the (easily dismissable) right. One song that particularly influenced me was by a band called *Crass*. It was entitled 'Bloody Revolutions', and was a direct challenge to the call for revolutionary action that I had so heartily assumed was the way forward:

> You talk about your revolution, well, that's fine
> But what are you going to be doing come the time?
> Are you going to be the big man with the tommy-gun?
> Will you talk of freedom when the blood begins to run?
> Well, freedom has no value if violence is the price
> Don't want your revolution, I want anarchy and peace

You talk of overthrowing power with violence as your tool
You speak of liberation and when the people rule
Well ain't it people rule right now, what difference would there be?
Just another set of bigots with their rifle-sights on me. [2]

A few other experiences were also important. I went to see a psychoanalyst at the Tavistock for a year. His transferential interpretations infuriated me (Why the hell did he think he was like my dad!), but his one (not very analytical) outburst at my tendency to dispute most of what he said did make me wonder whether I, and my family, might not be too stuck in a rigid system of beliefs. Then, when I got to University, I encountered 'hard left' activists who I experienced as dogmatic, closed-minded and simplistic, and felt that I wanted to have nothing to do with their politics. I stayed involved with politics just about (i.e. I joined the Labour Party), but became increasingly involved with personal development and therapeutic activities, much of it through the pro-feminist 'men's movement' that was burgeoning in the 1980s and 1990s.

WHY SOCIALISM NEEDS HUMANISM …

As I allowed myself to move further and further away from my communistic roots, I increasingly began to feel that there were fundamental problems with this political creed. First, whilst the socialist beliefs I had adopted as a child seemed to be about creating a society in which people were happier and more fulfilled, the socialists I encountered seemed to have little understanding of, or interest in, people's *psychological* needs or functioning. Questions like 'What makes people happy?' or 'What makes life worth living?' did not seem to be on the socialist agenda at all; and yet, to me, they seemed like the most fundamental issues of all: How could you create a society of happier people if you didn't know what happy was? Indeed, with the communists and socialists I met, the assumption seemed to be that if people had enough food, drink and shelter then that would be enough—there seemed to be little appreciation of what Maslow (1968) called human beings' 'growth motivations': their desires for creativity, change, stimulation and achievement. I remember, on a trip to the Soviet Union, being struck by the fact that there was just one type of jam in the supermarket: rows and rows of the same strawberry glop. It seemed lifeless, boring, uninspiring; and whilst I do not believe that a lack of adequate conserves led to the downfall of the Soviet empire, I remain convinced that it was the failure of the Soviet system to meet people's growth needs that led to its collapse. For all the problems of the capitalist West, its ability to provide people with challenges, variety, and the potential to achieve goals seems to me to cater more effectively for the whole spectrum of people's psychological desires.

---

2. Reprinted by kind permission of Southern Records.

Then there was blame. As a young boy, playground arguments about the viability of communism would almost inevitably come down to the issue of whether people were inherently good or not. 'People can't live without money,' my fellow pupils would say. 'If you didn't have any money, someone would just walk into a shop and take everything.'

'Ah, yes,' I'd retort, 'but people are basically good, so if they knew they'd be taking something away from someone else, they wouldn't do it.' (At this point, I'd usually get back 'So why don't your parents give away their film distribution company'!)

So, for me, the whole of communist thinking was based on a faith in the inherent goodness of humankind. And yet, when I listened to socialists talk, there seemed to be a great deal of distrust towards whole swathes of humanity: 'the media', the Tories, the police, and worst of all, right-wing Americans. Everyone was 'good', but there was a sense in which these people were selfish, power-hungry and inherently 'bad'.

So, to me, there seemed to be a basic contradiction here: were people inherently good or weren't they? And if the argument was that these people *could be* good, they had just been socialized to be bad, then essentially we (the good people) could just as easily be them; in which case, why were we giving them such a hard time? Moreover, this attitude of demonization seemed to me to lack political expediency. If we wanted to change these people's attitudes, we weren't going to be able to do it by relating to them in a way that inferred they were suspect or ignorant. They did that to us ('loony lefties', 'politically correct thought police', 'hooligans') and I knew it only made me more adamant in my opinions— so why should I expect them to be any different? And finally, when I began to talk to people on the right of the political spectrum, what I realized was, phenomenologically, these characterizations of them were just plain wrong. When I spoke to right-wing Americans, or policemen, or conservative-voting fellow students, it simply was not the case that their agenda was one of self-protection or self-enhancement. These were people who genuinely believed that what they were doing was for the good of others as well as for themselves: that communism was threatening people's freedom and they wanted to protect it, or that the miners' unions needed to be broken because they were holding the country to ransom. And the more I became immersed in a person-centred, phenomenological standpoint, the more difficult I found it to brush these self-reports aside and claim that I *really* knew what they were up to. I may not have agreed with them, but if I thought they were coming from a place of selfishness or malice, where was my trust in their ability to know their own experiencing?

Another set of contradictions seemed to exist in how working-class people were viewed. On the one hand, the message from the hard left was that these were the people who would free us from our class bondages; but on the other hand, they were the McDonalds-eating, football-watching couch potatoes, too passive, gullible and compliant to question anything they read in *The Sun* (unlike the people who read *The Guardian*!). A contradiction … and, again, ways of being that were entirely at odds with the phenomenological realities of the working-class people that I listened to.

For me, then, humanistic ideas provided an essential corrective to the radical, socialist views I had encountered in much of my youth. Here was a view of human beings which not only saw people as needing food, shelter and comfort; but also goals, challenges and new possibilities (Maslow, 1968)—a viewpoint that seemed to me to capture much more of the wholeness of human desires. And instead of seeing people as malevolent and power-hungry, it held fast to the idea that people were inherently constructive and pro-social—albeit that they might act in destructive ways (e.g. Rogers, 1959). Moreover, it was an approach that moved beyond blaming people or putting labels on them, and instead started with the concrete reality of each person's lived-experiences and the intelligibility of their behaviours. This, it seemed to me, was a much better starting point from which to try and change people's attitudes and beliefs.

… AND WHY HUMANISM NEEDS SOCIALISM

As a corrective to much socialist thinking, I found humanistic and person-centred ideas essential; and their deep faith in humankind, their commitment to non-hierarchical relations and their emphasis on freedom and liberation resonated with some of my most fundamental beliefs. In their own right, however, I was always troubled by their potential to approximate more reactionary standpoints. In particular, like many other authors from both within the person-centred field (e.g. Barrett-Lennard, 2005; Bohart, 2003; Holdstock, 1993; Mearns & Cooper, 2005; O'Hara, 1992; Stinckens, Lietaer & Leijssen, 2002) and outside of it (e.g. Geller, 1982; Sinclair & Monk, 2005), I have always been concerned by the individualism that seems to lie at the heart of person-centred and humanistic thinking. In his book, *Carl Rogers' Helping System*, Godfrey Barrett-Lennard (1998) shows how client-centred therapy grew out of the grounds of Rooseveltian 'New Deal' America, and its initial emphasis on individual actualization and personal achievement would seem to mirror, in many respects, the 'American dream' (Shaw & Colimore, 1988: 60). When I watch my daughters' Barbie® DVDs, I am often struck by the similarities between the morals and message doled out by corporate America—'Be yourself', 'Be who you want to be'—and humanistic ideas and principles. Here, there is little explicit regard for the needs or the rights of the Other, nor of a responsibility towards them. Rather, development is a move towards autonomy and independence. 'The primal choice, the fork in the road,' writes Maslow, 'is between others and one's own self' (1968: 52), and the path towards individuality that humanistic psychologists would seem to favour puts them very close, at times, to the libertarian right.

What also narrows this distance is the tendency within the humanistic field to neglect *structural inequalities* within society: the fact that different social groups and classes have very different capabilities to actualize their potential. A working-class, disabled Black woman, for instance, has very different opportunities to an able-bodied middle-class White man. When psychological difficulties are understood primarily in terms of conditional positive regard (Rogers, 1959), however, these socio-economic differences can easily be overlooked. The same can be said for the issue of *power*. Some groups in society have much more opportunity to enforce their way of doing things than others, but this is rarely talked about in the person-centred field (though see Proctor, 2002). Much is made of personal power, but power is not something that just exists at an individual or experiential level: it also exists by virtue of being part of particular groups and classes. Without an appreciation of these dynamics, then, the person-centred approach will be very limited in how much it can help *all* people to liberate themselves and overcome powerlessness.

The danger, however, is not simply that parallels exist between a person-centred and reactionary world-view, but that humanistic and person-centred ideas and practices may be used to justify, or shore up, reactionary political systems. If maturity, for instance, is defined in terms of the ability to act autonomously and independently (Rogers, 1961), then it is easy to deduce from this that dependence on others or the State—for such support as unemployment benefit or health care—is an immature, and hence undesirable, state of affairs. Certainly, Maslow was no fan of those he did not feel were achieving autonomy. He wrote in his journal: 'As far as the unemployed loafer today, in times of shortages of help, I'd simply be willing to let them starve ultimately. Short of this nothing will work. As with some nothing works but shooting' (quoted in Shaw & Colimore, 1988: 58). Along similar lines, if distress and unhappiness are attributed to intrapersonal factors such as conditions of worth, then it can be inferred from this that improvements to society need to happen at the individual level—for instance, through counselling and psychotherapy—rather than through wider political change. Here, the fact that most person-centred practitioners are engaged with change processes at the intrapersonal, rather than societal, level, suggests that our approach *has* become incorporated into a political system that views psychological distress in distinctly apolitical terms.

Of course, in defence of these criticisms, one could argue that Rogers was deeply committed to progressive political change (see Barfield, Chapter 22 and O'Hara, Chapter 12, this volume), and there is no doubt that this is true. Moreover, one could argue that at the heart of the person-centred and humanistic approaches lies a belief in 'synergy': a principle that if I do the best for myself, I will also do the best for others (Shaw & Colimore, 1988). A slight variation on this theme is to say that the actualizing tendency is inherently pro-social, such that: the more I allow myself to be guided by my inner directing force, the more I will act in ways that are helpful to others (Rogers, 1961).

But is it really true that following my own needs, drives and organismic valuing tendency will result in pro-social behaviour?[3] Take the following example: At four o'clock in the morning, my nine-month-old daughter Shulamith wakes up and starts crying. I now have a choice: Do I go downstairs, get some milk for her, and then feed her for the next half hour or so; or do I tell my partner, Helen, that I've got a really long day at work tomorrow and that it's her turn to feed the baby. Here, it would be too simplistic to say that my needs and Helen's needs are in total opposition. For instance, it might be that once Helen dragged herself out of bed to feed Shulamith she would have some profound moments of encounter with our new baby. But it would seem to me equally simplistic to assume that our needs are entirely consonant: that if I enhance and maintain my being by going back to sleep that this will also in some way enhance and maintain Helen's, or vice versa. The reality, in this and in numerous other situations, is that some of my needs will be consonant with the needs of others, and some will be dissonant. So whilst the humanistic notion of synergy is a useful corrective to a more Hobbesian view of human beings— as inherently pitted against each other—to simply assume that if I do what is 'right' for myself it will also be 'right' for others seems equally one-sided. Relationships, like life, are enormously complex, and it seems to me that the assumption of synergy can often be a means of avoiding the discomfort and exertion of having to think that complexity through. Emmanuel Levinas (1969), a postmodern philosopher that some person-centred writers are beginning to draw on (e.g. Cooper, in press; Schmid, 2002), argues that meeting an Other in an ethical and principled way gives something of great value to the 'self', but it also requires sacrifice,[4] effort, and a willingness to move beyond our own egocentric standpoint. This, it seems to me, is a much more balanced understanding of how one person's needs relate to those of another.

Just as humanism provides an essential corrective to socialist rhetoric, then it seems to me that socialism provides an essential corrective to humanism. By going beyond an individualistic perspective and acknowledging the socially embedded nature of our existence, it can begin to address the issue of the inequalities of opportunities that exist in our society and also the complex issue of the relationship between my needs and those of others. Here, a humanistic approach becomes much more than a vehicle for individual self-assertion; it becomes a means of creating more opportunities for all in a socially just way.

---

3. I am indebted to Pete Sanders here for pointing out to me the problematic nature of this assumption.
4. At a recent person-centred workshop, I was struck by how uncomfortable (even angry) many people were with the idea of 'sacrifice', on the grounds that it meant giving up some of your own needs for the needs of others. Yet, as I am suggesting here, perhaps it is important for us to reconsider the place of 'sacrifice' in person-centred theory and practice.

PSYCHOSOCIAL EXISTENCE: A SOCIALIST-HUMANIST UNDERSTANDING

Having argued that socialism needs humanism and humanism needs socialism, I want to sketch out a preliminary framework for understanding human needs and experiences that can underpin a socialist-humanist politic. It is based on a Rogerian (1951, 1959) understanding of human personality and development, but attempts to broaden it out to include social and political factors as well as intrapersonal ones.

The starting point for this model is that people have a whole range of different 'wants'. Coming from an existential background (Cooper, 2003, 2004), I prefer the term 'wants' or 'desires' to 'needs', 'motives' or 'drives', because it conveys a less mechanistic and deterministic understanding of how people come to act in the way that they do. That is, the person is not conceptualized as being 'driven' or 'needing' to behave in certain ways by some non-human force, but as having the capacity to make proactive choices against a backdrop of certain wants. To say a bit more about these wants: they can be conceptualized as existing in a hierarchy, with lower order wants being the means by which higher order wants are fulfilled. So for instance, a lower order want may be to complete this chapter, and this may be in the service of a higher order want, such as being seen as a successful academic, which might then be in the service of an even higher order want, such as 'being liked by people.' [5]

Within this model, no two highest order wants are seen as being inherently incompatible. Two of my most fundamental wants, for instance, might be for excitement and for security, and in an ideal environment there is no reason why I could not experience both of these to my satisfaction. In reality, however, our wants are often in tension with each other, because we inhabit an environment in which the achievement of one want frequently necessitates the subjugation of another. A person in a context of limited financial resources, for example, might only be able to achieve their desire for financial security by suppressing their desire for excitement and stimulation: for instance, by taking a job in a fast-food restaurant. Alternatively, in that environment, the person may be able to actualize their desire for stimulation by forming a musical group with their friends, but then they might have to compromise their desire for financial security. In other words, in an ideal world, no two wants need ever conflict. But we don't live in an ideal world, and in the real world, our wants may come into conflict because of the limited material resources of our environment.

This model of multiple wants may seem very different from Rogers' (1951, 1959) understanding of personality and human development, with its emphasis

---

5. Note, whilst the notion of 'wants' tends to convey the idea of something residing *within* the individual, in fact, we can also think of wants as being embedded within a socio-cultural context: for instance, the Western world's *want* for consumerism.

on the unity of the actualizing tendency. In reality, however, the model presented here is essentially just a broadening out of Rogers' original formulation, within which the specific developmental pathway identified by Rogers can be seen as one exemplar (see Cooper, 2000). For whilst Rogers (1959) describes the actualizing tendency as a singular source of energy, what he describes in his model of development is essentially the emergence of a tension between the desire to actualize the self-concept and a desire to actualize *other* aspects of the organism, brought about because the person inhabits a world in which to obtain positive regard from self and others they must deny certain experiences and desires. In other words, to achieve the higher order want of being liked, the person strives to see themselves in a way compatible with their conditions of worth (a lower order want); but in doing so, the person undermines the achievement of other higher order wants, such as their desire to be emotionally or freely expressive.

In this model, well-being is associated with the maximal satisfaction of wants whilst distress is associated with the minimal satisfaction of wants.[6] Why does such minimal satisfaction of wants come about? A first possibility is that the person lives in such a restrictive environment that only a very few of the person's wants can be satisfied at any one time. So, for instance, a young man living on an underprivileged estate chooses to deal drugs to have some financial mobility, but at the same time has to sacrifice his desire for physical security or to live ethically or to care for his children. Here, then, distress and dissatisfaction are primarily brought about by external factors. It may also be, however, that a person in a relatively benign environment is also experiencing a high degree of dissatisfaction, and this would suggest that they are not maximizing the actualization of their wants as much as their environment would allow them to. Why might this happen? If we accept the person-centred assumption that people are at all times striving to maintain and enhance their being, it must be that the person has configured their life in such a way that attempts to achieve certain wants and desires are undermining other wants and desires more than they need to.

By bringing together socio-political and intrapersonal 'causes' of mental distress into a single conceptual framework, the model outlined here also points to the value of both political and therapeutic activities as a means of enhancing mental well-being. Through political activities, social contexts can be reconfigured, such that people are more able to achieve more of their wants more of the time; and through therapeutic activities, people can find ways, within their particular environment, of getting more of their wants met at more of the same time. In particular, through counselling or psychotherapy, people can find ways of achieving certain wants without undermining others. Here, then, lower order activities and wants are reconfigured so that they allow the actualization of more higher order wants more of the time.

---

6. An alternative hypothesis is that well-being is associated with a feeling that one *can* satisfy one's wants (possibility or hope), whilst distress is associated with a feeling that one *can not* (hopelessness or despair).

Central to this process of increasing self-consonance, as many self-plurality theorists have argued (see Cooper, Mearns, Stiles, Warner & Elliott, 2004; Hermans, 2003; Rowan, 1990; Rowan & Cooper, 1999), is that the different 'parts' or wants of the person begin to communicate more openly and empathically with each other. Instead of dismissing, disowning or disparaging other 'voices', they start to listen to each other and see the legitimacy of each other's underlying desires. As the person begins to give their vulnerable side a voice, for instance, the other 'parts' of the person begin to see that this side is not merely 'weak' or 'disposable' but a manifestation of their desire for security or closeness. Here, then, the 'parts' of the person can begin to find ways of working together, rather than pulling in different directions.

So far, this model of psychosocial existence has focused primarily on the individual level, but this analysis can be easily extended to the social plane. If individual well-being is associated with the maximization of personal wants, then the well-being of a society can be associated with the maximization of wants across people (the humanistic agenda), distributed as equitably as possible (the socialist agenda). Here, social improvements can be brought about in a number of ways. For instance, campaigns can be fought to ensure that power (the ability to get what you want) is more equitably distributed, or laws can be enacted that lead to a greater maximization of wants overall.

As at the personal level, however, an increased achievement of wants across society may not necessarily require changes in 'external circumstances'; and, as at the personal level, the key here may be improved communication. The more effectively people can express to each other their wants and listen to the wants of others, the more likely it is that the achievement of wants will be maximized. It may be, for instance, that my partner Helen really does enjoy getting up at four o'clock in the morning to feed our baby, and it is only through open and honest communication that I would know about that; and if she does not want to be doing that, then the more we can talk about what we want in that situation— and listen to the other person's wants—the more likely a constructive compromise will be achieved. People, I would suggest, waste enormous chunks of their lives doing what they do not want to do because they believe that someone else wants them to do it, when, in fact, the other person does not want that at all. So the more people can communicate openly and honestly about what it is they want, the more likely they are to get those wants met, and the more able people will be to figure out how to maximize the achievement of wants across society.

Here, the basic anthropological assumption, along person-centred (Rogers, 1961) lines, is that people are not inherently 'evil'. In other words, that we do not have some higher order want to stop others getting what they want; and that, in many instances, one of our highest order desires may be to help others achieve their own wants. At the same time, and less consonant with a person-centred perspective (though not with a Piagetian one (see, for instance, Shaffer, 1996)), the model is underpinned by an assumption that people do have an inherent tendency towards egocentricity: that they tend to give greater weight and credence to their own wants, perceptions and experiences than those of others. I certainly see this clearly in my children: they do not intend to harm others, but they often struggle to fully conceptualize what others want or need. Similarly, as I have argued in a previous paper (Cooper, 2005), adults are often very poor judges of the experiences and perceptions of others, and have a tendency to assume that others see the world in the same way that they do, and therefore want what they want. Whilst human beings may have a basic desire to help others, it is only by knowing what others actually want that they can really do so. In other words, without communication, our chances of maximizing our collective wants are slight.

At the same time, this basic human egocentrism may be so strong that, at times, open and honest communication may not be enough to bring about a maximal and equitable distribution of wants. If I am an affluent person, for instance, the financial demands that a raise in taxes brings about may be so proximal (i.e. close) to me, and the opportunities it offers less affluent people so distal (i.e. far away), that no amount of communication may convince me to accept it. Moreover, I may be tempted to block out or dismiss the other person's experiences, and the more power I have, the more capacity I have to do that. The other factor is that, as at the intrapersonal level, the more limited the resources, the more genuine is the conflict between the satisfaction of my wants and those of someone else; so here, too, the impact of communication is limited. In other words, open and honest communication is not a substitute for political action, but it may be a very effective means of reducing the amount of conflict required, and of maximizing the achievement of wants that any one situation will allow.

A SOCIALIST-HUMANIST POLITICAL AGENDA

That is the theory, but what about the practice? It is my belief that we need a political force—perhaps a pressure group or even a political party—that can bring a humanistic agenda to the political table. This would be a progressive political voice that, alongside socialist and radical activists, would fight for equality and social justice—for instance, campaigning for the rights of asylum seekers— and against discrimination and abuses of power. But, unlike so many voices on the political left, it would also bring humanistic values and practices into the social arena: for instance, an emphasis on the value of good communication, a belief in the fundamental trustworthiness of human beings, and a willingness to challenge dehumanizing ideas and practices wherever they emerge. Most specifically, perhaps, it would be a radical progressive voice without the element of blame. A political force that challenges injustices and inequities at the socio-economic level whilst maintaining a phenomenological appreciation of why people act and feel in the way they do.

In terms of a political agenda, one key issue for such a force would be the development of emotional literacy in young people (see Hough, Chapter 26, this volume). As I have argued in this chapter, and as I devoutly believe, one of the most effective means of improving our society would be by helping our children and young people to learn to express their genuine feelings and wants, and to empathically receive the genuine feelings and wants of others. If they could learn to do that, if young people could learn to tell each other what they wanted as assertively as possible rather than expressing it in violence or in passive aggression, the reduction in the amount of social conflict and destruction could be enormous. And I can actually visualize this: classes in which young people are helped to identify their feelings, in which they have opportunities to practise assertiveness and negotiation with others, in which they can learn that it is OK to tell each other about their vulnerabilities and anger. Perhaps it is too much to hope that young men, tanked up with alcohol on a Saturday night, could learn to say 'I felt really hurt when you spilt my pint', but at least if they could identify those feelings or had learnt to take a few steps back from them, social problems could be dramatically reduced. Certainly, it seems bizarre to me that whilst young people are taught about virtually every subject under the sun at school, the one thing they learn so little about is themselves and their relationships with others.

And, of course, it is not just young people who have difficulties relating effectively with others. Indeed, perhaps one of the biggest contributions that a humanistic agenda could make to the political arena would be in terms of helping the politicians, themselves, to communicate more effectively with each other. Like many people, when I watch our politicians 'debating' on programmes like *Question Time* or in the House of Commons, I am aghast at their seeming incapacity to listen to each other or to treat each other with respect. With their agenda of point-scoring, name-calling and putting the other down, it seems a way of communication more appropriate to a primary school playground than the most powerful institution in our country. Imagine, then, if our politicians and leaders could actually listen to each other, to learn from the vast intelligence that so many politicians seem to have and to cooperate on political issues rather than compete. And imagine if that was also true for world leaders across national boundaries: that they could listen to the wants of other nations and see the legitimacy of their desires, rather than seeing things only from their own perspective. We are talking here about moving beyond a 'politics of blame' to a 'politics of understanding', and in the United States, former senator John Vasconcellos has begun to make such moves with his 'Politics of Trust' network (see <www.politicsoftrust.net/home.php> and Chapter 30, this volume).

CONCLUSION

As a person-centred trainer and therapist, I see the benefits every day that this way of being can have on clients, trainees and colleagues. It is no magic solution, but in terms of helping people cooperate more closely together and get more of their wants met more of the time, I know of no better approach. At a time when we are so in need of new ways of addressing old problems, when 'old style' socialist politics appears so dramatically to have failed us, it seems to me that person-centred understandings and practices have a unique contribution to make: one which is not about psychologizing or psychotherapizing socio-political issues, but about bringing humanistic values and practices into a radical political stance. Socialist humanism offers us a way forward that is both socially and individually sensitive, that understands the wants of the individual without forgoing the wants of the collective. It is an approach which, I believe, has the potential to become a major new force on the political scene: a truly progressive politics for the twenty-first century.

REFERENCES

Barrett-Lennard, GT (1998) *Carl Rogers' Helping System: Journey and substance*. London: Sage.

Barrett-Lennard, GT (2005) *Relationship at the Centre: Healing in a troubled world*. London: Whurr.

Bohart, AC (2003) Person-centered psychotherapy and related experiential approaches. In AS Gurman and SB Messer (eds) *Essential Psychotherapies: Theory and practice* (pp. 107–48). New York: Guilford Press.

Cooper, M (2000) Person-centred developmental theory: Reflections and revisions. *Person-Centred Practice, 8* (2), 87–94.

Cooper, M (2003) Between freedom and despair: Existential challenges and contributions to person-centred and experiential therapy. *Person-Centered and Experiential Psychotherapies, 2* (1), 43–56.

Cooper, M (2004) Existential approaches to therapy. In P Sanders (ed) *The Tribes of the Person-Centred Nation: An introduction to the schools of therapy related to the Person-Centred Approach* (pp. 95–124). Ross-on-Wye: PCCS Books.

Cooper, M (2005) The inter-experiential field: Perceptions and metaperceptions in person-centered and experiential psychotherapy and counseling. *Person-Centered and Experiential Psychotherapies, 4* (1), 54–68.

Cooper, M (in press) Person-centered developmental and personality theory. In M Cooper, P Schmid, M O'Hara & G Wyatt (eds) *The Handbook of Person-Centered Therapy*. Basingstoke: Palgrave.

Cooper, M, Mearns, D, Stiles, WB, Warner, MS & Elliott, R (2004) Developing self-pluralistic perspectives within the person-centered and experiential approaches: A round table dialogue. *Person-Centered and Experiential Psychotherapies, 3* (3), 176–91.

Dunayevskaya, R (1965) Marx's humanism today. In E Fromm (ed) *Socialist Humanism* (pp. 63–76). London: Penguin.

Fritzhand, M (1965) Marx's ideal of man. In E Fromm (ed) *Socialist Humanism* (pp. 157–65). London: Penguin.

Fromm, E (1961) *Marx's Concept of Man*. London: Continuum.

Fromm, E (Ed) (1965) *Socialist Humanism*. London: Penguin.

Geller, L (1982) The failure of self-actualization theory: A critique of Carl Rogers and Abraham Maslow. *Journal of Humanistic Psychology, 22* (2), 56–73.

Hermans, HJM (2003) The construction and reconstruction of a dialogical self. *Journal of Constructivist Psychology, 16* (2), 89–130.

Holdstock, TL (1993) Can we afford not to revision the person-centred concept of self? In D Brazier (ed) *Beyond Carl Rogers*. London: Constable.

Levinas, E (1969) *Totality and Infinity: An essay on exteriority*. (trans A Lingis) Pittsburgh, PA: Duquesne University Press (Original work published 1961).

Marx, K (1988) *Economic and Philosophical Manuscripts*. (trans M Milligan) Amherst, NY: Prometheus Books (Original work published 1844).

Maslow, A (1968) *Towards a Psychology of Being* (2nd ed). New York: D van Nostrand Co, Inc.

Mearns, D & Cooper, M (2005) *Working at Relational Depth in Counselling and Psychotherapy*. London: Sage.

Nord, W (1977) A Marxist critique of humanistic psychology. *Journal of Humanistic Psychology, 17* (1), 76–83.

O'Hara, M (1992) Relational humanism: A psychology for a pluralistic world. *The Humanistic Psychologist 20,* (2&3), 439–46.

Proctor, G (2002) *The Dynamics of Power in Psychotherapy: Ethics, politics and practice*. Ross-on-Wye: PCCS Books.

Rogers, CR (1951) *Client-Centered Therapy*. Boston: Houghton Mifflin.

Rogers, CR (1959) A theory of therapy, personality and interpersonal relationships as developed in the client-centered framework. In S Koch (ed) *Psychology: A study of science* (pp. 184–256). New York: McGraw-Hill.

Rogers, CR (1961) *On Becoming a Person: A therapist's view of therapy*. London: Constable.

Rowan, J (1990) *Subpersonalities: The people inside us*. London: Routledge.

Rowan, J & Cooper, M (eds) (1999) *The Plural Self: Multiplicity in everyday life*. London: Sage.

Schmid, PF (2002) Knowledge of acknowledgement? Psychotherapy as 'the art of not-knowing' —prospects on further developments of a radical paradigm. *Person-Centered and Experiential Psychotherapies, 1* (1&2), 56–70.

Shaffer, DR (1996) *Developmental Psychology: Childhood and adolescence*. London: Brooks/Cole.

Shaw, R & Colimore, K (1988) Humanistic psychology as ideology: An analysis of Maslow's contradictions. *Journal of Humanistic Psychology, 28* (3), 51–74.

Sinclair, SL & Monk, G (2005) Discursive empathy: A new foundation for therapeutic practice. *British Journal of Guidance & Counselling, 33* (3), 333–49.

Stinckens, N, Lietaer, G & Leijssen, M (2002) The valuing process and the inner critic in the classic and current client-centered/experiential literature. *Person-Centered and Experiential Psychotherapies 1,* (1&2), 41–55.

Chapter 11

THE SPECTACULAR SELF: ALIENATION AS THE LIFESTYLE CHOICE OF THE FREE WORLD, ENDORSED BY PSYCHOTHERAPISTS [1]

PETE SANDERS

This chapter explores the role of information technology and media in the development of personality and psychological distress—with radical implications for person-centred therapy (PCT). The theme of the chapter is alienation, taking Marx's writings on alienation (1844), and the development of that thesis by Gottlieb (1987) as a basis, with situationism (Debord, 1967) completing the analysis of alienation in contemporary society. I also ask how useful the concept is as it stands and what modifications may be required in order to bring it within the ambit of person-centred therapies. Furthermore I understand that the alienation discussed in this chapter is, to a large extent a 'luxury', possible only in a post-scarcity society.

Does self-psychology collude with modern-day alienation? If the very nature of the broadcast infomedia-saturated environment is qualitatively different from the human milieu of the pre-broadcast media age, we must discover how to rehabilitate psychotherapy practice so that it becomes a tool for genuine emancipation and freedom.

The title of the chapter takes the term 'spectacular' from the situationist thesis that life today has become a series of spectacles to be viewed, not actions to be lived. Its use is ironic, suggesting that we do not have the 'freedom' to 'choose' to consume these fabricated images of life. Alienated selves manufactured as necessary fodder for both post-scarcity consumer capitalism and the personal growth industry are anything but spectacular. If it ever claimed to be counter-cultural or emancipatory, self-psychology might now be another cog in the wheel of consumerism. In order to be a genuine force for emancipation and freedom, person-centred therapy must develop psychosocial practice.

THE PROBLEM IN BRIEF

Person-centred therapy has largely concerned itself with the internal world and small-scale social relations at the level of the interpersonal when developing an

---

1. My thinking and writing on this subject has progressed immeasurably as a consequence of various lively and thoughtful communications and discussions with Mick Cooper. Also, many thanks to Suzanne Keys for her helpful comments on a late draft of this chapter.

understanding of human distress. This horizon is too limited if we are fully to understand personality structure and human distress. What is missing is a real acknowledgement (and better understanding) of the relation between large-scale social structures and the material circumstances in which people live, and personality structure and human distress. I am not the first to suggest that Marx's theory of alienation (Marx, 1844) usefully broadens psychotherapy's limited view, reconnecting therapy theory, practice, therapists and their clients, to the social and material world. [2] However, such a connection has not been commonplace in PCT.

ALIENATION

ALIENATION ESTABLISHED—MARX AND ALIENATION [3]

Marx made his major contribution to our understanding of the possible links between consciousness and reality in his *Economic and Philosophical Manuscripts* written in 1844. This is not a complete or coherent theory of alienation, largely because the notes are sketches covering a number of themes, but I will select various themes to suit my purpose, whilst aiming not to distort or misrepresent Marx's ideas by omission.

Marx asserted that labour (work) in a capitalist system causes fundamental separations between 'real' life and 'life-as-experienced' largely because in capitalism the natural link between effort in our lives and survival, or enrichment of our human possibilities, is broken. This direct and natural link becomes mediated by, and soon dominated by, the activity of creating wealth for our employers. Instead of work being a means to survive, maintain, enhance or enrich a person's life, the product of the person's work belongs to someone else and soon the person becomes enslaved to work out of an unnatural form of necessity. Marx believed that labour is an aspect of self and so when what you produce by labour is made external to your life, it becomes alien to you.

An important consequence of work in a capitalist system is the externalization of aspects of the person since the first step is to experience the products of our labour belonging to someone else. Contrast this with a more natural order where, in order to survive or enrich our lives, we do and make what we need and want; thus using the products of our labour in ways that satisfy and enhance us, rather than making someone else more rich and powerful and the bonds of our enslavement stronger. The necessity of working in such a system dominates a person's life and eventually almost all of a person's experience is externalized, to the extent that their

---

2. For example, the work of Erich Fromm was an idiosyncratic mix of Freud and Marx (see e.g. Fromm, 1941, 1955, 1989). It is also clear that alienation was a central theme in the writings of R.D. Laing (Laing, 1961) but little explicit exploration of Marxist theory was evident in his work, although the anti-psychiatry 'movement' of the 1960s had broadly Marxist theses.
3. Students of Marxism will be familiar with this material.

experience of *life itself* becomes alien to them, since it no longer belongs to them.

A second effect is powerlessness, whereby the products of workers' labour only strengthen their enemies. Workers in a capitalist system do not control the process of work, have *no choice* but to live in order to work and produce goods that enhance their employer's wealth, not their own. None of the effort in life is turned directly to fulfilment, flourishing or actualization.

Third is the alienating effect of exclusion where the worker creates (through her labour) the world she does not own and therefore by extension, the world in which she does not really belong (and is constantly reminded of this). I deliberately use a gender-specific 'she' here, since feminists use this theme of alienation to illustrate the patriarchal nature of capitalism. Another topical example of this form of alienation is where older people feel they are not wanted in the world that they built through their labour.[4] In such a society, the person creates, but has no control over, and is not a part of, their world.

Unable to experience belonging or the power to shape our world, we are unable to define our identity, according to Kierkegaard (1959) we cannot say 'this is me, this is who I am, this is what I want'. Instead, alienated, enfeebled and disenfranchised, we are more likely to follow the suggestions of others and to live surrogate and vicarious lives.

ALIENATION PROGRESSED—GOTTLIEB AND CONTEMPORARY CRITICAL THEORIES

Roger Gottlieb's book *History and Subjectivity* (Gottlieb, 1987) is an attempt to revise Marxist theory in the light of the recent (1960s/1970s) history of the broad left, especially in America. In particular and most importantly for this chapter, he integrates socializing processes and reminds us of the importance of 'Marx's root conception of resistance to social exploitation and moral degradation, and to see both of these inscribed in relations of economic and political power' (Gottlieb, 1987: xix). He urges us to relate 'particular human experiences back to the social settings in which they are produced' (ibid.: xix).

Gottlieb uses Hegel's concept of relationship between the 'Master and Slave' wherein the Master's sense of self and social position derives from his coercion and subjugation of the Slave, who in turn loses his identity. But whereas Hegel has it that the slave comes to realize that his subjugated position is what makes the Master's sense of self possible, Gottlieb declares that any possible change in the political consciousness of the slaves has become arrested under advanced capitalism. He develops the idea of alienation in his analysis of how the self becomes dominated by a commodity-driven lifestyle to the extent that our 'sexuality, family and personal lives are unreal'. We, the oppressed, are permanently blocked from experiencing our lives as forms of action and we necessarily

---

4. Although Marxists will assert that every oppressed group will experience this by virtue of being a *worker*, rather than being 'different'.

'… turn to the greater reality of social authorities as sources of strength, control and direction …' (ibid.: 160). [5]

Gottlieb explains that alienation is rationalized as the price we must pay for material wealth and personal freedom. However, the circle closes when he reveals that 'freedom' turns out only to be the 'freedom' to choose and consume a lifestyle and express unorthodox opinions ('free speech'). He illustrates the vacuous nature of this 'freedom' thus:

> Because democratic ideology is combined with mass powerlessness in the worlds of work and politics, too much is loaded on to the family, fashion, hobbies, the latest VCR, mobile home, lace underwear or therapy group. (Ibid.: 159)

Gottlieb also points to modern telecommunications media as key in the control of democratic ideology. This is a development of classical Marxist theory and it provides us with the foundations for an analysis demonstrating that there has been a fundamental shift in how our identity is shaped by the environment in post-scarcity capitalism. In the past one hundred years, the methods by which news and commercial information are conveyed have changed, not only in speed and quantity of information transmitted, but also the *nature* of the information. [6] Our need to know what is happening in the world is met by media mediated by and representing commercial interests and the state. Media representations of lived experience are the vehicles for ideology. The media today present all structures, all relationships, all lives, all others, all realities and all possibilities.

Parenthetically, I am still shocked by how the media insidiously encroach on new domains of everyday life: recently we have had a spate of 'diagnosis-and-treatment-by-media' episodes, as access to medical treatment is decided by media, not medical opinion; and again as we are invited to view celebrities 'share' with us (live on our behalf, with us as mere spectators) the experience of having their parents grow old and die. Such representations of 'reality' were few in the early twentieth century and practically non-existent one hundred years before that.

These representations of reality now not only fill the void in the alienated self with desires fitted to the purpose of the system; desires tailored to induce us to consume the latest products. They also fill the gap between our desires and our lived experience. This is the message of situationism.

----

5. In the field of individualist self-psychology, person-centred theory describes such dynamics in its own vocabulary of internal and external locus of control and incongruent self-structure formed by conditions of worth. The point is that person-centred theory limits its analysis of the roots of tension and disempowerment to personal experiences, rather than social and economic relations.

6. Since Gottlieb's work was published in 1987, entertainment media have evolved further with the development of the Internet, computer games consoles and mobile phone technology. Later in this chapter I look briefly at psychotherapy's failure to engage with the possible effects of these technologies on human development and personality.

ALIENATION COMPLETED—DEBORD AND SITUATIONISM

Situationism as a movement was a diverse collection of groupings existing between the mid-1950s to the early 1970s, although its influence largely is felt (though largely uncredited) in cultural and political ideas to the present day. Readers unfamiliar with the history of the movement are referred to Hussey (2002) and Plant (1992). Guy Debord (1931–1994), artist, writer, filmmaker and political commentator, wrote the major situationist theoretical work, translated as *The Society of the Spectacle,* published in English in 1967. It consists of 221 numbered theses building to a theory of alienation, which situationists had claimed would 'wreck this world'. Debord's claim in the preface to the Third French Edition was slightly less ambitious: 'This book should be read bearing in mind that it was written with the deliberate intention of doing harm to spectacular society. There was never anything outrageous, however, in what it had to say' (1992/1994: 10).

The tone is set with the opening thesis: '1. The whole life of those societies in which modern conditions of production prevail presents itself as an immense accumulation of spectacles. All that was once lived has become mere representation' (p. 12). He goes on systematically to develop Marxist ideas of alienation in an advanced capitalist society. In such a society, however, everything is organized to perpetuate the system itself, not for profit or progress.[7] Alienation is complete (it has moved beyond mere alienation of labour to alienation from all experience) and extends to all areas of life, so all knowledge, art, culture, spirituality and leisure become reproduced as commodities. People in such a world have no authentic feelings; they are separated from themselves because the reality of human activity is replaced by images in every possible place. These images then 'become', i.e. are experienced as, 'reality'. The disembodied processes of alienation and their products become the entity known as 'the spectacle'.

As well as routine analysis of the broadcast and mass print media (this was published in 1967 and pre-dates mobile phones, twenty-four hour television and the Internet), Debord explains how the spectacle reproduces, renews, continues to represent itself and becomes stronger regardless of opposition or interference by co-opting and absorbing revolt and turning it into a commodity. Students at Strasbourg in 1966 explained, in a pamphlet translated into English as *On the poverty of student life,* 'revolt is contained by over exposure: we are given it to contemplate so that we shall forget to participate'. The spectacle is a complete manifestation of social organization that leaves us as mere spectators, worse still, passive consumers of the images of our lives, separated from real experience. The spectacle is how the modern state keeps people in their place without physical force.

---

7. The traditional philosophy of capitalism is based on the Enlightenment idea of progress; the large-scale social goal of unregulated capitalism is to make the economy wealthier and the people more affluent than they normally would be. This economic growth has no prescribed end; the purpose is for nations and people to grow steadily wealthier.

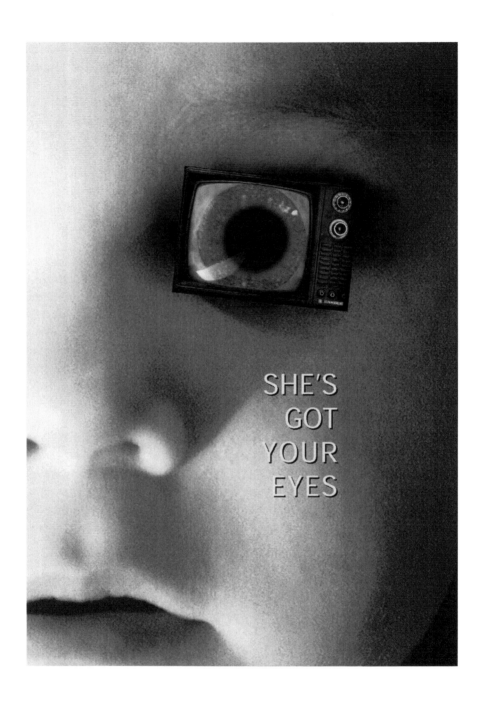

She's Got Your Eyes. Reproduced courtesy www.adbusters.org

Society of the Spectacle is a bleak, angry, desperate analysis. Andrew Hussey in his biography of Debord captures the essence perfectly: 'The defining mood of the book', Hussy writes, 'is … one of disgust' (2002: 217).

> 215. The spectacle is the acme of ideology, for in its full flower it exposes and manifests the essence of all ideological systems: the impoverishment, enslavement and negation of real life. Materially, the spectacle is 'the expression of estrangement, of alienation between man and man' … (Debord, 1967/1994: 151)

> 217. What ideology already was, society has now become. A blocked practice and its corollary, an antidialectical false consciousness, are imposed at every moment on an everyday life in thrall to the spectacle—an everyday life that should be understood as the systematic organisation of a breakdown in the faculty of encounter, and the replacement of that faculty by a *social hallucination*: a false consciousness of encounter, or an 'illusion of encounter'. In a society where no one is any longer recognisable by anyone else, each individual is necessarily unable to recognise his own reality. Here ideology is at home; here separation has built its world. (Ibid.: 152, original emphasis)

WHAT'S IT GOT TO DO WITH THERAPY?

There are several reasons why we should be interested in the ideas of Karl Marx, Roger Gottlieb and Guy Debord, and why we should look for links between these ideas and healing mental distress.

ALIENATION AS A BASIS FOR PSYCHOTHERAPY THEORY

Carl Rogers proposed that psychological distress (potential or actual) is caused by incongruence between self and experience. Rogers (1959: 226) expresses it thus: 'This, as we see it, is the basic estrangement in man.' The individual's organismic experiences have become alien to it, being rejected in favour of experiences mediated by conditions of worth. This is intrapersonal alienation—an alienation impelled by the dynamics of interpersonal relationships. If indeed we are intrinsically and essentially relational, it might suggest that this intrapersonal alienation is the *prime* alienation, since it springs from our relational essence. However, Mick Cooper (personal communication, 2006), points out that 'from a relational perspective, the primary alienation is from others and community, not from experiencing'. This is an important observation, since here we begin to make out a possible taxonomy of alienation (see below), and this would have implications for the domain of influence of psychotherapy.

One may ask 'alienation of what from what?' (M. Cooper, personal communication, 2006). How can I validate the authenticity of my experience? How do I know when I am in touch with my 'real self'? The problem identified here concerns the fact that 'authenticity' is a socially constructed concept and is likely to be imposed as a bourgeois ideology rather than be a genuine experiential referent. For example, when I wrote, above, 'the natural link between effort in our lives and survival, or enrichment of our human possibilities, is broken', I did not explain what 'natural' means. Am I writing with some image of the noble savage, or a return to nature, in my mind? It is surely no more 'authentic' to be a vegan smallholder than it is to be a city financier. These are of course bourgeois constructions that I would be seeking to impose as a prescription on working people. Cooper's solution is to invoke the more neutral idea of splitting of experiencing due to competing needs leading to a possible plurality of selves (Cooper, 1999) each with possibly conflicting needs. There is room here for many innovative person-centred theorists from Zimring and his notion of the healthy balance between 'me' and 'I' self-states (outward-looking and inward-looking respectively) (Zimring, 2000/2001) to Mearns' construction of configurations of self (Mearns, 1999; Mearns & Thorne, 2000). The issue of identifying 'authentic experience' is indeed important, but the point addressed in this chapter is not so much the *nature* of the experiential elements of personality as *how they come to be in conflict*. If psychotherapists only look for *relationally generated* incongruence, alienation or multiple selves, they will *at the very least* have a limited range of awareness.

Notwithstanding the need for more elaboration of the concept of alienation/splitting/configurations/plurality, I assert that there are more sources of 'alienation' in our contemporary society than are allowed for by person-centred theory. The theory falls short in two possible areas; first it fails to address the socio-cultural developments of the late twentieth century which serve to alienate humans more completely from their experience. Second, new theory must be formulated to embrace the dialogical perspectives of, for example, Schmid (2002) and Mearns and Cooper (2005). If person-centred therapy only engages with alienation at the level of interpersonal/family/social *relationships* it will be working with only one, possibly minor, source of alienation in our culture.

Karl Marx had it that when what we *do* in order to survive and thrive (collect things, make things, or the products of our *labour*) is wrenched from us, this leads to a form of alienation from our experience of ourselves as do-ers in the world. Since the experience of what we do for ourselves in order to live (from survival to flourishing) is an important foundation of our identity, when we suffer basic estrangement from the products of our labour, we have another form of alienation which also has psychological manifestations. Gottlieb and Debord then develop the dynamics of Marxist alienation to follow the trajectory of modern life whereby our identity is affected less and less by what we produce and more and more by what we consume.

Put another way, person-centred theory, previously fixated upon distress caused, and then masked, by close, usually familial interpersonal relationships is now being stretched to include the notion of being fundamentally and essential relational, i.e. identity as *relational in essence*. Marx was fixated upon how distress can be caused, and then masked, by the 'doing' aspects of our lives: working, providing for ourselves and seeking fulfilling authentic experience. Debord was fixated upon how this 'identity through production' has been changed by post-scarcity capitalism into 'identity through consumption'.

Now we have the foundations of an extended theory of alienation which, when fully developed, would embrace both the relationally driven alienation of Rogers and the dialogical theorists, and the doing-driven alienation of Marx and Debord. By addressing production/consumption-driven alienation in an extended theory we will open the door for genuine psychosocial practice in a person-centred way, and support efforts to develop theory in areas traditionally 'difficult' for person-centred therapy, such as trauma. Wider understandings of alienation from experience can only enhance the work of, e.g., Coffeng (2002) and Joseph (2005).

We can now appreciate the basic complementary propositions advanced by Marx and Rogers—Rogers dealing with interpersonal relationships of 'relating' and Marx dealing with interactions with the material world of 'doing'. Carl Rogers' (1957, 1959) hypothesis was that given the right interpersonal relationships, human beings would heal, flourish and fulfil their potential. Karl Marx's hypothesis was that given the right material, economic and social conditions, human beings would flourish and fulfil their potential.

As a first position for general consideration, I propose the scheme in the table below to stimulate thinking about alienation and distress.

	Rogers alienation from my experience of myself	Dialogical approaches alienation from others	Marx/Debord alienation from my experience of myself as a producer/do-er
Process of alienation	introjection	alienation from/ isolation from/ others	alienated labour → change from producer to consumer
Psychological well-being	congruent self-perception	in congruent relation with others	experience life as a form of action
Nature of psychological distress	incongruence between self and experience	isolation/withdrawal/ lack of social skills/ loneliness	passive consumerism, addiction, living through images, self-image dominated by spectacular images

FURTHER CONSEQUENCES OF AVOIDING THE MATERIAL WORLD

Another disturbing omission in theory development occurs when psychotherapy fixates on interpersonal relations as the sole context of personality development and simultaneously ignores the material world. Failure to appreciate any effects of the changing material environment in which young people develop will eventually render psychotherapy obsolete.

The last 30 years have seen several trends in telecommunications media which have the potential to alter the very nature of human relations. Mobile phone technology, computer games consoles and the Internet have similar effects upon the structure of human communication and relations. First they insidiously and relentlessly isolate and individualize the person. Second they mediate an increasing proportion of human *personal* communication, and third these technologies reinstate 'interpersonal' relations *on their own terms*, configured in and by their own images and meanings.

This increasingly removes direct immediate contact between people as the dominant method of interaction (in which people directly and spontaneously make meaning from experience) and replaces direct experience with simulated experiences or images (with ready-made insinuated meanings). Young children do not dance *together* facing and bumping into each other: they 'dance' in parallel, tapping their feet on coloured plastic patches, looking at a screen in an arcade game. Children do not play football *together*, making tackles, feeling the weight of the ball: they 'play' football with their fingers and thumbs whilst looking at a television screen. Children do not talk *with each other*, they 'talk' to each other often in isolation, or exchange photographs of where they are and what they are doing—sometimes within sight of each other—on a mobile phone. People do not make love *with each other*, they have sex by looking at someone on an Internet site whilst asking them to take off their clothes and masturbate. Dancing, sport, conversations, sex—simulations and images at every turn—all without directly and immediately listening to, looking at, touching, smelling or tasting another person and their context-in-the-world. Spectacular life will annexe *all of lived experience* in this way.

Whilst some may think nothing is *intrinsically wrong* [8] with these activities, psychotherapists have not asked how these fabricated and mediated developmental experiences might differently interact with human developmental processes.

THERAPY AS REVOLUTIONARY AND EMANCIPATORY ACTIVITY OR AS A COMMODITY?

It is often said by person-centred therapists, that person-centred psychology is revolutionary. In order to live up to this promise, it must explain how it avoids

---

8. This is true on one level, but we must also know that with mediation comes the possibility of control by an intermediary, whether this is a government, software corporation or Internet service provider. In addition, I have not commented on the violent, sexualized content of computer games available to children. I leave the reader to factor in these influences on development.

Debord's prediction that it will become absorbed into everyday reactionary practice to further oppress and control the public. In Andrew Hussey's words: 'The seamless global language of the "integrated spectacle" … endlessly falsifies the world so that nothing makes sense, absorbs dissident voices so they can no longer be heard' (2002: 372). There are many symptoms of commodification of therapy in general which will be explored later in this chapter, including the declaration of an 'emerging profession' and the approval of regulated practitioners.

The end of the Cold War saw the replacement of fake communism with the fake freedoms of consumer capitalism and the result is now, according to Debord, 'the world which cannot be verified' (ibid.: 372). The trend towards evidence-based practice is a facet of this unverifiable world—what counts as evidence is the spectacular presentation of 'information' by government agencies, drug companies and professional bodies. Meanwhile practitioners retreat into professionalism rather than organize revolt. Where is the organized person-centred resistance to the regulation and professionalization of therapy when there is 'absolutely *no evidence whatsoever* to demonstrate that the "accredited" or "registered" practitioner is any more competent than their non-accredited colleague' (A. Rogers, 2004: 12, original emphasis). I will return to a more chilling musing on registration later in this chapter. Meanwhile I remind myself that situationist theory challenges us to ensure that person-centred therapy does not become a spectacular image of change that we buy and consume as a commodity in place of change itself. [9]

Since the spectacle presents fabricated real experience as a commodity, what need have we for real therapy when media therapists queue up on daytime television to perform absent therapy on soap-opera 'stars'? Why struggle with real life when you can sit on your sofa and watch a celebrity live on your behalf and then have their psychology analysed by a lifestyle coach? 'Therapy' is becoming the pathetic consolation prize for what it has squandered: the claim to help people have contact with authentic lived experience. When people's access to emancipatory change is provided by viewing faux therapy with the stage persona of a media personality in their absence, alienation and separation from experience are complete. It is now too late for John Shlien's warning:

> Psychotherapy could suffer the worst possible fate. It could become part of the entertainment industry. (Shlien, 2003: 74)

---

9. Neuro-Linguistic Programming deals with this problem by self-consciously paradoxically conflating 'real' and 'pretend' change. If a client overcomes their public-speaking phobia by *pretending* that they are confident, does it matter that they haven't undergone a 'real' change process? (See e.g. Bandler & Grinder, 1979.)

THE CONSEQUENCES OF INSTALLING THE *ALIENATED* INDIVIDUAL AT THE CENTRE OF PSYCHOTHERAPY THEORY

I now turn to the points raised in the previous section with reference to the ethos of individualistic therapies and look at a selection of the literature that asks questions about the place of 'therapy-as-we-know-it' in our culture.

Humanistic therapeutic approaches, person-centred therapies and Kohut's self-psychology (Lee, 1991) present the individual as the centre of attention. But paradoxically, the alienated individual is effectively isolated, cut off from larger relations and not connected to social and economic structures. Such a view turns the world upside down since it is a matter of fact not theory that humans live in a social, material world. Such theories run the real risk of incorporating the fundamentals of separation, isolation and alienation into a model of human health. Put bluntly, this model locates that which makes us distressed and mad at the very centre of human health and wholeness.

If this analysis is correct, person-centred theory is positioned, not as a revolutionary emancipatory manifesto *empowering* individuals from the bottom up, but, rather in the worst possible case—a top-down capitalist ideological prescription masquerading as natural law.

Furthermore, this installation of the pathologically alienated individual as the apogee of humanity colludes with free-market economics to shift human consciousness and the roots of identity away from relations with others and social and economic structures, towards relations entirely within the self-structure. And who could then argue that the personal growth industry does not *require* alienated selves as customers? If therapy is truly revolutionary or counter-cultural, what, then, does the personal growth 'profession' do to prevent the manufacture of alienated selves on an industrial scale? [10]

Furthermore, psychology and the study of human inner life has, through its unerring focus on the individual, given theoretical backing to the lie that responsibility for the impoverished lives of people is not located in the economic and social conditions created by governments and global capitalism but that it is located in the minds and biology of the people themselves.

> [D]iverting attention from environments causing crime [and mental illness] is needed by the privileged economic classes and politicians seeking to absolve themselves of responsibility for the dreadful social and material conditions of a large part of the population. Their objective, as well as the objective of those whose research they

---

10. In the wider therapeutic community several academics, authors and practitioners remind us of the social and political contexts of therapy—many concentrate on the politics of the profession of psychotherapy (see House & Totton, 1997), while others ask what contribution psychotherapy might make to the political process (Samuels, 2001), and still others champion the identity politics of race, gender and gay issues.

underwrite, is to locate the causes of social problems within the bodies, minds and genes of the oppressed. (Joseph, 2003: 161)

We're working on our relationships constantly, and our feelings and reflections, but look what's left out of that. What's left out is a deteriorating world ... The buildings are sick, the institutions are sick, the banking system's sick, the schools, the streets—the sickness is out *there*. (Hillman & Ventura, 1992: 3–4, original emphasis)

Others go further and say that therapy's complicity is no random event. It is required in order to maintain the necessary illusions on which our entire system of 'democracy' depends. David Edwards is explicit:

The point is that the corporate consumer system needs us to 'go into ourselves', it needs us to be obsessed with the apolitical internal world of our psyche and relationships. Any identification of the *actual* source of our ill-being with the fundamental nature of our political and economic system is bound to be discouraged by that same political and economic system. (Edwards, 1995: 47, original emphasis)

Noam Chomsky is blunt:

A properly functioning system of indoctrination has a variety of tasks, some rather delicate. One of its targets is the stupid and ignorant masses. They must be kept that way, diverted with emotionally potent oversimplifications, marginalized and isolated. (Chomsky, 1991/1992: 369)

Nothing^{TM} Billboard. Reproduced courtesy www.adbusters.org

And how does psychotherapy serve the stupid and ignorant masses as they lie at the mercy of the political and economic system? To paraphrase Hansen, McHoul and Rapley (2003), we have expanded the forms of misery requiring our assistance with an ever-multiplying list of official afflictions, illnesses, syndromes and disorders. Now driving, shopping, eating, sex, reading, dressing, personal finance, home décor and holidays are open to diagnosis and therapy as we increase the ways in which we can find ourselves—and of course, we find ourselves wanting. When your self is found wanting, don't worry, therapists have the technology, we can rebuild you, just pick the model and we will quote you a price. We are at the centre of what Hansen, McHoul and Rapley (ibid.: 1–9) call 'the trade in the self'.

PERSON-CENTRED THERAPY AND WIDER CONTEXTS

We find that early in his career Rogers was fully aware of the role of social, material and economic factors in human distress. In 1942 he wrote:

> A moment's reflection will reveal the fact that some individuals are so weighed down by unfortunate circumstances or so weakened by personal inadequacies that no reorganization of attitudes would enable them to meet life on a normal basis. Here is a delinquent boy, living in a so-called 'delinquency area', where social forces encourage delinquent acts, residing in a home where he is rejected in favor of a younger brother, attending a school which makes no allowance for his retarded mentality, but continually makes him conscious of his failures. No amount of counseling or psychotherapy is likely to be successful in such a case. The strength of the destructive factors is such that a mere reorganization of the boy's attitudes is insufficient to make normal satisfactions possible. Even if he could achieve a high degree of insight into his situation, there are few elements of his life over which he could exercise control. *This is a case in which environmental treatment must be the primary approach.* Counseling can play only a secondary role. (p. 61, my emphasis)

Rogers used several examples to illustrate the same point, and later referring to research done by Alexander and Healy (1935) into young offenders, he wrote, 'in commenting upon this experiment later, Healy recognized that without better economic and social conditions, the insight gained from psychoanalysis in such cases is ineffective' (Rogers, 1942: 62). And again, referring to his own earlier work (Rogers, 1939) he asserts: 'The economic, cultural, and educational factors, both positive or negative, which have entered into the experience of this person are also important' (Rogers, 1942: 63).

By 1951, Rogers' gaze had turned almost exclusively inward. Nevertheless, he explained how the developing self-structure is built, in larger or smaller part, of material from the environment swallowed whole, rather than from the authentic experiences of the person; describing the continuing process of alienation from the world, from others and from one's lived experience. An alien self is imposed. Rogers stated that such experiences were 'as a result of interaction with *the environment*, and particularly as a result of evaluational interaction with others' (1951: 498, my emphasis). However, a distortion has been woven into this theory over the years. In the post-Freudian psychological milieu of the 1950s, it was assumed that such experiences practically exclusively (rather than 'particularly') originated in human relationships with significant others. The influence of psychoanalytic thinking determined that the introjection of values and 'conditions of worth' existed exclusively in such significant relationships as families, particularly parents. Rogers and the humanists might have wrenched some of psychology from the grip of psychoanalysis, but in the years that followed, 'the environment' came to mean 'the family' and particularly 'relationships with parents'.

Person-centred theory must reclaim the wider meaning of 'the environment'. There is no reason why we should not consider social, economic and material conditions (essentially including media representations of 'reality'), language and ideology to be part of the environment to which a developing person is sensitive. Indeed it is essential. Recent trends do not give much hope for development of a more socially orientated set of sensibilities amongst self-psychologists. To the contrary, since there is an increasing tendency to seek explanation in the biology of the individual's brain as writers queue up to make use of the tenuous 'discoveries' in neuroscience. It would appear that we would still much rather locate the problem in the individual rather than in the society that we have responsibility for co-creating. The social exclusion that we tolerate, and vote for, has psychological consequences and these are avoidable. Such solutions however are difficult, requiring struggle in community rather than instant fixes from experts in neuroscience.

However, some neuroscientists do not share this dash towards locating problems and solutions within the individual brain. Steven Rose (2005) cautions:

> Consider the worldwide epidemic of depression identified by the World Health Organisation (WHO) as *the* major health hazard of this century, in the moderation—though scarcely cure—of which vast tonnages of psychotropic drugs are manufactured and consumed each year. Prozac is the best known ... Questions of why this dramatic rise in the diagnosis of depression is occurring are rarely asked—perhaps for fear it should reveal a malaise not in the individual but in the social and psychic order. Instead, the emphasis is overwhelmingly on what is going on within a person's brain and body. (Ibid.: 5–6, original emphasis)

Rose further contextualizes the burgeoning reductionistic 'neurogenetic-industrial complex'—the darling of consumer culture as we chase designer lives, drugs, brains, genes and babies:

> The neurogenetic-industrial complex thus becomes ever more powerful. Undeterred by the way that molecular biologists ... are beginning to row back from genetic determinist claims ... psychometricians ... behaviour geneticists ... and evolutionary psychologists are claiming genetic roots to areas of human belief, intentions and actions long assumed to lie outside biological explanation. Not merely such long-runners as intelligence, addiction and aggression, but even political tendency, religiosity and the likelihood of mid-life divorce are being removed from the province of social and/or personal psychological explanation into the province of biology. With such removal comes the offer to treat, to manipulate, to control. (Ibid.: 6–7)

Rose's most chilling phrase is 'the offer to treat', since it is here we meet the potential complicity of the therapy profession when we repeatedly fail to ask who or what is manufacturing our clients. Offering to treat (depressed) people crushed by lack of opportunity, oppression, discrimination, poor housing and community services with individual therapy is plainly unethical. [11] Worse still, we find (in the UK) a soon-to-be-regulated helping 'profession' straining at the leash to compete for government funding to 'treat' such distress. What more dangerous scenario can there be than a state-regulated helping industry, funded by the state to provide the state-approved 'treatment' of distress. [12] Whilst keeping the church and judiciary free from state control, we follow the pied pipers in our professional bodies to state control of our mental life (see e.g. Postle, 2005). Is person-centred theory and practice revolutionary? For my sake I hope so, for I will not follow it if it leads down this road.

WHATEVER HAPPENED TO PERSONAL POWER?

Rogers' writings on personal power and the politics of individual emancipation might appear to answer many of my complaints. I agree that dealing with the issues of power in the therapeutic relationship *is* the strong suit of person-centred therapy (Proctor, 2002) and remains the revolutionary application. However,

---

11. I recently watched an item on local television about a young woman single parent living in a damp mould-infested house which the local council viewed as 'adequate'. She was 'depressed' and prescribed antidepressants, according to the report—another communiqué from the spectacle in the world that doesn't make sense.

12. But don't worry, with apologies to Kenny Everett, 'It's all done for the best *possible* reasons', namely for the 'safety' of our clients—it has nothing whatsoever to do with creating 'spectacular selves' and fabricated desires and an infrastructure with which to deliver them.

the exclusive focus on the individual can be used to predicate and launch reactionary practice.

Rogers' (1978) thesis is that a fully functioning person has more 'personal power', is able to understand and manage their lives better, is more likely to be able to resist social or ideological control and the socializing influences in the environment, and has a better 'bullshit detector' to emancipate their choices. He rejects what he calls the behaviourist position of the environment shaping the individual's behaviour, and suggests that the individual chooses to 'shape the environment for her own benefit' (ibid.: 19). He casts socialization against actualization as irreconcilable forces.

My assertion is that for the most part in *On Personal Power* Rogers underestimates the power of the spectacle. Tony Merry (2003), however, would have said that I underestimate the creativity and power of our tendency to actualize to raise us above being mere spectators in our own lives. I happily concede that many clients do have control restored to limited areas of their lives, but only sufficient to enable them to return to unfulfilling work and their prescribed role as passive consumers. Should we be satisfied with restoring to our clients the fake freedom to choose which brand of clothing to identify with? Earlier in this chapter I raised concerns about our lack of interest regarding how our clients are manufactured. Now I am disquieted by how we wash our hands of them as we return them to spectacular life; only to greet them (and their fees) with a concerned smile on their way back in to our consulting room through an ever-revolving door.

It is undoubtedly true that people, however oppressed, can experience being masters/mistresses of their own world for the first time as a consequence of therapy, but without a *social* dimension to *psycho*-practice, we are reconciled to returning the young mother in footnote 11 to her mould-infested 'home'. I return to the situationist prediction that any revolt is absorbed and returned to us as a commodity: 'Black power', 'skateboarders against the nazis', 'ecoactivism'. Can we ensure that person-centred practice does not become a commodity too? I do not know, but we ignore this analysis at everyone's peril.

> Leisure, culture, art, information, entertainment, knowledge, the most personal and radical of gestures, and every conceivable aspect of life is reproduced as a commodity; packaged and sold back to the consumer. Even ways of life are marketed as lifestyles, and careers, opinions, theories, and desires are consumed as surely as bread and jam. (Plant, 1992: 11)

CONCLUDING QUESTIONS: NO SOLUTIONS

In order to become a radical—or indeed *any*—solution to some of the issues raised in this chapter, how must person-centred theory and practice develop, or is it fit for the task as it stands? There are key issues to address in theory and practice.

When thinking about the genesis of personality and distress, what do we understand the 'environment' to be. Do we only include interpersonal relations, or do we embrace wider social, economic and material influences? We must continue to refine our understanding of how social and material circumstances affect individual psychology. In particular we must ask: if production/consumption-driven alienation propagates distress, what kind of intervention, therapeutic or otherwise, would be appropriate? Is one-to-one 'therapy-as-usual' to be prescribed?

What are the implications for our understanding of the necessary and sufficient conditions for emancipation? Could we be more effective psycho-practitioners if we developed a model of person-centred social action, removing some of the *causes* of oppression and how can PCT avoid becoming absorbed and commodified by the spectacle?

What do we mean by 'authenticity' and 'congruence' in terms of 'natural' human behaviour? How might we adjust our terminology to differentiate between authenticity, and openness to, and connection with, immediate experience? Do some interpretations of theory set actualization against socialization? How can we value both of these complementary vectors in development and maintenance of human beings, and even begin to embrace the notion of 'sacrifice'?

In short my enduring concern is to ask, 'Is PCT radical?' If it ever was, how can it be rehabilitated and remain so? Allied to this most difficult puzzle is another urgent, but less esoteric problem, namely what must PCT do to oppose and dismantle what it is philosophically set against: the installation of state-regulated mental life from birth to death, from lifestyle TV to regulated therapist? Whilst addressing these issues we must pull off a deft trick: to continue to wear our theory lightly, keeping it dogma-free. It would be unfortunate to find that we were oppressing our clients and ourselves with theory that was too narrow to embrace all of human distress, and then 'administer' it as ideology.

It is too early to suggest solutions—although it would be relatively easy to advise practitioners to do this or that according to my own preferences. There is no 'do this and everything will be alright' ending. Most importantly, the purpose of this chapter is to stimulate discourse not foreclose it with prescriptions or commodified off-the-shelf solutions. In particular, the person-centred therapies must work from their own first principles in creating person-centred psychosocial practice. There are social models of distress available, and psychosocial interventions crafted by practitioners in other therapeutic approaches, but how do we build our own, from Rogers' revolutionary founding principles?

It remains that in the twenty-first century, as always, the key to engaging with alienation in theory and practice is to *act*, not *spectate*.

REFERENCES

Alexander, F & Healy, W (1935) *Roots of Crime.* New York: Alfred Knopf.

Bandler, R & Grinder, J (1979) *Frogs into Princes.* Moab, UT: Real People Press.

Barrett-Lennard, GT (2005) *Relationship at the Centre: Healing in a troubled world.* London: Whurr.

Chomsky, N (1991/92) *Deterring Democracy.* New York: Verso. Updated edition, 1992. New York: Hill and Wang.

Coffeng, T (2002) Contact in the therapy of trauma and dissociation. In G Wyatt and P Sanders (eds) *Rogers' Therapeutic Conditions. Volume 4: Contact and Perception* (pp. 153–67). Ross-on-Wye: PCCS Books.

Cooper, M (1999) If you can't be Jekyll be Hyde: An existential-phenomenological exploration on lived plurality. In J Rowan and M Cooper (eds) *The Plural Self: Multiplicity in everyday life* (pp. 51–70). London: Sage.

Debord, G (1967) *The Society of the Spectacle.* English translation by Donald Nicholson-Smith, 1992. Republished in 1994, New York: Zone Books.

Edwards, D (1995) *Free to be Human.* Dartington: Green Books.

Fromm, E (1941) *Escape from Freedom.* New York: Holt, Rinehart and Winston.

Fromm, E (1955) *The Sane Society.* New York: Holt, Rinehart and Winston.

Fromm, E (1989) *Beyond the Chains of Illusion.* London: Abacus.

Gottlieb, RS (1987) *History and Subjectivity: The transformation of Marxist theory.* Philadelphia: Temple University Press.

Hansen, S, McHoul, A & Rapley, M (2003) *Beyond Help: A consumers' guide to psychology.* Ross-on-Wye: PCCS Books.

Harman, JI (1997) Rogers' late conceptualization of the fully functioning individual: Correspondences and contrasts with Buddhist psychology. *Person-Centered Journal, 4,* (2), 23–31.

Hillman, J & Ventura, M (1992) *We've Had a Hundred Years of Psychotherapy (And the world's getting worse).* San Francisco: Harper.

House, R & Totton, N (1997) *Implausible Professions: Arguments for pluralism and autonomy in psychotherapy and counselling.* Ross-on-Wye: PCCS Books.

Hussey, A (2002) *The Game of War: The life and death of Guy Debord.* London: Jonathan Cape.

Joseph, J (2003) *The Gene Illusion: Genetic research in psychiatry and psychology under the microscope.* Ross-on-Wye: PCCS Books.

Joseph, S (2005) Understanding post-traumatic stress from the person-centred perspective. In S Joseph and R Worsley (eds) *Person-Centred Psychopathology: A positive psychology of mental health* (pp. 190–201). Ross-on-Wye: PCCS Books.

Kierkegaard, S (1959) *Either/Or.* Princeton: Princeton University Press.

Laing, RD (1961) *The Self and Others.* Harmondsworth: Penguin.

Lee, RR (1991) *Psychotherapy after Kohut: A textbook of self psychology.* Hillsdale, NJ: Analytic Press.

Marx, K (1844) Economic and philosophical manuscripts. <www.marxists.org/archive/marx/works/1844/manuscripts/preface.htm>

McLeod, J (2003) *An Introduction to Counselling* (3rd edn). Buckingham: Open University Press.

Mearns, D (1999) Person-centred therapy with configurations of self. *Counselling, 10* (2), 125–30.

Mearns, D (2000) *Person-Centred Therapy Today.* London: Sage.

Mearns, D & Cooper, M (2005) *Working at Relational Depth in Counselling and Psychotherapy.* London: Sage.

Merry, T (2003) The actualisation conundrum. *Person-Centred Practice, 11* (2), 83–91.

Morotomi, Y (1998) Person-centred counselling from the viewpoint of Japanese spirituality. *Person-Centred Practice, 6* (1), 28–32.

Plant S (1992) *The Most Radical Gesture: The situationist international in a postmodern age.* London: Routledge.

Postle, D (2005) <http://ipnosis.postle.net/pages/ChurchFalsePromises.htm>

Proctor, G (2002) *The Dynamics of Power in Counselling and Psychotherapy: Ethics, politics and practice.* Ross-on-Wye: PCCS Books.

Rogers, A (2004) A radical departure. *Person-Centred Practice, 12* (1), 2–16.

Rogers, CR (1939) *The Treatment of the Problem Child.* Boston: Houghton Mifflin.

Rogers, CR (1942) *Counseling and Psychotherapy.* Boston: Houghton Mifflin.

Rogers CR (1951) *Client-Centered Therapy.* Boston: Houghton Mifflin.

Rogers, CR (1957) The necessary and sufficient conditions of therapeutic personality change. *Journal of Consulting Psychology, 21* (2), 95–103.

Rogers, CR (1959) A theory of therapy, personality, and interpersonal relationships as developed in the client-centered framework. In E Koch (ed) *Psychology: A study of a science, Vol. 3* (pp. 184–256). New York: McGraw-Hill.

Rogers, CR (1978) *Carl Rogers on Personal Power: Inner strength and its revolutionary impact.* London: Constable.

Rose, N (1985) *Psychological Complex: Psychology, politics and society in England, 1869–1939.* London: Routledge.

Rose, S (2005) *The 21st Century Brain: Explaining, mending and manipulating the mind.* London: Jonathan Cape.

Samuels, A (2001) *Politics on the Couch: Citizenship and the internal life.* London: Profile Books.

Schmid, PF (2002) Knowledge or acknowledgement? Psychotherapy as 'the art of not-knowing'—Prospects on further developments of a radical paradigm. *Person-Centered and Experiential Psychotherapies, 1,* 56–70.

Shlien, JM (2003) *To Lead an Honorable Life: Invitations to think about client-centered therapy and the person-centered approach.* Ross-on-Wye: PCCS Books.

Thorne, B (1991) *Person-Centred Counselling and Christian Spirituality: The secular and the holy.* London: Whurr.

Thorne, B (1995/97) The accountable therapist: Standards, experts and poisoning the well. *Self and Society, 23,* 4. Reprinted in R House & N Totton (eds) (1997) *Implausible Professions: Arguments for pluralism and autonomy in psychotherapy and counselling* (pp. 141–50). Ross-on-Wye: PCCS Books.

Thorne, B (1996) The cost of transparency. *Person-Centred Practice, 4* (2), 2–11.

Zimring, F (2000/2001) Empathic understanding grows the person ... *Person-Centered Journal, 7* (2), 101–13. Reprinted in S Haugh and T Merry (2001) *Rogers' Therapeutic Conditions. Volume 2: Empathy* (pp. 86–98). Ross-on-Wye: PCCS Books.

Chapter 12

THE RADICAL HUMANISM OF CARL ROGERS AND PAULO FREIRE: CONSIDERING THE PERSON-CENTERED APPROACH AS A FORM OF CONSCIENTIZAÇÃO [1]

MAUREEN O'HARA

On reading the *Pedagogy of the Oppressed* (Freire, 1972) as a graduate student, I recognized immediately a correspondence between what I took to be both men's humanistic world-views and my own buoyant humanism.

RADICAL HUMANISM

Throughout the work of both Freire and Rogers runs a single thread. Both unabashedly celebrate human existence and our evolutionary potential. They write of their fascination with human capacity for self-regulation, self-understanding and transcendence. Neither begs the intervention of a God, magic, manipulative technology, or supernatural forces. They are both radical humanists.

Rogers (1977) placed his faith in what he describes as 'the formative tendency' or 'actualizing tendency' for growth born in each person. He trusts that as long as life remains, this tendency remains. He even insists that the actualizing drive survives even in people so abusively dehumanized that it appears that nothing of their humanity remains:

> Belief in the worth of the free person is not something that can be extinguished even by all the modern technological devices—bugging of conversations, 'mental hospitals' to recondition behavior, electric tortures and all the rest. Nothing can extinguish the human organism's drive to be itself—to actualize itself in individual and creative ways. (Rogers, 1977: 261)

Rogers never gives up on people. Nor does Freire.

Freire has profound Christian and Marxist convictions. He sees both these convictions (often said to be contradictory) as expressions of his belief that the

1. Based on an article first published in *Journal of Humanistic Psychology, 29*, (1), 11–36, Winter 1989.

destiny of humanity is humanization and to become subjects of free and authentic experience. He sees human beings as responsible participants in the continuous evolution of consciousness. This vision and his work to bring it about are the basis of what he terms his 'comradeship' with Christ and with Marx (Freire, 1981).

Freire's faith, like Rogers', in the inextinguishable push for transcendence, is unshakable. Whether speaking of downtrodden peasants, hotheaded revolutionaries, oppressed women, or even life-negating torturers or agents of oppression, he insists that all are born to live human lives, to be subjects of their own experience in a world of their conscious beings. Freire admits he is a utopian:

> Conscientização is clearly associated with utopia. It implies a utopia. The more conscious we are, the more capable we are of denouncing the inhuman or dehumanizing, and proclaiming the human. This is thanks to the commitment we make to transformation. (Freire, 1979: 28, translated from Portuguese)

EMANCIPATION AND HUMANIZATION

One similarity in the work of the two men that strikes most people at once is the overtly emancipatory thrust to all their efforts. Both men have consistently presented their work strategies for use by those who wish to facilitate both the rehumanization process of alienated people, the liberation of the oppressed and achievement of full authentic human existence.

Rogers did not at first promote any particular model of *human*. He knew what a person was, more by its opposite—which he saw in the diminished and dehumanized people who sought his help as a counselor—than by any formulation about *health* or *personness*. Person-centered approaches have their origins in Rogers's search for strategies of liberation for people psychologically oppressed by dehumanizing ideologies, institutions, technologies, religious beliefs, personal myths, and orthodoxies. The end-goal of person-centered intervention is what Rogers terms 'becoming a person' (Rogers, 1961). Rogers is committed to helping people become who, in their deepest hearts, they know themselves to be, however different from the crowd. His view of the fully functioning person is essentially Euro-American, which sees humans as individually autonomous and radically free to allow the authentic expression of an actualizing tendency that Rogers believes is present in all of nature.

Freire, too, considers authenticity an essential aspect of full humanness. A Hegelian, he considers the oppressed as 'beings-for-the other', and the goal of his pedagogy is for people to become 'beings-for themselves' (Freire, 1972: 34)—subjects of their own authentic experiencing (p. 32). He suggests this is achieved through a process of critical education whereby the oppressed learn to read reality for themselves and to describe it in their own words.

Superficially, Freire's authenticity may appear to be the same as Rogers' 'becoming a person', but Freire's concept of person is actually quite different from Rogers'. For Rogers, a person is seen as distinct from society, separate, individual, and free to express him- or herself in unique ways. Rogers has an individualistic or egocentric concept of personhood. Freire's view, in contrast, is much more sociocentric. He considers a 'person' both as an individual center of consciousness and as a social reality. The 'authentic voice' described by Freire is not an isolated voice uttering idiosyncratic opinions, but one that begins in a specific sociopolitical context.

In his book *A importância do ato de ler* (1982) Freire describes his own early childhood experiences of learning to read and write. He shows us a little boy surrounded by a world he did not create, populated by people who were there before him, who described the world to him as it made sense to them. He learned the meaning of words through a combination of his own subjective experience and the labeling by others, and with each meaning came a dense matrix of associations carrying in them many of the cultural elements of life in northeast Brazil. Out of this emerged his first sense of what is 'real'.

Later, as an old man, a return to the backyard of his childhood was to reveal much about the origins of his understandings and misunderstandings of reality. His sense of identity as an adult was partially given by the world in which he first developed language. When Freire speaks of self (Freire, 1982) he speaks of a self that can only be adequately comprehended as emerging from and coextensive with the concrete contexts of its history. This includes people one has known, words and meanings used, experiences lived, ideas accepted, lies believed, and knowledge acquired. Authenticity in this view is not so much a question of being 'different from the crowd' and free to construe the world uniquely, as it is for Rogers, but it is to be to aware of the effects of one's context, to take a critical stance towards it and so become free from distortions in 'reading the world' created by myths, lies, and exploitation, perpetrated by one group for the purpose of maintaining domination of another.

Traditional psychological and sociological thinking suggests that many forms of 'inauthenticity' or dehumanization occur because there exists an uneven balance of power between an individual and a group. The needs of the group (family, school, church, etc.) are seen as pitted against the needs of the individual, and generally the group wins out at the expense of the individual. The group's norms, values and desires gradually become incorporated into the individual members in the form of 'introjections' that, especially in complex industrialized societies, are often antagonistic to many of the felt needs and desires of the individual. On the macro scale, dominated groups will, in the interest of survival, be similarly obligated to introject the desires and values of dominant groups, and then to reproduce them, even if this results in self-negation, as it has been shown to do for women, for instance (Bernard, 1981; Adams 1999).

When this happens, the individual or group lives under tension. Personal needs for self-assertion, individuality, integrity, and self-expression conflict with a sense of partness, the need to belong to a larger whole. Emphasis in humanistic psychology on autonomy, self-expression, self-fulfillment, self-assertion, uniqueness, and so on, can be understood as a challenge to unfair, coercive advantages society (or a group) has over an individual. Dominated groups, such as women, gays, ethnic groups, and so on, have yearned to express their truth, assert their identity, and achieve autonomy.

The work of both Freire and Rogers is aimed directly at this uneven balance of power; Rogers focuses on the disparity between the individual and various groups—family, community, culture, and so on, and Freire focuses on the disparity between dominant and dominated groups. As stressed earlier, both Rogers and Freire are committed to creating a society in which each human being is supported to become his or her full self. Although their stated or implied models of 'full personhood' may be quite different, both men share a conviction that what characterizes the fully human life is *consciousness*—and that the exclusively human activity is the *search for knowledge*. They share the belief that, to some extent, human evolution is in our own hands, and that history is made by human activity. More conscious beings create a more conscious world, and a more conscious world creates more conscious human beings. Both see human beings as architects of culture, and although both stress a secular, 'this-worldly' view of reality, both at the same time hold that a transcendent reality is at work in human nature.

Rogers approaches the achievement of consciousness through exploration of the inner world of the individual and the intimate environment of the therapeutic relationship. He works to help individuals explore the myths they have of themselves and their relations in the world, to become conscious of inner resources and mobilize them for the fight to become more fully *self*. His writings are full of examples of expansion of individual consciousness. In his later work, which deals almost exclusively with group settings, Rogers recognizes the importance of groups as well as therapists in the facilitation of individual growth. Even in a group situation, however, what draws Rogers' attention is the (usually emotional) behavior of individuals. He frequently quotes examples in which individual outpouring of emotional expression has been the pivotal event in a group. In his evocative style he tells us of such an event at the Rust, Austria encounter on the issue of Central America.

> Sunday morning the air was electric. The mood was different. The atmosphere in the general session was decidedly changed. There was recognition that there was hate, as well as pleasant feelings, involved. At different times several people expressed very bitter feelings against the United States; in one case, the person was surprised to discover how deep and strong his bitterness was. Two persons spoke of being torn between two cultures—Latin America and the United States. Passionate speeches were made by the Nicaraguans and by others,

but these were very different from presentations. Persons were talking to persons. (Rogers, 1986: 23–45)

In a group setting Rogers did not talk about 'group issues' and usually responded on a personal level to anyone who did ask group-level questions. For example, in one group encounter in Europe a woman wanted to discuss the male–female power dynamics in the group. Rogers responded to her by asking her to express how she was experiencing her own 'personal power' in the group at that moment. Gradually the focus shifted from 'How come the men seem to be in charge here?' to 'How can I get closer to Carl?' and finally culminated in a cathartic release as the young woman acknowledged a deep frustration in her attempts to get close to her military father. When an anonymous and 'massified' member of a group is given the undivided attention of a figure like Rogers or of the group itself, the experience can be very powerful (Bowen, O'Hara, Rogers, & Wood, 1979). In the above case everyone was deeply affected. Rogers gave the woman the gift of personal recognition, and in doing so facilitated the woman's 'rehumanization' in her own and in her society's eyes. What was left hanging, however, was the whole question of male–female power issues in that group in particular and in society in general, not as issues between individuals but as issues of institutionalized prejudice. What had begun as an attempt to examine some of the structural aspects of dehumanization ended as a private individual experience. Even the comments by observers who had been deeply affected were limited to personal identifications with the woman's emotional longings.

Freire, on the other hand, focuses much of his attention on the group, and on the relationships between groups in society, creating teaching strategies whereby people can explore the way groups function and how this has an impact on individual consciousness. Pedagogical approaches seek to create experiences whereby people may become aware of the ways in which groups can either enhance or damage the personness of their members and the ways in which the larger social forces sometimes promote, sometimes conspire against, full humanness. Freirian educators hope, and I think expect, that this process will lead people to denounce oppressive systems of human organization. They help the oppressed search for alternative ways to organize society, wherein the group does not parasitize the life force of individuals and where one group does not unfairly exploit the labors of others.

Freire's facilitators are interested in individual personal experiences, but unlike the Rogerian therapist who might simply ask, 'What is your experience?' they inquire 'Your experience is of what?' thus turning the focus immediately back to the concrete conditions of daily life and the relationship between external reality and subjective experience. When an illiterate peasant believes she is powerless, the Freireian wants to know how this was learned and whether it is really true or merely an untested myth promoted by the dominant group, and internalized. In our Rogerian experience above, a Freirian would not have left the process at the level of individual experience, but would have facilitated the cognitive exploration of the relationship between the actual sexual power dynamics within the workshop, how they might be isomorphic with those in the broader culture, how they were sustained by myths, ideologies, and practices to which the young woman and her father had been subjected throughout both their lives. The Freirian process would not end until some understanding had been achieved about how the authenticity and humanness of both was exploited by systems of economic and military power, that need men to see themselves as 'breadwinners' and protectors and women to see themselves as homemakers and defenseless.

Perhaps more than any other humanistic thinker, Freire has taught us to blame neither the victims—whether it be their 'unconscious motives', their 'biological inferiority', their basic 'lack of motivation'—nor 'divine plan' or 'supernatural entities' for the injustices of society, but instead to search for understanding about how societies work. For Freire (1970), liberation involves becoming aware of oppression, and understanding how this oppression is accomplished. This is not abstract or theoretical knowledge, but the kind of knowledge that is achieved through action. In attempting to improve the conditions of life, each new action brings the possibility of learning. Gradually the dynamics of society that either facilitate or impede achievement of humanization are confronted, comprehended and transcended.

For Freire, critical consciousness is an ongoing *achievement*, developing only through action in the world. By reflection upon the action, and its consequences in the world (and in their hearts), people become aware of their aspirations to become fully human, and aware of the forces (internal and external) that conspire to enslave the human spirit. This open-ended process of action, and reflection upon the learning from such action, Freire (1970) termed *praxis*.

Because critical consciousness is an activity, and because a person becomes ever more conscious by the exercise of critical consciousness, methodologies of facilitation must be consistent with these at all stages. It is a profound contradiction for a liberational educator, community worker, humanistic therapist or workshop convener to use techniques that, even momentarily, rely on the domination or objectification of another. In a world increasingly populated with manipulators— be they evangelists, gurus, Madison Avenue advertisers, party organizers, inspirational speech makers, or psychotherapists—this is a very radical stance: that all technique must be subordinated to the achievement of critical consciousness. Freire (1980) decries revolutionary leaders or educators who 'massify' the oppressed, practicing manipulation and indoctrination behind some rationalization:

> Propaganda, slogans, myths are instruments employed by the invader to achieve his objectives ... In that manipulation encourages 'massification' it categorically contradicts the affirmation by human beings as Subjects. Such affirmation can only come when those

engaged in a transforming action upon reality also make their own choices and decisions. In fact, manipulation and conquest, as expressions of cultural invasion, are never means for liberation. They are always means of 'domestication'.

True humanism, which serves human beings, cannot accept manipulation under any name whatsoever. (p. 114)

A Freirian educator relates to an illiterate farmer as a co-learner, a co-explorer of reality. They enter a true dialogical relationship in the Buberian sense; together they can explore and act upon their shared actuality. According to Freire, it is a meeting of teacher–student and student–teacher in order to solve some real problems (Freire, 1970). Freire, describing his work with peasants, calls this his *pascoa* or 'Easter', wherein he dies as he was before and is reborn closer in his common humanness to his partner in the discovery. The revolutionary educator and the oppressed peasant become transformed by their *mutual* grasp of their shared reality, thereby approaching one another. Freirian educators do not bring a ready-made truth to oppressed peasants, they bring themselves and they surrender to a true relationship with them, acting and reflecting as authentic people, to build a society together ever more closely reflecting the highest human aspirations.

This radical position has caused Freire's work to be rejected by impatient ideologues of both the political 'left' and 'right' who search for powerful new behavioral technologies to create their image of a better society, quickly and predictably. They claim that the situation is too urgent and that they care too much about the plight of the poor to wait until the poor get around to reinventing the wheel. Freire believes such arguments indicate these leaders wish to objectify the poor, enlisting them in the leaders' unilaterally determined aims. He believes such strategies stem from contempt or pity, not love. Transformational educators or leaders participate wholeheartedly even in reinventing the wheel, because they have faith that what liberates is the journey not the destination. Furthermore, they believe that because consciousness implies creativity, human beings never quite reinvent so much as create something unique (Freire, 1970).

Rogers has devoted a great deal of attention to describing what he sees as the essential attitude of the 'person-centered therapist', that of unconditional respect for the other. All tendencies to manipulate, control, interpret, persuade or prescribe run counter to Rogers' radical faith in an 'actualizing tendency' responsible for healing and growth. He has always maintained that the therapist does not position himself or herself as an expert, imposing will or values on the proceedings, but enters into a relationship that is real and present for both. Because he believes the actualizing telos is positive, the direction and outcome of therapeutic encounter can be allowed to emerge from the encounter itself. Empathetic contact implies participation in a shared actuality. As these parties (therapist and client, teacher and student, convener and workshop participant) bring themselves to bear on the same reality, they become united and they, too, undergo a *pascoa* in which previously held 'truths' or 'selves' yield, giving way to transcendent possibilities.

The work of a Freire educator or a Rogerian facilitator is theoretically very simple—surrender to the unfolding relational actuality, reflect upon the transformation, then be ready to act again, guided by the knowledge gained in reflection. In fact, it is very difficult to maintain. Vanities, greed, power, impatience, fear, laziness, naïveté, magical thinking, politics, status, and so on, all act to prevent the formation of true transforming relationships. It may be just this paradox, theoretical simplicity and the difficulty of achieving it (for more than just moments) that causes person-centered approaches to be written off as 'simplistic', even among humanistic psychologists. It is especially difficult for North Americans, accustomed as we are to responding to suffering by moving into action, simply to accompany a person in pain without feeling compelled to step in and solve the problem. As Farson puts it:

> ... practitioners are impatient. They are not satisfied with such a pedestrian approach. They argue that if it is beneficial for people to talk about their feelings then perhaps it is good to make sure that they do so. To accomplish this all sorts of gimmicks have been invented to elicit expression of feelings ... Authoritarian gimmickry seems irresistibly satisfying even to humanistic psychologists. Rogers himself sometimes seems to be caught up in this trend. Performance seems to be winning over safety, aggressiveness over acceptance, emotionality over dignity. (Farson, 1978)

But Freire and Rogers both know that when we resort to 'facilitative' expertise, we rob the other of the rich possibility for learning that exists in the actual difficulties we inevitably encounter any time we attempt to meet another in authentic dialogue. Even techniques that actually facilitate achievement of open, noncoercive dialogue, for example, may end up robbing participants of the opportunity to recognize for themselves the causes of coercion, and the reasons for silence, and so on:

> If you wish to keep the hungry dependent give them rice, if you want to set them free give them access to land and help them learn how to farm. If you want to enlist the silent in your cause tell them what to say, if you want to set them free, teach them to read and let them speak their own truth. (Brazilian cook participating in a Freirian literacy program, personal communication)

Person-centered approaches and Freire's liberational pedagogy are thus not then best understood as technologies of change, but rather as methods of inquiry and for systematic exploration of human reality. They are open-ended methods for searching for knowledge and for creative empowerment. Through painstaking, dialogic examination of actuality, the consciousness of all the parties to the dialogue expands. Both men believe that such a process is emancipatory. It leads people to a greater consciousness of the inner subjective experience, of the interpersonal process of dialogue, and of the broader social and (for Freire, if not for Rogers) political and historical realities of existence.

PERSON-CENTERED COMMUNITY GROUPS: RESOLVING THE CONTRADICTIONS

For those who worked closely with him during the later years of his life, it is obvious that by the 1980s Rogers had become somewhat of a contradiction. While he never modified his individualistic core theory about the nature of our consciousness, he nonetheless increasingly focused his attention on broader social questions and pushed his work ever further into frankly political arenas. In his last years he worked in over 20 countries, including South Africa, where he facilitated encounters between Blacks and Whites; Latin America, where North encountered South; Europe where Eastern Bloc Marxists met Western humanists; Ireland, where Protestants met Catholics; in Rust, Austria where he brought together diplomats, politicians, and peace activists from Nicaragua, the United States, and other Central American and European countries to consider the violence then raging in Central America; and the former Soviet Union, where participants met each other in new and more open ways. Experiences in these experimental communities permit us, in fact I believe, require us, to reconsider Rogers' theory in light of the actual practice. It then becomes possible to reconcile some of the contradictions in Rogers' own work, and between Rogers and Freire.

Person-centered approach workshops were originally developed as a way to test the hypothesis, which originated in Rogers' experience in individual therapy, that under certain conditions not only will individuals move toward self-actualization and growth but so will communities and groups. Rogers and others have written several descriptions of these programs (Rogers, 1977; Bowen et al., 1979; O'Hara & Wood, 1983). Findings from these experimental situations suggest the need to reconsider the meaning of such concepts as *person, self* and *society*, and the relationship between them. We have come to see that only a 'holistic' vision of *person* can provide an adequate base for a humanistic psychology. *Person* must imply a being who is at once autonomous, responsible, whole *and* who is a constituent part of, heir to, and creator of larger social entities such as relationships, families, groups, classes, societies, and so on. Human beings can only be fully understood when we acknowledge that any time someone expresses 'self' fully, both individually and belonging are perforce expressed at the same time. When I express myself authentically without reservations, my whole truth, as I *experience* it, *understand* it, and *articulate* it, I also express my gender, nationality, class, ideology, cosmology, and what all these mean about my place in the world. The words I use, the meanings I make, the form and content of my expression are both uniquely mine and part of an intersubjective world to which I belong. And whether I am aware of it or not these transindividual aspects of identity can be recognized and decoded by others and have their effects upon them.

That Rogers himself seems to have had some intimation of this without ever having articulated it fully is shown, perhaps, by his famous assertion that the 'most personal is the most universal'.

In person-centered workshops we have seen that in very special circumstances it is possible for the conflicts between the individual and the group and between conflicting groups to become resolved in ways that take nothing (although much may be given) from either the individual or the group. It seems possible, for example, for a group and the individuals who are part of it to establish a relationship in which a high-order harmony is achieved. This is not a static harmony in which no discord is heard, but is more like a conversation or a jazz group's improvisation, created by the contributions of individuals. Under these special circumstances the group consciousness becomes resonant and isomorphic with the consciousness of the individuals (O'Hara & Wood, 1983).

A truly dialogical I–Thou relationship may occur not only between individuals in a group but between the individuals *and* the group, and between groups. There are moments when something can be created that is greater than the customary struggle between opposing elements or the separate voices of individual participants. This kind of group process can be wiser than even the wisest person. In these moments it does not matter whether one speaks of someone's individual reality or of the group's reality, because at these moments they are identical. In other words, when the members of a group can understand how a particular 'voice' bears up on the collective predicament, the group as a whole takes a step toward knowledge and expansion of critical consciousness. The following example is from a multinational workshop in Europe.

> John, a black North American, although wishing to participate in a group task, was having difficulty accepting the views of a co-participant, a white South African. John eventually exploded into a spontaneous and whole-hearted (verbal) expression of his rage and anguish at apartheid. It was a moment of total self-assertion, experienced, however by everyone present as a moment of integration. For the first time John experienced himself and was experienced by others as *part* of the group. Everyone participated in the act, passive but integrated as a group. When Nigel, the South African responded in an equally autonomous and self-assertive manner, expressing the depth of his individual frustration at being a lawyer who had defended blacks challenging pass-laws (thereby incurring the suspicion of blacks

and whites alike), a sudden shift occurred. Separateness melted as mutual comprehension took the place of antagonism. Both John and Nigel had found an ally where they had seen an enemy. They experienced a oneness of purpose, not through trying to understand or integrate themselves, but through vigorous assertion of their separateness (within the context of a mutual commitment to the same group task). (O'Hara, 1984: 218)

The different individual 'truths' about apartheid were expressed without inhibition, censorship, reservation, or judgment. Everyone present became more conscious of apartheid at many levels of existence, from the uniquely personal to the broadly political. From that moment on, each individual person and the group, as a collective entity that is more than the sum of its parts, had a greater grasp of the issues, a subtler feel for their consequences, and a greater ability to live and function in a world where such situations exist. Both the individuals and the collective had undergone a *pascoa*—in other words they had undergone a transformational learning experience.

The context of Carl Rogers' working life differs markedly from that of Paulo Freire's. Rogers' work deals primarily with middle-class members of a dominant culture, people very much like himself. Freire's work deals mostly with dominated people, illiterate peasants and the disenfranchised in poor countries. These differences cannot be overlooked, especially when comparing the work of the two men on the level of ideology, techniques, or methodologies; approaches that may be emancipatory in one context may be oppressive in another. It is not, in my view, Freire's Marxist/Christian view or his passionate commitment to the struggles of the poor that make it transformational—there are plenty of examples of people who share his ideology and speak equally passionately on behalf of the oppressed yet continue the tactics of domination. Freire's work is transformational because of its commitment to truth and the achievement of critical consciousness. Rogers' person-centered approach is also, at base, a process by which persons and groups can search for truth. It is not the famed Rogerian axioms regarding the 'necessary and sufficient conditions', nor 'non-directiveness', nor the expression of emotions that makes person-centered approaches effective; it is knowledge or critical consciousness of oneself (in both individual and transindividual aspects) and of one's place in the world, which heals. Beyond that, when individuals become aware not only of their own psychological reality, but how it participates in larger systems either in resonance with it, or as a dissident, they contribute to an advancement of collective consciousness too, thereby, furthering the advancement of human society as a whole.

What both Freire and Rogers offer us, separately and together, is the faith that truth both heals and emancipates; the uncompromisable position that we are all capable of becoming conscious, the conviction that we achieve this only through dialogue with each other, and the hope that through such dialogue, whenever, wherever, and however we have the opportunity, we may create a world where each may live in dignity and may exercise our natural vocation to become even more fully human. As humanistic psychology reaches out further into the wider sphere of social and international relations, person-centered approaches, grounded in the work of Carl Rogers, sharpened by the more political thinking of Paulo Freire, have much to offer. They offer a non-sectarian praxis based in the most human of all activities, dialogue, which embraces both the private unique world of the individual and the public intersubjective world of groups and societies. A praxis that aims at conscientização, when deepened by the individual psychological insights of person-centered processes, offers facilitators of social transformation a way to aid people seeking to emancipate themselves from both public and political oppression and from their own internalized patterns of compliance. Such work is truly revolutionary.

REFERENCES

Adams, H (1999) *Tortured People: The politics of colonization.* Penticton, BC: Theytus Books.

Bernard, J (1981) *The Female World.* New York: Free Press.

Bowen, M, O'Hara, MM, Rogers, CR & Wood, JK (1979) Learnings in large groups: Implications for the future. *Education, 100,* 108–77.

Farson R (1978) The technology of humanism. Presentation at Center for Studies of the Person, La Jolla, CA.

Freire, P (1972) *Pedagogy of the Oppressed.* New York: Herder & Herder.

Freire, P (1979) *Conscientização.* São Paulo: Cortez & Moraes.

Freire, P (1980) *Education for Critical Consciousness.* New York: Continuum.

Freire, P (1981) Unpublished transcript of a talk given in Itaquaquecetuba, SP, Brazil.

Freire, P (1982) *A importância do ato de ler.* São Paulo: Cortez & Moraes.

O'Hara, MM (1982, July) The Person-Centered Approach as Conscientização: The works of Carl Rogers and Paulo Freire. Paper presented at the First International Forum on the Person-Centered Approach, Oaxtapec, Mexico.

O'Hara, MM (1984) Person-centered gestalt: Toward a holistic synthesis. In RF Levant & JM Shlein (eds), *Client-Centered Therapy and the Person-Centered Approach: New directions in theory, research and practice* (pp. 202–21). New York: Praeger.

O'Hara, MM & Wood, JK (1983) Consciousness and the group mind. *The Gestalt Journal, 6* (2), 103–16.

Rogers, CR (1961) *On Becoming a Person: A therapist's view of psychotherapy.* Boston: Houghton Mifflin.

Rogers, CR (1977) *Carl Rogers on Personal Power.* New York: Delacorte.

Rogers, CR (1986) The Rust workshop: A personal overview. *Journal of Humanistic Psychology, 26* (1), 23–45.

Chapter 13

PSYCHOTHERAPY: THE POLITICS OF LIBERATION OR COLLABORATION? A CAREER CRITICALLY REVIEWED [1]

Dave Mearns

Politics is something that lefties do—we don't have politics, only rightness.

Thus whispered the President of the Escondido Rotary Club after my fifteen-minute address in 1972. This was my first experience of 'redneck' country. Far from being restricted to the mid-west of the USA, 'redneck' territory starts east of a 20-mile coastal strip down the length of California. The same address had been well received in a dozen other clubs, but they had been in that 20-mile coastal strip. Certainly, there had been my unwitting faux pas in San Diego when, in answer to the question, *'What have you noticed about Rotary in California?'*, I innocently observed that, in all the clubs I had visited, I had not seen a Black person. The next week I was taken to the Rotary Club of South-East San Diego where *all* the members were Black! My talk in Escondido was not, in my 'leftie' view, particularly 'political', though there was a joke about Nixon and I had forgotten to smirk when I mentioned McGovern. That afternoon I was taught a lesson when I was a guest of the Rotary Club President at his avocado farm. He sent for his Mexican-American farm manager. When the manager arrived the farmer told him to 'go away and come back again *quicker*'. The man was being humiliated as a political lesson to me that 'this is what life is like'.

Even in our counselling community I have found a fairly widespread disregard of 'politics'. People seem even offended by the juxtaposition of the terms 'counselling' and 'politics'; some are positively irritated by the concept; and very few are skilled in analysing the politics of counselling settings. Yet, such analyses reveal new perspectives and possibilities. In analysing the politics of a situation we are encouraged to empathize with all the various stakeholders in that social system. So, the Practice Manager in the clinic where we work as a counsellor is not just 'being mean because that's the way she is', rather she is deeply concerned about the job she does—she loves the work, takes enormous satisfaction in running the Practice efficiently and wants to exert what early authority she has on this

---

1. This paper was presented as the 99th 'Associates of the University Counselling Service' Lecture at the University of East Anglia, Norwich, on March 28, 2006.

new counsellor who could potentially disturb her tidy process.

Carl Rogers was not a great politician but he did have a considerable political impact, though that impact was more on individuals than institutions. In *Carl Rogers on Personal Power* (1978), he told the story of how, at one talk when he had said he was not 'political', a man came up at the end and said,

> ... I began to read your material, which upset everything I had learned. You were saying that the power rests not in my mind but in his [the client's] organism. You completely reversed the relationship of power and control which had been built up in me ... And then you say there is no politics in the client-centered approach! (p. 3)

Rogers liked this story—he liked to think that he had, indeed, had such a political influence. Shortly after this experience he started to apply the label 'quiet revolutionary' to himself.

Yet, for all his political influence on individuals, Rogers did not have a significant influence on institutions. He challenged institutions but he did not really understand them and he certainly did not value them, so his influence seldom outlasted his presence. Rogers was an 'individual psychologist' not a sociologist or a social psychologist. He would challenge institutions for not being person-centred while failing to empathize with their need to be institution-centred. Unlike his work with individuals, he could not meet institutions where they were and understand and value them for what they were. He also mistook his success in micro politics for potential in macro politics. In his last twenty years he worked in South Africa, the USSR and numerous other countries to apply the encounter group method in work towards conflict resolution on an international scale. His thesis was that if people could meet each other as persons they would be moved by each other and shift out of their polarized positions. Of course, he was right in this thesis—people are moved by the humanity of others and by connecting with their own humanity. But if this is all that is done—if the work is only at the level of the individuals and the institutions are ignored—the institutions have a tendency to exact a powerful retribution on their dissidents. It is argued that the most powerful macro political influence of Rogers was on the way President Carter approached the Camp David talks between Egypt and Israel. Carter was a long-time admirer of Carl Rogers and sent him a personal message at his 80th birthday celebration. The meeting between the representatives of Egypt and Israel was expected to be a difficult negotiation with not much hope of success. Carter set it up in an unusual way, getting the delegates to arrive some days before the negotiations would start. This 'acclimatization period' was not to do with jet lag. It created an informal situation out of sight of the media and other stakeholders where the persons on the two sides found themselves having some informal contacts—like the Israeli and Egyptian negotiators who were seen showing each other photos of their families in the grounds of the ranch.

Amazingly to the rest of the world an 'accord' was struck at Camp David between the negotiators, Begin of Israel and Sadat of Egypt. The two most alienated countries in the world at that time had come to an agreement. Even more amazing is that the Camp David Peace Accord is still in place today.

Of course, the main protagonists were made to pay. Begin was soon deposed and Sadat was assassinated. Politics is not only about individuals meeting as persons—Begin and Sadat had failed to represent the prejudices of their peoples.

Carl learned something about the boundaries of his 'person-centred' ideology in the making of a powerful documentary in 1973. Equal numbers of protagonists of the Roman Catholic and Protestant communities were put into an encounter group for three days and the proceedings filmed. It was too dangerous to do the filming in Belfast, and London or Dublin were out of the question for one or other faction, so everyone was flown to Pittsburgh for the filming. I was involved at the editing phase because, when the producer, Bill McGaw, got the tapes back to California for editing, I was the only one who could understand the Belfast accent!

One of the most powerful moments in that movie is when one participant describes an explosion outside his house and him going out to pick up the remains of his sister. When gently challenged on his seeming lack of emotion in telling the story, the man says something like: 'When I revisit that event a steel shutter comes down between me and my emotions. That steel shutter needs to stay there—or else I don't know what I would do.'

This experience affected Carl—it helped him to see one of the boundaries of the person-centred philosophy he had developed. Previously, his emphasis had been one-directional—that opening out to our experiencing is totally positive. But, in this example, he saw the dialectic—that there were limits and an opposite imperative. To his and the producer's enormous credit they honoured this boundary by naming the movie, *The Steel Shutter* (Rogers et al., 1973).

Incidentally, that movie had a scary history thereafter. Six cellulose copies were initially printed. Two were retained in California, three went to Belfast and one was held by me in Scotland. The three Belfast prints were used in numerous cross-faction meetings led by Pat Rice. One by one the three prints were lost. One was stolen and two were ceremonially burned when meetings were abruptly brought to an end—one by masked protestant militants and one by members of the Provisional IRA. Just as eerie is the story about my print. I lent it to a Swedish colleague who was going to organize showings in her country. After 6 months she had still not returned it, nor responded to my letters. I found that she had been killed in a road traffic accident and the print was never found!

So, it is difficult to evaluate Carl Rogers' impact on macro politics and my own contribution in that regard has been zero or perhaps even less than zero. You can get a less-than-zero score when you evaluate your achievements and find that they may have been working in the wrong direction. My last involvement with direct action politics came around 1969 when, along with colleagues in the 'Youth for Peace in Vietnam' movement, I organized a sizeable demo with a concluding event in docklands Glasgow. I stood in the front row of the large gathering growing more and more furious at first one speaker, then another, then another. I was passionate about the atrocity of the war and it meant not one damned thing to any of those speakers—they were just using the event as a vehicle to promote their own politics. The speaker who happened to be 'on' when I finally broke down wore a nice white jacket which was not improved by the impact of the half-eaten orange I hurled at point-blank range. I was physically ejected from my own demo and I retired from macro politics.

If truth be told, the end had been coming for a while. I was having a hard time coping with the dissonance between my deep passion about the humanity of people and the fact that colleagues not too far to the left of me might even be willing to kill for what they/we believed in. That to me went right against what I believed in—the medium must, in my view, be consistent with the message—often a problem in macro politics. What I had found is the so-called '*horseshoe*' of politics: the political spectrum can look like a straight line from left to right but, in fact, its extremes are bent towards each other.

I was looking for some other, more consistent, medium for my valuing of humanity—strange that I found it in psychology. But Rogers' writings offered huge resonances for me. Here was a man who cared so deeply about humanity that he did not try to use his power, even subtly, to steer others. He even valued their difference from him. He had developed a way of working in therapy that was powerful in helping people to find their own power. This was micro politics rather than macro politics—it wasn't going to change the world, except by a slow person-to-person evolutionary process. But, although it might be small, I felt I could trust it for two reasons: the medium was consistent with the message and the effects, though small, were consistent. It did not look likely that one day I would discover that politically it had actually been working towards repression, though you never know …

When I later spent time with Rogers I was amazed how consistent he was with his message. He was a genuinely warm person, interested in those around him and expansive enough to give others space. I had to go through my own struggle in relation to him. When you meet someone whose writing has led you to change your whole life there can come a time when you begin to resent them—you find it difficult to make the transition to just being with them as another person in your life. I took my struggle with this to Carl and he came out with a wonderful offering (which I later learned that he had adapted from a new book title). He said: 'When you meet the Buddha you have to kill him in order to meet the person.' Anyway, it worked, and I joined the group of people who shared a genuine friendship with him. I used him well in my supervision—he was exactly what I needed and I needed to move fast as a young therapist. I had no time for the gradual developmental process I *now* emphasize. He was perfect for that, because he gave so much *space* for my development. A small piece of dialogue I remember verbatim gives an example. One of the hospital patients I was working with was profoundly traumatized—very closed off to communication—indeed mute. (This wasn't Rick in Chapter 6 of *Working at Relational Depth in Counselling and Psychotherapy* (Mearns & Cooper, 2005) but quite like him). The dialogue with Carl went as follows:

Carl: *Do you know what you are doing with him* [the patient]?

Dave: *Not a bloody clue, Carl.*

Carl: *That's alright then.*

In these days of treatment plans and expectations about what it means to work 'professionally', such an exchange might be seen as bordering on the unethical and Carl would certainly be seen as deficient as a supervisor. Yet, this short exchange describes the core of what we are trying to do in person-centred therapy—we are trying not to 'do' anything with or to the client—we are trying *not* to have an agenda for the client. Instead we are trying to relate with the client in a way that gives him space enough to do almost anything. The work is perfectly reflexive too—Carl was giving me the same huge space.

So, person-centred therapy has for me, over these past 35 years, been a vehicle for my politics. My politics are entirely directional: I want to move things in a direction that empowers people. Person-centred therapy can do that—it can help people to be more fully aware of themselves, even aware of the different and sometimes competing 'parts' to themselves. Knowledge is power (an ancient socialist principle) and self-knowledge can be powerful in its impact particularly when it is being discovered in a context that is genuinely prizing of the person— of the *whole* person. The mix is made even more powerful by the fact that the partner in the exploration is not seeking to usurp any of the power.

In general, this empowering process works in a direction that is opposite to that of totalitarian capitalist democracies such as pertain in the USA and in Britain. Of course, the doctrine of the right *appears* to emphasize 'freedom', 'self-sufficiency', and even the word 'empowerment' is sometimes used, but, as is well recognized by many South American countries in 'discussion' with their northern neighbour, those freedoms are only permitted within the context of a capitalist economy—indeed, it is freedom of the capitalist economy and its running elite that is being furthered, not freedom for the people. A capitalist economy cannot permit such general freedom because it relies on an enhanced level of deprivation. Deprivation motivates the few to use the economy to escape and demotivates the many to be subservient to it. For a time Thatcher tried to peddle the illusion of the 'trickle-down economy' but, at least, political and economic consciousness has now risen above such platitudes. The problem with an economically engineered disempowerment is that, because of its totalitarian nature, it is easier to see it than to remediate it. This is the problem that is being faced by Chavez in Venezuela, Morales in Bolivia and Bachelet in Chile.

Although the task of this chapter is to focus on micro politics more than macro politics, it is important for my purpose to note one key mechanism that can seriously disempower people at both the macro and the micro levels. The mechanism is contained within the term 'totalitarian capitalist democracy'. Initially, the terms 'totalitarian' and 'democracy' might appear to be at odds with each other, particularly with the spin given to the word 'democracy' in the past 80 years in the West (but not in the East or the Middle East). After all, democracy means that we all have a vote and everyone's vote is equal—so the people have the power to change things. Sounds good, doesn't it? It sounds good because it is oft repeated 'unspeak' as Steven Poole (2006) describes in his fascinating new book of the same title. Poole defines 'unspeak' as 'a mode of speech that persuades by stealth', e.g. 'climate change' (instead of 'global warming'), 'war on terror', 'ethnic cleansing', 'freedom is on the march' or 'repetitive administration of legitimate force' (US army on the beating to death of a prisoner in 2003). 'Unspeak' is language that attempts to socially construct reality. So, the apparently wholly positive connotation of the term 'democracy' masks the fact that no power is actually being given—the 'free vote' is a complete fallacy. The way to make the giving of a free vote safe for a totalitarian capitalist regime is simple—*make all the political parties the same!* It is fascinating to see how well this has been achieved in the USA and in Britain—you can have a vote, but all the parties are the same—they all occupy only a tiny sector of the political spectrum. People were surprised in the 1990s when multinationals began to contribute heavily to New Labour, favoured even above the Conservative Party. But this move of Labour to New Labour was much more important to capitalism than simply having one party to support, for if you can have *both* big parties you have achieved the ultimate switch from a capitalist democracy to a *totalitarian* capitalist democracy, such as was accomplished in the USA many years previously.

The same mechanism can exist in micro politics within institutions—we appear to have freedom but only in the context of all the possible choices being, essentially, the same, because none of them steps out of tight parameters set by the institution. This is not something to moan about—I never moan about politics—instead, it is valuable knowledge if we are seeking to engineer change.

Political awareness is so important at the micro level. Probably we should run courses in it. An awareness of the 'politics of helping' can make the difference between feeling impotent and depressed or effecting meaningful development.

THE POLITICS OF HELPING

THE PRIMARY OBJECT OF HELPING SERVICES IS NOT TO HELP, BUT TO BE *SEEN* AS HELPING

This is the first premise of the politics of helping. 'Image' is everything where reality for the vast bulk of the population is decided by the tabloid press, which now includes most television news services. I have coined the term 'tabloid politics' to denote the kind of deficiency-model political thinking which derives initially from the tabloids but is now pervasive even in macro politics where legislation is designed in response to headlines. 'Tabloid politics' is pervasive within micro as well as macro politics—how things *appear* is more important than how they actually *are*. Hence, the first premise: that helping services are primarily there to be *seen* to help. A corollary, within health services, is that it is better to spread a service for 100,000 people out to 200,000—that way we are being *twice* as helpful! I recall being faced with this suggestion by a commissioner of our counselling provision. I directed my response to the only doctor in the room and asked what would happen if we had enough of a drug to treat 'x' people, but we then 'cut' it to treat '2x' people. 'It wouldn't help anyone!' was her reply. 'Precisely', I said.

My reaction to the first premise is to understand it, and how it is mediated by administrators. A reaction of frustration is dysfunctional if it inhibits constructive response. Instead, I want to take five steps comprising a positive response:

First, I want to understand these politics as fully as I can;

Second, I want to understand the power by which the politics holds its administrators;

Third, I want to *value* those administrators—in my experience they are human beings trying to make the best of their job, just as I am mine;

Fourth, I want to know what I want in the situation;

Fifth, I want to engage in a process of '*articulation*' with the administrators.

'Articulation' is a process described initially in Chapter Two of *Person-Centred Therapy Today* (Mearns & Thorne, 2000) and further elaborated in Mearns (2003). It is a process of genuine dialogue. I am concerned to be as clear as possible about what I want and my limits, but I am equally concerned to find out as much detail about the needs and limits of the other. Most important is that I want to *learn* from the articulation process. There are many possibilities for learning: I may learn from the expertise of the other; I may learn about some of my own inadequacies; I may learn how better to communicate within the articulation process.

So, this is what I am trying to do in articulation, but what about the response of the other? It is rare for the other to consistently fail to participate in the dialogue. Often the other will start out as guarded, even unnecessarily defensive. But my valuing of the other and my efforts at empathy towards their position are powerful within human relating and a guarded but positive response usually ensues. Once the other realizes that I am genuine in this process, even genuinely learning, they generally begin to dialogue—which means that they genuinely listen to me. We have then established the conditions for coming to the 'best fit' of both our needs. I will not necessarily get all of what I want and they will not get all of what they want, but together we can get what *we* want (or, indeed, genuinely decide that it is not good for us to do business).

The reader will recognize that what we are talking about in this articulation process are powerful dimensions of humanity. We are doing political 'business' together, but we are using our humanity to do it. My experience, consistently, is that we *both* get more out of the 'deal' and that we genuinely look forward to further such meetings. We can welcome those because we are both being 'real' in relation to each other. The politics is not an obstacle to us being real—it is merely the context in which we meet.

Once an articulation process is established with the other, I want to be able to take the initiative in future situations. I want to consider the situation in advance, not only mapping out my own initial position but also anticipating the needs of the other.

The opposite of articulation would be to stick rigidly and defensively to what we want, with no learning resulting and achieve a result that will probably not be the most creative. After the event we can always retreat into moaning about the world. We probably will not look forward to further encounters with the other.

HELPING IS GENERALLY A DISGUISE FOR SOCIAL CONTROL

Our colleagues in the once noble profession of social work know all about this, the second premise in the politics of helping. During the past 30 years they have seen their role change from 'potentiality model' to 'deficiency model'—from 'social work' to 'social police'. They have been *devoured* by tabloid politics. Their whole profession has been defined by the 'extreme case'. A child is taken away from the family under fears of child abuse that later cannot be established and the resultant publicity shouts about the rights of parents and their abuse by social workers. The next week the case is of a child abused by parents—and social work is blasted for knowing about the danger but failing to remove the child! It is no wonder that the profession has become traumatized. As with victims in serious cases of abuse, some workers have even internalized their own guilt and begun to represent the voice of the abuser. The once respected early 1970s 'model' for the profession, Florence Hollis, now becomes regarded as naïve—a figure of ridicule for some in the profession; a director of social work, last week, suggests that parents should be drug tested; 'defensive practice' becomes the norm—touching children in care homes becomes explicitly forbidden and de facto regarded as unethical. One certain prediction is that in 20 years' time there will be scores of litigations taken out by former residents of children's homes against practitioners and authorities on the ground of their systematic denial of natural human physical contact, despite the huge body of evidence that shows how critical it is for development.

I deeply want to emphasize my regard for social workers—my most enjoyable teaching experiences were in that sector before I withdrew from it in 1990. Thousands of social workers continue to seek to work with integrity and humanity. Many others have joined us in counselling. But the profession has largely been subverted to a 'deficiency model' having started life as 'potentiality model'.

Tabloid politics finds 'potentiality' boring—'deficiency' and the 'deficient' sell newspapers, provide easier headlines and stimulate the salivation of the right-wing majority. Most approaches to counselling and psychotherapy are oriented towards 'potentiality' rather than 'deficiency'. Probably we are the only profession thus oriented—though a strong case can also be made for medicine, but not within mental health, of which I will say more later. Therefore, we need to be politically aware in respect of Premise 2. We can expect to be expected to 'correct' the 'deficiencies' of our clients—to be agents of 'social control'.

Once again, we could respond to these politics by throwing our hands in the air, shaking our head, and retreating into principled indignation. Principled indignation is a comfortable place—but it sure as hell does not help other people.

There is nowhere that is more pervaded by the social control political premise than in work with young people. Great Britain hosts arguably the worst context for the valuing and the empowering of young people. It is considerably more oppressive for the young than most other cultures and in this instance Britain is much worse than the USA. Database searches linking terms such as 'self-esteem' and 'education' provide a huge response in American publications and very little in Britain (except in Special Educational Needs where the link is well understood).

One of my earliest 'quests' (and that word is well chosen because in the early days I felt like Don Quixote) was to bring counselling into education. The story is in two parts. The first part was when I worked with my friend, Professor John MacBeath, on the so-called 'Guidance and Home' research project, financed by the then Scottish Education Department. We were genuine researchers and our finding in relation to counselling in schools went against our own hopes. We concluded that counselling in schools was not possible. Our rationale is given in our book entitled *Home from School*:

> It is difficult to ask the guidance teacher also to fulfil a counselling
> role in the fullest sense of that term. It is, after all, unreasonable to

expect pupils to confide in someone whose accountability is to the authority of the department, the school, the Scottish Education Department, or to parents. The pupil cannot, therefore, either expect confidentiality or assume that his own individual needs will be given the highest priority by the guidance teacher. The fact that the pupils [in our research] tended not to see guidance as a source of counselling is perhaps unsurprising. (MacBeath, Mearns & Smith, 1986: 283)

Interestingly, our research finding was contradicted in a simultaneous (1986) publication by the Consultative Committee on the Curriculum, entitled *More than Feelings of Concern*. They were positive about counselling in schools as long as the counsellor was also a teacher, so together we set up a pilot. The counsellor was an experienced teacher who also held an appropriate counselling qualification. We abandoned the pilot after four months. The counsellor had established a service that allowed pupils who were to be 'suspended' (and there were many) to spend some time with her before they departed the school. Her rationale was that they should, at least, feel that they had had 'a hearing' before they left. The deputy head teacher disagreed and in a final instance he locked the counsellor in her room before suspending a pupil!

Fifteen years later I was encouraged to take up the quest once more. In a pilot project, financed by Greater Glasgow Health Board, we designed a counselling service for three large schools. We insisted that the pilot be over two years, because a counselling service, in any sector, generally takes two years to become fully established. The result has been dramatic. After a detailed clinical outcomes evaluation the project has been rolled out from 3 schools to 23. Yet, the existence of counselling in schools is politically problematic because of the social control premise. Politically, young people are expected to be controlled. They are essentially regarded as 'deficient'; certainly on matters of ethics and development (though I suspect that they are actually more sophisticated in those areas than was the generation that now judges them). Even the most 'potentiality model' oriented teachers are in a difficult position in schools because they stand 'in loco parentis' and, therefore, are expected to enact the social control norms of 'parents' in our culture.

Learning from our mistakes of fourteen years previously, we took a more confrontational approach to the social control norm. There was no question of us 'articulating' with social control—it is ethically at variance with counselling and a clear stance must be taken. Articulation happened in other areas, for example with respect to the enormous 'child protection' expectations (more unspeak, incidentally), but in regard to allowing counselling to reinforce a social control agenda a firm stance is essential.

In the knowledge that this was a critical issue for work in schools, we set up a service that was defined as '*in* the school, but not *of* the school'. This is a critical political distinction—the service is physically located in the school but it is governed by the University and operated under the ethic of the British Association for Counselling and Psychotherapy which prohibits a social control agenda for counselling.

I use this example to illustrate the fact that if we are working politically we will be seeking a process of articulation, but there are also limits to articulation. These limits should be as few as possible—but they are important and it is important we stand firmly for them (and justify them by argument and evidence). In one school we found an insistence on a social control agenda becoming clear only after the service had started. Our service manager engaged in weeks of dialogue but then withdrew the service—there can be no compromise between counselling and social control.

So, politics is important because it gives us knowledge and understanding not only of the context in which we are working but of the colleagues with whom we are working. An awareness of the politics is also important because, in the profession of counselling and psychotherapy, we are being, whether we like the term or not, 'political subversives'. In the vast majority of contexts we are working in institutions where our ideology does not belong—indeed, it is often at odds with the prevailing ideology. We are oriented towards 'potentiality model' while most institutions to which we attach are 'deficiency model' oriented. A while ago I talked with two person-centred counsellors whom I will rename Bill and Ben. They run a successful drug counselling project. They had just had their funding doubled. I knew the way they worked—I had trained them. I read their funding bid which was full of behaviourally specified objectives regarding symptom reduction and problem remission. It was the language of symptom-oriented practice. I questioned them on their practice in the light of the document. Their response was: 'We do PCT as we have always done. OK, we monitor the client's drug-taking behaviour because we need that for the reporting. But the therapy is not aimed at the drug taking—it works with the person. Of course that works its way through to the symptoms, but only indirectly.' Bill and Ben were politically astute. They were well aware that service provision contracts in their setting are not given to services that are 'potentiality' oriented. Tabloid politics is not interested in the 'potentiality' of drug addicts—only in changing their disgusting behaviour—so Bill and Ben presented their work in that way, while seeking to work in an empowering fashion.

Within mental health the same politics applies. The counselling profession has achieved a remarkable feat in significantly infiltrating a domain that is politically at variance with counselling's 'developmental' imperative. Many might argue that its foothold within mental health is weak—and it is. But, each year, many hundreds of thousands of patients experience a significant therapeutic benefit from the counselling offered. One of the clever things counselling has done is to attach itself to *primary* care rather than the secondary tier. This has been critical because of the slightly different politics of 'health' that operates in the primary and secondary contexts. Within primary care the predominant concern is with physical health. In physical health care the 'symptom' is seen as an indication of an underlying problem. The physician will certainly treat the symptom, essentially to reduce the discomfort of the patient. But they will *also* attend to the underlying problem and will see the symptom as offering clues about that. Now this is very close to the orientation of the therapeutic counsellor, so the physician and the counsellor can potentially develop a common language.

However, the politics within secondary mental health services are considerably different. Perhaps the, usually small, department of psychotherapy is an exception, but most other services are geared to symptom reduction. They did not always start there, but the process of institutionalization has gradually pushed them there. Probably therapeutic counselling could not have survived in the secondary sector, unless it also followed the path of institutionalization. Incidentally, this difference in perspective between the physician and others on the 'symptoms' in mental health care goes back many years, at least to the time of Shakespeare, as witnessed in this exchange between Macbeth and his wife's physician in the Scottish play:

> Macbeth: How does your patient, Doctor?
> Doctor: Not so sick, my lord, as she is troubled with thick coming
>   fancies;
>   That keep her from her rest.
> Macbeth: Cure her of that;
>   Canst thou not minister to a mind diseas'd;
>   Pluck from the memory the rooted sorrow;
>   Raze out the written troubles of the brain.
>   And with some sweet oblivious antidote;
>   Cleanse the stuff'd bosom of that perilous stuff;
>   Which weighs upon the heart?
> Doctor: Therein the patient must minister to himself.
> Macbeth: Throw the physic to the dogs—I'll none of it.

> (*Macbeth*, Act V, Scene III)

THE POLITICS OF 'EVIDENCE-BASED PRACTICE'

This takes us to the politics of 'evidence-based practice' and how we might approach that challenge expansively rather than defensively. The phrase 'evidence-based practice' sounds so good, does it not? How could any reasonable person take a position *against* evidence-based practice? Straight away our 'unspeak' sensors should be alerted; when some statement—in what is such a controversial area—sounds so incontestable, it is usually unspeak, as it is in this case. It is unspeak because of how 'evidence' is defined. Firstly, in the consideration of sources of evidence, only *reliability* and not validity is considered. 'Evidence' that is higher in reliability is more valued, even though its validity might be contested. So, an ordering of 'evidence' is drawn up, placing RCTs (Randomized Controlled Trials) at the top; followed by non-randomized but controlled trials; then comparison group studies; pre- and post-test studies; and, at the foot of the evidence ladder, the opinions of expert practitioners. The idea is that *all* this evidence should be considered, with more weight being given to studies higher up the hierarchy because of their greater reliability. However, the way such levels of evidence tend to be *applied* is to look no further than RCTs (see Hutschemaekers & van Kalmthout, 2006). The problem with this is that very few RCTs have been done in the domain of counselling. Many more RCTs have been done, in-house, by CBT (Cognitive Behaviour Therapy) practitioners evaluating their own approach against other approaches. This explains what is in fact a political consequence, bizarre to most in the profession of counselling and psychotherapy, that CBT is often regarded as the treatment of choice within the health service.

This kind of political challenge (more political than scientific) calls on us for a political response. What arguments can we develop to help us to dialogue with different people? Here, the most important question is: *What stakeholders are we speaking to?* We have a range of argument, but the form of argument must fit the stakeholder. There is no point in arguing the above points on evidence validity and reliability in discussions with the commissioners of our counselling service. They would rightly respond with a wry smile. Equally, it is pointless to send evidence of our patients' appreciation of our service and even the outcomes evaluation of our practice to NICE (the 'National Institute for Clinical Excellence'—more 'unspeak', incidentally). *But*, if we have different kinds of argument we can fit these to the different stakeholders.

One argument I have found useful comes from the work of Robert Elliott, most recently described in Elliott et al., (2004). In analysing the slightly more positive research findings favouring CBT over PCT, Elliott takes into account what are called 'researcher allegiance factors', applying an accepted correction factor (Luborsky et al., 1999) to the 'effect sizes' (literally, the size of the effect the treatment appears to have) for both conditions. Once the correction factors for researcher allegiance are applied, the differences between CBT and PCT disappear, basically because such a high proportion of CBT studies have been performed by CBT protagonists.

Another study, useful to quote in discussions on effectiveness is that of King et al., (2000). Costing £½ million, this was the largest RCT comparing CBT and PCT. It was not aligned with any approach and it was conducted in Britain (for some stakeholders that is important, though it should not be so). This study threw up a number of interesting findings, one of which was that there was no difference between CBT and PCT, but that there was patient preference for PCT. (The politics in this is that patient preference is given weight, but only when the 'evidence' is equal.) Incidentally, another interesting finding from the King study was that the differences between PCT and CBT over 'usual practitioner care' disappeared at 12-month follow-up. I asked Michael King what proportion of the control group found a counselling-type intervention between 4 and 12 months (because that is a likely explanation of the loss of effect). Unfortunately he did not have any qualitative dimensions to the study, so no light could be cast on this question.

A very recent paper (Stiles et al., 2006) could prove to be of particular political value in this struggle to challenge the NICE view that CBT should be preferred over other counselling approaches. It analyses CORE (Clinical Outcomes in Routine Evaluation) data for 1309 patients and reports no differences in effectiveness between CBT, PCT and indeed PDT (psychodynamic therapy). Time will tell what the political response to this is. It could be that the science becomes questioned on the grounds that 'effectiveness' studies are regarded as less reliable (though, arguably more 'valid') than 'efficacy' studies, but this is certainly a useful new reference in the political debate. Incidentally, this whole 'use' of science within the political arena could be seen as yet more unspeak.

It is politically important that this research work continues. But this is not the kind of evidence that will, on its own, convince other stakeholders, such as local commissioning bodies and general medical practitioners—they need something closer to home—for example, a clinical outcomes evaluation as part of clinical governance expectations. Now, a common response from counsellors to this demand for an outcomes evaluation is to sigh with frustration and to put in place a simple 'patient satisfaction' inventory. However, such a minimal response fails to grasp the political opportunity that lies in every apparent threat like this. The best way to respond to this, politically, is to say: 'Yes—we will do an ongoing evaluation—and it will be the best Goddamn ongoing evaluation they have ever seen!' Over many years in the University of Strathclyde we have tried to do that in our Counselling Service provision projects. We want to provide the best practise-based evidence we can to the various commissioners of our services. Interestingly, when we make our presentations of results, it is not the convincing statistics which the commissioners focus upon—it is the individual patients. Our service manager will display a scattergram showing hundreds of 'dots', each of which represents a patient. Every time the result is the same—those attending ignore the statistical evidence and instead pick first one 'dot' then another and another so that the manager can click on them to reveal the whole history of those patients through their treatment. What the administrators get enthused about is humanity—tracking individual people and trying to work out why they were helped so much or not. In all political work within institutions it is important to remember that administrators are people too!

CONCLUSION

So, I have presented a thesis that political awareness is critical if we are to work in relation to the institutions of our society in order to achieve the humanistic goals behind our counselling and psychotherapy offerings—offering a widening and deepening consciousness; offering a therapeutic relationship that is healing rather than damaging to the human spirit; and offering a relationship that genuinely empowers. An important human dimension embodied in the concept of articulation is the expansive rather than defensive relationship we offer to colleagues within the social systems, colleagues who, from a defensive perspective, might be seen as part of the opposition. To a great extent we can view the political challenge to us as one of whether we can be strong enough to offer the other person in the political dialogue the same kind of humanistic presence that we offer elsewhere. This is the critical question. As person-centred practitioners we are used to offering our client our genuine empathic valuing. But, when we are faced with administrators, there is a tendency suddenly to become non-empathic and judgemental. I know that this switch is because we feel threatened and sometimes inadequate and therefore defensive and negative, but can we change that to become genuinely more confident of our offerings, so that we can be expansive rather than defensive in relation to the other? Of course, we can duck such a political challenge and retreat into a safe but sure private practice. A retreat into private practice is comfortable for us and good for our clients, but it will probably mean that there are no counsellors, except 'social control counsellors', available for our grandchildren.

But am I a political fool? Have I simply, within the domain of counselling and psychotherapy, repeated the cycle I described in my earlier political 'career'? Has my work actually served the opposite of my desire? In believing that I have been politically shrewd and skilful in articulating with the world of deficiency model and social control politics while retaining a potentiality model and developmental impact, have I been deceiving myself? Have I, like the originators of 'New Labour' who sought to work *within* the system and are now judged as collaborators, been doing more to undermine social development than to facilitate it? Is my concept of 'articulation' just 'unspeak' for conformity? It is easy to deceive oneself. From my social psychology roots I know how easy it is for the individual to become socialized into doing the want of institutions while falsely believing they are an effective dissident. I know how the psychology of conformity and the social construction of reality work. On a personal level I know that I once signed the punishment book to corroborate the reality of two senior colleagues in a List-D school that a boy had been appropriately 'reprimanded' when, in fact, he had been mercilessly beaten.

OK—I have used a lot of fancy words, like 'empowerment', 'potentiality', 'articulation'. I have spoken positively, even warmly, about representatives of mainstream institutions such as health, social services and education. Yet I also know that, within totalitarian capitalist regimes, concepts such as 'empowerment' and 'potentiality' are reserved only for the capitalist elite. For the rest of the population, providers of such 'helping agencies' are not there to help but to control—to quell potentially disruptive dissonance; to disguise the impact of disempowerment; to institutionalize the victim's self-blaming; and, in the case of education, to produce more compliant fodder for the capitalist economy.

Have I, in fact, simply been a mildly subtle, self-deceiving collaborator to that system? It is a horrific question—it would have been better to have done nothing than to actually use my skills and effort to further such humanistic abuse.

The answer?—the honest answer?—I don't know.

REFERENCES

Consultative Committee on the Curriculum (1986) *More than Feelings of Concern*. Edinburgh: Scottish Education Department.

Elliott, R, Greenberg, CS & Lietaer, R (2004) Research on experiential psychotherapies. In MJ Lambert (ed) *Bergin and Garfield's Handbook of Psychotherapy and Behavior Change*, 5th edn, (pp. 493–539). New York: Wiley.

Hutschemaekers, G & van Kalmthout, M (2006) The new integral multidisciplinary guidelines in the Netherlands: The perspective of person-centered psychotherapy. *Person-Centered & Experiential Psychotherapies, 5* (2).

King, S, Sibbald, B, Ward, E, Brower, P, Lloyd, M, Gabbay, M & Byford, S (2000) Randomised controlled trial of non-directive counselling, cognitive behaviour therapy and usual general practitioner care in the management of depression as well as mixed anxiety and depression in primary care. *Health Technology Assessment, 4* (19), 1–84.

Luborsky, L, Diguer, L, Seligman, DA, Rosenthal, R, Krause, ED, Johnson, S, Halperin, G, Bishop, M, Berman, JS & Schweizer, E (1999) The researcher's own therapy allegiances: A 'wild card' in comparisons of treatment efficacy. *Clinical Psychology: Science and Practice, 6*, 95–106.

MacBeath, J, Mearns, D & Smith, M (1986) *Home from School*. Glasgow: Jordanhill College Press.

Mearns, D (2003) The humanistic agenda: Articulation. *Journal of Humanistic Psychology, 43*, 53–65.

Mearns, D & Cooper M (2005) *Working at Relational Depth in Counselling and Psychotherapy*. London: Sage.

Mearns, D & Thorne, B (2000) *Person-Centred Therapy Today: New frontiers in theory and practice*. London: Sage.

Poole, S (2006) *Unspeak*. London: Little, Brown.

Rogers, CR, McGaw, WH Jr & McGaw, AP (1973) *The Steel Shutter* (motion picture). Available from University of California, Santa Barbara Davidson Library, Department of Special Collections.

Stiles, WB, Barkham, M, Twigg, E, Mellor-Clark, J & Cooper, M (2006) Effectiveness of cognitive-behavioural, person-centred and psychodynamic therapies as practised in UK National Health Service settings. *Psychological Medicine, 36*, 555–66.

Chapter 14

PERSON-CENTERED THERAPY WITH CHILD AND ADOLESCENT VICTIMS OF POVERTY AND SOCIAL EXCLUSION IN BRAZIL [1]

ELIZABETH S FREIRE, SÍLVIA H KOLLER,
ALINE PIASON, RENATA B DA SILVA
AND
DEBORAH GIACOMELLI

Psychotherapy, in Brazil, is frequently considered a 'luxury' which may be appropriate only for upper-middle-class individuals. The underlying assumption is that the powerless groups of society need to have their material needs like housing, sanitation, adequate nutrition, physical health care, jobs and education met, rather than to have psychotherapy. However, we think that this is a patronizing and disempowering view of the victims of poverty and social exclusion. The perspective of the person-centered approach, conversely, is that every human being, regardless of her social, cultural or economic condition, has within herself vast resources for growth and for constructive fulfillment of her inherent possibilities (Rogers, 1977). Therefore person-centered therapy can become a very important agent in the promotion of self-empowerment and resilience of the socially excluded population. As person-centered therapists and supervisors working in a private institution in Brazil, we decided, therefore, to develop a program that might expand our work to reach the impoverished group of our society that had been excluded from the benefits of psychotherapy. Before describing this program, though, we think it is important to introduce some aspects of Brazil's socio-economic structure and culture.

BRAZIL'S SOCIETY TODAY

Brazil is a country of 176 million people. It is a highly stratified society resulting from colonialism and slavery. The relatively high GDP per capita (US $2,593 in 2002) masks deep inequality because Brazil has a highly skewed income distribution, which is among the world's worst. Poverty is most pervasive in the

1. This chapter has been amended from ES Freire, SH Koller, A Piason & RB Silva (2005) Person-centred therapy with impoverished, maltreated, and neglected children and adolescents in Brazil. *Journal of Mental Health Counseling, 27* (3), 225–37. Reproduced here with kind permission of the authors and publisher.

rural parts of the northeast, but there are also pockets of urban poverty in the largest cities in the developed regions in the southeast and south. The number of people who live below the national poverty line was estimated in 2001 to be about 17% of the country's total population. Twenty-two per cent of the population survives on less than US $2 a day. Due to the high unemployment levels and widespread informal economic activity, the lowest strata continue to be excluded from full participation in markets and full access to government services (Hudson, 1997; Human Development Reports, 2004). As a result of the acceptance of interracial unions, Brazilians form one of the most heterogeneous populations in the world, constituting a trihybrid population with European, African, and Amerindian (i.e. South American Indian) roots. Based on self-declared ethnicity, in 1991, Brazilians were 55.3% White, 39.3% mixed-race (*pardos*), 4.9% Black, and 0.6% Asian (Parra et al., 2003).

Regarding youth and their education, in Brazil, 28.3% of the population is under the age of 15. If compared with developed countries, Brazil has a relatively young population. There are 32 million children and adolescents who live in families with incomes of less than US $40 a month. The widespread poverty creates a breeding ground for malnutrition, abuse, maltreatment, and violence against children (Soca, 2004). Primary school is free and compulsory for children between the ages of 7 and 14, but high drop-out rates and grade repetition are endemic problems. In 1990, school enrollment reached about 90% of school-age children, although there was wide variation, with lowest enrollment among rural and low-income populations. However, only about one-third of students enrolled in primary school finish eight years of mandatory schooling. Students in Brazilian public schools receive an average of four hours of class time per day (Hudson, 1997; Human Development Reports, 2004).

Public access to medical care increased after Brazil's constitution of 1988 granted all Brazilian citizens the right to access free medical assistance. The management and organization of health services was decentralized from the federal to the state and, particularly, municipal level. Although the public domain oversees basic and preventive health care, the private non-profit and for-profit health care sector deliver the bulk of medical services, including government reimbursement and subsidized inpatient care. Therapeutic treatment in hospitals tends to dominate funding at the expense of health promotion and disease prevention programs (Hudson, 1997).

Brazil's mental health care system has been traditionally based on large psychiatric hospitals and asylums. Since the 1970s, debates about the state of the psychiatric hospitals and the mentally ill have given rise to the creation of alternative social resources for mental health care such as halfway houses, shelters, leisure centers, community centers, day hospitals, night hospitals, psychiatric units in general hospitals, and psychiatric emergency units. Also, multiprofessional staff, including psychologists, nutritionists, nurses, and social workers, have been created to attend to patients in these alternative settings

(Vietta, Saeki, Santa Roas & Ferriera, 2000). It is important to note that in Brazil the profession of mental health counselor does not exist, as will be discussed more fully below.

The public health institutions were decentralized after the 1988 Constitution and renamed Basic Health Units (*Unidades Básicas de Saúde*). These units focus on primary health care and prevention and employ few psychologists. According to Dimenstein (1998), throughout Brazil, the mainstream psychotherapeutic approach is psychodynamic therapy, which is taught in all universities and used by most psychologists both in private and public practice. Although there is no systematic research available on the psychologists' work in the public health field, Dimenstein (1998), Silva (1988), and Boarini (1995) point out that patients' drop-out and poor treatment outcomes are common problems faced by psychodynamic psychologists working in the Basic Health Units.

THE DELPHOS INSTITUTE

The Delphos Institute is a person-centered private institution, located in Porto Alegre, [2] which offers both internships for undergraduate academic students of psychology and a training program for already licensed psychologists. Brazil's legislation permits only psychologists and psychiatrists to work as psychotherapists or mental health clinicians. After completion of a five-year academic program in psychology, university students obtain a bachelor's degree, which allows them to work as psychotherapists. During the last year of their academic program, students usually have internship training in clinical psychology. After obtaining a bachelor's degree, most psychologists who decide to practice psychotherapy enroll on private training courses in order to further develop specific skills of the psychotherapeutic approach they will apply in their practice.

At the Delphos Institute, undergraduate academic students of psychology can enter internship training in the person-centered approach. In the first two months of training and before providing therapy, they study the person-centered approach by reading Rogers' most important publications. This study is continued throughout the internship training. In addition, the students have weekly group supervision with two or three other students. They audio-record and transcribe almost all therapy sessions, with the client's consent, and bring the transcripts to the supervision meetings. Trainees read their transcripts to the group and receive feedback about how they respond and relate to the client. Thus, the supervision meetings provide trainees with the opportunity to improve the quality of their person-centered attitudes in the therapeutic relationship with their clients.

---

2. Porto Alegre is the capital of the southernmost state of Brazil. It is one of the biggest cities in the country, with a population of 1.5 million inhabitants.

THE LAUNCH OF THE PERSON-CENTERED PROGRAM FOR
AT-RISK CHILDREN AND ADOLESCENTS

In 2002, as supervisors of the Delphos Institute, we launched a program that provided person-centered therapy for impoverished, maltreated and neglected children and adolescents. Therapists volunteering to work in this program were psychology students undertaking their one-year internship in clinical psychology at the Delphos Institute. This program started in 2002 with only two therapists and two supervisors, with more therapists and supervisors joining the program in the following years. Each therapist trainee, during her one-year internship, was assigned at least four clients, and some have worked with up to twelve clients. The therapists and the supervisors were not paid for this work. Between 2002 and 2004, sixteen therapists, fourteen female and two male, and five supervisors, all female, have participated in the program. Their ages ranged from 23 to 54 years old. The group of therapists and supervisors reflects the intermingling of ethnic groups in Brazil, making it difficult to describe them using single-ethnic categories.

The program was first launched at a long-term residential shelter providing care to children and adolescents from age 6 to 18 years old who were legally committed to the shelter due to abandonment, neglect, abuse, or death of their parents or guardians. These children and adolescents were also victims of poverty and social exclusion. Many of them were living on the streets before going to the shelter.

The shelter is a non-profit private institution that can house up to 70 children and adolescents. Most of its financial resources come from a Norwegian non-governmental organization. The shelter is located in a small village in a rural area in the southernmost state of Brazil, Rio Grande do Sul. The children and adolescents who are committed to the shelter come from small and medium-sized cities in this area. They attend a school in the village, where they have the opportunity to foster social relationships within the community. On weekends and vacations, when it is possible, they visit their families.

Before the program was launched, we had thought that group therapy would be more effective than individual therapy, because the former would reach a larger number of children and adolescents. Soon, however, we realized that these children and adolescents needed individualized attention and a private space-time of their own, because they live in a group situation 24 hours a day. Therefore, we decided that an individual therapeutic setting would be of greater help. At the very least, it would provide an experience of privacy for them.

The shelter provided two rooms for the therapy sessions, which the therapists converted into play-therapy settings. The therapists came to the shelter once a week, from Porto Alegre—which is two hours away by car—to provide 50 minutes of therapy for each of their clients. The children and adolescents were referred to therapy by one of the directors of the shelter after conversations with the staff, mainly because of relationship problems with support staff and peers, such as defiant behavior, aggressiveness, and social isolation.

THE FIRST OUTCOMES

The non-directivity of person-centered therapy produced a strong impact at the very beginning of the program. The children and adolescents were accustomed to being questioned by a multitude of professionals, including psychologists, social workers, psychiatrists, support staff, and directors of the institution. They were so accustomed to answering questions that the non-directive climate of the therapeutic relationship surprised them. For instance, Paul, [3] a 14-year-old boy, said to the therapist in his first session, 'Are you not going to ask me questions?' Similarly, Jane, a 13-year-old girl, said in her first session, 'I don't know what to say … I have nothing to talk about … there were so many psychologists with whom I talked, so I have already talked a lot with them, but then I was quiet and they asked me questions … They asked a lot of things that they wanted to know. Now it's just me who has to talk … So, what am I supposed to do? I have nothing to talk about.' Despite this puzzled initial response to the therapist's non-directive attitude, Jane talked a great deal during the whole session, freeing painful and deep feelings, sharing them with the therapist, without the therapist asking a single question. The therapist's only utterances were empathic understanding responses (see Temaner, 1977).

The puzzled initial reaction to the non-directive person-centered relationship suggests that these children and adolescents were not used to being allowed to experience autonomy and self-determination. They were not accustomed to experiencing their personal power within a relationship. Nonetheless, they soon came to realize that the relationship with the therapists of this program was unique, quite distinct from anything they had experienced before. For instance, when Carlos saw his therapist in front of the dining hall while waiting for the door to be opened for lunch, he asked her,

> *Tia* ['tia', aunt, is the affectionate way children in Brazil address adult women], this 'psychology' is different, isn't it? We do not have to keep answering questions because the *tia* does not ask us questions. We talk whenever we want. If we do not want to talk, we can just play. It's *we* who choose what to do.

When the therapist agreed with him, Carlos turned to another boy next to him and said, 'You see? I told you!'

Not surprisingly, after the program was operating for a few weeks, many

---

3. All names are fictitious in order to preserve the client's confidentiality.

children and adolescents came on their own initiative to the therapists asking for therapy, demonstrating that the space-time of therapy and the therapeutic relationship were of great value to them. The following client utterances illustrate their appreciation: 'I'm so happy that now I have someone who listens to me', 'It's so good that I can talk about these things with someone. That relieves me' and 'I would like you to attend my friends too. It's so good here!'

Six months after the beginning of the program, the first outcomes were shown to be quite positive. The children and adolescents who had received therapy made noticeable improvements in their relationships with the shelter's staff, their peers and their families.

The case below illustrates the nature of these first outcomes.

JUDY

Judy is a 13-year-old girl. Her mother died when Judy was 12, and then she had to live with her grandmother. The relationship with her grandmother was conflicted, and Judy got involved with drugs and robbery. Eventually, she ran away from home. She was living on the streets when she was committed to the shelter and was referred to therapy because she was having relationship problems with her peers and was perceived as 'too quiet' by the support staff. In the first session, she said to her therapist:

> I'm alone now. Sometimes I start to cry, and I cry a lot, and I don't want to talk with anybody. I don't want to talk. Talking doesn't help. The more I think, the more I talk, the more I want to cry … It feels so bad.

By the 4th session, she showed a significant improvement in her mood:

> [Now] I feel better talking than crying … Before, any little thing that I thought would make me cry. Now it's different. Now everything has changed. Now I feel much better. I feel good when I'm alone. Sometimes, when I was thinking and I was alone, I cried. Now, I don't cry. Now, when I'm sad, I know that I have someone to talk to, and that feels so good!

After the 8th session, Judy went to her grandmother's house for the summer vacation. She stayed at home the entire time and did not try to run away, as she used to do. After the vacation she told her therapist that she had helped her grandmother with the housekeeping and had taken care of her little sister. Moreover, she said that when an old friend invited her to run away to go to a party she refused the invitation. She said:

The vacations were pretty good! ... I had the experience of having my family and I felt much better ... I have my home. Before, I wouldn't think about family ... [when I was] on the streets I used to do a lot of wrong things ... Now I'm going to live my life. I've decided that I do want to go back home, I want to be accepted, I don't want to do wrong things any more ... Now I think about my own life, and I give more value to what I have ... I have grown up.

THE IMPACT OF THE PERSON-CENTERED APPROACH ON THE SUPPORT STAFF

The unique characteristics of the person-centered approach also impacted on the support staff. Most of them had expected that the therapists would apply a medical-like model, formulating diagnoses and assuming the role of mental health experts in the relationship with the children and the staff. Some support staff even showed a skeptical attitude in the beginning of the program, as if it was hard for them to believe that this kind of psychotherapy, with no 'treatment plans', nor 'diagnosis' might really work. We chose to avoid confrontation and we attempted to be empathic and non-judgmental, not only towards the children, but towards the support staff as well. Perhaps one might say that we 'walked softly through the shelter' (paraphrasing Rogers (1977) who referred to himself as 'walking softly through life'). This proved to be a very successful 'strategy'. A few months after the beginning of the program, the support staff were respecting and valuing our work and perceiving person-centered therapy as being really helpful to the children.

As we wanted to contribute to the growth of the support staff as well as to the children, we offered to facilitate a monthly person-centered group with them. We told them that this would be a space-time for them to share their experiences, thoughts and feelings in relation to their work with the children. The director of the shelter supported the idea and allowed them a two-hour slot in their monthly work-time schedule to participate in these group meetings. Although the very initial 'instruction' for them was to talk about issues related to their work with the children, the members were actually free to talk about any issue that was important to them and the facilitators attempted to be consistently non-directive. The groups were initiated at the beginning of 2003, and at the end of the year the facilitators were asked by the support staff to continue the groups in the following year. It was an experience of empowerment and growth for the support staff. In these groups they realized their capacity to make positive changes in their relationships with the children as well as in their relationships with the directors of the shelter. There was a big shift in their attitudes from a position of 'complaining' to an attitude of 'striving' for their objectives in their work in the shelter. Also they became more empathic and less judgmental towards the children and adolescents who they had perceived as 'problem-causing'.

THE EXTENSION OF THE PROGRAM TO OTHER INSTITUTIONS

The positive outcomes achieved at this shelter motivated us to extend this program to two other institutions in Porto Alegre, which provide community day programs for impoverished and at-risk children and adolescents from the outskirts of the city. One of the institutions is a state and public facility while the other is a non-profit private, Catholic institution. Both provide programs [4] for children and adolescents from age 7 to 14 years old, during the daytime when they are not at school. These programs include sports, music, handicrafts, educational and leisure activities. The children and adolescents also receive two meals during the time they are in the institutions. The Catholic institution also provides a program for pre-school children (0 to 6 years old) and vocational courses for adolescents aged 14 to 18 years old.

For the implementation of the program, each institution provided one room for the therapy sessions, which the therapists themselves converted into play-therapy settings, as they had done in the shelter. The referral to psychotherapy was similarly made by the directors of the institutions after conversations with support staff, and the reasons for referring were mainly relationship problems with support staff and peers, including defiant behavior, aggressiveness, and social isolation.

FEATURES OF THE THERAPEUTIC PROCESSES IN THE INSTITUTIONS

From August 2002 to August 2004, 98 children and adolescents, aged 5 to 18, have participated in this program. In the shelter, there were 47 children and adolescents, 17 female and 30 male; there were 34, 14 female and 20 male, in the Catholic institution setting; and 17, 6 female and 11 male, in the public institution setting.

According to the principles of client autonomy and self-determination in person-centered therapy, it is the client who decides when to terminate therapy. In the shelter, 3 children (6.38%) decided to discontinue therapy before the 4th session. The other children terminated therapy because their therapists had finished their one-year internship or because the children left the shelter to be re-united with their families. Up to August 2004, the number of therapy sessions per client ranged from 2 to 39, with an average of 14 sessions.

In the two nonresidential institutions, the children and adolescents missed more sessions than the children in the residential setting because of scheduling conflicts. In these two institutions, 9 children (17.64%) decided to discontinue

---

4. These programs, named Socio-Educational Service Care (Serviço de Atendimento Sócio-Educativo—SASE), are funded by the municipality.

therapy before the 4th session. The number of sessions per client ranged from 1 to 27 sessions, with an average of 10 sessions. The reasons for client drop-out in this program are not well understood. One hypothesis is that the therapists, who were inexperienced and still beginners in their training, were not able to implement the person-centered therapeutic attitudes adequately. Another hypothesis is that the children and adolescents did not appreciate the unstructured feature of the person-centered interaction and might have experienced it as psychologically threatening or boring.

In the person-centered approach, the non-directive and empathic attitude of the therapist makes each therapeutic session and each therapeutic process unique. In this program, the children and adolescents interacted with their therapists in a multitude of ways. They played games, with the therapist or alone, talked, or remained silent. The topics that the children discussed within a session also varied from subjective and emotional experiences, to their daily activities (e.g. school, family or friends) and mundane issues like movies and sports. This multitude of ways of interaction occurred because the therapist attempted to accept unconditionally whatever the child did or said in the session. The therapist did not lead the child in any pre-determined direction and did not impose any professional agenda. The child led the therapeutic process, and the therapist just followed.

The outcome of this person-centered program has been assessed through interviews with support staff and directors of the institutions and also through analysis of the clients' utterances and behavior within the therapy hour. These interviews and analyses showed that, in general, the children and adolescents who received therapy achieved: (a) important and relevant improvement in interpersonal relationships, with more positive attitudes towards others (e.g. peers, family, institution staff); (b) better performance at school; and (c) improvement in mood and emotional functioning, encompassing the accomplishment of a greater and more constant well-being. The following case histories illustrate these outcomes.

TONY

Tony is a 9-year-old boy committed to the shelter because he was wandering and begging on the streets. He would not attend school and did not know how to read. Tony lived with his mother who beat him; his father having left the family. When Tony came to the shelter, he behaved aggressively and violently towards support staff and peers, beating, kicking, and shouting at them. He did not develop any friendships and made sexual advances towards the other boys in the shelter. After six months of therapy, the director of the shelter said that Tony's behavior had improved significantly. He became calm, tranquil, and 'self-controlled'. He developed friendships and respect with peers and support staff. Also, the sexual harassment towards peers ceased. The director believed that the therapy was fundamental to that change. She had previous experience at the shelter with similar cases of children who lived on the streets and had sexualized behavior, but these children did not adapt to the structure and rules of the shelter and eventually had to leave.

JULIANO

Juliano is a 6-year-old boy who received therapy in one of the non-residential institutions. He was referred to therapy because the support staff perceived him as troublesome, agitated, and aggressive, with difficulties relating to peers and teachers. After six months of therapy, the teachers said that he had become calmer and more sociable, engaging in constructive interactions with others. Furthermore, his change triggered positive changes in his family too. He lived with his mother and four siblings in conditions of extreme privation and poverty. His mother was rather neglectful about herself and her children, as if she had simply given up taking care of herself and their lives. The family lived with no hygienic care at all, and the institution staff said that their home was extremely dirty. Following the positive changes in her son's behavior, Juliano's mother asked his therapist for psychological help for herself. She started therapy, and soon her behavior also changed quite positively. The institution staff described her as 'another woman' after she started therapy, and as actively engaged in taking care of herself, the children, and the house. The change in her appearance was quite impressive: from being someone who was dirty, with tattered clothing and disheveled hair, to a 'good-looking woman, clean, and well dressed'.

MARIA

Maria is a 13-year-old girl who was committed to the shelter because of family negligence. She was referred to therapy because she had episodes of violence and aggressiveness towards peers and support staff. Also, her moods were very changeable, and she had sudden episodes of crying. Some support staff said that they could not trust her because her behavior was quite unpredictable. The support staff were also concerned about her sexual behavior for they observed that she seduced and 'dated' many boys, although dating was forbidden in the shelter. After six months of therapy, the support staff noticed a great change in her behavior and mood. She was calmer, and the episodes of violence, crying, and aggressiveness ceased. Before she started therapy, she was taking antidepressants with no improvement at all. As her mood improved after she began therapy, the psychiatrist who was treating her decided to discontinue medication because it had become unnecessary. The support staff also observed that Maria had discontinued her somewhat 'promiscuous' behavior. She developed a love relationship with one boy at the shelter and has no longer been sexually involved with other boys.

These cases illustrate the pattern of change and outcomes that have been achieved with the implementation of person-centered therapy in these institutions. This pattern of change reflects the achievement of important aspects of resilience (Garmezy, 1996) with the children and adolescents establishing a more powerful social and emotional network with peers and staff. Also, the multitude of distinct ways of interacting that were developed by the children and adolescents in their therapeutic sessions supports the Rogerian hypothesis that it is the therapist's unconditional acceptance of the client's experiential world that ultimately promotes growth and therapeutic change (Rogers, 1959). The successful outcomes described above were found in children who only played cards or other games with their therapists during the therapeutic hour, without any talk about their feelings or experiences, and also in children who only talked about movies, sports, and such with their therapists, as well as in children who talked about themselves in the more culturally expected way of doing therapy. In fact, these results support the assertion that whatever way the client behaves, if the therapist is unconditionally accepting and *present* with the client, then the actualizing tendency is promoted.

CONCLUSIONS

The outcomes of this program support the conclusion that person-centered therapy is an effective factor in the promotion of children's and adolescents' resilience in the context of multiple adverse conditions such as socio-economic disadvantage, neglect, maltreatment and abandonment. Moreover, the resiliency processes found in these children and adolescents who achieved positive adaptation, despite exposure to significant threat or severe adversity, is ultimately due to the underlying functioning of their organismic actualizing tendency.

It was also found that the person-centered approach can really 'empower the oppressed':

> ... when power is left with persons, and when we are real with them, understanding of them, caring toward them, constructive behavior changes occur, and they exhibit more strength and power and responsibility. (Rogers, 1977: 287–8)

In fact, these children and adolescents, through the experience of their personal power within the person-centered therapeutic relationship, were enabled to change the history of their lives, from being victims of poverty and social exclusion to becoming empowered individuals with capacity to organize themselves out of impoverishment. Also, the experience of the support staff in the person-centered groups contributes to the conclusion that the person-centered approach can really be a 'ferment' for social change (see Rogers, 1977).

Finally, the effectiveness of this program also supports the conclusion that person-centered therapy is a multicultural approach. It is the multicultural feature of the person-centered interaction that explains the effectiveness of person-centered therapy with this distinct population of Brazilian lower-class and non-white children and adolescents. Also, the outcomes of this program suggest that the person-centered approach should be widely developed in service programs for other oppressed populations in different cultural settings and minority contexts.

REFERENCES

Boarini, ML (1995) The psychologist's work in basic health units: Some notes. *Cadernos de Metodologia e Técnicas de Pesquisa, 6,* 65–96.

Bozarth, JD (1998) *Person-Centered Therapy: A revolutionary paradigm.* Ross-on-Wye: PCCS Books.

Bozarth, JD & Brodley, BT (1991) Actualization: A functional concept in client-centered psychotherapy. *Journal of Social Behavior and Personality, 6,* 45–59.

Bozarth, JD, Zimring, F & Tausch, R (2002) Client-centered therapy: The evolution of a revolution. In D Cain & J Seeman (eds) *Humanistic Psychotherapies: Handbook of research and practice* (pp. 147–88). Washington DC: American Psychological Association.

Brodley, B (1997) The nondirective attitude in client-centered therapy. *The Person-Centered Journal, 4,* 18–30.

Carvalho-Silva, DR, Santos, FR, Rocha, J & Pena, SD (2000) The phylogeography of Brazilian Y-chromosome lineages. *American Journal of Human Genetics, 68,* 281–6.

Dimenstein, MD (1998) The psychologist in basic health units: Challenges for the professional training and practice. *Estudos de Psicologia (Natal), 3,* 53–81.

Garmezy, N (1996) Reflections and commentary on risk, resilience, and development. In R Haggerty, L Sherrod, N Garmezy & M Rutter (eds) *Stress, Risk, and Resilience in Children and Adolescents* (pp. 1–15). New York: Cambridge University Press.

Goldstein, AR (1973) *Structured Learning Therapy: Toward a psychotherapy for the poor.* New York: Academic.

Hudson, R (1997) Brazil: A country study. Retrieved July 20, 2004 from Library of Congress, Federal Research Division website: <http://www.country-data.com/cgi-bin/query/r-1675.html>.

Human Development Reports (2004) Retrieved July 20, 2004 from United Nations Development Programme website: <http://hdr.undp.org/statistics/data/cty/cty_f_BRA.html>.

Moon, KA (2001) Nondirective client-centered therapy with children. *Person-Centered Journal, 8,* 43–52.

Parra, FC, Amando, RC, Lambertucci, JR, Roca, J, Antunes, CM & Pena, SDJ (2003) Color and genomic ancestry in Brazilians. *Proceedings of the National Academy of Sciences of the USA, 100,* 177–82.

Patterson, CH (1984) Empathy, warmth and genuineness in psychotherapy: A review of reviews. *Psychotherapy, 21,* 431–8.

Patterson, CH (1996) Multicultural counseling: From diversity to universality. *Journal of Counseling and Development, 74,* 227–31.

Pedersen, P (1976) The field of intercultural counseling. In P Pedersen, WJ Lonner & JG Draguns (eds) *Counseling Across Cultures* (pp. 17–41). Honolulu: University Press of Hawaii.

Rogers, CR (1959) A theory of therapy, personality, and interpersonal relationships as developed in the client-centered framework. In S Koch (ed) *Psychology: A study of science: Formulation of the person and the social context Vol 3* (pp. 184–256). New York: McGraw-Hill.

Rogers, CR (1977) *Carl Rogers on Personal Power.* New York: Delacorte Press.

Rogers, CR (1986) Rogers, Kohut, and Erickson. *Person-Centered Review, 1,* 125–40.

Rogers, CR & Dymond, RF (1954) *Psychotherapy and Personality Change.* Chicago: University of Chicago Press.

Silva, RC (1988) The psychologist's work in health units: Some thoughts about the function of psychology. Unpublished doctoral dissertation. Instituto de Psicologia da Universidade de São Paulo, São Paulo.

Soca, R (2004) Children—Brazil: Hunger, poverty create breeding-ground for social ills. *Inter Press Service News Agency.* Retrieved July 25, 2004 from <http://ipsnews.net/interna.asp?idnews=24213>.

Sue, DW & Sue, D (1990) *Counseling the Culturally Different: Theory and practice.* New York: Wiley.

Tausch, R & Tausch, AM (1990) *Client-Centered Therapy.* Gottingen: Hogrefe.

Temaner BS (1977) The empathic understanding response process. *Chicago Counseling and Psychotherapy Center Discussion Papers,* Chicago, IL: University of Chicago.

Vietta, EP, Saeki, T, Santa Roas, D & Ferriera, L (2000) Halfway house: An alternative to rescue the rights and citizenship of the mentally ill person. *International Journal of Psychosocial Rehabilitation, 5,* 19–28.

Wardle, F (n.d.) Of race and racism in Brazil. *Interracial Voice.* Retrieved July 25, 2004 from <http://www.webcom.com/intvoice/wardle5.html>.

Chapter 15

NOT JUST NAMING THE INJUSTICE— COUNSELLING ASYLUM SEEKERS AND REFUGEES

Jude Boyles

In 2003 Amnesty International estimated that there were 35 recognized conflicts and 132 countries still practising torture (Amnesty International, 2003). At the start of 2005, worldwide there were 19.2 million asylum seekers/refugees and 'others of concern' according to the United Nations High Commissioner for Refugees (UNHCR, 2005). Internationally, women and children experience violence, sexual abuse and trafficking on a massive scale.

These women, men and children fleeing war, violence and oppression are claiming asylum in the UK and are increasingly seeing counsellors for support with their pre-flight experiences and with the losses and multiple difficulties of exile.

Following the Immigration and Asylum Act (Home Office, 1999), asylum seekers (someone who is fleeing persecution in their homeland, has arrived in another country and made themselves known to the authorities and exercised their legal right to apply for asylum under the 1951 UN Refugee Convention) were dispersed away from the South East of England to other parts of the UK. The term 'asylum seeker' is widely used to describe individuals within this group and has been used in recent years to undermine the credibility of those who seek protection in the UK. In this chapter I shall use the term 'refugees' to describe both those who are seeking protection and those who have been granted it.

What struck me was how this group of people were most in need of health and welfare resources and did not have access to either, including to the statutory mental health counselling service in West Yorkshire and Humberside where I worked as a counsellor at that time. Person-centred therapy in the West is largely utilized by one group of people, the White middle class. This is the same group, in fact, who access most other resources as well. This is a fundamental issue of social justice, particularly in the increasingly hostile and racist climate into which refugees arrive. I believe that therapy can be a vehicle for addressing injustice. It was this belief that led me to work towards my service becoming accessible to refugee communities.

The first time I saw a refugee who was a survivor of torture for an assessment remains a vivid memory for me. I witnessed his confusion at this 'strange' relationship I was describing. What I offered seemed to him to be rude and intrusive on the one hand, and awkward and embarrassing on the other. Whilst reflecting on his feelings the first time we met, he said he had a headache and the chair was very uncomfortable! My hope that he could describe to this helpful stranger the huge range of overwhelming feelings that he was struggling to understand was profoundly inappropriate. The question had a very different meaning to him and his cultural understanding of what he was experiencing was so very different to mine. He had been in the UK for just two months; he hadn't been socialized into seeking help from a stranger in this way as most communities are in the UK. It was not acceptable or familiar to describe how he was feeling and his private thoughts to a 'professional helper'.

The language of counselling and trauma is now part of UK culture and most communities have some knowledge of it, but it is more widely used and provided by UK British nationals. An expectation that he would tell his story to me could easily have replicated his experience during the Home Office interview when he first arrived. The distance that counsellors often maintain could have been experienced as rude and rejecting.

Prior to my first assessment, I was concerned that therapy could further oppress this individual and inadvertently support him to adjust to oppression and injustice in the UK. This concern remained active throughout my relationship with him and remains so in all my work with refugees. This sat alongside a further concern that therapy could separate and reduce his experiences of torture and the UK asylum process as being his alone rather than the experience of communities, in his case in Iran and others seeking asylum in the UK. By individualizing his responses, counselling could dampen any sense of collectivity or community and the reassurance that can bring.

I was also concerned that I could simply replicate, maintain or further the injustice if I imposed my model of help without naming and addressing those injustices. Too often in counselling we fail to notice when we inadvertently impose our own cultural framework, including help-seeking and offering models of 'care', on those who we seek to support. These models of counselling and care often ignore traditional concepts of healing and survival.

As a feminist, I understand our societies from a feminist perspective. Therefore, my understanding of my clients' experiences is framed in that way. To sit with a woman who had been raped and see her receive no justice through our Criminal Justice System has sadly been a regular experience and one that arouses in me a huge sense of anger and outrage. The legal system that frequently allows such violations to go unpunished is the same one that refuses and removes many 'failed asylum seekers' to countries where they will face further violations of their human rights, including torture and persecution.

As a feminist, I had explored what must be familiar themes to any political activist who chooses counselling or therapy as a career. How can I ensure that I don't further oppress the people I work with? How can I develop a way of working that ensures that injustice isn't just named but justice is fought for? How can I work from the cultural framework of my client, with an understanding of the structural positions we both have?

DEVELOPING A MODEL

The ethos outlined above has formed itself into an active human rights model in my work with survivors of torture and organized violence at the Medical Foundation for the Care of Victims of Torture in the North West. I can clearly remember working with the young man described above who had been detained and tortured for two years in Iran and sitting with his grief and outrage at his experience. We sat together shocked and appalled when he came to a session having been refused asylum. The Home Office hadn't believed him. It was another year before he was granted 'Indefinite Leave to Remain'.

This was five years ago, in 2000, prior to beginning work at the Medical Foundation; but Home Office decision making remains poor. I am now familiar with the asylum system that our clients go through on arrival into the UK and expect refusals, often followed by lost appeals. In Amnesty International's research report (Neil, 2004) Home Office decisions are shown to be based on inaccurate and out-of-date country information, unreasoned decisions about people's credibility and a failure to properly consider complex torture cases. Government figures themselves show that the Home Office got the initial decision wrong on nearly 14,000 asylum cases in 2003 (Neil, 2004).

Those seeking asylum are housed and supported under separate arrangements to UK citizens. This is funded and administered by a special government department, the National Asylum Support Service (NASS). Those supported by NASS receive cash payments worth 70 per cent of income support. A lost appeal can result in the termination of peoples' accommodation and allowance and for some, destitution or removal to their counties of origin often results.

At the time when this young man was refused asylum, it was a horrific shock to me. It was, of course, a profound shock to my client who, in the months that followed, tried to understand a system that responded to his experiences in this way. The grief and disappointment in this democracy he had fled to, and how it had treated him, shook him to the core. It shook me too. I sat with him in his grief and that was my role. However it soon changed to asking myself, do I have a wider role, not just as a witness to his experiences, but shouldn't I act? Not just in relation to the knowledge I now held about his experience and its profound effect on him, but about how he had been treated in the UK. Or was I acting primarily because I couldn't bear to sit with his and other clients' sadness and hopelessness as the system fails them?

INCORPORATING CASEWORK INTO THE COUNSELLING RELATIONSHIP

For those who work with refugees, there are many challenges. It will be a familiar experience to many who have worked with refugees to sit with a client who brings with them a bag of documents from the solicitor for you to read or asks you to help with their housing. This can happen at a first appointment or a year on; perhaps the client is confused about your role, or does not know who else to ask or trust to help. You may want to suggest an advocate and realize there is no one available to advocate, or at least no one who will have the knowledge and understanding of the client necessary for effective and prompt action.

It can be a shock for counsellors to learn at first hand the asylum and support system in place for refugees and the extent to which it renders their clients powerless with few rights. It can be anxiety provoking too, once it becomes clear how vulnerable people are to detention and removal. The asylum system is processing people increasingly quickly and the system changes regularly; this is frightening for clients and counsellors alike.

It is hard for a refugee to ask for help, particularly when they are unfamiliar with or don't understand the systems and culture they are now living in or don't have the language to ask. Providing information can be the most useful thing a counsellor can do as the relationship begins, as well as assisting access to community support and networks.

It can sometimes seem that you are the only person who can act to defend, protect or to ensure basic rights. It is important for you to have access to local refugee organizations and advice agencies, including refugee community organizations that can provide vital support for your clients. Having access to this information and knowledge of the system will reassure both you and the client.

I was in the process of building a new relationship with a heavily pregnant woman from Sierra Leone, who was very distressed and withdrawn following her experiences. At our fourth session, she informed me that NASS had housed her in a top flat in a block without a lift, with no fridge or cooker, and only one chair and one blanket on the bed. She did not yet speak English and she wasn't sure if the way her housing had been organized was right. She knew others lived in better places with cookers, but she was just so relieved to be in the UK and was too frightened to complain, just in case they left her with no home at all. She had been in the country six weeks. I had the knowledge and the power to act and her situation was resolved with a letter from myself, as a practitioner, about her basic rights and physical and mental health needs.

Some of my colleagues looked on suspiciously; was this counselling? They asked what the impact of my actions on the counselling relationship might be.

What my client said to me about this was that it meant that somebody cared. It also said to her that she was right to be outraged at where she was expected to live and at the conditions she was housed in. While I worried about disempowerment, she was hugely relieved that she was going to be safe and warm that night and was able to cook African food for the first time since she had fled to the UK!

How did it impact on our relationship? Before this, I believe that she had felt both ambivalent and confused about coming to speak to me every week. I think this was the first time the relationship felt helpful, and that perhaps she had found someone she could trust and who was interested in what she said. But there was a much more fundamental message to her in my actions. The cause of her distress was social, and needed a practical solution. By not acting, I risked leaving her in her distress, seeing it as private pain, not an unjust situation.

To talk about empowering her to act in this situation could possibly have left her in an appalling situation for many weeks, maybe months, and would ignore her position of powerlessness. There are times when it is possible to refer to other agencies for advice, and this will widen the support network for your client; at other times it is necessary to act.

It was this learning and dialogue with clients that enabled me to answer so many of the questions raised by this work. Working from a human rights perspective was the framework I adopted when I first began this work, prior to working at the Medical Foundation, as an instinctive response to working with refugees. I watched some counselling colleagues instinctively do the same, usually those working from within a person-centred model where the core conditions are based on an essential humanity and a search for understanding within a respectful relationship.

For other counsellors around me it was a confusing time; some withdrew from the work saying 'asylum seekers can't make use of counselling' or 'it isn't appropriate to offer counselling when their lives are so unstable'. Others lost their focus and became purely advocates, wondering what had happened to the therapeutic relationship with the client but feeling relieved that they could actually do something practical to help, having felt de-skilled and powerless to change their clients' situations.

THE MEDICAL FOUNDATION

The Medical Foundation is a human rights organization and offers counselling within this context; to be neutral in the face of human rights violations at home and internationally can be felt as a violation in itself to our clients. Our role is to challenge the use of torture and raise awareness of its consequences. In the aftermath of September 11th 2001, the global debate around torture and its use has intensified and this includes torture perpetrated by the West. Our work remains as important as it was 20 years ago when the Medical Foundation was founded.

Our clients rarely see justice, and perpetrators are not brought to trial for their actions. However justice, both social and political, would often be more therapeutic than anything I could offer.

THE RESPONSIBILITY TO ACT

What survivors of torture will find in the room with my colleagues and myself is a sense of justice, a counsellor who holds strong beliefs about human rights and the right of refugees to seek protection and be treated humanely in that process. These beliefs are stated. They will also find someone who wants to understand their experience both pre-flight and in the UK and who may be able to act, sometimes in very small ways and sometimes to protect.

Our model involves a process of assessment that is holistic, and aims to understand the full extent of our clients' experiences. This assessment process can often take four sessions, as you explore together their history and life in the UK. It involves exploring what might help with what can often feel a huge and overwhelming set of difficulties and a history so horrific it is hard to understand how the person could have survived.

Many of the problems may be social and/or medical and have practical casework solutions. Part of the dialogue of the assessment will be thinking together about how they might use your support to name and explore their struggles and what else may help with the multiple difficulties they may be bringing. The dialogue can be used to try and make sense of this new relationship they are embarking on, exploring from whom and how they sought help at home and how they understand what it is you are offering.

Sometimes what may be brought to the session is an issue concerning poor housing or an inattentive lawyer, but listening to these experiences is often the start of building a trusting relationship. Survivors can experience relief at sharing these difficulties and may be validated by your concern and even sometimes by your outrage. Often they will feel relieved by the information you may be able to provide, even if it is only the address of an advice agency or a map and the bus route. Once trust is built, a survivor can begin to bring to you their experiences of war, torture and loss that cause such profound distress.

As the relationship develops, there is a need to be flexible in order to respond to the changing world of your client. This flexibility and commitment to follow your client's experience is familiar to person-centred counsellors but the sudden changes can be dramatic when working with refugees. One week can be spent exploring the grief of being separated from family; the following week with the panic that arises when your client's NASS support is terminated and your client has walked to the session, has no bus fare and is hungry.

There can be consequences for the therapeutic relationship in acting to protect and advocate for a survivor of torture. Acting to protect may ensure your client's safety, but may leave a sense of indebtedness that in itself may be an obstacle in the therapeutic process or it may strengthen and deepen the relationship. By protection, I mean the most fundamental protection, to act to stop a client being removed to a country where it is likely they will face further torture, conflict or death.

For me, questioning my role in protecting clients started before I began to work for the Medical Foundation, whose ethos around protection is clear. Our ethos is that we have a role in ensuring survivors of torture are protected from further torture and violation. I remember asking myself; what is my responsibility as somebody 'safe' who is in a position to use responsibly the testimony shared in the session?

I believe counsellors do have a responsibility. This in most cases means writing a report about your client that may have a direct impact on their asylum case. It means stating an opinion, something that person-centred counsellors don't usually do in this context. The testimony that is shared, with a survivor's permission, doesn't remain between you. All of your client's experiences in the country they fled from that have been explored during counselling are used to write a report that is submitted as part of their asylum case.

As a human rights counsellor I believe my dialogue with clients should further human rights. I have a responsibility to use responsibly the testimonies of my clients.

BEARING WITNESS

Torture is an attempt to break the spirit of a person so that they question humanity and lose trust in themselves and others. It induces shame and holds not only individuals, but also communities, in fear. The founder of the Medical Foundation, Helen Bamber (2001/2002: 1) has said; 'torture can be described as the act of killing a person without their dying. As such, it destroys trust, belief and hope.'

Society has much to learn from these testimonies of our clients as the experiences of survivors are historically often questioned, ignored or denied. If we don't use such information responsibly, it becomes an individual experience and not the collective experience of thousands of people. Within the Medical Foundation this forms part of an archive of human rights atrocities, which informs our national and international work. Counselling must hear the individual survivor, but the collective voice of survivors and their allies is the voice that will effect change.

> Many come to see that the testimony they provide in the process of bearing witness carries a responsibility towards the past. (Helen Bamber, 1993: 4)

The action of writing a report is often felt to be hugely validating for clients but can also impact on the counselling relationship. Sometimes, however, we make it too complicated. I remember struggling with how grateful a client was, following the writing of a report that she felt heard and understood her experiences. I explored this in supervision and together we wondered why shouldn't she want to thank me, human to human, for being one of the few people who acted. Does our concern around power cloud our work when in its simplest sense we are using testimony to protect individuals and to understand and challenge violations internationally?

In a fundamental sense, what we should be offering is our humanity and understanding, and ultimately a commitment to hear what has happened. Our skills in supporting exploration and listening are integral to that.

RESPONSIBILITY TO LEARN

For those working with refugees there is a responsibility to try and keep up to date with information about countries where human rights are violated or where there is conflict. A commitment to understanding the political and social contexts our clients have fled from is integral to the work. How can we understand our clients if we hold no information about the world they have fled and the violations that continue?

How can I understand an Afghani client if I don't have a basic understanding of the political history of the country and its neighbours? Those who say they seek to understand the client, without this knowledge, are at risk of separating the individual from their history and culture and imposing a Western concept of the individual on clients from collective or community-based cultures.

I remember a 40-year-old man from Afghanistan, from the Pashtun tribe, spending week after week giving me a history of his tribe and country. My supervisor at the time 'wondered' whether this need to tell me was about his avoidance of 'difficulty'.

I thought then and now that my client was right to tell me. How could I understand him if I didn't understand who he was by how he had lived and what he had lived through? It helped me to understand him and his place in his society. It also helped me understand the situation of his wife and children left behind in a refugee camp in Peshawar. In his mind, he knew that I couldn't understand his world and the pain of what he had lost if I didn't try and understand what it meant to be him.

Often we impose onto our clients what we consider to be traumatic, or empathize and validate when the client has begun giving a testimony before we have come to understand their experience. For this Afghani man, having lived through two wars, and survived poverty, oppression and deprivation, the risk was that I would silence him when he was only just beginning to share his experiences. If we respond too readily with our own shock and distress, often disguised as empathic understanding, we risk silencing our clients.

Alongside country research and commitment to cross-cultural practice should sit an understanding of power, of your position within structural oppressions. A commitment to working within a human rights framework also means naming and exploring such issues of power and privilege, such as my power as a UK citizen, as a White person, and other structural powers I may have, as well as elements of personal power and how they might impact on the relationship. It may mean naming your or your family's shared refugee history.

When counselling refugees, there are additional layers of power issues to be explored. Refugees are among the most disempowered and marginalized in the UK. Often I have been saddened by the huge amount of gratitude that simply ensuring our clients have choice about their interpreter has produced. Even the most basic right to be understood through the voice of a person you have had some choice in and trust can seem rare. We have a responsibility to name our position and explore the impact of advocating for the most basic of rights, the right to communicate.

Human rights counsellors can name the social and political processes that leave clients in poverty and can create a dialogue to help survivors understand the process whereby refugees are deliberately kept in poverty to discourage 'others' from coming.

Refugees describe living half in one world and half in another; knowing that human rights violations and conflict continues, with their families, neighbours and communities remaining at risk. We must remember that many do not survive or cannot flee. Increasingly, as refugee rights are violated in the UK, I wonder too if increasing numbers will survive exile. In my current caseload, most survivors hold the idea of killing themselves as a realistic option, were they forced to return. For many it seems the one choice left for them if they were facing removal.

FINDING MEANING

Exploring experiences of oppression here in the UK and in their countries is a crucial part of finding meaning. Pat Bracken (Bracken & Petty, 1998) emphasizes that what is important in recovery is finding meaning, social and political meaning. War, persecution and torture are political processes.

When a country has been at war or a regime/opposition is in place that tortures and kills and the international community stands by—that is political. I believe that engaging in political debate with our clients is crucial to them finding meaning. Giving expression to anger about the neglect that lets genocide, war and human rights abuses continue with little action from the international community is important. Included in this is the part the British Government did or did not play, and the part British colonization may have had on a client's country of origin. Shying way from these debates can keep our clients silent and replicate oppressive relationships both in exile and from the past.

Recovery and healing are terms frequently used in both the counselling and mental health fields. Refugee clients have often challenged the idea of 'healing and recovery'. A Kurdish client once asked me how he could possibly recover when his community remained oppressed: 'How can I think about this when they are killing us? I will get better when it stops. My people will carry this with them for ever.'

We cannot think those experiences of torture and/or organized violence can be treated in isolation from the rest of their lives. From collectivist cultures or community-based cultures, 'a people' are being wounded, and the assault is felt even though the person may be physically in the UK. It is important to suspend our beliefs about what might help and what we hope to offer in counselling.

What I often hope for is that the person finds their own way of understanding and living with their experience. Often it is justice, not individual recovery that is wanted, both for them and their communities. Survivors want social justice: the right to decent housing, a good lawyer and the right to work. (Those seeking asylum are not allowed to work under recent asylum legislation.) Survivors also want an end to the nightmares, flashbacks and sleeplessness that is the daily experience of many.

Finally, the very act of bearing witness is a political act in itself and furthers human rights. What we witness must inform how we live our lives. It is our responsibility to use that knowledge, whichever environment we counsel in. As a counsellor at the Medical Foundation, our clients' histories are held and play an important role in the documentation and verification of torture.

CONFIDENTIALITY OR SILENCE

The concept of confidentiality is familiar to us as counsellors, but in some societies there may not even be a word for it—the concept may not exist. On many occasions I have described and explored our code of confidentiality, and clients have been shocked and sometimes insulted; 'There must be no secrets, I have left a country of silence and secrets, I don't want you to keep this secret.' This client was stating my responsibilities as the listener and she was right.

FACING REMOVAL

Many counsellors, after an initial interest, are withdrawing from this work. In this hostile climate, it can feel sad and complex work, leaving counsellors feeling overwhelmed and de-skilled. Those counsellors who are refugees themselves often find the daily stories saddening and very close to their own histories and those of their families.

Often asylum seekers and refugees don't understand or particularly respect what counselling is. When an exhausted client is asking for justice: decent housing, somewhere safe to live, access to a fair and independent system that will look at her case without bias—it can be difficult to imagine how talking might help.

Refugees often won't know the rules of help-seeking in the UK as they have fled societies with other forms of helping and framing/expressing distress. They bring legal documents and social and practical issues to sessions and ask you to help them to stay. It's a mysterious model of help we are offering, a model in which there is an assumption that to talk is important and fundamentally that by sticking to the core conditions, the counselling process will be helpful. It often is, but for those counsellors working with refugees, the reality of the removal of their clients to face possible further persecution or re-traumatization can make the work painful and distressing.

Many clients will be refused, lose appeals and face removal to war-torn countries, conflict and further persecution. Alongside this they are often given hope and support through community networks and new friendships/relationships with those of us who are appalled at what they have experienced and the erosion of their rights in the UK. They may also have a counsellor with a commitment to standing alongside them throughout the process of exile.

Survivors of torture have endured a great deal to get here, but they will bring with them the knowledge that most don't make it. As a country we receive a tiny proportion of refugees. (Asia hosted more than a third of all the people of concern to the UNHCR in 2005 (36%), followed by Africa (25%)—Europe hosted just 23%. The UK hosts just 2% of the world's refugees. Two-thirds of the world's refugees are living in developing countries, often in camps. Africa and Asia, between them, host over 60% of the world's refugees.) Most don't manage to escape. They are killed, 'disappeared', displaced within their own countries or remain at risk. This is particularly so for women.

When we are faced with a survivor of torture or war, it can be easy to re-victimize. Survivors often have immense strength and coping abilities. This person might not see in the beginning how sitting in front of you for just an hour a week at a set time is really going to help. Nevertheless, for many, the relationship that is formed in counselling can be the beginning of finding hope and trust in another person.

What we offer, as human rights counsellors, is a belief in human rights and a belief in counselling relationships. We also believe that the person has a right to be in this country and to be treated with dignity and respect. If we offer that justice in the room, then the hour can be very important indeed.

REFERENCES

Amnesty International (2003) *Combating Torture—A manual for action*. London: Amnesty International.

Bamber, H (2001/2002) Breaking through the walls. A message from the director. *Medical Foundation Annual Review* (p. 1).

Bamber, H (1993) The Medical Foundation and its commitment to human rights and rehabilitation. Paper presented at the conference 'The Internal Struggle Against Torture and the Case of Israel' organized by the Association of Israeli–Palestinian Physicians for Human Rights (p. 4). Tel Aviv, 13–14 June 1993.

Bracken, P & Petty, C (1998) *Re-thinking the Trauma of War*. London: Free Association Books.

Home Office (1999) *Immigration and Asylum Act*. London: HMSO.

Neil, S (2004) *Get It Right: How Home Office decision making fails refugees*. London: Amnesty International Research Report (February).

UNHCR (2005 Edition) *Refugees by Numbers*. Geneva, Switzerland: UNHCR.

Chapter 16

DISABILITY, MULTIDIMENSIONALITY AND LOVE: THE POLITICS OF A COUNSELLING RELATIONSHIP IN FURTHER EDUCATION

Suzanne Keys

INTRODUCTION

Frederick [1] and I met at a sixth-form college in London where I was his counsellor for three years. This chapter consists of a transcript of a discussion between us followed by my learnings from this relationship in terms of personal, relational and institutional politics, empowerment and advocacy, service and love, multidimensionality and limitations.

Frederick and I are different in many ways: he is a 19-year-old single young man with cerebral palsy from a Pakistani and Muslim family. He joined the college on an entry level course and is now at university. I am a 36-year-old married woman who is able bodied, middle class, a university graduate and from a Northern Irish and Protestant family. These differences have an impact on the language we use, the ways we see the world and on our counselling relationship.

THE POLITICS OF THE PROCESS

The process of writing this chapter has paralleled the issues within it. I have had a real struggle to know how both Frederick's and my voice can be heard authentically—at times over-facilitating and trying to erase my power in an effort to allow his voice to come through. I have been caught between re-presenting and representing (Wilkinson & Kitzinger, 1996) and with the fallacy of providing an opportunity which is uncontaminated for Frederick's voice to be heard: 'the practice of giving research subjects a "voice" within academic texts, whether by speaking for them or by letting them speak for themselves, is always and inevitably a textual device that retains and reinforces, rather than weakens, the academic author's authority' (MacMillan, 1996).

---

1. Frederick has read and given his written and verbal consent for this chapter to be published and chosen his own pseudonym. All other names have been changed.

I have been very aware of the power differentials and at times have wanted to equalize something which cannot be equalized, not wanting to recognize the limitations which are there and the fact that equality is more to do with recognition and authenticity than with sameness. I have got very caught up in getting it right. I have wanted Frederick to feel empowered to write. He, on the other hand, has felt that my voice will always carry more weight, although he sees the writing of this chapter as a political act, which he hopes will change how people think about disability, counselling and education.

The idea for writing the chapter together came from me. Frederick agreed to do it but mentioned several times that he was so grateful to me for our relationship that he was only too happy to repay me in some way. I felt awkward about this and kept checking this out and reminding him that he could opt out at any time and that I didn't need any 'payment' from him for what had gone on between us. It was as if I was trying to second-guess his consent, see if there was something hidden there, not trusting his words or honouring the trust we had established in our relationship. On reflection, I realize I may have been quite ungracious about my lack of acceptance of his desire to give something back and his feeling that this is a way that he can do it. I am aware that clients need their love and appreciation to be heard as well as to receive this from their therapist (Thorne, 2002). Frederick also said that he felt happy that I had come to him to ask for something as he has the sense that he is always the one who has to go to others and make things happen.

The following discussion took place specifically for this book, after we had finished counselling. I have chosen the beginning and end and two extracts from the middle where Frederick talks about his difference as a disabled person and his relationship with others. I have tried to cover the sections left out in the rest of the chapter. Frederick also says how 'tricky' it would be for him to write or tape something on his own and how long it would take him and how he wants me to write it and for him to have a look at it. We also talk about confidentiality and his fears of being political and how that might jeopardise some of his relationships in college.

DISCUSSION TRANSCRIPT

Extract 1: Beginning of tape

> F1 *I really valued it and some of the things you did for me were a turning point in my college career and I'd just like to say that the way you have helped me physically, if I look back on it, you have done more than what any other counsellor would do and, you know, it's like, it's kind of, it's basically what it is, is, it's love for me. If you didn't have the love for me you wouldn't do what you did. (S: uhm) I deeply thank you from the bottom of my heart.*
> S1 *(quietly) Uhm, I can hear that.*

F2 That's why I've dragged it on for a few more days because I wanted to do justice to everybody. (S: right, yeah) I'm dragging it on.

S2 'Cos you want to do justice to everybody? (F: yeah) In terms of thanking them? Is that what you mean?

F3 Yeah, I think it's only right and proper. The unfortunate thing is that they won't be there for me (S: they won't be?) come September. (S: right) That's another issue.

S3 Yes, so the first issue's about thanks and also you feel cared about. It sounds like you feel loved by me, anyway, and that has made a difference to you.

F4 It's made a psychological difference (S: yes) it's also been an empowering, I thought I'd never say this (smiling).

S4 (laughing) What? The word empowerment?

F5 It's been self-empowering.

S5 You never thought you'd say that Frederick?

F6 Nah, I'd never thought I'd say that. (S: right, uhm hmm) But empowering in the sense that I haven't been able to do things for myself but I've instructed other people (S: I see) to do them for me.

S6 Right, so you've found the power to do that?

F7 Yes. That power in a sense has only come from you knowing me inside out.

S7 Hmm, that's really interesting so somehow me knowing you has allowed you to feel more powerful about yourself so that you can ask other people to help you to do things. That's really interesting.

F8 Because what I mean is that at least I've got some legality.

S8 Legality? What does that mean?

F9 That means legal justification. (S: right) If I ask you for something you're inevitably going to give it to me. (S: uhm) I'm not going to say it's a given because it's not. (S: right) But you're inevitably, well not inevitably, nine times out of ten you're going to give it to me. (S: right) But if I ask other people they might say 'no' but I might say to them, 'Look, Sue supports my view'. (S: yeah) And it'll be like, 'OK then we must do something about it.'

S9 Right, so that gives you some kind of credibility or something, back up?

F10 Yeah, but it's only small, only personal credibility it's not public credibility. All the years I've been here I've been trying to fight for public support, public legality, public justification (S: right) but I've ended up getting personal.

S10 And what's the difference for you between public and personal?

F11 The public is where everyone knows, everyone connected to your studies or development as individual, they know but private or personal is just like you and another person, in this case you.

S11 So that works. The kind of personal works but (F: but) but you don't think the public is working that's what you've been

F12 (interrupting) yeah but the public needs to work because in some cases you're in the pound seats, in some cases they're in the pounds seats but I am never in the pound seat.

S12 And the pound seat, what I understand by the pound seat, is the place of power and you don't feel you're ever in that place of power.

F13 No.

S13 So your chair is never a pound seat?

F14 No, it can never be.

S14 It can never be?

F15 Because of my status.

S15 And your status is?

F16 I'm a student, you're not.

S16 It's your student status that means you don't have the power?

F17 Yes.

S17 Right, uhm.

    Silence

Extract 2

F18 Because namely, see see again this is where I'm different, where disabled people or people with special needs are different (S: yeah) because your able-bodied colleague, not colleague, students, would probably say that in one or two sessions max.

S18 You reckon?

F19 But it's taken

S19 (interrupting) so you see yourself as slower?

F20 It's taken me, it's taken the realization three years to kind of say that but my peers would say that in two or three sessions.

S20 But that's not my experience Frederick. It takes a lot to say what you've said. The feedback I got from the meeting we were at this week as well was how articulate you were and you know and I, my sense is that you are able to put into words very difficult things which I don't always find that other students can. You know everyone has different ways of expressing themselves but

F21 yeah, I appreciate that.

S21 I kind of find you have a very deep thinking.

F22 But I just feel that my able-bodied colleagues although they are able some of them are not willing.

S22 Able but not willing.

F23 But I'm not able but I am willing.

S23 Willing?

F24 Willing to say stuff, say things.

S24 It takes quite a lot of courage some of the things that you say.

F25 Yeah, because of the way I see the land. Nobody sees the land like I do. Go out there now and ask some people, ask some able-bodied people how they see themselves, how they see the system?

S25 And it wouldn't be the same as you.

F26 Yeah, probably they see it as fine blah blah blah blah.

S26 Whereas your perspective on it, well it sounds like it's unique but due to your disability you'll see it in a particular way

F27 Yeah and

S27 it sounds like you feel very alone with that Frederick.

F28 Yeah and that takes a lot of other things away in terms of socializing and all that kind of stuff (S: yeah) because because every day it seems I'm fighting. I'm not maturing other sides, I'm not maturing my social element. (S: I see) I'm not maturing

S28 (interrupting) like all your energy is focused on the kind of just surviving, fighting, getting your needs met so you don't get a chance to develop your social side?

Extract 3

S29 Do you feel I'm fighting with you?

F29 No, it's just that it's, that what you're saying to me is alright, yeah but I've got other people who serve me that are fighting me as well. (S: right) My carers are fighting me.

S30 What do you mean 'fighting you' Frederick?

F30 They are kind of challenging every view, (S: I see) concept and the fact is that person is able-bodied and I'm disabled. (S: right)

S31 So therefore your views are the ones that matter—oh there's an ant!

F31 You don't like ants?

S32 Not particularly crawling all over me. What about you? Do you like ants?

F32 Not really no.

S33 So what you're saying from what I've understood, if I've understood you correctly, is that you know about disability issues because you're disabled and that able-bodied people like your carers don't really know and they're not really listening to you and they're coming up with their own opinions from an uninformed place. Is that what you mean?

F33 Yeah, but what makes it more—what time do we finish? 1.15? (S nods) What makes me more sad about it (S: right) is that they know, he knows, he is aware rather of the disability issues (S: right) in terms of what causes spasm, what causes, you know, people to talk in a certain way, people to eat in a certain way so he knows all about the stuff but it's amazing that he doesn't kind of concur

S34 How come he doesn't agree on the more political stuff is that it?

F34 Yeah and it's not

S35 (interrupting) he's got the information, uhm, but he doesn't seem to hold the same views as you.

F35 I'm not asking him to hold the same views, I'm just saying or asking him, not to hold the same view but take my view and when he goes into the outside world spread what I've told him. Don't argue with it because if you argue with it you're just like the rest of them. It's like me saying to you, 'Oh I've got a problem with Greg [a member of staff]' and instead of you doing something about that or you trying to resolve it by getting him in here you go around telling the whole college, 'Oh Frederick has a problem with Greg'. (S: right) That is the equivalent.

S36 Yeah, so it's kind of like you're saying he's not really engaging with the issues and he's not spreading the word about it?

F36 Yeah it's like when I told you that months ago, years ago that I had a problem with Gemma [F's tutor], you didn't say to people, 'Oh he's got a problem with Gemma guys. (S: mhmm) Let's do something about it'. You actually got her in here and actually sorted it out.

S37 So that's something about, is that something about acting on it?

F37 Not only acting upon it but listening and not wanting to, (S: right, yeah) not wanting to have the same view as other people.

S38 So listening to you and taking you seriously.

F38 Yeah, and kind of giving classical but workable solutions as well.

S39 That's important.

F39 It's like you didn't kind of—if I said to you, 'Look I've got a problem with Gemma'— you didn't kind of say to me, 'Oh she's on the payroll why have you got a problem with her?' You didn't jump.

S40 Mhmm, right I didn't try and contradict, change your mind is that what you mean?

F40 You didn't kind of like challenge me. You said, 'You've got a problem with Gemma. Alright what's the problem?' I told you the problem and you took it from there.

S41 Right, listening to you, believing you, taking you seriously, acting on it (F: it's) trying to find solutions.

F41 It's not only believing, I mean, I mean, I mean, I mean it's like me saying I've got condoms in my bag (S: right) do you believe me? (F smiling) or do you think I'm having a bit of a joke you know what I mean?

S42 That's not that kind of believing then?

F42 Yeah.

S43 Right.

F43 I mean there's different kinds of

S44 Do you have condoms in your bag?

F44 No.

S45 Would you like to have condoms in your bag?

F45 Uhm (sigh) possibly. See there's a difference between wanting and having.

S46 You know that difference don't you?

F46 Yeah.

S47 Big difference for you.

F47 I might want Gemma to teach me but is she teaching me is another matter.

S48 Yeah, you might want to have sex but whether you have it or not is different.

F48 Yeah.

S49 Uhm.

Extract 4

S50 Well, if you had a list you wanted to leave with me I could pass it on to Zena [a college manager].

F50 Yeah, but it's all administration, it's PR, man, trust me. (S: right) Public relations rubbish.

S51 PRR (F: yeah, sigh) right Frederick?

F51 PRC actually.

S52 Crap?

F52 *Public Relationship Crap.*

S53 *Is that going to be your last word? Crap?*

F53 *Yeah, this* [college life] *has been ten weeks or twenty weeks equivalent of a Big Brother house. (S: really) Trust me. But it's, it's—you know I can't bring myself … that I'm leaving.*

S54 *Uhm, it's like really hard to take in?*

F54 *And the thing is I spoke to Anna* [learning support assistant] *and I gave her a little thank you kind of thing and she said, 'Oh Frederick, I'm trying to avoid you because I don't want to say goodbye' and I said, 'Well, how do you think l feel? I'm leaving here next year at least you're coming back here next year to teach.' I'm not even coming back next year for God's sake.*

S55 *Yeah, I know it's really hard to believe that you won't be here next year. Like you can't really believe it.*

F55 *(quietly) No.*

S56 *And maybe that's the way it's got to be that you won't believe it. It is sad.*

F56 *Most people would love to see the back of me I'm sure.*

S57 *Well, I'll miss you.*

F57 *Most people, not you, but most people. (S: right)*

S58 *Will be glad that you're gone?*

F58 *Yeah, they won't probably say it to my face but I know I have been a pain in the arse. (S: uhm) I know that I've been a pain in the arse.*

S59 *And that's a hard thing to (F: yeah) know.*

F59 *I've been a pain in the arse but if it wasn't for this puppet inclusion policy, yeah, they'd probably think, 'Just get on with it son'—you know what I mean? Because of this puppet inclusion policy, you know, they have to be seen to be doing the right thing.*

S60 *You don't quite buy it?*

F60 *It's not about buying it, it's about what's on the packing? They say it's GM but is it GM? No, it's not. It's just more expensive.*

S61 *So what's on the packet doesn't match what's inside?*

F61 *Yeah. Sue, you're good, man.*

S61 *I'm good, I get you?*

F62 *You're seriously good. (both smiling) You get all the connotations and everything.*

End of tape

POLITICS: PERSONAL, RELATIONAL AND INSTITUTIONAL

Politics was a word Frederick used often during our relationship so it was an intrinsic part of the content that he brought especially in terms of where the power lay in the institution and how powerless he felt. He talked a lot about his experiences of being a young man who uses a wheelchair in an institution and a society where his concerns are not heard or understood and where he encounters many disabling barriers (see social model of disability e.g. Sinason, 1992; Hawkins, 2002; Daly, 2003).

This highlighted the power dynamics between him and the institution but also between him and me in terms of my role as a counsellor in the same system. In talking and writing for this chapter the complexity of the public and private interweaving of the personal, relational and institutional political dynamics has become apparent. When talking about these three dynamics, Frederick's way of putting it was:

> F   *… institutional is preventable (S: right) and this kind of politics or whatever,*
> *relationship politics helps people. (S: right) So you've got P and you've got H, which*
> *stands for prevent and help and you've got—what was the other one? I've forgotten*
> *the other one already. It was like your own politics and you've got F*
> S   *What's F?*
> F   *Fight.*
> S   *And that's your own politics is it? So it's P, H, F.*
> F   *P, H, F, yeah.*

So, for Frederick, the politics of our relationship is about helping, Frederick's political involvement in the institution is about prevention and his personal politics is about fighting and it is fighting which seems to underline everything in terms of relating. Frederick's sense that he has to fight for survival (F28) has been predominant throughout the time that I have known him. His imagery from the beginning of our relationship has been of him living in a continual state of emergency, fighting alone, often on a bloody and sweaty battlefield where he has two options: fight or die. He has to fight to be heard and seen, to get his needs met. In a previous taped discussion Frederick said:

> *The only way the actual individual gets any say is when he or she is in an institution and*
> *it's up to that institution to cater, or in this case, either to cater or for the student to fight*
> *for themselves which I personally have had to do practically from birth and I know that*
> *sounds very strong but I've had to practically do it all of my living life. Because my*
> *interpretation is 'if I don't do it nobody will' … if we don't apply ourselves or challenge*
> *the status quo in the political circles then I feel that disabled people, or less able people,*
> *lets put it this way, will die without a trace or their education will die without a trace.*

This is how I understand Frederick's sense of prevention: he is not only fighting for his own survival but also has a sense of duty to fight the system he is part of to try and get his voice heard on behalf of disabled people as a whole in order to make changes.

I can see visible flaws and I feel it as my duty as a disabled student and as a student at this college that I highlight these flaws in their full glory because I don't want people to go round walking blindly to these situations.

This means raising his voice and getting angry and being aware that he is seen as a 'pain in the arse' (F58). Frederick is aware too that often the more he shouts and the more persistent he is the less he gets heard. He feels he has no choice. He cries out in desperation.

It means that his vulnerability and fragility often go unnoticed and in this transcript, although it is a discussion and not a counselling session, it is clear that there are many instances when I lack empathy. I do not pick up on his sadness or his sense of impotence (e.g. S1, S12, S20) and get caught up in quite a combative relationship (e.g. S30ff, S44ff). It is perhaps inevitable that, in terms of the relational politics between us, there was fighting.

In S29, when I ask Frederick if he feels I'm fighting with him, what we have been discussing is my suggestion that we list some of the things he has been talking about in terms of what he would like to change in the institution and that he passes it on as feedback to staff at the college. He is convinced that, like reports he has seen others write, it won't go anywhere and it would be a waste of time. I cling on to my practical solution to his practical problem, in a retrospectively embarrassing way, and to make matters worse, bring it up again in Extract 4. I am aware of how slow I am at understanding what Frederick is saying and how caught up I get in fighting the preventative fight. On reflection, I am aware that Frederick's fighting touched my sense of wanting to engage in prevention politics in the institution: the part of my personal politics that wants to see things changed, that believes passionately in voices being heard and valued within a system. I wanted to join the cause with him, make a difference, change the world. Unfortunately, I think at times this meant I didn't hear what Frederick was saying. I was too busy joining in the fight to change the world that I lost contact with the fullness of my empathy. I missed changes of tone, physical gestures, contradictions with fighting vocabulary. This of course echoes what often happens in party politics when people get so caught up in a cause or vision or even a laudable desire for social change that they become single-tracked and lose their empathy for the other. Relationships become oppositional and combative. Person-to-person contact and the complexity of relationship are lost and, with them, ironically, any hope of constructive and lasting change. It also echoes Frederick's own difficulty in empathizing with his colleagues. We had an ongoing and long-running debate about whether it was acceptable or not to reverse out of my room in his wheelchair without being able to see who was walking past. There was space to turn round in the room and have a clear view down the corridor but he always maintained that if he rode over people's toes it was a way of showing them what it was like not to be seen and not to be respected.

EMPOWERMENT AND ADVOCACY: LOVE AND SERVICE

An example of my limited empathy in our discussion is Frederick's definition of empowerment in both extract 1 and 3. He says that he feels slower than his able-bodied colleagues who would have got this quicker (F20) and yet it is I, whom he assumes is more 'able' than he, who have been the slowest to understand. This shows how dependent we are on each other to challenge some of the assumptions and stereotypes we have about the 'other group'.

It is only in studying this transcript after our three-year relationship that I am finally beginning to understand what Frederick means by empowerment and what that meant in our relationship. Empowerment is not a fixed entity but rather an experience which is co-defined within a relationship. It is not about some kind of power that I, or anyone else, can bestow on Frederick. It is not even about him being able to do things for himself necessarily: 'empowering in the sense that I haven't been able to do things for myself but I've instructed other people to do them for me' (F6). For Frederick looking back at our relationship he sees it as his voice being heard in the world. It is about ad-vocacy: his voice going forward. I and his carers 'serve' him (F29). It is not my job to have opinions about what Frederick says or believes. This, of course, is very much in keeping with a non-directive, phenomenological person-centred approach to counselling. But with Frederick the added dimension is that he wants me, and his carer, to 'take [his] view ... into the outside world' (F35), whatever we think about it. He wants us to be his voice in the world as he does not believe his voice carries any power or authority. Empowerment involves both the private and the public (F11).

In Extract 1 I noticed that I feel comfortable about Frederick feeling empowered because I know him 'inside out' (F7) and that gives him confidence. So this would fit more with my ideal and my assumptions about the importance of 'power-from-within' and our collective 'power-with' and even 'power-to' (Proctor, 2002). However, I am less comfortable about the idea that he 'instructs' others to do things for him because of that. It becomes his 'power-over' and I somehow give him 'legality' because he feels I'll do whatever he asks and he has me as a back-up if he is challenged (F9). It is easier to understand in terms of a favourite phrase of Frederick's: 'pound seats' (F12). He knows that within the system we are both part of, both in terms of the education system and the society we live in, I have more role and societal power (Proctor, 2002) than he has. I am in the 'pound seat'. He wants to use this to get his voice heard. The question for me is whether, in his service, I am prepared to be 'used' like that?

My discomfort is to do with the dynamics of power in our relationship. Although Frederick feels powerless in the world he was also very powerful in our relationship and I often felt powerless not only within the educational system but also within our relationship. Although our 'power bases' and the 'power processes' may seem at first glance to endow me with more power in the relationship, this was not always the case nor did it always determine the 'power outcomes' (Proctor, 2002). Part of my sense of powerlessness was to do with my desire to follow Frederick's agenda, whatever that meant about mine and I think this is a common misinterpretation of the person-centred approach to therapy. It was as if I felt the most helpful thing for Frederick was if I negated my opinions and views, i.e. 'my power-from-within'. Thus my voice and authenticity are sacrificed for the sake of hearing Frederick's voice and struggles, allowing him to have 'power-over' me.

It is this fine balance of power in our relationship which we struggled with and which challenged the interplay of empathy, acceptance and congruence within me. It also emphasized for me the importance of the relationship in counselling. Our relationship gradually came to be based on an ethic of relational trust (Frederick described it as more 'two-way') as opposed to an ethic of autonomy. That was how we dealt with the basic ethical challenges of a therapeutic encounter: inequality, difference, risk and uncertainty (Bond, 2004). It was the quality of our relationship, the love, which was empowering, and part of that quality was my authenticity. I had to be continually mindful of finding a balance between entering Frederick's world and following his direction and expressing my views, particularly when it came to issues to do with the college. I knew that I had an attitude of 'principled non-directivity' (Grant, 1990) with Frederick and I think Frederick recognizes that with his use of the word 'love' in F1. I was not trying to tell Frederick what to do nor did I think I knew what was best for him. Nevertheless, that didn't mean that I didn't offer suggestions or express my opinions or that an onlooker observing our interchanges might not think I was being directive or unempathic at some points (e.g. S20, S44). I endeavoured to be in Frederick's world, to share my understanding of it with him, to accept him and believe in him but also to respect him by being myself in the relationship.

This is where therapy as 'service' (the definition of the word therapy, see Schmid, 2001) makes more sense to me. It is not about one person having 'power-over' another but rather about love.

> In the interpersonal encounter which we call therapy, when addressed and asked to respond, we assume a deep responsibility, an obligation in which our fellow man [sic] expects us to render the service we owe to each other: nothing else but love. (Schmid, 2001: 62)

I was very moved by Frederick's recognition that 'if you didn't have the love for me you wouldn't do what you did' (F1). Here I am recognized as a person who loves him, who wants to serve him out of love not out of submission. Love is a concept we had looked at before in terms of different kinds of love in different relationship but this was the first time Frederick said it about our relationship. In the last months of our counselling together he did talk about the fact that he could 'feel' that 'your spirit is right'. The adjectives he used were 'warm, kind, generous, deep, honest, genuine'. He could sense 'evil' in other places but the counselling room was the safest in the college and he didn't have to be a 'tough nut' there. He could be 'broken' and 'vulnerable'. This gave an added spiritual dimension to his constant struggles on the battlefield. In a subsequent session he talked about how certain people made him feel good because they seemed interested in his world and he could feel their spirit too. He talked about how important it was for him to feel loved. I understood this as a recognition that he had allies and that it was something to do with spirit and that there might be some respite from the fighting, however momentary. Reflecting now on these glimpses of a spiritual dimension to our work it seems crucial to me that we are here in a different kind of connection—interconnection—where there is sameness as well as difference, where there is interdependence as well as in/dependence and where Frederick feels recognized and validated as a lovable human being, a member of the human race. He links this sense of being loved to his feeling of empowerment, a word he thought he'd never use (F4). Loving becomes political.

Frederick's acknowledgement of this underlying bedrock of our relationship deeply moves me and helps me to keep my 'mistakes', 'misunderstandings' and 'oversights' in perspective. I would not have been able to articulate love as my motivation and commitment to him if he hadn't verbalized it, thereby enabling me to recognize it in myself. I can easily concentrate more on my own sense of failure and powerlessness, much like Frederick himself.

MULTIDIMENSIONALITY

As I said to Frederick on different occasions our relationship challenged me in many ways. It took me beyond my usual boundaries into new territory where I had to discover the idiosyncratic nature of this relationship: what the particular boundaries were for this particular relationship in this particular setting (Keys, 2003 b).

Frederick once described me as a multidimensional counsellor and I find that an increasingly helpful concept. Being multidimensional is about being fully human. When Frederick first talked about me being multidimensional he said it was because we looked at a range including 'moral, relationship, temperament, sexual side and academical side' and also because I challenged his opinions. He brought many dimensions of himself and I found myself responding with many dimensions of myself. The relationship became multidimensional. In subsequent discussions Frederick has talked about wanting to experience the dimension of therapeutic touch with, for example, a 'physio/counsellor' who could communicate understanding 'from the heart through the hands'.

Our counselling relationship took place within the context of an educational institution in the broader political agenda of 'widening participation'. With Frederick I learnt both about widening the dimensions of me, the counsellor, as well as the counselling service so as to provide a more accessible service to a diverse range of students. For example, in the first evaluation we did of our counselling relationship Frederick commented on the physical barriers in my room: although I moved the chairs around when he came the room was not set up for someone in a wheelchair to 'drop-in' as other students can, or to turn their wheelchair around so as to not have to reverse out. I learnt first-hand what being 'anticipatory' [2] means. He also taught me a lot about having accessible publicity and about being available. I have an open-door policy so that when I am not with someone students can drop-in or, as in Frederick's case, pass by regularly and say hello and 'check-in'. In terms of my personal and professional widening I have found myself growing in my flex-ability, response-ability, connect-ability, political-ability, resourcefulness, humility and empathy (Keys, 2003a).

My growing multidimensionality took me beyond the traditional idea of 'the counselling room' and in this way more physically into the political arena. I got involved in Frederick's politics of prevention and help, beyond being in the room and listening actively. This is about responding to a client with all of myself, including my political awareness. It is about being empathic to the person in their environment. It is about being 'for' the client as well as 'with' him/her (Kearney, 1996). Moreover the counselling room does not exist in isolation. It is not disconnected from the corridors, rooms, people and systems around it. The challenges lie in negotiating those connections without losing sight or site of Frederick in the context of empathy, acceptance and congruence.

Frederick mentions in Extract 3 the way I acted at the beginning of our relationship when I invited one of his tutors, with whom he felt unable to communicate, into the counselling room. This was hugely significant for Frederick in that I actually did something for him. It took me a while to realize it was the physicality of this which was so powerful for Frederick (F1), not arguing with him or trying to change his mind (F35, F40) or talking to people but actually doing something (F36). It makes sense that as Frederick feels physically unable to do so many things because of his cerebral palsy somebody prepared to act physically on his behalf, taking his views forward, is very meaningful and powerful. He often reiterated the importance of the 'act' during our counselling and this for me is about agency and social change.

LIMITATIONS

The other side of availability, accessibility and multidimensionality is the issue of boundaries, limits and how far the dimensions go. It often felt very confusing and messy with Frederick as I navigated what felt like new territory. Supervision

---

2. Race Relations (Amendment) Act 2000 and Disability Discrimination Act (2005) both underline the legal duty of educational establishments to be anticipatory and make reasonable adjustments.

was invaluable in this process as I questioned myself and wondered whether this was 'counselling' or not.

On reflection, I realize how hard it has been for me to be aware and accepting of my own limitations, the limitations of my role and the limitations of the system. Frederick, for example, reminded me of the implications for me of being 'on the payroll'. Frederick is constantly aware of limits and that is part of his fighting politics. We shared a political idealism and desire for social change but he is able to accept limits in a way that I, coming from my particular personal, physical, social and political background, don't. He constantly reminded me that for him it isn't a 'level playing field', that there are 'double standards':

> ... *double standards in terms of, 'Oh I've got an able-bodied colleague who is here at this level and I need to get to this level'. The harsh reality of life is, if I am going to be there, up there, then my able-bodied colleague is always going to be up there, always higher. (accompanied by hand gestures) Yes, he or she is always going to be higher. (Extract from taped discussion)*

He is never in 'the pound seats' (F12), he is 'not able' but he is 'willing' (F23) and he knows about the difference between 'wanting and having' (F45). In a follow-up conversation he talks about having 'censored choice' and that choice for him doesn't mean choice as it does to able-bodied people. Part of me didn't want to accept these limitations. I want him to be on a level playing field, be able to have what he wants, be able to match his will with his ability and to have the same choices as other people. He is much more realistic about the world he lives in. He is aware of his social positioning (Kearney, 1996) and the conditions of worth imposed on him from society (Chantler, 2004). The question is how I, as a person-centred therapist both recognize and accept these constraints and also challenge their internalization and believe in the potential for equality both within the counselling relationship and beyond. Working with Frederick taught me a lot about learning to live with both a sense of acceptance of limitations as well as the desire to fight. It is a central dilemma for person-centred theory and for many spiritual and existential writers: the desire for change, coupled with the acceptance of the present and its limitations (Hill & Keys, 2006). A key paradox of person-centred theory is that it is only through acceptance that change happens (Rogers, 1961). It is something that I struggle with in all areas of my life. Frederick and I struggled with it in our relationship.

As I have said to Frederick on several occasions I believe that the institution and I failed him in some ways by not alleviating some of his distress and responding more practically to some of his criticisms of what he felt was wrong with his educational environment. I have wondered too if therapy itself was disabling. Frederick continually asked me to come out and see what it was like for him, see the 'injustice' and 'devastation'. For Frederick 'seeing is believing'. Visibility is, understandably, of immense importance. I never felt I could leave the counselling room and go into the corridors and classrooms with him and be a witness and an advocate in the way that he asked. It felt like a limit I couldn't cross. I wrote letters on his behalf, made links with a local disability advocacy service, invited staff in to the room to meet us and invited Frederick to take part in a meeting I organized for staff and students to look at designing a tutorial on confidence building (S20). But somehow it never seemed enough. I couldn't accept both my and the institution's limitations. This is where some of my personal struggles often get enmeshed both in my politics and therefore, of course, in my practice as a therapist: striving for there to be enough for everyone and for me to be and do enough. For Frederick too there is never enough.

CONCLUSION

My experience of working with Frederick has changed my practice in terms of my awareness of the personal, relational and institutional political dynamics that are inevitably the context of a counselling relationship. I realize the challenging reality of Kearney's assertion that:

> [T]here is no politically neutral fence available for us to sit on, and that our attempts to do so have the consequence (intended or not) of supporting the existing political system. When we try to be politically neutral, not only do we end up by being 'conservative' (in the sense of not challenging the status quo) but even more importantly we do this 'out of awareness', by default, and in this way we fail to take personal responsibility for the consequences of our actions or non-actions. (Kearney, 1996: 59)

She quotes Yalom's introduction to *A Way of Being* where he picks up on Rogers' challenge to school psychologists not only to treat those damaged by the educational system but to change the system (Rogers, 1980). As I conclude this chapter, this country is gearing up for general elections. I awoke this morning to the news that a mother of a child with autism has challenged the prime minister on live television about the government's inclusive education policy which she claims is under-resourced, excluding and not delivering 'what's on the packet' (F60). I hope Frederick hears about this news story and takes some hope from it that the issues he feels so passionately about are on the political agenda and that he is not alone. I am sad however, that individuals who have on-the-ground experiences of government policies, have to get to a state of desperation before their voices have the remotest chance of being heard.

I hope too that I have the courage, humility and discernment to keep taking these issues forward within the institution where I work as a counsellor, an advocate, an agent of social change, but above all, as a human being. However, as Frederick said to me in a recent discussion about this chapter the important question is: 'Who has the last word?'

REFERENCES

Bond, T (2004) An introduction to the ethical guidelines for researching counselling and psychotherapy. *Counselling and Psychotherapy Research, 4* (2), 4–9.

Chantler, K (2004) Double-edged sword: Power and person-centred counselling. In R Moodley, C Lago & A Talahite (eds) *Carl Rogers Counsels a Black Client* (pp. 116–29). Ross-on-Wye: PCCS Books.

Daly, T (2003) Acceptance, power and the velveteen rabbit. In S Keys (ed) *Idiosyncratic Person-Centred Therapy: From the personal to the universal* (pp. 17–36). Ross-on-Wye: PCCS Books.

Grant, B (1990) Principled and instrumental nondirectiveness in Person-Centered and Client-Centered Therapy. In *Person-Centered Review, 5* (1), 77–88. Reprinted in DJ Cain (ed) (2002) *Classics in the Person-Centered Approach* (pp. 371–6). Ross-on-Wye: PCCS Books.

Hawkins, J (2002) *Voices of the Voiceless: Person-centred approaches and people with learning difficulties.* Ross-on-Wye: PCCS Books.

Hill, M & Keys, S (2006) Longing in practice: Prayer and therapy. In J Moore and C Purton (eds) *Spirituality and Counselling: Experiential and theoretical perspectives* (pp. 180–9). Ross-on-Wye: PCCS Books.

Kearney, A (1996) *Counselling, Class & Politics: Undeclared influences in therapy.* Ross-on-Wye: PCCS Books.

Keys, S (2003a) Making counselling accessible to all. In *AUCC Journal*, Winter 2003, 45–6.

Keys, S (ed) (2003b) *Idiosyncratic Person-Centred Therapy: From the personal to the universal.* Ross-on-Wye: PCCS Books.

MacMillan, K (1996) Giving voice: The participant takes issue. In S Wilkinson and C Kitzinger (eds) *Representing the Other: A feminism and psychology reader* (pp. 141–6). London: Sage.

Proctor, G (2002) *The Dynamics of Power in Psychotherapy: Ethics, politics and practice.* Ross-on-Wye: PCCS Books.

Rogers, CR (1961) *On Becoming a Person.* Boston: Houghton Mifflin.

Rogers, CR (1980) *A Way of Being.* Boston: Houghton Mifflin.

Schmid, PF (2001) Acknowledgement: the art of responding. Dialogical and ethical perspectives on the challenge of unconditional relationships in therapy and beyond. In J Bozarth and P Wilkins (eds) *Rogers' Therapeutic Conditions: Evolution, theory and practice, Vol 3 Unconditional Positive Regard* (pp. 49–64). Ross-on-Wye: PCCS Books.

Sinason, V (1992) *Mental Handicap and the Human Condition: New approaches from the Tavistock.* London: Free Association Books.

Thorne, B (2002) *The Mystical Power of Person-Centred Therapy. Hope beyond despair.* London: Whurr Publishers.

Wilkinson, S & Kitzinger, C (eds) (1996) *Representing the Other: A feminism and psychology reader.* London: Sage.

Yalom, ID (1980) Introduction. In CR Rogers *A Way of Being* (pp. vii—xiii). Boston: Houghton Mifflin.

Chapter 17

UNVEILING THE UNSPOKEN: WORKING TRANSPARENTLY WITH SOUTH ASIAN COMMUNITIES

KAMER SHOAIB

INTRODUCTION AND BACKGROUND

When I was approached to write this chapter, I wondered how I, a second-generation, working-class, British-born Muslim female of Kashmiri descent, could convey the value of a person-centred way of working with individuals who are substantially culturally different from oneself. Although twenty years of professional and personal life experiences have significantly informed my therapeutic practice, the most significant influence on my development as a therapist has been my knowledge of economic factors, class, cultural, religious and social attitudes surrounding such communities.

Working as a 'person-centred' therapist with clients from different cultural backgrounds has raised numerous issues. In particular I have struggled with the inappropriate use of Eurocentric models, which are neither visible nor even acknowledged as part of the therapeutic process when working with such clients. However, working in a person-centred framework means *being with* the client from their viewpoint, allowing the flexibility of connecting with the client, their experiences and their world—but how, and in what context this is applied, is the crucial issue.

Terminology also remains problematic—not only has terminology changed with time, but the meanings of words which encompass a variety of political, social, racial and ethnic meanings have also changed. In this chapter I will not define terminology except to describe the ethnicity of 'South Asian', a term which refers to people who themselves, or their ancestors, have originated from the geographical areas of Pakistan, particularly Azad Kashmir.

WHAT LED ME TO WHERE I AM

In the late eighties I was employed as a welfare rights advisor and initially the service experienced a low uptake, even though it was conveniently located in the heart of a large South Asian community. The situation changed within four weeks of me taking over the post from a White male. The surgeries became immensely popular; South Asian people, mainly originating from the Indian subcontinent, especially women, would attend the surgeries initially for benefit advice but then would return regularly not just for benefit advice. Certain obstacles that had hindered access were removed; it was an open surgery and no referral was necessary. I was a female, I spoke their language and I had an understanding of their cultures. These were all important factors especially for first and second generation South Asian women—some did not speak English, some were dependant on others, and still more were oppressed in their homes and their extended families—they did not have to 'educate' me about their culture and family systems.

Most important it was confidential service, where trust could be established, and people could talk about a variety of issues which were causing them psychological distress ('*parshani*'). Many times I would hear the expression '*mari sir ne undar vazan heh*' (inside my head I have a weight) or they would talk about physiological symptoms they were experiencing, that the GP had given them medication for because they said '*meh sohch niya*' (I'm thinking). With hindsight I realize that, as a welfare rights advisor, I was using the core conditions, but not within the specific therapeutic contract and boundaries I do now as a counsellor.

What was being highlighted in this service were the numerous social, cultural, economic and political barriers that existed for (mainly) British South Asian clients living in Britain. Nevertheless, for people who accessed it, their benefit needs were met, there was accessible information, awareness of available support relating to their issues, and an access point that channelled them into other services. Two domains of person-centeredness became apparent, both of which inform my current practice when working with South Asian clients. First is the practical element (the way the service is run) which attends to external issues that impact on a client and secondly the therapeutic element (the way the therapeutic relationship is enacted) which attends to internal issues.

RACE, CULTURE AND ETHNICITY

We live in a dynamic and evolving multi-ethnic, multiracial, and multicultural multi-faith society. It may appear that races and cultures are merging, and that we are practically neighbours as we rub shoulders via films, fashion, music, telecommunications media, Internet and television. Yet therapists may find themselves working with people whose race, ethnicity and culture are substantially different from their own. Academic training in psychotherapy is supposedly designed to incorporate and promote the ethic of equality, but we find there is limited information or guidance available to professionals (Billington et al., 1998).

Fernando (1991) refers to *race* as grouping people together based according to their biological and physical characteristics—most predominantly the colour of skin. He defines *culture* as the ways of thinking and feeling of groups of people; their beliefs, traditions, values and their social habits—a complex framework of interaction between an individual, their social groups and their societal environment, with each element of this interactive process impacting on or influencing others. Attempting to predict or draw assumptions about an individual's cultural context purely from knowledge gained through books or listings of behaviours or even from people of the same cultural group as the subject may lead to false conclusions.

Fernando (1991) describes *ethnicity* as a sense of belonging, noting that ethnic identity is not static and may change with age, time and life cycle stage. Furthermore, Wallman (1979) suggests that ethnicities and cultures are not internal possessions, but *ongoing* psychosocial processes that emerge out of larger socio-historic processes. In addition, my own experiences in therapeutic relationships suggest that although a person can lean more towards one core identity, equally they can construct and reconstruct multiple identities that are not fixed but adjust and change in the different social contexts the person moves in.

PRESENTING SOCIAL AND POLITICAL FACTORS

The socio-economic factors and environmental pressures facing people in lower classes lead to an increase in incidence of psychological distress (Modood et al., 1997). Kearney (1996) asserts that person-centred therapy should include awareness and understanding of the social constraints on people's lives. Although Asian families experience the same factors as their host culture, i.e. increased demands, past history of abuse, relationship issues in their lives, differences between the genders and between the generations (Kohen, 2000), these factors are then compounded by a series of other issues, which are different across all communities. These include various forms of racism, and inadequate recognition and understanding of the complexities of, for example, language, culture, religious differences and inter-generational conflict that can contribute to psychological distress.

Migration can be a cause of psychological distress in itself—affecting an individual's perception of their own ethnicity. Frustration, loneliness, the inevitable clash of values, problems integrating and the processes involved in settling into a new country all contribute. Some literature asserts that these difficulties are usually regarded as problems of adaptation and not as mental illness. This process of adaptation—termed 'acculturation' (Berry et al., 1992)—is a multidimensional, psychosocial phenomenon that occurs *in* the individuals as a result of their interaction with a new culture (usually the majority culture).

It is important to recognize the many effects of acculturation and ethnic identity when working with an individual from a minority group, as a number of symptoms can be attributed to these factors. In addition, the degree of acculturation is associated with styles of expressing distress, experiences and expectations of services. Duration of residence in the UK (first, second, generation etc.), whether born in the UK or not, the circumstances of entry, (refugee, political asylum, *Mangetar* (visa obtained through marriage), torture victim), attitudes towards statutory services, and quality of life in the UK, will all colour the style of presentation of symptoms and may even determine the type of issue and symptom content (e.g. post-traumatic stress disorder if they are a torture victim). Furthermore it must be remembered that whilst cultures are not static and the process of acculturation is not static, both individuals and communities hold on to cultural and community values from their homeland, which might stay static to a point, even though in their homeland cultural attitudes may have moved on.

LANGUAGE, CONCEPTUALIZATION AND IDIOMS OF DISTRESS

Language and communication are also variables that can hinder understanding both outside and inside the therapeutic relationship, and affect the accessibility of services (Shoaib, 2001). There is scant information to help us understand how psychological distress may be differently perceived and expressed *specifically* in South Asian groups, and consequently still less is known about how professionals interpret these communications. In holding a universal meaning of distress, a therapist may neglect the web of meanings that an issue has for a particular sufferer in a particular culture.

One explanation could be that GPs fail to recognize psychological distress in ethnic minority clients (Bhui, Christie & Bhugra, 1995). However it has been said that counselling and psychotherapy are not appropriate for minority groups because of their lack of 'verbal facility' or the ability to understand and 'work through' their problems in a way that accords with the Eurocentric psychological models.

Individuals are reluctant to reveal their religious and or spiritual beliefs since often they are dismissed, or seen as a symptom of mental health or can even lead to being sectioned under the Mental Health Act (Ghafoor, 2002). Therapists must actively assume responsibility in looking for common language, and more crucially, must learn about their client's belief systems or the problems that culturally different clients face in communicating their emotional distress in another language (Kearney, 1996). They must reach out to understand how, for example, South Asian clients conceptualize and express their distress. Understanding the language used by the client enables the therapist to enter their internal frame of reference. As conceptions of distress (illness, discomforts, disturbances, diseases) and their presentation are socio-cultural in origin—and specific to particular groups and situations—they are unlikely to be similarly interpreted across cultures and ethnicities.

There are many general references to the way in which psychological distress may be differently expressed in different ethnic groups by describing emotions using physiological metaphors, similes, evocative phrases and analogies (Krause,

1989; Fenton & Sadiq-Sangster, 1996; Shaikh & Reading, 1999). South Asian women were found to describe and express their feelings according to *how* they experienced them, describing emotions in a physiological or in a metaphorical way (Shoaib, 2001). South Asian people have many words for love and Western society has a huge vocabulary for the various shades of mental ill health and associated processes. The language of emotion is very rich in many Asian languages, for example Urdu and Bengali are both languages of great love poetry. Clients may simply make use of the vast number of well-worn phrases that exist in all languages to describe their feelings and descriptions of emotionalism. As the main Asian languages are littered with references to the heart, head and pulse, the meaning of many such phrases can be far from transparent.

When Asian clients present their emotional problems in physiological terms, a Eurocentric therapist may label their problems 'psychosomatic'. However the terms 'psychosomatic' or 'somatization' in the Western health belief system have negative connotations inasmuch as they refer to physical symptoms not fully explained by a general medical condition. Somatization is often used to argue that such communities lack the adequate linguistic or psychological sophistication to communicate their feelings; therefore they somatize their distress (Raleigh, 1995; Chaturvedi & Venugopal, 2001; Green, 2001). In fact it is only a different idiom to convey emotions, so Asian mental health or emotional issues are best understood in accordance with Asian health belief systems in which mind, body and soul are connected, and may be 'heart-orientated' (Malik, 2000). As a therapist one needs to be aware when 'being with' an individual, you may be working with a client surrounded by family, culture and society, around which orbits the person's spiritual world.

> Complicated personal, cultural and social meaning complexes may fashion the way in which emotion is expressed through behaviour; and the socio-cultural context in which an emotion is felt and expressed may affect the outcome. Not only that, but emotions may be suppressed, distorted or exaggerated for psychological, social or cultural reasons; and some feelings, or the way they are expressed, may be designated as illness. (Fernando, 1991: 101)

Along with others, I argue that quality of communication and rapport between therapist and client is heavily dependent on the therapist's understanding of the patient's cultural idioms and his or her interpretation of them as culture plays a major part in the idiomatic expression of distress (Lemert, 1997). The potential gap in understanding can be bridged by knowledge. However, the expression of emotion and the diverse ways of coping with distress cannot adequately be dealt with by listing behaviour patterns of each culture since cultures are not static.

> A culturally skilled counsellor is one who is *actively* in the process of becoming aware of his or her own assumptions about human behaviour, values, biases, preconceived notions, personal limitations, and so forth. (Sue & Sue, 1990: 47)

Cultural differences between client and therapist are inevitable in a multicultural society. Where the cultural distance between client and therapist differs even more because of differing language, customs, religion, health beliefs and value systems, the potential for misunderstanding in the communication of distress is increased. Furthermore we need to recognize that the majority of our professional frameworks are supported by beliefs and practices of Western society. Influenced by Eurocentric professional and academic institutions which regulate training, the possibilities for poor practice are manifold.

POWER AND CONTROL STRUCTURES WITHIN CULTURE, GENDER AND SOCIETY

The South Asian community can operate as a cohesive force, conditioning, sanctioning and reinforcing the concepts of honour and shame (honour being integral to maintaining patriarchy) which prevail amongst South Asian families regardless of religion, caste and class. The existence of notions such as '*izzat*' (honour) and '*sharam*' (shame) can be used as powerful ideological weapons (Crescent Life, 2003), both playing a pivotal role in policing, controlling and containing women's behaviours and lifestyle, particularly their sexuality (Southall Black Sisters, 2004; Shoaib, 2004). Ironically an illusion of respectability, status and reputation is created as women are considered to be the upholders of this 'system'.

Once tainted, shame can stay with the family for generations (Adams, 1998). The fear of hostility, loneliness, lack of support and general ostracization is intense. For example, the stigma of divorce—being isolated and/or rejected from their own family, relatives and the wider community—is a terrible prospect for an Asian woman. She may have never lived on her own and will be ill-prepared practically, emotionally and psychologically. Responses to the dishonour of the family vary. In most cases women are rejected and blamed; this can have detrimental emotional and psychological effects on the woman. In addition, there are societal oppressions, including fear of racial discrimination which can pressurize the woman into staying.

As a result of these many factors, Asian women may choose to stay silent and internalize issues (Shoaib 2001), thus experiencing psychological and physiological symptoms. Alternatively they may hide the abuse from society, 'live with it', and hope that 'one day things will get better' (Shoaib, 2001). Shoaib (2004) stresses that these factors could make some individuals more vulnerable to long-term psychological and emotional effects, whilst others would describe this as kismet (fate), and many may not know the protocols to follow if they are a victim of domestic violence. Having said that, some women feel liberated and self-empowered after a process of rehabilitation; some even resume links with their families after a gap (Shaikh & Reading, 1999).

RACE AND GENDER POWER STRUCTURES

In addition to oppression inside the family, Almeida et al. (1998) refer to society's invisible veils (Sue & Sue, 1999) of homophobia, gender and racism that orbit around the interior oppressions of relationships; forces that control and dictate individual lives. The impact of social intolerance, gender isolation within cultures and the legal system are important factors that should not be overlooked.

With regard to social control, Pilgrim (1983) stresses that doctors exercise power and control in the National Health Service, and it could be said that professionals, including therapists, provide and execute gatekeeper roles in the distribution of society's material and social resource.

Nearly all the South Asian women interviewed in my study did want to access counselling (Shoaib, 2001). However lack of knowledge, and language and communication barriers prevented accessibility and several professionals, including GPs, believed that their services were not 'appropriate'. Although patients from this group are more likely to approach their GPs, key findings from two national health surveys (Modood et al., 1997; Bajekal, et al., 2001) indicate that these groups may also be more prone to suffer from psychiatric illness. Findings also suggest (Shoaib, 2001) that there was a preference by some Asian male GPs to promote cognitive therapies, rather than person-centred therapies, as these seemed less threatening in the wider cultural context.

Like GPs, therapists are in positions of professional power and may have understanding and knowledge that can be shared with the client of what is accessible and available and how help can be channelled, including obstacles that may be encountered. Some may ask whether this is 'therapy proper', but I argue it is person-centred practicality and it does promote client autonomy. Therefore I do exercise this position of power in the interest of the client *with the* client so that they are able to lead a more resourceful life.

A mature Asian female client, who has been subjected to domestic violence from her partner and extended family, pointed out that since coming to the UK in the early 1960s she had approached GPs several times (all of whom had been Asian males) and 'begged' for help but not received any until her youngest child got married and left home. Some Asian communities have a great respect for health professionals to the extent that they will not confront, disagree, conflict or point out problems they are facing. These factors are woven in subtle omnipresent threads for all South Asians but more so for women who are oppressed and simultaneously trapped at different levels. The dynamics of power in primary health care in Asian communities reveal not so much power dynamics of class or race, but simply the power over, and dominance of, women. Beneath the professional cloak of the healthcare professional, an Asian male heart still beats.

INDIVIDUALISM/COMMUNALISM

The individualism associated with Western society stresses the person's individuality thus omitting family and community, whereas a distinguishing feature of South Asian cultures is communalism/collectivism (Palmer & Laungani, 1999). In counselling approaches where there is an emphasis on the self it is important to place the self within the wider context of the client's world: the culture of the family, the culture of their community, their area, the town in which they live and so on. Layered over this are the influences of gender, sexual orientation, class, religion, status, race, each with its impact on the client—how they experience themselves and how they must be understood. Typically, issues of belonging, conformity and about 'the unspoken' find their way into the session. In fact, more often than not, when I am 'with' a South Asian client I know many a time we are not alone in the room—we have the psychological presence of family and community in the room with us.

IMPLICATIONS AND CHALLENGES FOR PERSON-CENTRED THERAPISTS WORKING WITH SOUTH ASIAN COMMUNITIES

In his overall hypothesis Rogers says the following:

> If I can provide a certain type of relationship, the other person will discover within himself the capacity to use that relationship for growth, change and personal development. (Rogers, 1967: 33)

The key in Rogers' hypothesis is the term 'a certain type of relationship'. The core conditions are present from the first meeting if psychological contact is made. With South Asian clients initially, it would mean a person-centred way of being a gatekeeper/advocate and meeting practical needs whilst simultaneously establishing the therapeutic relationship. Some might say that this is not part of therapy as such, however in the early stages some clients may need a more direct approach until they familiarize themselves with the process.

By 'being with the person' the client feels heard and understood but the therapist is in a position to 'initiate constructive personality change' not just by being the incubator but also by being practically active with the client, being a funnel and gatekeeper through which individuals can pass, connect with, and access wider opportunities. This might involve giving information on services, making referrals, helping with childcare arrangements so that they can attend sessions, etc. Counselling professionals are in positions of power by virtue of their knowledge of services and support, and as gatekeepers to accessing other support mechanisms and opportunities.

Some South Asian clients do not respond as well to a non-directive approach which focuses on feelings and the quest for self-actualization. They may prefer a logical, rational and structured approach (Sue & Sue, 1999), especially if their understanding of psychological distress is closely entwined around their religious and spiritual beliefs. Some of these beliefs focus on the internal world whereas others place the spiritual or healing factors external to them. Here a more direct approach could incorporate exploration of spiritual routes, consideration and involvement of a religious framework which might include sources of strength such as activities, recitations, reframing thoughts by looking at role models within their faith or other dimensions that tune into and underpin that client's belief system.

To be person-centred culturally skilled therapists we need actively and regularly to examine our own values and beliefs and have an awareness and understanding of our own internalized attitudes and ideologies, academically, culturally, racially and historically. Only through such knowledge and awareness as therapists will we be able to have a sense of our effect upon others as well as access to an understanding of the dynamic process that unfolds between ourselves and our clients. Without an understanding of self, 'we will neither be congruent nor accurately able to understand the way others see themselves' (Proctor, 2004: 132).

Therapists can enable clients to release blocked energies, not just by creating an environment *in* the therapeutic relationship but by understanding and applying our power-in-authority to help optimize resources that can be available to client. This provides the social opportunities for the client to maximize their potential and take more control and responsibility for the own lives from their own sources of reference. It is clear that for some clients it is easier to go with those they know where there is shared history or areas that are familiar where they find a safe place and a sense of belonging. However there is no assurance that there can be a successful outcome for the client working with a therapist from a mutual cultural background as the counter issue is that it can create collusion. So 'difference within culture' is at least as important as 'difference between cultures' (Lawton & Feltham, 2000).

AN ETHICAL DILEMMA

Person-centred therapy, working in the world of the client, can easily touch on oppressions and inequalities. I find from my experiences of working with South Asian clients that although there can be short-term internal change in the individual, we then come to a glass ceiling, where the external factors shaped by socio-cultural or political factors oppress the person and they feel trapped. In these instances South Asian clients may need access to long-term counselling.

This can pose a number of challenges for a therapist who works in time-limited therapeutic settings for an organization or where there are limited resources, especially if the client has not worked through their issues in a short space of time. With White clients and those who speak English or have no preference regarding the cultural background of the therapist, it is more likely that there will be long-term counselling services available. My ethical dilemma is that unless there is long-term support available I am reluctant to 'open their hearts' and leave them on the table after a few sessions. When initial assessment indicates that long-term work is necessary, but support unavailable, I sometimes reluctantly turn clients away. I believe that it can do more harm than good, bringing issues into awareness and leaving the client exposed, unresolved and sometimes suicidal.

CONCLUSION

I agree with Jordan (1997) when she stated that anyone who wrote about therapy should 'say what is actually happening in the therapy relationship, not what theory prescribes or what sounds smart or clever or theoretically formed', however I would add that what orbits around the therapy is also of relevance and may at times be more important. One does not have to be a cultural *expert* to work with forms of difference as the type of relationship is primarily determined by the attitudes and skills of the therapist, but in order to be more effective and competent it is beneficial to have an understanding of the client's world as well as acknowledging and valuing their world and those differences.

My experiences of working with South Asian communities have informed my therapeutic practice whilst remaining grounded in person-centered ways of working. I find that it is sometimes not enough just to offer the core conditions but that I have to draw on concepts that underpin client's belief systems which take me outside the realms of the Western world and Western thinking.

I have also found that over time I am becoming more in tune with how power and oppression are represented at different levels in relationships, in communities and in society especially when the impact of these issues and resulting conflict feed into the core of the self structure. More and more I find it comes in guises that are best described as microscopic and can change shape and form according to the environment. Yet these processes are omnipresent, unspoken and invisible. These processes insidiously harm individuals who are then more susceptible to further long-term psychological and emotional damage.

Professionals, services and society collude and contribute to the very oppressions which cause these long-term effects, by promoting the idea that if individuals do not 'fit the mould' then the problem lies with and in the individual, not the model, professional or service. The person-centred therapist has to identify and locate factors outside of the individual client in order to be effective in these circumstances.

REFERENCES

Adams, CE (1998) Asian survivors of domestic violence. *British Journal of Criminology, 36,* 34–41.

Almeida, R, Messineo, T, Woods, R & Front, R (1998) The cultural context model. *Journal of Family Practice, 23,* 426–7.

Bajekal, M, Primatesta, P & Prior, G (eds) (2001) *Health Survey for England.* Department of Health.

Berry, JW, Poortinga, YH, Segall, MH & Dasen, PR (1992) *Cross-Cultural Psychology.* New York: Cambridge University Press.

Billington, R, Hockey, J & Strawbridge, S (1998) *Exploring Self and Society.* London: Macmillan Press.

Bhui K, Christie Y & Bhugra D (1995) The essential elements of culturally sensitive psychiatric services. *International Journal of Social Psychiatry, 41* (4), 242–56.

Crescent Life (2003) Issues of Domestic Violence [Online], Available from <www.crescentlife.com/psychissues/domesticviolence.html> Accessed 12/06/03.

Chaturvedi, SK & Venugopal, D (2001) *Somatisation and Somatic Neurosis—Cross Cultural Variations.* Department of Psychiatry, National Institute of Mental Health and Neurosciences, Bangalore, India <www.priory.com/neuro.htm>.

Department of Health (2004) *Organising and Delivering Psychological Therapies.* (July 2004) Department of Health.

Fenton, S & Sadiq-Sangster, A (1996) Culture, relativism and the expression of mental distress: South Asian women in Britain. *Sociology of Health and Illness, 18,* (1), 66–85.

Fernando, S (1991) *Mental Health, Race and Culture.* Hampshire: Macmillan Press.

Ghafoor, R (2002) *Mental Health Information Need of Black and Ethnic Communities in Central Manchester.* Manchester Health Promotion Specialist Service, Central Manchester NHS Primary Care Trust and Manchester Race and Health Forum.

Green, B (2001) *Neurotic Disorders and Somatisation* (14/3/01) Consultant in Psychological Medicine, Halton Hospital, Runcorn, Cheshire, UK <www.priory.com/neuro.htm>.

Jordan, JV (1997) Relational development: Therapeutic implications of empathy and shame. In JV Jorden (ed) *Women's Growth in Diversity: More writings from the Stone Center, New York* (pp. 138–61). New York: Guilford Press.

Kearney, A (1996) *Counselling, Class and Politics: Undeclared influences in therapy.* Ross-on-Wye: PCCS Books.

Kohen, D (2000) *Women and Mental Health.* London: Routledge.

Krause, I-B (1989) Sinking heart: A Punjabi communication of distress. *Social Science and Medicine, 29* (4), 563–75.

Lawton, B & Feltham, C (2000) *Taking Supervision Forward: Enquiries and trend in counselling and psychotherapy.* London: Sage.

Lemert, C (1997) *Social Things: An introduction to the sociological life.* Lanham, MD: Rowman

& Littlefield Publishers, Inc.

Malik, R (2000) Culture and Emotions: Depression among Pakistanis. In C Squire (ed) *Culture and Psychology* (pp. 147–162). London: Routledge

Modood, T, Berthoud, R, Lakey, J, Nazroo, J, Smith, P, Virdee, S & Beishon, S (1997) *Ethnic Minorities in Britain: Diversity and disadvantage. Fourth National Survey of Ethnic Minorites*. London: Policy Studies Institute.

Palmer, S & Laungani, P (1999) *Counselling in a Multicultural Society*. London: Sage.

Pilgrim, D (1983) Politics, psychology and psychiatry. In D Pilgrim (ed) *Psychology and Psychotherapy: Current trends and issues* (pp. 121–38). London: Routledge & Kegan Paul.

Proctor, G (2004) *Encountering Feminism: Intersections between feminism and the person-centred approach*. Ross-on-Wye: PCCS Books.

Raleigh, SV (1995) *Mental Health in Black and Minority Ethnic People: The fundamental facts*. London: The Mental Health Foundation.

Rogers, CR (1967) *On Becoming a Person: A therapist's view of psychotherapy*. London: Constable.

Shaikh, Z & Reading, J (1999) *Between Two Cultures: Effective counselling for Asian people with mental health and addiction problems*. Middlesex: EACH.

Shoaib, K (2001) Kashmiri women's perceptions of their emotional and psychological needs and their access to talking therapies. Unpublished thesis, Liverpool John Moores University.

Shoaib, S (2004) Professional South Asian women's perceptions of causes, effects and service issues on domestic violence. Unpublished dissertation: University of Salford.

Southall Black Sisters (2004) *Domestic Violence and Asian Women: A collection of reports and briefings*. London: Southall Black Sisters.

Sue, DW and Sue, D (1990) *Counselling the Culturally Different* (1st edn). New York: John Wiley and Sons, Inc.

Sue, DW and Sue, D (1999) *Counselling the Culturally Different* (3rd edn). New York: John Wiley and Sons, Inc.

Wallman, S (1979) *Ethnicity at Work*. London: Macmillan.

Chapter 18

PERSON-CENTRED THERAPY, CULTURE AND RACISM: PERSONAL DISCOVERIES AND ADAPTATIONS

Indu Khurana

I have been working with the person-centred approach for some eight or nine years, and consciously with issues of culture for the last five or six. Over the course of these years my use of the person-centred approach has moved from aspiring to be completely faithful to what I believed to be the prescribed theory, to moving towards an approach that feels more person-centred in a practical way, for me.

In keeping with Rogers' thinking, the uniqueness of each relationship is paramount in my work. I find it important to develop a strong relationship based on trust and honesty, over time with my client. Within that relationship, as the therapist, I am as genuinely myself as I can be. Often when working with clients from differing cultures, I have found that practice following from what I take to be a narrow view of person-centred theory is not sufficient. I have increasingly realized that the core conditions had themselves started to become a condition of worth for me and I had struggled to fit into them.

In my work, I repeatedly encounter clients from all age groups and backgrounds, who want to be heard and understood and acknowledged but then want something more. This is sometimes tied in with the fact that today's society is fast-paced and results-focused. Consequently I have found that the clients' organismic self has been stifled to such a degree that they are completely disconnected from any experience of it. This translates in reality to a situation where the client has no 'knowledge' of how to break cycles of behaviour, or indeed to be in touch with their true feelings. Whilst this sometimes happens, in accordance with theory, because of internalized conditions of worth and introjected self-concepts, at other times it is the result of ethnic culture that emphasizes authority, and where 'respect' has a different meaning than in Western Anglo-American culture. The result is a person who in their culture of origin is deemed acceptable, but feels at odds within mainstream British culture. When they take up therapy, they experience a reinforcement of mainstream Anglo-American thinking underlying most therapeutic approaches, i.e. the individual is more important than the collective, and elders and tradition are not held in high esteem.

In contrast, the client may come from a culture where authority is held in the highest esteem and so comes looking for help in a manner that assumes, indeed acknowledges, the authority of the therapist and *requires* the therapist to give them advice and suggestions. As a person-centred therapist, I can choose to not take this mantle of authority that is offered. But I have found that this is a very 'foreign' way of being for many people from a variety of cultures and backgrounds. Clients have struggled so much with this alien way of being that they have often found therapy unhelpful or useless and have walked away without any feeling of assistance or relief or having been 'met'.

Initially I had frequent personal tussles with this particular 'more' that my clients demanded from me. I thought this was a sign that the client was perhaps not ready for therapy or that they were not ready for the person-centred approach. However, I came to think that in the twenty-first century, being listened to, understood, accepted, and allowed to make one's own decisions are still not familiar feelings for many people. I found they often could not cope with having such a different climate (as advocated by Rogers), since this is in direct contrast to what they know and are familiar with from their native culture. They find this contrast at the least puzzling, and sometimes stark and threatening.

As a consequence, I began to feel that perhaps I was being too rigid with my application of the person-centred approach and was trying to make the person fit the theory rather than working with the individual in front of me and with their needs. I was behaving as if I was the expert and knew better than they that this approach and my application of it was best for them—I was claiming to know better than they, what was right for them. Certainly this was how I felt I came across in my *actions*, in contrast to my *belief* that they were their own experts and I was simply the person facilitating their growth and access to their own internal resources.

Taking this into consideration, I gradually adapted my practice and now try to weave the core conditions of the person-centred approach in and around the person sitting in front of me. This means I am different with each client, adaptable to the point that sometimes I will accept the role of authority that they assign to me. But in doing so, I try to amend it so that it fits in with my understanding of the person-centred approach. So I might initially offer a different way of looking at things or a creative method in response to their request. I believe this to be an intuitive way of working in greater harmony with both my client and myself, whilst also hearing my client in their plight.

I have had to devise a way of working that initially uses a combination of the person-centred approach with a more proactive element blended in to each session depending upon the client's needs. In this way of working, the passing over of power and control back to the client has to be a gradual process and can only occur over time in direct correlation to the growth and expansion of their organismic self. Hand-in-hand their locus of evaluation becomes progressively more internalized: throughout this process, I have faith that the client will sense and trust their actualizing tendency.

Putting this process into words makes it sound more fixed and 'programmed' than it is in practice, but it allows the client and myself to look at their goals then work towards achieving these in a practical way, attuned to their cultural expectations. Alongside this we examine the psychological impact of such actions and goals including any fears that may be out of awareness. The client can then develop concrete strategies. All along the way however, the client is offered the core conditions of empathy, congruence and unconditional positive regard.

In addition I consciously take into account the client's culture by asking about their culture and how it might impact the process we are examining. I also try to *demonstrate* my understanding that their culture as well as their social environment will have an impact on the process, and I encourage them to become aware of such factors. We work in a flexible way, bending in the wind of the client's changing needs; I am thus modelling for them how to be more flexible in themselves in their circumstances.

I find this a more holistic way of working, helping me to be open and aware of the social and organizational contexts, the community as well as the individual. This can entail the utilization of other tools to elicit the qualities Rogers talked about in his theory but did not address in a practical way. These can include artwork, play work, and visualizations.

SUMMARY

The client's self-worth increases gradually throughout the process because the practical and strategic elements are not used directively, but offered as ideas to consider and amend as appropriate and only to be used if the client wishes to. The client is still in control but does not feel alone in the process, because there is proactive interaction with another human being. When a person has been starved of the ability to think creatively about their own lives and situations they may have no knowledge of a range of opportunities that might help them. Gradually I pass the baton back to them as they become more confident in their actualizing tendency and organismic self, so they learn to listen and trust themselves and their processes. The locus of evaluation, whilst starting off external gradually becomes internal as they increasingly clearly and overtly take charge of their own decision-making process. Their sense of empowerment can be visibly seen to increase.

When a client looks expectantly at me for direction, I can explain or even 'demonstrate' the person-centred theory in action as much as I want, but they want more from me. This very gentle way of meandering through their process using a modified person-centred approach—modified to fit their needs—feels more substantial for them and the client is more likely to return to sessions and find value in the relationship.

Chapter 19

WHITE COUNSELLOR RACIAL IDENTITY: THE UNACKNOWLEDGED, UNKNOWN, UNAWARE ASPECT OF SELF IN RELATIONSHIP

CoLIN LAGO AND SHEILA HAUGH

how disappointing

If we examine critically the traditional role of the university in the pursuit of truth and the sharing of knowledge and information, it is painfully clear that biases that uphold and maintain white supremacy, imperialism, sexism and racism have distorted education so that it is no longer about the practice of freedom. (hooks, 1994: 29)

The power of silence is so massive ... there is a value in calling these 'Black issues' because it is a re-prioritizing something, highlighting the fact that everything taught are White issues, we don't actually say that, we just call it theory and practice. We don't say everything we are talking about is White, because it's invisible. (From a lecturer interviewed in Isha McKenzie-Mavinga's (2005) Doctoral Dissertation 'Understanding Black Issues in Counsellor Training')

INTRODUCTION

During the last decades of the twentieth century, serious concern emerged on both sides of the Atlantic to ensure that sensitivity and efficacy of therapeutic delivery within mixed 'race', culture, and ethnicity dyads, (where client and counsellor originate from differing backgrounds) was addressed in practice. Several research efforts and subsequent publications emerged in the United States on this topic, many of which travelled well, conceptually speaking, to the multiracial, multicultural situation in Britain. (See e.g. Pope-Davis & Coleman, 1997; Pedersen, 1987; Sue, 1981; Lago & Thompson, 1996; D'Ardenne & Mahtani, 1989; Eleftheriadou, 1994.)

Reflecting, inevitably, national aspirations towards equality of opportunity in all arenas of socio-cultural activity, (e.g. health, education, the law, employment, etc.) counselling/psychotherapy qualification and continuing professional development courses began to address such issues, first from a perspective of 'multiculturalism', the mode in currency during the late 1970s. Later developments and emphases withi appreciation and respe such as racism, discrimi these were replicated via th in focus led to the emerg 1980s. arena shifted from this position of cultural knowledgement and incorporation of subjects d power differentials within society and how l and professional organs of the state. This shift of anti-racist policies and practices during the

Early initiatives by the ritish Association for Counselling (now British Association for Counselling d Psychotherapy) included the establishment of the Race and Cultural Education (RACE) subcommittee, (later to become the RACE division) to stimulate, advise and offer post-qualification training within this field of application. From this caucus of committed practitioners and their activities came the formal adoption and implementation of ethical guidelines in relation to the delivery of therapy in this 'multicultural' arena. During the same period, (in the 80s and 90s) Sue et al. (1992) worked on and then published a set of 'multicultural counselling competencies' for the Professional Standards Committee of the American Association for Multicultural Counseling and Development. These were published simultaneously in two leading professional journals, a unique cooperation to ensure a widespread dissemination of the ideas. (These competencies are listed in tabular form in Lago, 2006: 124–5.)

During these more recent phases of development within the therapeutic field on both sides of the Atlantic, the awareness of 'power' and its connectedness to whiteness, both at an individual as well as societal level, and how it related to the 'diverse' counselling relationship, began to be explored. A complex emotional reaction often occurred within and emanated from White participants of training courses exploring these issues where they began to recognize, often for the first time, the enormity of the implications arising from this new awareness. Common reactions included feelings of guilt and sometimes denial, distortion, defensiveness and withdrawal. Buckley has more recently recorded these strong emotional responses within White therapists in her doctoral research (2004). Other generic research related to the 'anti-racist' training approaches popular at that time suggested that its effects were often contradictory and indeed did not achieve the desired outcomes (Pedersen et al., 2005). That is, in striving to facilitate participants' understandings of racism and its mechanisms, many participants retreated back into their formerly held views, finding this new awareness too painful and confronting of their existing attitudinal positions. This particular period of anti-racism training lasted only a few years and was soon followed by what some multicultural theorists consider to have been the rather more conservative decade of the 1990s.

Power is clearly still an issue as is the complex power of whiteness. How does being a therapist, (even if you are White?) differ from being a 'White-aware' therapist? How come practice suggests, and research reveals, that the issues of 'race', culture and ethnicity are frequently matters of concern and consideration within Black/White and Black/Black therapeutic relationships, yet so infrequently figure within White/White relationships, (Tuckwell, 2002)? White people clearly do not consider themselves as 'raced', that is, relative to other groups. Dyer (1997) and Bonnett (1999), amongst others, have drawn attention to this popular (and manifestly false) conception of whiteness as 'normal', the standard, humanity itself!

This 'blanket' unawareness frequently operates implicitly on training courses, causing great hurt and anxiety to Black trainees, already in the minority on the course as well as having few, if any, Black or aware White teaching staff for support. Recent research by Watson reveals the significant and disabling impact of unaware processes upon Black trainees (Watson, 2004).

The emergence in the USA of the cultural, racial and ethnic identity development models (during the last decades of the twentieth century) has provided a set of useful and detailed templates for exploring (one's own) identity in relation to other groups within society. (Lee, 2006, offers an updated synthesis of these models.) Though only researched within the American milieu, the ideas are stimulating both for members of 'minority" and 'majority' groups in other Western countries. Despite these developments, those within the majority group within society (i.e. White practitioners) frequently tend to be less, if not completely unaware of the impact of their relative 'socially constructed positionality' on minority groups.

This chapter, thus rooted in the above historical developmental phases, attempts to deconstruct the nature of 'whiteness' itself, how it operates through counsellors and their theories and practices in a manner that has potential significant impact upon therapeutic outcomes—yet which is often outside of awareness and beyond conscious control. Whiteness is neither neutral (an idea frequently postulated) nor an absence of 'something'. It has strong, all-pervading, determining and frequently harmful effects.

WHY UNDERSTANDING 'WHITENESS' MATTERS

> It would be hard to imagine writing a book about what it means to be White. Most White people don't consider themselves to be part of a race that needs examining. They are the natural order of things. Bonnett (1999: 200)

> Whiteness, as a set of normative cultural practices, is visible most clearly to those it definitively excludes and those to whom it does violence. Those who are housed securely within its borders usually do not examine it. Frankenberg (1993: 228)

Therapy is a social process (Lago & Smith, 2003; Tuckwell, 2002; Schmid, 2001). It therefore constitutes a location in which the larger society's dynamics are inevitably present within the attitudes, concerns, beliefs and behaviours of both participants in the interaction, the therapist and the client. Carter provides data, both from his studies of therapeutic dyads and from relationship type studies that suggest that a therapist's actions (i.e. intentions) and affects, perhaps because of their position of power, have a greater impact on the psychotherapy process than the client's reactions (Carter, 1995). These findings, Carter asserts, 'strongly indicate the importance of training a therapist to explore the meaning and significance of their own race and to understand how race influences perceptions of self and the client' (1995: 228).

If we shift our attention, momentarily, to the wider society, we will discover a very extensive range of research evidences that demonstrate unequivocally, consistent and disturbing patterns of discrimination towards various groups in society frequently described as 'diverse' and 'different.' (See e.g. Skellington & Morris, 1992; Troyna, 1981; Coker, 2001; Husband, 1982; van Dijk, 1993; Smith, 1977; Institute of Race Relations, 2002; McKenzie-Mavinga, 2005; Curtis, 2005, 2006; Phillips, 2006.) Given that these discriminatory practices have occurred right across the whole range of organizations, professions and organs within society, the psychotherapy/counselling profession cannot afford to either ignore these findings or repeat the mantra 'As carers and trained professionals, how could we be discriminatory or racist?' Such frequently cited and indeed genuinely felt (though profoundly uninformed) opinions expressed by psychiatric staff were strongly challenged as long ago as the early 70s by the book *Racism and Psychiatry* (Thomas & Sillen, 1972). Without attention to these ethnic inter and intra group phenomena in society and within self, therapists are in danger of repeating these discriminatory patterns.

In focusing attention on her understanding of how her whiteness had affected her life experiences, Peggy McIntosh listed forty-six special circumstances and conditions which 'she did not earn but which she had been made to feel were hers by birth, by citizenship and by virtue of being a conscientious law-abiding 'normal' person of good will' (McIntosh 1988: 5–9).

Amongst her statements appear the following:

> I can choose accommodation without fearing that people of my 'race' cannot get in or will be mistreated in the places I have chosen.
> I can be sure that if I need legal or medical help, my 'race' will not work against me.
> If my day, week or year is going badly, I need not ask of each negative episode or situation whether it has 'racial' overtones.
> I can do well in a challenging situation without being called a credit to my 'race'.
> I can turn on the television or open the front page of the newspaper and see people of my 'race' widely represented.

The sheer inequity of the above statements (and the remaining 41 in her original list) compared to the everyday experiences of 'non-White' people is shockingly obvious.

WHAT IS WHITENESS?

Decoding 'whiteness' has proved a challenging and elusive task, a point that is made time and again in the edited text *White Reign*, (Kincheloe et al., 1998). For example,

> Even though no one at this point really knows exactly what whiteness is, most observers agree that it is intimately involved with issues of power and power difference between white and non-white people. (Ibid.: 4)

> This collective white denial of privilege inhibits questions and public reflection on how being white may provide benefits. (Ibid.:15)

> One difficulty in studying the white self is that, until recently, it was an invisible and non-researched category, even difficult to name and not perceived as a distinctive racial identity. Even today, most white Americans either do not think about their whiteness at all or else think of it as a positive or neutral category. (Ibid.: 78, cited in Vera, et al., 1995: 296)

> White skin privilege and the advantages that accompany it are not necessarily obvious to those who are White and middle class. (Ibid.: 80)

An examination of 'whiteness' holds the potential for illumination and symbolic decoding of the skin colour as an identified identity within society alongside other identities. Whiteness frequently operates as a veil that conceals and thus disguises its essence. Whiteness is manifestly not just a blank sheet or a sphere of neutrality, as is often implied, but it clearly occupies a position in relation to others, and most often that position is one of relatively more societal power.

The relationship of whiteness to power is explicitly addressed within the working definition of 'diversity' that has been adopted by the British Association for Counselling and Psychotherapy (BACP, 2005). This document details groups within society that are deemed to constitute the 'advantaged/norm'. These include people who are 'White, male, heterosexual, able-bodied, and of working age'.

Substantial change will not occur until such time as the White majority group members in society fully recognize and appreciate the conditions and circumstances created for others by their present way of being. Studying whiteness is more than timely. This chapter invites readers to explore from what identity position within society they are living, looking and judging. In other words, continue to 'know thyself' and your many facets particularly (in relation to this chapter) your own sense of ethnic identity and your attitudes to those who are 'different' and 'diverse'.

SO WHAT IS IT TO BE WHITE?

Almost twenty years ago, with two other colleagues (Jean Clark and Shantu Watt), we ran an evening class at Leicester University (that was, incidentally, tied in as an option to the Diploma in Counselling being headed there by Michael Jacobs). An experiential exercise that we used to conduct there involved the exploration of the processes and stages of transition of oppressed groups from the earliest moments of sensing something was 'not quite right' through to striving for and achieving recognition of their felt injustices and thus gaining a sense of parity within society. For those within the dominant group, there is no problem, nor indeed even an inkling that there might be a problem! However, as the critique grows in the 'minority' group and begins to achieve recognition, the dominant group is then forced to begin to recognize the challenges (and hopefully accept the truths) as presented. The following is a prime example of such a transitional process.

Perhaps one of the most significant (and still ongoing) developments in social history during the last one hundred years or so is the evolution of the women's movement, from the early days of suffragettes seeking to obtain the vote, to seeking equal pay and promotion prospects and most importantly, equality of opportunity with men. This long-term process was strengthened and informed through the raising of consciousness through meeting, relating, uniting, talking and writing.

This societal transitional process, as indicated above, is fuelled by the cumulative experiences of injustice and powerlessness in members of the minority oppressed group, strong motivators to inspire and energize steps to change. By contrast, where might the energy come from to understand themselves from within groups who already occupy the power position? There is little to drive such understanding (no sense of oppression, injustice, moral outrage) other than perhaps amongst those few who are sensitive to minority group experiences. Certainly, the exercise referred to above revealed how those members of majority groups who become sensitive to the expressed needs of the minority group can become also subject to ridicule and alienation. Barriers to such exploration can therefore be most potent, violent and fear inducing.

WHITENESS, IDEOLOGY AND CONTRADICTIONS

... any person-centred consideration on what is 'healthy' or 'fully
functioning' must include a theory of social criticism. (Schmid, 2005:
76)

Whiteness often operates in a manner explained by Marx when he described the
function of ideologies as concealing the contradictions that lay beneath them.
From the perspective of whiteness as a veil, a norm, a neutral zone in which all is
apparently possible, then clearly there are a multitude of other contradictory
dimensions not being seen, recognized or confronted.

The contrast between the position of being White—and not recognizing
the 'invisible weightless rucksack' described by McIntosh (1988: 6), 'of special
provisions, assurances, tools, maps, guides, codebooks, passports, visas, clothes,
compass, emergency gear and blank cheques' that accompany the colour—and
being 'non-White' is stark. For those who are not White, who suffer
discrimination, the effects go very deep, leading to what West has described as a
'collective clinical depression' that affects minority groups (West, 1993: 17).

As Dupont-Joshua (1997) has noted, racism works from the outside in,
from society to the individual's internalization of those values. If society
continually sends out messages to minority groups that they are second-class
citizens, this accumulated message inevitably impacts upon the self-esteem and
self-worth of those individuals in receipt of such messages. The pernicious external
judgements of society become strongly introjected by those in receipt of such
messages. Members of minority groups are thus doubly sabotaged.

Though startlingly obvious, the corollary of the above position also rings true.
That is, that 'Whites', by virtue of being White in a White-dominant society,
introject societally reinforced values ranging from 'being normal' to 'being superior'.

WHITENESS AS A COMPONENT OF POWER

... in every circumstance my whiteness will play a role in the outcome,
however 'liberal' or 'anti-racist' I imagine myself to be. White men
have enormous economic advantages because of the disadvantages
faced by others, no matter what any individual white men may intend
... You do not have to be racist to benefit from being white. You just
have to look the part. (Jay: 1998: 3)

Adding the above societal positioning of whiteness to Carotenuto's definition of
therapist's power (below) presents a graphic picture of the (societally and
professionally reinforced) White therapists' power position relative to the client
from a minority group. He asserts:

> We often tend to conceal the fact that no other profession involves a greater inequality of power than the psychotherapists, in which one of the two poles is always, by definition, psychologically weaker than the other. For reasons intrinsic and structural to the psychological field, when a person is overwhelmed by suffering or convinced that his/her rational dimension which up to that moment had qualified him/her as a human being, has failed, asks someone stronger than s/he is to save him/her, s/he places that person in a position of power and superiority. This could be why we undertake this profession: it is the only one that allows us to deal with weaker individuals, in partial identification with the omnipotent figure of saviour offering a hand to the suffering. (Carotenuto, 1992: 51)

The above statement constitutes a challenge of the highest order to therapists. What motivates them to be a therapist? How aware are they of the exercise of their 'personal power'? Are they at all aware of the 'role power' they carry? A role power, incidentally, that is both societally and professionally sanctioned. In addition to these other aspects of power, this chapter forcefully asks the question, what is the power of a therapist's White identity? And to what degree does this power reside within the therapist, within the client's perception and within the relationship?

WHITENESS AND THE PERSON-CENTRED APPROACH: WHITENESS, IDENTITY AND THE SELF

The concept of whiteness has been identified above as an aspect of identity.

Having opened this section with the previous clear sentence, we were somewhat halted in the writing process by our general wish to link the notion of 'identity' to that of 'the self' and subsequently to go on to question the relationship between whiteness and congruence. The barrier to developing this theme was the complexity that potentially existed between the concepts of 'self' and 'identity'. Much of psychotherapy literature is concerned with the self, what it is, how it is constituted, constellated and configured. The term 'identity' however, appears much more in the wider social sciences literature and in some usages this term refers to aspects of the person, e.g. the cultural values or perspectives an individual most strongly relates to, their religious beliefs, their social affiliations, etc.

Searching the Internet delivered comments supportive of our own confusion! For example, 'usages of the self differ between theorists and fields of study, but in general the self refers to the conscious reflective personality of the individual' (from one definition of self, <http://en.wikipedia.org/wiki/Self>). 'The notion of identity has many uses throughout the social sciences. In cognitive psychology, identity is discussed in terms of whether or not an individual is self-reflective' (from one definition of identity, <http://en.wikipedia.org/wiki/identity>).

Other definitions were of great interest and reflected, perhaps inevitably, the complex relationship uniting and differentiating the two concepts. Some are offered below, followed in brackets by the definition from which they came.

- 'The distinct personality of an individual regarded as a persisting entity.' (definition of 'Identity')
- 'The individual characteristics by which a person is recognized by.' (definition of 'Identity')
- 'Your consciousness of your own identity.' (definition of 'Self')

(All three above from <http://wordnet.Princeton.edu/perl/webwn>)

- A single autonomous being, seen as a unity of multiple selves within any individual person. (definition of 'Self') (From <http://method.vtheatre.net/dict.html >)

The recurring unifying element contained within the above definitions seemed to us to be the component of self-reflectivity.

However, within the context of exploring White self-identity, we contend there is a need to explore outwards as well as inwards. That is, to pursue a 'self-other-society' reflectivity. Identity is socially constructed, a never-ending elaboration and, hopefully, exploration of who one essentially is. Whiteness, as stated above, is one aspect of identity.

- If you are White, are you White-aware?
- How does that awareness inform you?
- What impact might your whiteness have upon your clients?
- What does your whiteness mean, to you?
- How do you behave, in your whiteness, with others who are White? Who are Black? Who are 'other'?
- How often have you considered this aspect of your identity in supervision, training groups and therapy?
- If asked how you developed your sense of White identity, could you reply?

One Black respondent reported her excitement that her White therapist had expressed sensitivity to her (the client's) ethnicity, yet this was followed by disappointment that the therapist, when asked, could not describe her own journey of becoming ethnically aware (Dhillon-Stevens, 2004). In this story we hypothesize that the therapist, by virtue of her personality and training, was somewhat aware of the challenges facing clients from minority groups. However, it seems that she had not subjected her own ethnic and cultural origins to reflection and discovery through therapy, education, reading and relationships.

THE WHITE BODY

The geneticists Walter Bodmer and Luca Cavalli-Sforza have noted that, amongst lay people, 'race' is lamentably salient (1995). By contrast, they assert, 85% of human genetic variation consists of differences between one person and another within the same ethnic group, tribe or nation. Another 8% (only) is between ethnic groups and a mere 7% is between 'races'. In other words the genetic difference between, say, two randomly picked Swedes is about 12 times larger than the genetic differences between the average of the Swedes and the average of Worperis and Apaches. In short, within-group differences are 12 times greater than between groups!

The fantasy of a 'White race' with historical origins in classical civilisation whitewashed the complexion of Greece and Rome (whose people were a mixture of Mediterranean, Semitic and African populations each bringing unique cultural traditions to the table) (Jay, 1998). Research has even revealed that paintings of Christ became whiter over the centuries!

Authenticity also has eminent bodily aspects according to Peter Schmid (2001: 222) as he draws attention to the significance of body as the organismic processor of experiences. Communication exists only within the bodies involved, (not outside of them). The power of non-verbal behaviour within the communication process is enormous. Within the setting of therapy, the body of both the therapist and the client are significant. With our bodies we can sense and be sensed. Both connection and separation, visibility and invisibility (through hiding psychologically) are possible. 'The body both reveals the person and also can hide him or her. There is no authenticity without the body' (Schmid, 2001: 222).

The impact of skin colour and perceived ethnic identity, as visual depictors of the body, can have enormous implications upon the therapeutic encounter, precisely because of the cumulative effects of previous experience on attitudes, behaviour, self-esteem, confidence and so on. The therapist who experiences difficulties and strong feelings in relation to attitudes towards ethnically different others will be greatly challenged in the company of such clients. The minority-group client who has experienced previous discrimination may well hide their real self from the therapist for a long time. In working with a White therapist—a symbolic representative of White society and thus representing all that this might mean in terms of discrimination and racism—the Black client may project an acceptable 'front', a 'proxy self', that they have developed to cope within a White majority culture. (See Lago & Thompson, 1997, for a further elaboration of this notion.) Only after an appropriate time has elapsed and trust has been established, might the client reveal aspects of their truer self.

Research by Robert Carter (1995) revealed that the outcomes of inter-ethnic therapeutic relationships were most successful when the therapist was at the equivalent or at a more advanced stage of identity development than the client.

(See Lee, 2006, for further references to the ethnic identity development models referred to above.) This suggests that the therapist's own sense of working through and comfort with their own issues of identity, which are, at some level, depicted by the body, is a critical requirement in enhancing their capacity for therapeutic accompaniment and effectiveness.

WHITENESS AND CONGRUENCE—'OPENNESS TO SELF BEGETS THE POSSIBILITY OF OPENNESS TO OTHERS'

> Authenticity essentially is an encounter attitude ... it is a precondition to enter dialogue. (Schmid, 2001: 213)

For person-centred therapists, at an early stage of understanding, congruence has traditionally been seen as the experiencing and possible expression of one's truth, one's essential being. By contrast, Schmid's statements position the quality of congruence within an interpersonal dimension. True dialogue can only occur between authentic persons—revealing the 'two unrenounceable dimensions of human existence: the substantial or individual aspect of being a person and the relational or dialogical aspect of becoming a person' (Schmid, 2001: 214).

Within the dialogical relationship, openness to self begets the possibility of openness to others (Lietaer, 1984; Truax & Carkhuff, 1967; Bozarth, 2001). Thus the more one can accept (the many aspects and experiences of) oneself, the more one can be open to the variety of experiences expressed by the client. This poses a considerable challenge to the therapist from the White, majority group (a) if they are completely or relatively unaware of this aspect of their identity, and (b) their client, either by virtue of the representation of their differing ethnicity, or through their explorations, raises this subject. When such moments occur within the therapeutic relationship, the therapist's capacity to stay open, congruent and thus relational are severely restricted. Critical experiences such as these were reported by the White therapists in Buckley's research (2004), and may also subsequently lead to the therapist's avoidance of this subject (Thompson & Jenal, 1994)—any loss of openness to his/her self at this point will impact upon the therapeutic process.

A critique of one of Rogers' filmed interviews with an African-American client is that he was 'race-avoidant', i.e. his responses acknowledged all aspects of the client's experience other than the client's multiple references to his 'race' (Moodley et al., 2004). Thompson and Jenal report (a) more frequent and early retreat from therapy by clients experiencing this difficulty in their therapists, and (b) that some clients learn not to incorporate this particular element in their future therapy with this therapist. To not be aware of one's White ethnic identity is to put at risk, for some clients at least, their confidence:

1. in the therapeutic process;
2. in raising and exploring their own issues surrounding identity;
3. in validating their concerns;
4. in you, as the therapist.

In short, this would be a gross and unethical disservice to any client.

WHITENESS AND THE THERAPIST'S UNCONDITIONAL POSITIVE SELF-REGARD: 'OPENNESS TO OTHERS BEGETS THE POSSIBILITY OF OPENNESS TO SELF'

A corollary to the above perspective may be stated as: 'Openness to others begets the possibility of the discovery of self'. However, we are *not* saying that therapists, in being open to others, should rely solely on clients to bring these gifts to their own self-knowledge! Rather, it is morally, ethically and professionally incumbent upon therapists to commit to their training, ongoing personal development, supervision, personal therapy and so on to maximize their learning and awareness. However, when therapists experience uncomfortable moments or discomfiting feelings with their clients, they are offered a real opportunity for development, if they can seize it. This is not to minimize, though, the crisis experienced by the therapist's self and their ensuing (lack of) confidence in their capacity to maintain the relational work with the client.

Schmid discusses the ever-present inherent challenge concerning the capacity of therapists to truly being open to the 'other', thus being open to have their 'objective' previous knowledge and attitudes changed. In short, this challenge, within the focus of this chapter, is to the real openness of the 'White' therapist to be personally impacted by the relationship (2001).

Seeman (2001: 208) quotes research by Swan (1970) on a study of congruence. He proposed, supported by his research, that persons who display a self-concept in which they accept, trust, and value themselves, would also behave interpersonally in ways that would be seen as highly accepting and effective. Swan's hypothesis was that within-person functioning and interpersonal functioning are connected aspects of a larger unity of functioning and that such connectedness would be revealed in communication processes. This research supports the importance of the therapist's unconditional positive self-regard as a precondition for unconditional positive regard for the client. Within the context of this chapter, the therapist's appreciation of their unconditional positive White self-regard is of great value in meeting the client acceptantly and genuinely.

Sadly, within the field of 'diversity' training, we have already noted the extremely complex dynamics that are triggered and sometimes-resistant tendencies evoked in participants when invited to explore matters connected to race, ethnicity, diversity, power, discrimination, etc. (Pedersen et al., 2005). Despite these matters being signalled as critical and profoundly important elements within many professional codes of ethics, the reality and integration of such provision by training institutes is sorely lacking. An informal straw poll of counsellor training courses conducted by BACP in 2004/5 revealed that a high proportion of courses reported their training ventures in this arena as inadequate and frequently not integrated with other aspects of the course (personal communication with a senior staff member at BACP).

CONGRUENCE, DIFFERENCE AND DIVERSITY

> Thinking about congruence implies difference. You cannot reflect on being congruent if you don't experience and consider diversity. If there was no difference there would be no process and progress. (Schmid, 2001: 218)

Schmid, in his chapter on authenticity, introduces the little known work (in the person-centred world) of the Lithuanian encounter philosopher, Emmanuel Levinas (2001: 218–9). Levinas extends Buber's 'I–Thou' concept to 'I–Others'. Or, more accurately, in Buber's terms, 'Thou–I', and in those of Levinas, 'Others–I'. These latter reconceptualizations are in recognition that the 'other' always comes first, (phenomenologically, developmental psychologically and ethically). From the ethical perspective, Levinas argues that service towards the other comes first and consequently, (authentic) dialogue proceeds from this basic conviction and attitude. However, this is not a dialogue that emanates from the position of authenticity of the 'I felt it so I said it' syndrome critiqued by Haugh (2001). Rather, this authentic capacity comes from a deeply considered and somewhat more complex position.

Levinas uses the concept of the 'Third One', this being symbolic of the social and group-based understandings of humans. Rogers (we are reminded by Schmid, 2005), had already noted that human beings are 'incurably social'. To be in relationship to several significant others, the group, demands of person-centred therapists that they cannot relate at the 'primitive' levels of 'simply' accepting and understanding. A comprehensive grasp of (Levinas') 'triadic' understanding requires a deliberate acknowledgement of and compassion to the 'other/s'. This can only be achieved, Schmid argues, after an extensive reflective process on the nature of the 'other/s' which can facilitate the process of actively opening up, in an adult way, to the mystery of the other anew, trusting him or her and being impressed by his or her otherness.

This open capacity to enter afresh and reflectively informed into the relationship with the 'other' facilitates and enhances the therapist's capacity for presence (Rogers, 1986) and relational depth (Mearns & Cooper, 2005).

CONCLUDING THOUGHTS: THE THERAPIST, THE CLIENT AND SOCIETY

The goal here is not to elicit White feelings of guilt for White racism but to encourage insight into the nature of historical oppression and its contemporary manifestations. (Kincheloe et al., 1998: 19).

The overall thrust of this chapter is to encourage and urge White colleagues to undertake a process of reflection and introspection into what their whiteness means, implies, communicates, symbolizes, etc. However, an inherent danger, lurking within this pursuit of White identity awareness, is the reaffirmation (for some) of feelings of superiority over others as a reaction to, or defence from, the pain of their discovery. This urge to examine whiteness is therefore a thrust to situating whiteness alongside other identities, not to reassert its dominant power position.

The focus of the profession (of counselling/psychotherapy) and thus its training courses, though necessarily reflecting upon the direct therapeutic relationship, has never sufficiently taken into account (with exceptional circumstances) the contextual factors of society and how these impinge upon the therapeutic dyad. Sanders (2005) radically extends this critique by acknowledging both the psycho-noxious effects of society upon humans (e.g. malnourishment, poverty, discrimination, social exclusion) and our vocationally driven, narrow, psycho-biological views of individuals which remove us from responsibility in engaging in the difficult political and community processes of change. Our 'over-focused', professionally biased ideological view of the person and their pathology as originating in personal rather than social circumstances shields us from all the contradictions beneath our ideological (and thus naïve, simplistic) views.

Are we able, as (White) therapists, to dare to look at the particular challenges raised by this chapter? One finding in the research by Thompson and Jenal (1994) was that European-American therapists (i.e. White) consistently failed to respond to issues of identity, when discussed by clients, but African-American therapists openly engaged with these issues. There is great discomfort (this is certainly too mild and bland an adjective for the gamut of strong emotions reported) consistently evoked in White therapists by the whole field of race relations. In this discomfort, there is potentially huge learning. Are we up to the challenge? Do we truly dare to review and reflect upon our relationship to the other, as urged by Schmid and Levinas? How might we implement the research-derived knowledge embedded in instruments such as the ethnic identity development models to enhance our therapeutic capacities with all clients?

As a profession grounded upon the premise of the necessity for awareness generated through reflection, introspection, therapy and group work, we, (White therapists), need to embrace these wider meanings and understandings of ourselves and our relative identities that are embedded in and determined by society. Only through so doing might we have a chance of not repeating familiar and well-evidenced old patterns of discriminatory and stereotype-reinforcing behaviour. Only through so doing might we have any real opportunity of meeting the other, as they fully are.

> Authors [in this case White therapists] know that gaining authorship is a process, not an instant flash of lightning. Therefore authentic people are patient, curious and full of the ability of being astonished and surprised. They know that the task is to learn and improve congruence, not to have it or not. (Schmid, 2001: 222)

The authors are indebted to the radical scholarship of all colleagues cited in this chapter and particularly wish to record their gratitude to Peter Schmid for his profound conceptualizations on the nature of congruence.

REFERENCES

BACP Equality and Diversity Forum (2005) *Definition of Diversity*. Rugby: British Association of Counselling and Psychotherapy.

Bodmer, W & Cavalli-Sforza, L (1995) *The Great Human Diasporas: The history of diversity and evolution*. New York: Addison Wesley.

Bonnett, A (1999) Constructions of whiteness in European and American anti-racism. In RD Torres, LF Miron & JX Inda (eds) *Race, Identity and Citizenship* (pp. 200–18). London: Blackwell.

Bozarth, J (2001) Congruence: A special way of being. In G Wyatt (ed) *Rogers' Therapeutic Conditions: Evolution, theory and practice. Volume 1: Congruence* (pp. 184–99). Ross-on-Wye: PCCS Books.

Buckley, J (2004) Cross-ethnic therapeutic relationships: A qualitative study of therapists' experiences. Unpublished dissertation. University of Sheffield, Department of Psychology.

Carotenuto, A (1992) *The Difficult Art: A critical discourse on psychotherapy*. Wimetta, IL: Chiron Publications.

Carter, R (1995) *The Influence of Race and Racial Identity in Psychotherapy: Towards a racially inclusive model*. New York: J Wiley and Sons.

Coker, N (ed) (2001) *Racism in Medicine: An agenda for change*. London: Kings Fund Publishing.

Curtis, P (2005) 'Jobs for the white boys.' *The Guardian (Education)* November 22nd (p. 10).

Curtis, P (2006) 'Segregation, 2006 style.' *The Guardian (Education)* January 3rd (pp. 1–2).

D'Ardenne, P & Mahtani, A (1989) *Transcultural Counselling in Action*. London: Sage.

Dhillon-Stevens, H (2004) Healing inside and outside: An examination of dialogic encounters in the area of anti oppressive practice in counselling and psychotherapy. Unpublished PhD thesis, Metanoia/ Middlesex University.

Dyer, R (1997) *White*. London: Routledge.

Dupont-Joshua, A (1997) Working with issues of race in counselling. *Counselling, 8* (4), 282–4.

Eleftheriadou, Z (1994) *Transcultural Counselling*. London: Central Book Publishing.

Frankenberg, R (1993) *White Women, Race Matters: The social construction of whiteness*. Minneapolis: University of Minnesota Press.

Forgas, JP & Williams, KD (eds) (2002) *The Social Self: Cognitive, interpersonal and intergroup perspectives*. New York: Psychology Press.

Haugh, S (2001) The difficulties in the conceptualisation of congruence: A way forward with Complexity Theory? In G Wyatt (ed) *Rogers' Therapeutic Conditions: Evolution, theory and practice. Volume 1: Congruence* (pp. 116–30). Ross-on-Wye: PCCS Books.

hooks, b (1994) *Teaching to Transgress*. New York: Routledge.

Husband, C (ed) (1982) *Race in Britain*. London: Hutchinson.

Institute of Race Relations (2002) IRR News: Fact file on racial violence <www.irr.org.uk>.

Jay, G (1998) Who invented White People? A talk on the occasion of Martin Luther King, Jr Day, 1998 <www.uwm.edu/-gjay/Whiteness/Whitenesstalk.html>.

Kincheloe, JL, Steinberg, SR, Rodriguez, NM & Chennault, RE (eds) (1998) *White Reign: Deploying whiteness in America*. New York: St Martin's Press.

Lago, C (2006) *Race, Culture and Counselling: The ongoing challenge*. Maidenhead: Open University/McGraw-Hill (2nd edn). (See also Lago & Thompson, 1996.)

Lago, C & Smith, B (eds) (2003) *Anti-Discriminatory Counselling Practice*. London: Sage.

Lago, C & Thompson, J (1996) *Race, Culture and Counselling*. Buckingham: Open University Press.

Lago, C & Thompson, J (1997) The triangle with curved sides: Sensitivity to issues of race and culture in supervision. In G Shipton (ed) *Supervision of Psychotherapy and Counselling* (pp. 119–30). Buckingham: Open University Press.

Lee, C (2006) Updating the models of identity development. In C Lago *Race, Culture and Counselling: The ongoing challenge* (pp. 179–86). Maidenhead: Open University/McGraw-Hill.

Lietaer, G (1984) Unconditional Positive Regard: A controversial basic attitude in Client-Centered Therapy. In R Levant & J Shlien (eds) *Client-Centered Therapy and the Person-Centered Approach: New directions in theory, research and practice* (pp. 41–58). New York: Praeger.

Mearns, D & Cooper, M (2005) *Working at Relational Depth in Counselling and Psychotherapy*. London: Sage.

McIntosh, P (1988) White privilege and male privilege: A personal account of coming to see correspondences through work in Women's Studies. Wellesley College Center for Research on Women, *Working Papers Series 189*. Reprinted in M Andersen & PH Collins (eds) (1992) *Race, Class and Gender: An anthology* (pp. 70–82). Belmont CA: Wadsworth.

McKenzie-Mavinga, I (2005) Understanding Black issues in counsellor training. Unpublished PhD thesis. Metanoia/Middlesex University.

Moodley, R, Lago, C & Talahite, A (2004) *Carl Rogers Counsels a Black Client*. Ross-on-Wye: PCCS Books.

Pedersen, A, Walker, I & Wise, M (2005) Talk does not cook ice: Beyond anti-racism rhetoric to strategies for social action. *Australian Psychologist 40* (1), 20–31, March.

Pedersen, P (1987) *The Handbook of Cross Cultural Counseling and Therapy*. Westport, CT: Greenwood.

Phillips, T (2006) 'Stop pretending it isn't happening.' *The Guardian (Education)* January 3rd (p. 2).

Pope-Davis, DB & Coleman, HLK (eds) (1997) *Multicultural Counseling Competencies: Assessment, education and training, and supervision.* Thousand Oaks, CA: Sage.

Rogers, CR (1965) A humanistic conception of man. In R Farson (ed) *Science and Human Affairs* (pp. 18–31). Palo Alto: Science and Behavior Books.

Rogers, CR (1986) A client-centered/person-centered approach to therapy. In IL Kutash and A Wolf (eds) *Psychotherapist's Casebook: Theory and technique in the practice of modern times* (pp. 197–208). San Francisco: Jossey-Bass.

Sanders, P (2005) Self-examination. *Person-Centred Quarterly,* November, (pp. 1–5).

Schmid, P (2001) Authenticity: The person as his or her own author. Dialogical and ethical perspectives on therapy as an encounter relationship. And beyond. In G Wyatt (ed) *Rogers' Therapeutic Conditions: Evolution, theory and practice. Volume 1: Congruence* (pp. 213–28). Ross-on-Wye: PCCS Books.

Schmid, PF (2005) Authenticity and alienation: Towards an understanding of the person beyond the categories of order and disorder. In S Joseph & R Worsley (eds) (2005) *Person-Centred Psychopathology: A positive psychology of mental health* (pp. 75–90). Ross-on-Wye: PCCS Books.

Seeman, J (2001) On congruence: A human system paradigm. In G Wyatt (ed) *Rogers' Therapeutic Conditions: Evolution, theory and practice. Volume 1: Congruence* (pp. 200–12). Ross-on-Wye: PCCS Books.

Skellington, R & Morris, P (1992) *Race in Britain Today.* London: Sage.

Smith, DJ (1977) *Racial Disadvantage in Britain: The PEP Report.* Harmondsworth: Penguin.

Sue, DW (1981) *Counseling the Culturally Different.* New York: Wiley.

Sue, DW, Arrendondo, P & McDavis, R (1992) Multicultural counseling competencies and standards: A call to the profession. *Journal of Counseling and Development, 70,* 477–86 (March–April).

Swan, AC (1970) Personality integration and perceived behavior in a sensitivity training group. Unpublished doctoral dissertation. George Peabody College: Nashville, TN.

Thomas, A & Sillen, S (1972) *Racism and Psychiatry.* New York: Bruner and Mazell Inc.

Thompson, CE & Jenal, ST (1994) Interracial and intraracial quasi counselling interactions. When counselors avoid discussing race. *Journal of Counseling Psychology, 41* (4), 484–91.

Troyna, B (1981) *Public Awareness and the Media: A study of reporting on race.* London: Commission for Racial Equality.

Truax, CB & Carkhuff, RR (1967) *Toward Effective Counseling and Psychotherapy: Training and practice.* Chicago: Aldine.

Tuckwell, G (2002) *Racial Identity, White counsellors and therapists.* Buckingham: Open University Press.

Van Dijk, T (1993) *Elite Discourse and Racism.* Newbury Park, CA: Sage.

Vera, H, Feagin, JR and Gordon, A (1995) Superior intellect? Sincere fictions of the White Self. *Journal of Negro Education, 64* (3), 295–306.

Watson, V (2004) The training experiences of Black counsellors. Unpublished PhD thesis, University of Nottingham.

West, C (1993) *Race Matters.* Boston: Beacon Press.

Chapter 20

CLIENTS' EXPERIENCES OF HOW PERCEIVED DIFFERENCES IN SOCIAL CLASS BETWEEN COUNSELLOR AND CLIENT AFFECT THE THERAPEUTIC RELATIONSHIP

JANE BALMFORTH

INTRODUCTION

As someone who comes from a mixed social background I've always been interested in class and aware of it as a presence in my life. My mother is from a middle-class background; my father was the first in his family to go to university. He won a scholarship to Oxford and my granny, a single mother who worked in the Yorkshire weaving mills, was so embarrassed he wasn't going out to get a job that she didn't tell anyone about his achievement.

Many years later, as a person-centred counsellor, I had the opportunity to carry out some research for an MSc in Counselling, and chose a class-related study. This chapter is the 'story' of that research.

A considerable amount of research already exists on differences between counsellor and client such as gender, race, sexual orientation, disability and the effect these differences have on the therapeutic relationship. Such differences can exert a powerful influence on the relationship if the counsellor is from a traditionally more powerful group (male, White, heterosexual, non-disabled) and the client belongs to a group that has experienced discrimination and oppression. The danger is that the inequality already inherent in the counsellor–client relationship will be intensified by the influence of one (or more) of these differences.

By contrast, I could find little research into the impact that a difference in social class might have on the relationship between counsellor and client, even though there is a similar historical imbalance of power between middle-class and working-class people.

I felt that class might have a similar impact to these other differences. I decided to find out how clients who identified themselves as working class, and perceived their counsellor as middle or upper class, experienced this difference and whether it had an impact on the therapeutic relationship.

BACKGROUND

The influence of class in our lives today is generally underestimated, and yet it has been well-documented that social class still has a major impact on factors such as our mental health, the education we receive, the jobs we go into and how long we live (see e.g. Argyle, 1994; Pilgrim, 1997; Kearney, 2003; Isaacs, in press).

In the world of counselling, there has been a tendency for class to be considered less relevant to the therapeutic relationship as a difference than gender, race or sexuality (see e.g. Kearney, 1996; Isaacs, in press). It has been assumed that counsellors leave this aspect of themselves outside the counselling room (Kearney, 1996) and become politically and ideologically neutral in how they observe and react to clients' issues.

One important theme in the literature relates to the danger of class differences in the therapeutic relationship heightening feelings of powerlessness in the client. In other words, if middle-class counsellors ignore the effect of the difference in class in the therapeutic relationship, this can reinforce the social inequality and disempowerment which working-class clients may already be suffering (see e.g. Proctor, 2002; Isaacs, in press).

For a working-class client having counselling with a middle-class therapist there are many issues that can affect the relationship. Kearney (1996) describes how the all-pervading nature of class can be perceived in clothes, houses, accent, language codes and vocabulary. For example, which part of town a counsellor lives in, or the size of the house can indicate how much choice, and therefore power, she has in her life compared with the client. This dynamic can remain in the relationship as something that is taken for granted (by both counsellor and client) or resented (by the client) unless it is challenged and the inequality is addressed.

Another important theme relates to the danger of middle-class assumptions by a counsellor rupturing the relationship with a client from another social class. Hargaden and Summers (2000) and Kearney (2003) highlight an example of this. A middle-class counsellor reflects back the words of a working-class client but adds the phrase 'in the car'. The client does not have a car, is overcome with shame and confusion, but feels unable to challenge or correct the counsellor. The counsellor has 'missed' the client by making an assumption based on their own frame of reference rather than the client's, and the therapeutic relationship is 'ruptured'.

I have now identified some of the themes about class and counselling that have already been written about. I felt that the voice of the client had received relatively little attention, and this confirmed my decision to make this the focus of my research.

FINDING PARTICIPANTS FOR THE RESEARCH

I chose to carry out a qualitative study in order to hear the clients' stories and make them the focus of the research, to hear about their 'life-world' (McLeod, 2001). I wanted to speak to clients who had experienced the dynamic of a perceived different social class in therapy and hear how this had affected their relationship with a counsellor and how it had affected the therapy. I also wanted the research to be a person-centred study; by offering the core conditions to the participants I hoped to ensure that the interview was a positive and enriching experience for all those involved (Mearns & McLeod, 1984).

I interviewed six clients who identified as working class and perceived their counsellor to be middle or upper middle class. I did not verify the actual class of the counsellor him/herself as the important element was that the client experienced a difference.

I advertised for participants on counselling websites, mail bases and in journals. The participants were counsellors or trainee counsellors (all person-centred except for one) who had been in therapy and experienced that the difference in social class had affected the relationship. The participants all spoke about therapy that had concluded before they began counselling training, except for one participant whose therapy had overlapped with the training. I chose to focus on recruiting counsellors or trainee counsellors who had experienced being clients in therapy because they were easier to contact than other clients (who were not counsellors); clearly, this will have affected how the participants responded and I would like to carry out a similar study with non-counsellor clients to observe any differences in the responses. I will return to this later in the section 'Points for Future Research'.

Four of the six participants were female and two were male; they were all aged between 30–55 years. They had had therapy with counsellors from various schools of counselling: person-centred, Gestalt, psychodynamic and integrative.

GATHERING THEMES FROM THE INTERVIEWS

I carried out semi-structured interviews, which I recorded and then transcribed. The key question that I asked was: 'Has there ever been a time when you feel that a different social class has affected your relationship with a counsellor?' I then explored this in depth with the participant, using other guiding questions: how the participant felt about the difference of class being voiced by them or by the counsellor, how the participant felt about being in therapy with a counsellor from a different class background, and how they might have felt if the background had been similar.

I started analysing the transcripts by intensive reading and re-reading and identifying themes. The 'immersion' and 'categorization' stages are the first steps in the process of analysis described by McLeod (2003). I focused on the 'feel' of the participants' words and then categorized the material to reach a phenomenological reduction, or 'essence', of the clients' experiences.

At the end of the categorization stage I had a huge list of about 60 or 70 themes from the interviews, such as 'I felt stupid', 'the therapist seemed to have her own agenda'. The number of themes felt quite unwieldy and unmanageable, so I looked for a way to organize the themes into groups that expressed the effect of a difference in social class on the therapeutic relationship. Looking through the list of themes, three main groups seemed to emerge:

- the clients' feelings about themselves
- the clients' feelings about the therapist
- the clients' feelings about the therapeutic relationship

Figure 1 illustrates the interrelationship and overlaps between the three groups of themes.

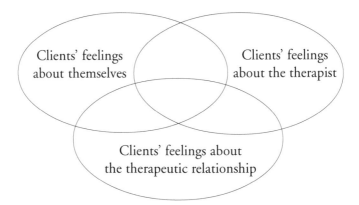

Figure 1 Main Groups of Themes

In order to organize the themes, I experimented with putting all the themes on cards, spreading them out on the table and moving them round to gather them into sub-groups, for example 'feeling disempowered', 'feeling misunderstood by the therapist' and then fitting the sub-groups into one of these main groups. There were, however, themes that fitted into more than one group, for example, 'the client feeling the need to prove herself to the therapist'. I could not decide whether this was the client's feeling about herself or the feeling about the therapist and eventually decided that this fitted into the overlapping section in between, as it belonged to both groups.

FINDINGS: HOW THE CLIENTS FELT ABOUT
THE DIFFERENCE IN CLASS

I found the whole experience of listening to the clients' experiences and then re-listening to the recordings and transcribing their words to be very moving. Sometimes while the participants were speaking my mind jumped back to the words of other interviewees, recognizing common themes; I felt indignant as one interviewee described a lack of empathy shown by the counsellor and excited when another interviewee used especially powerful phrases to describe their experience. I felt I was uncovering rich material that had lain undiscovered.

The quotations from the interviews that follow are the voices of the clients, which is the heart of the study. Their words explain how they felt about the perceived difference in social class. I have changed the names of all the participants for anonymity.

CLIENTS' FEELINGS ABOUT THEMSELVES

The clients' feelings about themselves had four sub-groups:

1. Feeling inferior

> I feel that because of the difference in our social class that I often feel quite inadequate. (Fran)

2. Feeling unable to be fully self

> ... some things are just holding me back from being me because I think she [the therapist] might judge me because of who I am, just a normal bog-standard person, as I put myself, and yet I try to appear to be so perfect, dress-wise, make-up wise. (Fran)

3. Feeling discomfort

> It was just really uncomfortable and so I felt like there was nev ... instantly there wasn't going to be an equality between us. (Lucy)

4. Feelings about voicing the difference in social class

> It wouldn't have occurred to me to have mentioned it, um, I just accepted it. (Jamie)

> ... because she was of a different class to me automatically changed the dynamic for me ... and I would've ... I wouldn't have thought about

saying to her 'what's going on here?' or 'I'm feeling different' or 'there's this thing between us that's, that's making it uncomfortable for me,' because she's ... upper class and so you don't challenge that. (Lucy)

CLIENTS' FEELINGS ABOUT THE THERAPIST

The clients' feelings about the therapist had four sub-groups:

1. Feeling misunderstood by the therapist

It was obvious every time I ... came out of my sort of process or she [the therapist] would ask me anything, it would be like these jarring moments when it would feel like 'She's miles away'. (Steve)

2. Therapist as authority figure

Along with her class and the status ... was the power thing and an authority thing, so it kind of felt like she was the figure of authority and I was this wee person that needed help. (Lucy)

3. Therapist's lack of awareness

I think he just didn't understand what it was like for a young working-class boy who didn't have a good vocabulary. (Jamie)

I experienced it that I've been expected to go into a middle-class world ... and that hasn't been reversed. (Molly)

4. Client experiences negative response from the therapist

Acceptance ... it wasn't really quite there. It was like: 'You're a strange man', you know. (Steve)

CLIENTS' FEELINGS ABOUT THE THERAPEUTIC RELATIONSHIP

The clients' feelings about the therapeutic relationship had three sub-groups:

1. No psychological connection due to inequality of power

There just didn't seem to be ... there was a barrier up which was tangible and palpable in the room and yet which we never acknowledged ... (Ros)

Because of what was going on with class differences, there was no
equality in it, you know, there was one person who had a place and
another person who had a different place, and how two people can
meet at relational depth in that, I don't know, I don't know ... (Lucy)

2. How the relationship might have been different with a therapist from a similar (i.e. working-class) background

I think then it felt like the world of therapy is a middle-class world
and [the therapist] being the way she was kind of went with the
territory and maybe if I'd gone to somebody similar it would have
been a bit cosy. (Ros)

I think I would have got to the shame a lot earlier and I think I would
have sensed a recognition ... (Molly)

3. The effect of the issue of class being voiced in therapy

I think I would project onto middle-class or upper-class people my
prejudices consciously or unconsciously unless it is addressed in the
counselling relationship. (Jamie)

ATTITUDES TO CLASS

As well as the themes I've described above, there were other powerful strands that
emerged from the interviews.

Several clients spoke about their attitude to their working-class background
and how this affected the relationship with the therapist. Some clients felt ashamed
of what their background revealed to the therapist; one interviewee spoke about
not understanding a word the counsellor used and yet feeling too embarrassed
and ashamed to ask her to explain. For other clients their background was a
source of pride and one participant spoke powerfully about her sense of struggle
against what she perceived as the class-based assumptions of her therapist:

... it felt to me like kind of a battle of wills and intellect and class
warfare. (Ros)

Clients referred to their therapist's lack of awareness of a different social
background in many different ways. Several participants drew a parallel with
Black/ethnic minority clients and White counsellors to highlight that this felt
like an unknown area for the counsellor who had needed educating:

> ... 'It's not really my job to educate you [the therapist]'. Um, and I mean I'm aware now that people from different racial backgrounds quite often have the same sense of ... of ... when they're working with someone from a different race ... (Steve)

This parallel draws attention to the similarity of 'difference' causing oppression of one group by another, whether by sexism, racism or disability discrimination (Isaacs, in press).

All the participants felt that being working class was another world for counsellors and they had had no feeling that the therapist could enter into their frame of reference of poverty, deprivation and financial struggle:

> It felt like outside of their experience so that they could get a grasp of it from the outside, but they couldn't really be there with me on the inside, or the opposite thing of I couldn't feel safe enough to take them into that world ... (Molly)

Some clients had even experienced the counsellor finding their values curious:

> ... she struggled with my values, um, she found them quite novel ... she couldn't ... it's like 'Oh, how interesting!', she'd say things like 'Oh, how interesting!' and I'd be thinking 'What do you mean "interesting"?!' (Jamie)

REFLECTIONS ON THE FINDINGS

I had the overwhelming feeling from meeting the participants and listening to their experiences in therapy that counselling is definitely not politically neutral. There are many unspoken assumptions and prejudices, many codes and myths that one class has about another. These can corrupt the development work of the therapy if they are not voiced, or if the client feels from the therapist's responses that he or she is being 'missed' because of these influences.

Many of the participants mentioned the delicate, sensitive nature of discussing class, of bringing it into the counselling room and had differing views on whether and how class should be voiced in the relationship. Some interviewees felt class would need to be addressed very carefully to avoid the therapist sounding patronizing; however, all the participants felt the issue needed to be voiced in some way to address any risk of the counselling relationship reproducing the power dynamic of one class over another.

Clients mentioned feeling unable to cry in the therapy for reasons related to the difference in class and the issue of power. One client felt that, for her, crying would be 'capitulation' to the powerful middle-class therapist. Another client felt sure her counsellor would despise her for giving way to tears, as crying would confirm the shortcomings of her working-class upbringing.

Clearly, a perceived difference in class between these clients and their therapists gave rise to a number of barriers in the relationship. I found it interesting that, although some participants said they would prefer a counsellor from a similar social class, others didn't feel this was necessarily the solution. Again, it was the lack of awareness of difference which seemed to create the feeling for the client that the counsellor just didn't 'get' him or her.

Clients said that they gleaned the counsellor's different class from such details as speech, clothes, surroundings (especially if the therapy took place in the counsellor's home) and from information that the counsellor disclosed about themselves, such as education.

One participant said she felt that the difference between herself, being working class, and her counsellor was that as a middle-class person, her counsellor was always on 'safer ground'. This gave me a very visual image of the counsellor standing on dry land and the client in a bog trying to balance on clumps of grass with the water creeping up. It seemed to sum up so well how the difference felt for many of the participants.

POINTS FOR FUTURE RESEARCH

The limitations of this study show that there is plenty of scope for further studies on counselling and class. The fact that the research focused on the stories of clients who had experienced a difference in social class meant that I was hearing from a self-selected sample of clients. Their responses or stories were therefore more certain to be powerful and to highlight the negative aspects of their experience than a random selection of clients speaking about class.

I would also not claim to be able to generalize about counselling and class from a sample of six clients. The aim of the study was to listen to the stories of these particular clients and extract the essence of what they experienced, rather than widen out the findings into statements that can be generally applied.

Earlier in this chapter I referred to the impact on the research of interviewing clients who are also counsellors about their experience, as opposed to clients who are not counsellors. Interviewing counsellors about therapy meant that their insights and thoughts about the therapy they had had were inevitably affected by their knowledge and practice of counselling. Another interesting future study would be to interview clients who are not counsellors about their experience of social class in counselling, and then interview their therapists to compare how they experienced the class dynamic. It would be fascinating to explore the similarities and differences that might emerge within the two groups.

CONCLUSION

All the clients I interviewed experienced the perceived difference in social class as a disempowering influence. This was the single most important conclusion of my research.

Where the difference was most powerfully felt in the therapeutic relationship was in the counsellors' lack of understanding of different life experiences, different access to opportunities, and how a lack of financial resources restricts, or at least affects, life choices. The inequality already experienced by the client in his or her life was then tacitly reproduced in the counselling relationship.

As person-centred counsellors I feel we need to be aware of our attitudes and feelings about class and of the signals that we send about our social class. For me personally, I found that exploring my own class background helped me to uncover how I felt about these issues.

The powerful words of the participants in this study show how counselling, a therapeutic relationship between two people, can still be affected by unspoken assumptions and beliefs about class in our society.

REFERENCES

Argyle, M (1994) *The Psychology of Social Class*. London: Routledge.

Hargaden, H & Summers, G (2000) Class, shame and self-righteousness. In Conference Papers *Embracing Life's Differences*. ITA Conference, 2000.

Isaacs, M (in press) Class dynamics, counselling and psychotherapy. In S Wheeler (ed) *Difference and Diversity in Counselling: Contemporary psychodynamic perspectives*. Basingstoke: Palgrave.

Kearney, A (1996) *Counselling, Class and Politics—Undeclared influences in therapy*. Ross-on-Wye: PCCS Books.

Kearney, A (2003) Class and Counselling. In C Lago & B Smith (eds) *Anti-Discriminatory Counselling Practice* (pp. 109–19). London: Sage.

McLeod, J (2001) *Qualitative Research in Counselling and Psychotherapy*. London: Sage.

McLeod, J (2003) *Doing Counselling Research*. London: Sage.

Mearns, D & McLeod, J (1984) A person-centred approach to research. In RF Levant and JM Shlien (eds) *Client-Centred Therapy and the Person-Centered Approach: New directions in theory, research and practice* (pp. 370–89). New York: Praeger.

Pilgrim, D (1997) *Psychotherapy and Society*. London: Sage.

Proctor, G (2002) *The Dynamics of Power in Counselling and Psychotherapy: Ethics, politics and practice*. Ross-on-Wye: PCCS Books.

Chapter 21

THE PERSON-CENTRED APPROACH: A VEHICLE FOR ACKNOWLEDGING AND RESPECTING WOMEN'S VOICES

BEA WHITE

My focus is on women and power and how person-centred therapy can enable women to develop their personal power. My writing comes from my work as a counsellor at a low-cost practice and from my own experiences in counselling.

HOW WOMEN MAY EXPERIENCE POWERLESSNESS AND DISTRESS

In this chapter I explore women's experiences of powerlessness. This is a particular issue for women living in a patriarchal society with assumptions of women's roles. I am linking powerlessness to experiences of abuse.

Women experiencing powerlessness may be aware of a range of feelings including anger, depression, shame and anxiety. In order to survive and manage distress, they may adopt coping mechanisms such as self-harming, eating disorders and dissociation.

There has been some honest and challenging writing recently linking women's experiences of abuse (sexual, emotional and physical abuse predominantly in childhood but also in adulthood) to psychological distress.

As a woman attempts to resist oppression she may self-harm in order to maintain some control. Proctor and Shaw (2004) outline how such women may receive a diagnosis of Borderline Personality Disorder (BPD). Symptoms used to diagnose BPD include an 'uncertain sense of identity', 'inappropriate anger' and 'impulsive behaviour such as self-harming' (Roth & Fonagy, 1996, cited in Proctor & Shaw, 2004). Proctor and Shaw offer an alternative perspective, that anger and coping mechanisms are understandable in the context of a woman's history, and outline psychiatry's tendency to coin concepts such as BPD to define a woman's pathology whilst ignoring the perpetrator of sexual violence and the relational nature of distress. Sadly a woman is viewed to have a mental disorder and her experiences of abuse are neither acknowledged nor understood. Walker (2004) clarifies that if a woman has experienced abuse and hurt from others then self-harm can be a way of regaining 'control' of her body. She talks about escaping from overwhelming feelings in order to be safe and writes,

> We all survive in different ways and if self-harm didn't serve a
> function, then women wouldn't do it. (Walker, 2004: 21)

Experiencing abuse in childhood can have substantial implications on women's lives with regards to not meeting their own needs, relying on external authority, self-blame and self-esteem issues.

As a result of traumatic experiences a child may learn to please the parent in order not to be punished further or be on the receiving end of violence. Hawkins (2005) reflects upon the conditions of worth present in early childhood. If a baby's needs are not met with love and acceptance they may learn not to trust their needs and believe that feelings are dangerous. Hawkins touches on the impact of assault,

> When an adult is unwilling or incapable of taking responsibility for
> their assaults, physical and verbal, on children, the child will pick it
> up and carry it through their lives. (Hawkins, 2005: 231)

Another potential psychological consequence of trauma is dissociation. Mearns and Thorne (2000) clarify that the aim of dissociation is to reduce painful, out-of-control experiences. Women can refer to parts, which are frozen or paralysed. As they risk bringing these parts, they may experience anxiety and vulnerability, and a stuck part, which can keep a woman safe and slowly reduce anxiety.

PERSON-CENTRED THERAPY AND POWER

Proctor (2002) refers to Starhawk's concepts of power: *power-over, power-with* and *power-from-within*. *Power-over* is control over others, *power-with* is the power of a group of people who recognize that they are equal and can both participate and listen. *Power-from-within* refers to an individual's personal power.

Proctor clarifies that the aim of person-centred therapy is to use *power-with* and that the core conditions encourage a woman to develop her own *power-from-within*. As a counsellor is empathically accepting of a woman, she has the opportunity to understand herself better and take greater control. As a counsellor is free to be herself, a woman can perceive this and adopt the same attitude towards herself.

AVOIDING POWER-OVER IN MY WORK

Women can enter counselling with experiences of *power-over* in relationship and may expect the same in counselling. I aim to be aware of power in the relationship and work non-directively. I used to believe that I was being helpful by answering a client's questions. I now believe that I am helpful and expressing my own personal power when I stay alongside her with her struggle and explain my reluctance to provide direct answers as my choice may differ from hers. I may offer suggestions but they are purely my suggestions and may not be the most suitable solutions for her. From such relating a woman may start to understand how she gives her power away. I am in awe of the resources women find, which reminds me that I do not hold the answers to another's life.

I aim to offer a safe space based on understanding and acceptance, be aware of my own attitudes and values and be open to continue learning. Sometimes this means being patient until a woman can face her experiences of abuse, which may touch upon oceans of hurt and pain. Staying with her imagery can help her to explore without touching on painful feelings.

Empathic acceptance is fundamental to avoiding *power-over*. This means accepting the whole spectrum of a woman's feelings. This gives equal validity to both socially acceptable and unacceptable feelings and acknowledges a woman's dissociated parts and her process. For me it can be like opening up a long-lost treasure trove, valuing all the different 'objects' inside and being with another as she starts to own them. It is my experience that a woman can be released to listen to and start accepting herself.

I aim to be real and with one client risked more self-disclosure in our work and I shared my tears at our ending. This felt acceptable as she moved on to validate some of her own experiences.

Limitations

By focusing on a woman's distress person-centred therapy does not acknowledge the context of the abuse and has the potential to individualize and isolate a woman. If a woman has felt isolated due to her experiences of abuse, person-centred therapy may unwittingly reinforce messages that she is to blame, as the focus is on her individual distress rather than acknowledging the distress originating from being in relationship.

Another limitation that Proctor (2004) touches on is *role power* and the power that society gives to therapists as having the ability to define a woman's problem. However hard I have tried to maintain equality, I have worked with women who have been confused about my role as I am both a human being (committed to equality) and a counsellor (with *role power*).

INTERNAL POWER

I will explore two themes relating to internal power—difficulties in asserting needs in relationships and difficulties in expressing anger. I will illustrate these with the experiences of a client I worked with, whom I shall name 'Anna', and with my own experiences.

DIFFICULTIES FOR WOMEN IN ASSERTING THEIR OWN NEEDS IN RELATIONSHIP

Proctor (2004) acknowledges 'gender role socialization' and wider social conditions of worth for women, coming from the media and other adults. She looks at the impact of 'societal power' on gender in patriarchal society. One obvious example is motherhood and childcare and the expectation that women will assume this role. There are less obvious examples where, due to experiences of abuse, a woman continues to blame herself for others' actions.

Without awareness, beliefs and values may be introjected from society and passed down the generations. Any injunctions from childhood may be difficult to resolve in adulthood as a woman struggles with her internalized rules and regulations. Common examples are 'I can't say no' (I don't have needs) or 'I can't ask for help' (I'm meant to care for others).

Women with experiences of abuse may similarly have internalized others' judgements. Hawkins (2005) refers to the internalized abuser, who is self-loathing and the judge of the vulnerable child, who is afraid and powerless. Some of the women I have met have felt powerless as they remain in a place of self-blame with beliefs such as 'I deserve the punishment'.

Impact on relationships

By taking care of others a woman may use her resources to meet external needs and is unable or at best partially able to meet her own needs. If she is living with self-blame then she may believe that others are 'normal', in other words, not distressed, and this can lead to greater isolation. One potential consequence of these dynamics is that a woman may decide to stay in an abusive relationship, as this is a familiar place for her and safer than change, and she is not used to prioritizing her own needs.

In the counselling relationship a woman may give her power away to the counsellor and she may expect the counsellor to provide her with answers as others have been willing to. She may be shocked to find that someone is willing to listen and not wanting to have *power-over*. She can experience intimacy that is neither threatening nor punishing, but welcoming, safe and enabling.

As a single parent with two young sons, Anna had learned to put her needs last. She felt responsible for the absence of one of her son's father and tried to fill the gap. She likened her life to that of a hamster on a wheel and I wondered how it might be for her to get off this wheel for a while. She had never tried but gradually started to relax her own rules and allowed herself some time-out. For this chapter Anna has written,

> *I used to 'beat myself up' because my son doesn't have an active growing and loving relationship with his father. I know now that this is not my fault and am learning that thinking about this absence is damaging only to me and doesn't alter the facts of their relationship.*

Anna compared her life to being in a lift—previously stopping only on the ground and top floors but now she was choosing to tentatively step out onto other floors. She writes,

> *I have learned a lot about myself and have made considerable changes within myself towards those individuals with whom I have emotionally intimate relationships. I am learning to take responsibility for my own words, thoughts and actions and to separate these from others' issues. I have recently been unwell and cancelled my visit to my mother. Prior to counselling I would've continued with the arrangements to please her and would've been both resentful towards her and angry towards myself for not stating my own needs and accepting responsibility for my decisions.*

Moving onto my experiences, I learned at an early age to rely on external authority and to please others. At 32 I fell ill with Epstein Barr virus (which is similar to glandular fever). Working through familiar patterns, the accompanying anxiety, being overwhelmed by feeling responsible for others and the painful awareness of not getting my needs met has been an ongoing journey. The turning point was my counsellor's refusal to give me answers but staying with me as I find my own. She has often been the testing ground for my growth, which has entailed risk as I learn to assert myself and say no. I can struggle with my own critic whilst supporting myself by a resilient and bold part. I have learned that others are responsible for their own anger and as I regain my power in relationships I move from reacting to others' judgements to standing back and responding from my own frame of reference.

DIFFICULTIES FOR WOMEN EXPRESSING ANGER

Shaw (2004) outlines the historic approach of Electro-Convulsive Therapy (ECT) or hospitalization with which society and psychiatry have punished women displaying anger, as anger does not fit with the expectations of feminine passivity. Psychiatry responds to women showing anger or self-harm by labelling them with BPD, which I believe, invalidates women's feelings and implies that they are unwell. I can imagine that their anger is only fuelled when the finger of blame is repeatedly pointed at them.

Impact on relationships

As women can expect to be punished or stigmatized, they are not being heard and may carry beliefs such as 'I do not matter'. If anger is judged to be a disturbance then women may become more isolated or adopt a façade to cope with life, or turn it in on themselves.

In the counselling relationship a woman may be afraid of bringing her own anger. It may be too much of a risk to do so in case of rejection or punishment. It may take time until she hears the counsellor valuing her. She may want to look after the counsellor and wonder if she is strong enough to receive her anger. What might it be like to share her anger?

Anna started counselling after several stays in hospital following bouts of depression, more recently post-natal depression. She tried to suppress her emerging feelings but referred to her self-destruct button and how she would turn her anger inwards and self-harm. She likened her anger to a balloon surrounded by knives and risked bringing it to counselling. She was angry with her ex-partner for not assuming his responsibilities in the care of their son. As she brought her anger, she checked out if I was afraid of it. I wasn't afraid of it and was experiencing her power. Anna felt heard and valued and this was the starting point for not turning her anger inwards. She began listening to and validating her anger and noticed that she no longer felt depressed. She committed herself to valuing any future depression.

My experiences of anger at a younger age tended to be unsafe and accompanied by some physical assault, which was described as discipline. In my need to release my anger as an adult, I would turn it inwards and beat myself up mentally and physically. Once I understood that I was harming myself I decided to look after myself more and am at a place where I am learning to accept and value my anger more. From my own counselling I have learned to trust my anger, which can be about creativity or regaining space and power in relationships. It can be a sign that something is wrong for me and that I need to assert myself. Anger mobilizes me.

SOME FINAL THOUGHTS

The above examples illustrate the effectiveness of the person-centred approach. Women can experience an alternative intimacy where they can learn to trust, value, assert themselves and regain a sense of their internal power. There are issues of power in the counselling relationship which the counsellor needs to be aware of.

I am becoming more aware of the potential for healing in group work. I believe the power of the therapist is reduced as women share experiences and are validated by hearing others' experiences, which reduces isolation. I recently attended an only child conference and this was the start for me of acknowledging my own shame, validating my experiences of enjoying my solitude at times and recognizing my own qualities for facilitating groups. Finally, I have found reading a wonderful source of validation, in particular, recent articles by Jan Hawkins.

REFERENCES

Hawkins, J (2005) Living with pain: Mental health and the legacy of childhood abuse. In S Joseph and R Worsley (eds) *Person-Centred Psychopathology* (pp. 226–41). Ross-on-Wye: PCCS Books.

Mearns, D & Thorne, B (2000) *Person-Centred Therapy Today.* London: Sage.

Proctor, G (2002) *The Dynamics of Power in Counselling and Psychotherapy.* Ross-on-Wye: PCCS Books.

Proctor, G & Shaw, C (2004) BPD under the microscope. *Asylum, 14* (3), 6–7.

Rogers, CR (1978) *Carl Rogers on Personal Power: Inner strength and its revolutionary impact.* London: Constable.

Shaw, C (2004) Sexual abuse: The psychiatric response and the construction of better alternatives. In G Proctor and MB Napier (eds) *Encountering Feminism: Intersections between feminism and the person-centred approach* (pp. 141–53). Ross-on-Wye: PCCS Books.

Walker, T (2004) Why cut up? *Asylum, 14* (3), 20–2.

Chapter 22

A PASSION FOR POLITICS IN CARL ROGERS' WORK AND APPROACH

GAY BARFIELD

PRECEDENTS FOR POLITICAL ENGAGEMENT

The person-centered approach (PCA) is a professional practice and personal and political philosophy that embodies principles which are deeply needed by humankind today in its search for inner peace, relational peace and global peace. Carl Rogers' exquisite triad of empathy, genuineness and unconditional positive regard reflect familiar ancient values and virtues recognizable by both formal religious faiths and by the natural human inclinations within us all around the globe toward more loving kindness and a safer sense of intimacy among us. No panacea, but a moment-to-moment renewable and correctable process, this elegant constellation of attitudes allows us, no matter what our particular cultural orientation or world-view, to practice and live out peace-making in our personal relationships as couples, family members, work colleagues, friends or enemies.

In this chapter I will explore the development of the work of Rogers and his colleagues in relation to politics, particularly around conflict and peace-building as a means of easing the stresses arising between people of different points of view. Simple and profound, but certainly not easy, these ways of being at least lend hope and the possibility for the healing of rifts and the lifting of our spirits in the uneasy moments between us, both individually and globally. Not to attempt to apply them predicts failure.

EARLY INDICATIONS OF ROGERS' SOCIAL AND POLITICAL CONCERNS

Some authors have criticized Rogers' approach as superficial, naïve and focused too much on self-sufficient individualism rather than on larger relationships and global concerns. (For reports of this, see Holdstock, 1990 and Thorne, 1991.) If this were so, it would seem to follow that such a position might encourage self-involvement and selfishness, isolation and an apolitical consciousness among both PCA clients and practitioners, and Rogers himself. However, it has been my experience for over 30 years, and continues to be so, that involvement in world issues and social justice has long been the leading developmental edge of our work. Certainly in Carl's writings, speeches and programs worldwide, he had been speaking to the issues of equality, peace, justice, and other fundamentally pro-social topics since the early 1940s, a long history of writing about political issues. His courage was present throughout his life and in his writings, stretching the parameters of his work decade after decade, often within the confines of traditional academic and psychological circles, organizations and departments. Currently, other prominent PCA leaders and authors such as Steve Olweean (2002) and Peter Schmid (1998, 2001, 2004) proceed in this same direction of expanding the PCA's engagement with global social concerns and relationship with the 'Other' in the broadest sense, recognizing the nature of Carl's work and approach as being far beyond mere involvement with the Self. Clearly, as indicated by the following, Carl Rogers' larger political interests were not a last-minute phenomenon or deviation off-path which appeared suddenly in his late years. For instance, as early as 1944 he was writing about his work with returning servicemen from World War II (Rogers, 1944a, 1944b, 1945; Rogers & Wallen, 1946) up until his final dialogue with David Russell (Rogers & Russell, 2002); in a 1952 presentation which later became a chapter in *On Becoming a Person*, 'Dealing With Breakdowns in Communication: Inter-personal and Intergroup' regarding the Soviet–American conflict; 1960 saw his paper 'Social Implications' again discussing our attitudes and roles in the world as well as an article in the *Journal of Applied Behavioral Sciences* in 1965 titled 'Dealing with Psychological Tensions' and the threats of the nuclear situation worldwide. In each of these, and other later articles and chapters not cited here, and whether writing of early conflictual meetings between health providers and consumers in a community or Chicanos and Anglos, or the Camp David meeting analysis, or the Cold War, or the politically charged multinational El Escorial (Spain) meeting in 1978, or Blacks and Whites in turmoil in South Africa, or of meetings with ex-presidents and political leaders in Central America, or even at our meetings at Seven Springs, California in 1984 about the pending national presidential election in the USA, Carl never wavered in his belief that the person-centered approach had something to contribute to the dilemmas of humankind.

Thus, in much of his general writings outside of therapy he made reference over many decades to the human potential for destroying ourselves if we could not resolve our inter-cultural and global animosities. Particularly when faced with the enormous power of scientific discoveries that could be used malevolently to destroy all of humankind and the environment with it, his hope and belief was that the person-centered approach might be applicable to each of these tragic potentials. He risked his entire professional credibility as he increasingly spoke about and acted upon his belief that person-centered principles could help ease tensions in these troubled areas of the world.

ROGERS' VISION

As I wrote at length in a letter to *TIME Magazine* in the year 2000, nominating Carl for 'The Person of the Century':

In a quote Carl made on August 8, 1984, which was used in an invitation to a fund-raising dinner we held in 1985 for the peace project's then upcoming 'Central American Challenge' gathering to be held in Rust, Austria with leading world diplomats, Carl Rogers stated: 'It seemed a little foolish at times to be thinking of starting the Peace Project at my age [then 82]. Yet I, like many others, feel that at the present time the problem of preventing a nuclear holocaust has top priority in my mind ... in my heart ... and in my work. That's why I am devoting myself to this project.'

In yet another memo addressed to me as Co-director with him and dated September 19, 1986, written less than five months before his death, and titled 'Priorities,' Carl stated unequivocally again: 'my primary objective is to continue the activities of the Carl Rogers Peace Project ... My work in the direction of peace has been the central theme of my life for a number of years now and it will continue, and the Peace Project is the major expression of that desire.'

In that same memo, he went on to speak of wanting to consolidate all of his peace activities work in Russia, South Africa, Central America or elsewhere 'under the umbrella of the Peace Project' to ensure decent funding for its continuation. During this same period, Carl Rogers' peace efforts were being publicly acknowledged in professional publications and journals, at national professional conventions by his colleagues, by peace organizations such as 'Beyond War,' by political figures and bodies such as President Jimmy Carter, Senator John Vasconcellos, the State of California, the City of San Diego, and by countless other individuals and organizations working to lessen the threat of nuclear holocaust and national, racial and ethnic hatreds. Carl was touched and heartened by these honors.

At the apex of his career, at 85 years old, Dr Rogers was able to fully participate in catalyzing, convening and facilitating the first Central American encounter in Rust, Austria with the Peace Project staff and the co-sponsorship of the University for Peace in Costa Rica. The four-day event was attended by some 50 political figures and diplomats from 17 nations, and influential lay persons of every political persuasion. Shortly after returning from the encounter, in the final weeks before his unexpected death, he and his team members at the Peace Project in La Jolla and elsewhere around the world were busy planning additional follow-up gatherings in Russia, Central America and South Africa, actively seeking funding from major foundations to realize these plans.

Unfortunately, Carl did not live to see the realization of these plans, nor of his dream of a well-funded and consolidated peace program through his institute for peace. Our major grant sources and possibilities disappeared almost immediately and completely after his death in 1987, due to a constellation of mitigating factors. It was only through the generous one-time gift of $100,000 from Mrs Joan Kroc to the Peace Project and through other self-generated fund-raising events that we were able in 1988 to re-convene a second Central American Dialogue in Costa Rica with diplomats from 11 countries, including the then President Oscar Arias, the Nobel Prize winner for that year. Without funding since that time, much of the work of the Carl Rogers Institute for Peace [was] dramatically limited, localized, nearly invisible, and ultimately closed down.

The final recognition of his impact on world peace in the 20th century was the formal nomination of Dr Rogers for the Nobel Peace Prize, which we received during his hospitalization. With both sadness and joy, we read aloud the announcement to Carl as he lay in a coma and dying on February 4, 1987. It is my belief that he heard us.

PUBLIC GATHERINGS ON POLITICS AND PEACE WORK

Specific large public events were also held over the years to share Carl's views on global issues, with always 500 or more people in attendance. In 1982 Marilyn Ferguson, Rogers, Sanford and myself, along with the support of other CSP staff and illustrious guest speakers, presented a large public gathering titled 'Two Humanists—Two Generations: A day to honor the planet, its people and our preservation' to celebrate Carl's 80th birthday and to report on Carl and Ruth Sanford's work in South Africa. A similar event was held in Orange County in November of 1986 at the University of California at Irvine, with Senator John Vasconcellos, Carl and myself speaking of our work in Central America. For Carl's 85th birthday and as a fundraiser for our continuing peace work to come, a final gathering took place just a month before his death where Carl focused on his visits to the Soviet Union, Central America and South Africa, and his hopes to return again to each of those volatile areas. Further fund-raising events were held after Carl's passing to attempt to realize these goals.

Thus, it is clear that Carl Rogers' ideas, expressed over many decades in his writings, films and videos, public conferences and lectures, indicated an on-going concern for social justice, equity, peace and dialogue across differences. His practical applications of these values became increasingly overt and political as he moved into his 70s and 80s. At this time he explicitly claimed in many international cross-cultural groups and settings that his major focus at that point in his life was the application of his approach to that of international peace, whether in Russia, Northern Ireland, South Africa or Central America. He grounded that hope in the establishment of the 'Carl Rogers Institute for Peace'.

Rogers said himself many years ago that *self*-development leads to an ethical engagement with others and all life. This sense of enfolding with others is particularly well expressed in us due to the very pro-social component of the actualizing tendency which he posited leads us toward *more* ethical and *more* socially conscious behavior, rather than to self-involving narcissism. As we become more self-confident in our positive behaviors and attitudes toward ourselves, and guided by our own internal locus of reference, we become more inclined toward adding to the general well-being of others.

Brian Thorne supports the sense of connectedness implicit in Carl's work when he quotes 'he [Carl] embraces the concept, first introduced by E.E. Sampson (1983) of "ensembled individualism": an individualism which is defined by its participatory involvement in the surrounding field and not by its separateness from it' (1991: 186). Thorne continues, 'It is possible I believe, to see Carl's work with encounter groups and then with cross-cultural communities and the peace movement as his gradual discovery of the glory of human beings when they are truly interconnected and find their fulfilment in participation which enhances rather than denies their uniqueness.'

ROGERS' 1978 STATEMENT: 'MY POLITICS'

Perhaps Carl's most important statement about politics, power and the PCA, and perhaps the least well known or quoted or analyzed, is in his *very* short statement published in *The Journey*, a short-lived newsletter edited by John T. Wood, John K. Wood and David Meador at CSP. The statement is excerpted from an unpublished paper that Carl delivered in El Escorial, Spain during Easter week, 1978, when asked by the 175 participants representing 26 countries to make a more explicit statement about his views on politics.

In considering the political, social and gender egalitarian aspects of the PCA, I invite the reader to take in slowly and carefully this brief but 'thick' half-page statement by Rogers on democracy and power, which I see as a watershed moment in Carl's political engagement. I believe that within this statement are embodied the most precise delineations of his view of PCA as politics that he ever articulated.

MY POLITICS
Carl R. Rogers
To me politics involves the question of where power is located, who makes the choices and decisions, who carries out or enforces those decisions, and who has the knowledge or data regarding the

consequences of those decisions. It involves the strategies involved in the taking of power, the distribution of power, the holding of power, and the sharing or relinquishing of power.

Let me summarize my own political 'ideology,' if you will, in a very few words. I find that for myself, I am most satisfied politically:

When every person is helped to become aware of his or her own power and strength.

When each person participates fully and responsibly in every decision which affects him or her.

When group members learn that the sharing of power is more satisfying than endeavoring to use power to control others.

When the group finds ways of making decisions which accommodate the needs and desires of each person.

When every member of the group is aware of the consequences of a decision, on its members and on the external world.

When each person enforces the group decision through self control of his or her own behavior.

When each person feels increasingly empowered, strengthened.

When each person, and the group as a whole, is flexible, open to change, and regards previous decisions as being always open for reconsideration.

I am sure that many of you regard these statements as hopelessly idealistic. But in my experience, especially when a facilitative climate is provided for a group, the members *choose* to move in somewhat the ways that I have described.

In some of my writings, particularly in my recent book, *Carl Rogers on Personal Power* [1977], I have given examples showing the effectiveness of this kind of politics in the marriage relationship, the family, in schools, in workshops, in the management of a business. I do not know of any political party or government which operates fully on this basis. But I do believe there is movement toward more participation in government, and a growing distrust of authoritarian institutions of every kind, so I do not despair.

This political creed of mine does not grow out of any political tract, or any general ideology. It developed out of my own experience, in which I discovered how richly rewarding it was to entrust persons with power, with responsible freedom of choice. (Rogers, 1982)

Here, Carl shows us once again that the basic premise of the PCA as expressed through his personal sense of politics and power within that approach is one that honors and respects the preciousness of each life, individually *and* collectively, a premise inherent in Carl's principles. This includes the preciousness of all peoples, even those with whom we disagree, the sanctity of the search for peace that includes each person's perspective which results in a sense of vivid living and engagement and respectful dialogue among us across our differences, an attitude so lacking today in our political discourse and our media reporting styles.

THE 'LIVING NOW' INSTITUTE

It is from such a philosophy and perspective of respectful dialogue across differences that I and other women began the first Women's Center at CSP in 1974, and then together with male colleagues, the 'Living Now Institute' in 1976 and the Carl Rogers Institute for Peace in 1984 as vehicles for social change. I have written at length about the Women's Center in the book *Encountering Feminism* (Proctor & Napier, 2004), but would like to elaborate below on the revolutionary social-action nature of both the Living Now program and the Peace Project.

After the development of a Women's Center at the Centre for Studies of the Person (CSP) in the early 1970s, the second tangible and ultimately quite long-lived (for over 22 years) result of my own commitment to the integration of social action and the PCA was the 'Living Now Institute' (LN) which I founded in 1976 with other CSP members. Nurtured originally by the earlier small women's group led by Betty Meador, and followed by the social activism of the Women's Center at CSP and by the increasing numbers of women involving themselves with CSP, I began to hold larger visions of how I would like to work in the world.

Founded with Andre Auw, John K. Wood and myself as co-directors, for over 20 years the core staff/team of LN remained Alberto Zucconi, Norman Chambers, Charles O'Leary, Arlene Wiltberger, Nel Kandel and myself, as several thousands of participants came from around the world to attend a ten-day live-in summer program held at the University of California at San Diego. Each summer, Living Now dealt specifically with socio-political issues, with participants from around the globe and notable speakers including Carl, and provided the first major context for person-centered discussions of major social issues of the time.

Admittedly, as noted earlier in this chapter, Carl had written and spoken with indignation about racism, and politics and corruption, and had begun international workshops with Chuck Devonshire and other colleagues in cross-cultural communications in the early 1970s, and with his daughter Natalie and others had held intensive socially conscious encounter gatherings beginning in the mid-1970s. But LN, begun in 1976, was, I believe, the first continuous annual expression within the PCA world speaking to the larger complex social issues beleaguering our nation and the world. Each annual title and topic for the 10-day-long gathering was explicitly political or socially conscious. Thus, LN became the first major fusing of content and culturally sensitive issues with the PCA process, creating a new form of 'topical encounter'. Carl used this platform willingly as a vehicle for voicing his increasingly political concerns and reporting on his international travels and work 'behind the Iron Curtain' in Poland and Russia, in Northern Ireland, South Africa and other 'hot spots' of the world.

Not everyone was happy about this 'innovation' at CSP and some members felt that we were no longer representing the PCA purely enough, and that Carl, by participating in it annually, was colluding in that impurity by becoming the key 'star attraction' that drew other famous speakers and writers of the era to the program to work with him. This seemed a contradiction to PCA principles of non-structured open-ended dialogue among equals. However, if we are honest about it, I believe that Carl had always been the main attraction and 'star' in any and all of our previous programs at CSP and worldwide. And, I suspect that it was an uneasy fit for many in the PCA community to deal so overtly with politically charged issues and cultural themes in flux at the time.

These socially relevant themes included aging, death and dying, racism, sexism, remaining humane in the nuclear age, life stages and transitions, men and women's relationships, planetary peace, diversity and living simply, among many others. Some years the focus was on one of Rogers' three conditions, either that of empathy, genuineness or unconditional prizing. Spiritual issues came to the fore as the years went on, and ultimately the politics of world peace, citizen diplomacy and conflict resolution were foreground concerns.

A key socially conscious aspect of LN was our staffing system. At all times in the past at CSP, the major programs there were run and staffed by men, particularly the La Jolla Program, the grandfather of encounter groups for Carl and CSP. The single extraordinary exception to that general rule was the important program created and convened by a woman, Orienne Strode (now Maloney), called 'Human Dimensions of Medical Education', which trained physician interns all across the country in the PCA, to increase their compassion and humanity as healers, and which Carl supported from its inception. The ripples of that program are felt today in physician education programs across the country. Other than that, the male-run and male-led program was the norm of the time.

I hoped to change that in my own work. Therefore, in every program thereafter that I convened or designed, I consciously made certain that both the guest speakers and the resident facilitative staff were balanced equally between men and women, and that men and women co-facilitated the small groups in all cases. This value statement and action about equal, cross-gender, co-leadership would become even more important in the development and staffing of the Peace Project in the 1980s, particularly when working on the Central American issues, and in our attempt to create ethnic, gender and political balance between the participants and staff wherever possible.

Our search for such equity and balance reached its zenith in the early 1990s in our effort to establish local Urban Diversity Dialogue groups (which evolved out of the Peace Project after Carl's death in 1987), the development of the Urban Diversity Council in San Diego, and our cross-border Mexican–USA Living Room Dialogues, the final closing expressions of the Peace Project. In spite of the limitations we faced after Carl's death, the Peace Project received a human relations award from the County of San Diego in 1992 for our pro bono work in improving dialogue in local communities about the volatile border immigration issues.

A MORAL ECOLOGY

We now know and trust from our years of experiences worldwide in the person-centered approach that dialogue and personal contact constitute a major pathway through to the perceived 'Other'. Thus, although the Peace Project itself no longer exists as a working entity, I still believe that a PCA-based dialogical process in every hamlet in this country and worldwide would be a timely re-beginning and continuation of the work. I trust and believe that on-going local and national gatherings of community dialogues in every village and city worldwide, convened by persons competent in person-centered listening and dialogue, along with spiritual and political leaders, and neighbors and lay people of good will and open minds and hearts, might be a beautiful start for renewing our sense of social contract to one another and the world.

Making room for and including diversity of thought through an open dialogue process, not narrowed by one pre-digested truth or dogma expressed in sound-bite thinking, censorship of ideas, or even outright purposeful distortions, but emerging from among peoples in charge of their own process of connections to one another, would be a revolutionary act in the spirit of Gandhi and Martin Luther King's movements of millions of people seeking to re-empower themselves through loving kindness and peaceful means. As important as our meeting together may be the quality of vitality with which we engage one another as the underpinning of our connection, for it is vitality that creates and enhances life in all its forms.

If we can come to some understanding of one another through such non-coercive and independently generated processes and perspectives, we might create an 'ecologically based morality' that is inclusive somehow of all perspectives within a tapestry of diverse but linked human systems, the outcome not defined as 'moral relativity' but what I term a 'moral ecology'. In so doing we might thus even enlarge the concept of what constitutes moral and ethical behaviors among a totally connected but widely diverse global family, and be able to articulate that clearly and respectfully to one another. If so, perhaps there is some hope.

To our credit in the PCA community, it is my experience over 40 years of working worldwide that even if we have not always been capable of living out our values together perfectly on those issues which had the capacity to separate us, our philosophical base invites us to attempt to do so by approximation. We PCA people are as human as anyone else after all, and, as does everyone, must daily face the difference between our aspirations and stated values, and our actual choices and behaviors, and the resulting outcomes. However, we keep giving ourselves the chance to change, again and again, thus more closely approximating our hopes for how we can be together.

In the final analysis, the entire world is at risk right now. We see clearly that at the global level, or any other level, without a mutual desire to listen, understand, genuinely meet and self-examine, hear other perspectives, acknowledge responsibilities, compromise, offer retribution and restorative acts and attitudes toward one another, and thus heal, repair, forgive and seek forgiveness, there is scant possibility of anything better happening than mutually agreed stand-offs, no-fly zones and bars not bridges between much of humankind.

In an effort to counterbalance those relentless invitations into psychic numbing that decrease our compassion and civility with one another in our public and private lives, I offer a different invitation for us to consider.

I invite us to call forth from ourselves and each other the voices and actions from those among us who would speak in alignment with a thirst for life and love, not death and destruction, who prefer to stand publicly and privately for high human (and I would claim more truly patriotic and universal) values such as peace, justice, equality, ethics and integrity, and who thrive on the love and respect for family, friendship, and humankind beyond our artificially created borders, and thus who cherish the life of earth in all its forms.

All of this may require a re-definition of our sense of courage. For example, henceforth, before going to war, courage may need to mean something quite different for young men and women and their families about to consider making their sacrifices. Courage may well be required to stand up against the exploitation of our psyches by rejecting those de-humanizing 'entertainment' modalities that train us in violence to become better, more compliant fodder for the beginning phases of this next hundred years' war. It will take another order of courage to fight a war already begun in the name of yet another 'crusade' by fundamentalist religious and political mentalities on both sides of the pointed spears, for such a war dishonors the spiritual callings of our deepest natures. It will also take enormous courage and idealism to say 'no' to participating in such a war.

As a start for activating our hopefulness and our own courage, each one of us might begin by expecting more from our corporations, our popular media and our professional politicians and religions. We might require of them and ourselves that we self-monitor our greed, be it material or for power, that we speak to and write articles and editorials and laws and sermons that hold accountable individuals, businesses, governments and religious movements for our thirst for excess profits and power or a place in heaven, at the expense of others.

At the same time, we will expect of ourselves as well that we no longer allow or support economically the cynical training of a generation made numb to their own inhumanity by bombardments from toddlerhood to their teens with media that teach a total disregard for pain and humiliation in another to the point of callousness and insensibility. Such idealism and courage will demand of ourselves a sense of proactive and responsible citizenship as watchdogs for our cultures, a role long abdicated by the passivity of too many of us.

In altering these downward cultural directions, we might even then elect presidents and prime ministers and legislative bodies and governments that truly believe in responsible ethics and integrity, service and compassion, fair economic systems, equity and justice, a free press, religious and cultural diversity and our own personally devised constitutions. I, for one, await with great anticipation such articles and actions and idealistic leadership from among us, and offer these thoughts as a personal beginning of my own.

YES

Yes, it could happen any time, tornado,
earthquake, Armageddon. It could happen.
Or sunshine, love, salvation.
It could, you know. That's why we wake
and look out—no guarantees
in this life.
But some bonuses, like morning,
like right now, like noon,
like evening.

William Stafford
The Way It Is: New and selected poems, 1998[1]

---

1. Reprinted by kind permission of the publishers, Graywolf Press.

REFERENCES

Holdstock, TL (1978) From client-centered therapy to a person-centered approach. *South African Journal of Psychology, 8,* 20–9.

Holdstock, TL (1990) Can client-centered therapy transcend its monocultural roots? In G Lietaer, J Rombauts & R Van Balen (eds) *Client-Centered and Experiential Psychotherapy in the Nineties.* Leuven: University of Leuven Press.

Kirschenbaum, H & Henderson, VL (eds) (1989) *The Carl Rogers Reader.* New York: Houghton Mifflin.

Olweean, S (2002) The Other. Psychological concepts of 'The Other': Embracing the compass of the self. In C Stout (ed) *The Psychology of Terrorism: Clinical aspects.* New York: Praeger/Greenwood Publishers.

Proctor, G & Napier, MB (2004) *Encountering Feminism.* Ross-on-Wye: PCCS Books.

Rogers, CR (1944a) Psychological adjustments of discharged service personnel. *Psychological Bulletin 41,* (10), 689–96.

Rogers, CR (1944b) Wartime issues in family counseling. *Journal of Home Economics, 36* (7), 390–3.

Rogers, CR (1945) Dealing with individuals in the USO. *USO Program Services Bulletin.*

Rogers, CR (1977) *On Personal Power.* New York: Delacorte.

Rogers, CR (1982) My politics. *Journey, 1* (6), 8

Rogers, CR & Russell, DE (2002) *Carl Rogers: The quiet revolutionary: An oral history.* Roseville, CA: Penmarin Books.

Rogers, CR & Wallen, JL (1946) *Counseling with Returned Servicemen.* New York: McGraw-Hill.

Schmid, PF (1998) Nouvelles perspectives pour l'évolution de l'approche centrée sur la personne. *Mouvance Rogérienne, 14,* 3–22.

Schmid, PF (2001) Interpellation et réponse. La psychothérapie centrée sur la personne: une rencontre de personne à personne. *Mouvance Rogérienne, 24,* 2–18.

Schmid, PF (2004) De la connaissance la reconnaissance. Défis que pose et que devra affronter l'approche centrée sur la personne dans une perspective dialogique et éthique en ce début du XXIᵉ siècle. In *Carriérologie. Revue Francophone Internationale 9,* (3&4), 401–21. English version 'From knowledge to acknowledgement: Challenges of and for the Person-Centered Approach from a dialogical and ethical perspective at the beginning of the 21st century, revised version of a lecture given at the conference 'Le Centenaire de Carl Rogers. Actualité de son message personnaliste', Paris, January 27, 2002.

Stafford, W (1998) *The Way It Is: New and selected poems.* St Paul, MN: Graywolf Press.

Thorne, B (1991) *Person-Centred Counselling: Therapeutic and spiritual dimensions.* London: Whurr Publishers.

Thorne, B (2002) *The Mystical Power of Person-Centred Therapy: Hope beyond despair.* London: Whurr Publishers.

Chapter 23

TRANSFORMATION IN TRANSYLVANIA

REINHOLD STIPSITS

I don't for a moment think that we have done things that will have a world wide impact. What we have done is to show, on sort of a smaller test-tube basis, that change is possible, reconciliation is possible, reduction of tension is possible, if a person-centred, facilitative climate is present. And that means a great deal to me. What we have worked on is more basic than the solution of problems; we have worked on helping people to understand one another, communicate with one another, and that, I feel, represents a much more realistic base for the solution of specific issues. (Carl Rogers, in Rogers & Russell 2002: 306)

Rogers' plea for a small step rather than a giant leap into unknown territory seems a particularly apt way to introduce a further example of the potential political impact of the person-centred approach (PCA). Obviously convinced of the effectiveness of the PCA, Rogers affirmed the ideas of freedom and human rights as its highest goals, freedom being an essential condition of a psychological climate in which healthy growth processes can take place. Creative teaching may be yet another goal however. The following paper deals with a personal experience which took place in 2004 during a guest professorship in that magical-sounding but relatively unknown place, Transylvania. I was offered a position for the spring term at the Babes Bolyai University in Cluj-Napoca, situated in the heart of Transylvania, teaching in the Faculty of Political Science and Public Administration, at the German department of Communication and School of Journalism.

THE BURDEN OF HISTORY

There are not many areas in the world today which are so unknown to Western or Central Europeans as Transylvania so I would like to begin with an overview of its historical development. Historically, this region of Romania has always been associated with that dark creature, Count Dracula, from Bram Stoker's classic novel of the same name, but even the facts do little to brighten its image. Today, 15 years after the 1989 assassination of the dictator Ceausescu, which ended fifty years of communism, Romania still ranks as one of the poorest countries in Europe. Eight out of ten of the poorest regions in Europe are in Romania, according to an official EU poll, with the average income at about 80 to 100 Euros a month. In light of this, Romania will require a transformation in order for it to join the circle of the more highly developed countries in the EU. A rich country in terms of natural beauty and resources, it has been exploited over centuries and ruined by various land reforms, which always resulted in the rich becoming richer while the masses remained bitterly poor. Romania's agriculture benefits from its climate of four distinct seasons, and the country would also theoretically have access to an unspoiled sea, had not ancient, leaky oil pipelines turned the industrial areas into an ecological disaster zone.

Towards the north west of the country there is Cluj-Napoca, the capital of Transylvania, founded by the Romans. It is also the location of the oldest Hungarian university, which was founded in 1581 and is older than the University of Bucharest, the capital of modern Romania. *Transilvania*, the Latin name for the region, has had a multi-ethnic society since that time. There are Romanian people, with their own distinct language of Romanian—a language related to the other Roman languages, French, Spanish, Italian and Portuguese. Since about the year 1000 AD Hungarians have lived here too, again with their own language, and split into at least two different groups. One of them, called the Szekler, (a strongly independently minded Catholic group, which has never been part of Hungary), has enjoyed the privilege of landownership, while continuing to speak Hungarian. For more than eight centuries Transylvania has also been home to the German groups of Saxons and Swabians, with minorities of Gypsies, Greeks, Serbs, Croats, Ruthenians (from Ukraine), and further Germanic groups such as Sathmar Swabians, and Landler (former Austrians). Last, but not least, there is a Jewish community.

For a long time the Hungarians claimed to make up the majority of the population in Transylvania, that is, until the transmigration of Romanian farmers and workers was promoted by the communist regime in order to establish a Romanian majority. People from the remotest areas of Moldavia were forced to settle in the Cluj Basin. The city promised work but a mass of industrial proletariats was the outcome, and for a while the number of Hungarians dropped to approximately 20% of the population. The number of German speakers went down to an estimated 110,000, or less than 0.4% of a nation with more than 22 million inhabitants. An interesting sequel to this is that between 1991 and 1994, about 700,000 people from the German-speaking areas of Romania left for Germany, Canada, Austria, or the US. The German government offered them—generously, one might think—a German passport and the equivalent of about 7,200 Euros, and for many, Germany (seeking to attract educated people and thereby achieve economic growth) seemed the Promised Land. They left Romania, leaving behind their old relatives and only a few children. For many emigrants this move resulted in unhappiness due to disappointment with low paid jobs and living, cut off from their roots, deprived of their functioning village structures and customs, in the anonymous suburbs of Western Europe. And for Romania itself, this meant the loss of well-educated people. A further problem was that many of the abandoned villages, where entirely German-speaking communities had lived for centuries, were taken over, literally overnight, by the Gypsies.

Apart from general economic deprivation, Romanian society is facing two major problems linked with ethnic issues. Probably the main problem and one for all ethnic groups is that the representatives of the Gypsies are not really willing to co-operate with any other groups in society. In fact the Gypsies dismiss all offers of public help, perhaps due to the fact that they have been treated as second-class citizens for too long. They were always forced to live in separate communities and were not accepted because of their very different attitudes towards manual labour, different views of private property and different views regarding democracy. Even today there are Gypsy kings living in huge castle-like buildings, ruling over their people. Demographically the development of the Gypsy population is a serious concern with many young teenage mothers, often pregnant again, begging with their babies in the streets. The rapid increase in number of the poorest of the population will remain a huge human problem, regardless of the general economic development and the EU projects teaching Gypsy children literacy skills, when many parents are illiterate and suspicious of the value of education.

The second ethnic conflict simmers beneath the surface and springs from the intense rivalry between Hungarians and Romanians. The struggle between these two groups has become more evident since the absence of the Germans, whose presence acted as both a buffer and a link. Without them they are now like a head and a body, with no functioning connections. One could call it a culture clash between two ethnic groups, who never got along very well. For example, a former King of Hungary, Mathias Corvinus, was called 'the Just' by the Hungarians, as the period of his reign was the only time when all Hungarian people lived in one empire. The Romanians, however, consider him a descendent of a Romanian *Voivod* (Count), who was born in Hunedoara, a definitely Romanian area, in which case he could not possibly have been a Hungarian king. Sibling rivalry is a mild metaphor for the problems between the Romanians and Hungarians. There is a general mutual fear of being quite literally overruled, a fear, which unfortunately is justified as history has proved over and over again.

After all the tragedies resulting from the nationalist ideas and ideologies of the nineteenth century, one can see manifestations of that cultural clash written in the very stone right in the city of Cluj. The architecture of Cluj-Napoca reveals all sorts of chauvinism regarding the influence of various landowners or the ever-changing majority of the city. [1] Even today there are many great buildings in Cluj

---

1. Today one can find a Romanian National Theatre and a Hungarian Theatre as well. Both houses employ excellent ensembles, which perform Shakespeare dramas or Beckett plays. One can enjoy Italian Opera or the works of the great Russian writers, in either Romanian or Hungarian. There are no German and hardly any English theatre performances. The educated audience nevertheless watches everything, including American blockbuster movies at the cinema, in English with subtitles in Romanian.

of a very Central European style, which attest to the influence of the by-gone Habsburg dynasty administration. Subsequent history right up to World War I has seen Romanian–Hungarian cultural battles for freedom of the press, religious freedom, power in royal courts and artistic freedom.

After World War I Hungary lost one-third of its land, namely the province of Transylvania, to Romania. The Hungarians took this loss to heart, but as in most similar cases the borders of one's emotional home are never clearly defined. Such things give rise to nationalism. Tumultuous times continued and in 1943 during World War II, from one day to the next, Romania withdrew its support of Germany and allied itself with Russia. The Communist period followed, resulting in millions of victims from all ethnic groups.

Not everything in that picture however gives reason to despair. As in art, there is another controversial field of struggle for the ordinary man, that of religion. Spiritual convictions are a very personal choice and an area of political and ideological debate. This is nothing new. The prime law for the German-speaking people in Transylvania dates back to 1486. Privileges and rights, such as electing local bishops, organizing free markets and collecting tolls were granted by the king. One of the little-known facts about Transylvania is that freedom of religious belief was guaranteed as early as 1568. That law predated any other such law in Europe. Transylvania can boast that it is one of the first areas in the world to allow its people religious freedom. It was even an inspiration to the young men who drew up the Declaration of Independence in the new transatlantic provinces of New England, known today as the United States of America.

It might therefore be surprising to learn how strong the influence of organized churches in this former communist country has always been, and still is. It is important to note that there are four faculties of theology acknowledged at the University, (the Orthodox, the Roman Catholic, the Protestant or Reformed Church, and the Greek Catholic Church). The Jewish community has a newly renovated synagogue and its members are well respected in the outside community. In spite of this seeming harmony, there is widespread distrust between the ethnic groups. The real danger to minorities therefore does not exist so much in public life as in people's emotional experience. The reality of assimilation and the difficulty of retaining one's ethnic identity merely by speaking a language of the minority are evident. I came across this in my contact with the German-speaking minority, and it is a problem aggravated by the shortage of teachers able to speak and teach (in) German. Not only this, it is also a situation which requires that such teachers practise objectivity and refrain from spreading any political propaganda. Gone is the time of colonies and one cannot promote freedom and commitment to humanist goals in the name of one single race, ethnic group, nation or spiritual belief.

A ROLE FOR THE PERSON-CENTRED APPROACH

It is at this point that I see a chance for the PCA to make a valuable contribution as an approach supporting multi-ethnical diversity and equality among different opinions and cultures. The diversity of religious backgrounds and the demand for the modernization of this so-called reform state creates pressure but is also a unique chance. It is a time of great transitions. PCA can be used as a tool for mediation and conflict resolution, as it was practised by Rogers in countries such as Northern Ireland, South Africa, and the Soviet Union. The 1985 Rust Conference in Austria, which focused on Nicaragua and its neighbouring states, is another example Rogers dealt with at length (Rogers, 1986; Swenson, 1987). Probably the staff group there was slightly too optimistic, but Larry Solomon said the conference 'was not a wasted effort. It was a step in the right direction' (Solomon, 1987: 347). Nevertheless John K. Wood criticized the event as succumbing to the 'pitfall [of] modelling an application instead of seeking creative experience together' (Wood, 1999: 154).

In the tradition of PCA there is a long forgotten book *The Person-Centered Approach and Cross Cultural Communication* edited by McIlduff and Coghlan in 1993. In their article 'On becoming a political person: a person-centered view' (1993: 114) Frenzel and Przyborski explore this same topic. Neither that article nor Alberto Segrera's and Mariano Araiza's work, who discuss some 'Proposals for a person-centered model of conflict resolution' remained in the focus of discussion. In the same volume you find also a thoughtful contribution by Colin Lago and Mhairie MacMillan—amongst the few who have taken up the challenge of diversity studies and intercultural work. Recently there has also been some work by a group of Austrians, who have offered training courses in client-centred therapy to colleagues in Romania (see Kinigadner, 2004). Credit should also be given to the effort to employ the PCA in a prison in Bucharest (Bonatiu & Din, 2004). Despite this, in Romania, like everywhere else in the world, the political consequences of a thoughtfully applied PCA are greatly underestimated. Politicizing the PCA demands that one focuses on promoting diversity, and this means providing a climate of understanding rather than just practising and applying a theoretical concept called the PCA. A positive attitude towards diversity would be grounds for hope and change in Romania, which aims to become a member of the European Union by 2007. Universities play a significant role in this transformation, too.

SOCIAL REPORT AND CONFLICT RESOLUTION

My first objective as guest professor in the German department of Communication and School of Journalism was to instruct a group of about twenty students in social reporting. I immediately got in touch with a variety of institutions, which accepted the students, who were to write a so-called 'social report' based on their observations there. It was an overall mutual learning experience. Not only should the students learn how to interview people in an unobtrusive way, but they were also asked to write a critical report on their experiences. Altogether we planned reports on the four following themes: travel, milieu studies, public services and local customs. All reports were documented carefully. As I had the pleasure and the privilege to accompany them, I gained insights into a variety of institutions I would never have expected to learn about.

I would like to mention only a few examples. One student was allowed to visit a psychiatric clinic. She was impressed with the caring attitude she found there towards all the senile patients one would commonly diagnose as Alzheimer cases. Besides the necessity of drugs to calm or strengthen some patients, she felt the care present in this isolated world too. With another student we visited a surgical department in the general hospital of Cluj. The highly qualified doctors shared with us their daily problems on their wards. State-of-the-art microsurgery with micro cameras is daily routine. There is, however, a lack of basic items such as surgical gloves, which are not always available. Another example was the fact that the first call in the morning goes to the blood bank. If there is none of the required blood group on hand, then of course an operation is not possible. Surrounded by such uncertainty, trust between doctors and patients is essential.

One report dealt with a foster home for juveniles whose parents are in prison. The young reporters encountered a very depressing situation. It is a difficult task to observe with keen interest and a non-judgemental attitude and proceed to write about a system where the inconveniences of poorly organized and poorly structured working conditions are obvious. One could clearly see the absolute need for conditions of worth. Children in bunk beds, trembling with fever, needed the warmth and care of their 'social mothers', as they were called, as did those young adolescents, who, in a primitive studio, organized a sort of private radio program for the foster home. Acceptance, unconditionally provided, was a rare experience for these children, and so strongly desired by all of them.

Here too a general dilemma becomes apparent: unconditional acceptance and genuineness can appear contradictory at times, but empathy can provide a sort of balance between the two. Whether it was the case at a special nursery for blind children, or at a vocational school for deaf students, my students had to study the impact these two attitudes may have on people, as well as their own personal power. If students, as ongoing but already firmly devoted journalists, wrote about their experiences in a genuine way, they would be torn between honesty and unconditionally accepting the misery they had to face. Critical journalism is a sensitive job. One does not need to be involved in a denunciatory style of investigative journalism to realize how strong one's impact on a social situation can be. The role of the journalist as a generator of views, values and opinions is so important. I see young students of journalism in a crucial position in a society that is undergoing transformation. Will old values survive along with a system that honours the party line more than individual freedom, or will success go to the new entrepreneurs, who are being seduced by quick money in amounts they had never dreamed of? Is there a third way? Corruption is an ever-present danger in a society in transformation and it is not always in the form of money. Corruption is primarily a question of morality, consequently public virtue is at stake. I see the person-centred approach as extremely demanding, with high standards to live up to. Self-criticism is also necessary within our so-called Western-oriented institutions, however we sometimes forget this in our attempts to be non-judgemental. Economic concerns and other interest-driven decisions very often occupy us in a way that contradicts the PCA. The politics of the PCA are humanism *and* commitment to its values.

Besides closely observing institutions, the students obviously had a great need to feel accepted by their teacher, and one way for me to show this was to ask them to publish their experiences. Up until this time they had never had any of their own writing published. The project however took a decisive turn when I offered to find a publisher for the students' findings. Students began to withdraw and, interestingly enough, the reasons for not wanting their work published were expressed in such statements as: 'I do not want to see my home country, Romania, shown in a bad light', or 'Somebody might think of us as a backward country. We know what is wrong here, we do not need your pity, we need your help.'

Who would not be touched by these attitudes and words? Do they represent self-censorship or humility?

Nevertheless this was the beginning of a mutual exchange of ideas between the students and myself, and something we have continued up to this day. Teaching at a university offers the opportunity to be part of a community. It illustrates the unifying aspect of an old idea, that of *Universitas,* the learning community of teachers and students. Publishing a work resulting from the efforts of a group is also a political gesture and, regardless of some of the difficulties due to inadequate information technology support or the inexperience of the writers, the outcome seems valuable enough to be pursued.

My second objective during my stay was a workshop called 'conflict resolution', addressed to the German-speaking group. However as soon as I passed the outlines of my workshop on to my colleague, Vasile Docea, a good friend of mine from the Romanian Department of Communication, he asked me to have his students from the Romanian Department invited as well. This was then the first time in this faculty that students of two language departments were put together in one course. We chose the workshop format as an example of what we wanted to demonstrate. I, as the facilitator, assumed the position of the third party mediating in the conflict. It was of course necessary to use the language of the third party too, which was English, so we had a workshop in English for a body of Romanian and German students. Fortunately it went very well. Not only did the students learn, at their request, something about the basics of Rogers' conflict theory, but we also had some other material and examples from previous group conflicts within the School of Journalism. These involved the German-speaking and Romanian groups studying Public Relations in the field of Communication Science. During the workshop we had awkward silences, we had times of wariness and aggression, and we had joy and understanding. As in any process of mediation the third party must carefully balance the interests of the conflicting groups.

What struck me most was the openness of the students, novices to the person-centred approach, a factor that allowed me to start afresh myself. Our experiment was appreciated by several faculties and seems to have created some ripples. I have since received an invitation from a professor at the Department of Philosophy inviting me to continue next year. This would mean working with Romanian and German students just beginning their course, and students of the Hungarian department would be invited too. A professor of psychology, the Vice-President of the Academic Council, has also expressed his interest. It would be naïve at this point to expect students of Gypsy heritage, but what Rogers said seems to be true: change is possible, reconciliation is possible, reduction of tension is possible, if a person-centered, facilitative climate is present. And I like to use his words to describe the situation I found in Transylvania: 'What we have worked on is more basic than the solution of problems; we have worked on helping people understand one another, communicate with one another, and that, I feel, represents a much more realistic basis for the solution of the specific issues' (Rogers & Russell, 2002: 307).

Transylvania has provided me with a time-warp-experience that I am grateful for. It has made me realize again the importance of trust in the potential of people despite difficult circumstances. I know the PCA is not a simple application of a value system and I have seen how, by embracing diversity based on a person-centred approach, creative solutions may be found to familiar problems.

PSYCHOLOGY AND SOCIAL CHANGE

Of course this essay could have been written much more academically. One would only have to mention the different roles of therapy as a curative enterprise, and the role of journalism or public relations as preventive enterprises. One could elaborate on the difference between prevention and care, but one would hope for sustainability. Politicizing the PCA would mean acting locally but with a global perspective, and the global perspective would be, in turn, universal. Politics deal with *interests*—they are not a matter of natural growth nor do they possess a self-actualizing tendency. Politics are a question of will, and viewing personal will as universal can become dangerous and totalitarian. Therefore politicizing the PCA always requires a great deal of education, and the will for community needs to be cultivated; it is social education.

One could also refer to one of the unknown heroes of modern psychology, a man who had an enormous impact on Rogers. Otto Rank, a psychologist, stands directly between the orthodoxy of a Freudian psychoanalysis and the 'Quiet Revolutionary', the 'good guy from La Jolla'. In his last book *Beyond Psychology*, Rank presents the eternal dilemma of our problem regarding political impact as 'the question as to whether a change in the people themselves or a change in their system of living is the better method for improving human conditions' (Rank, 1941: 17). He continues to explain that there are two dynamic forces inherent in this human conflict of the individual striving against the social impact of the civilization into which he happens to be born. This eternal conflict of humanity's striving for control of uncontrollable circumstances is dramatically epitomized in times of world war. (Not much has changed in this respect if we consider the present war on Iraq.)

Rank goes on to say:

> Bound by the ideas of a better past gone by and a brighter future to come, we feel helpless in the present because we cannot even for a moment stop its movement so as to direct it more intelligently. We still have to learn, it seems, that life, in order to maintain itself, must revolt every so often against man's ceaseless attempts to master its irrational forces with his mind. No matter in what terms this presumptuous aim is attempted, sooner or later a reaction sets in, be it in the form of intellectual scepticism and pessimism—through which, for example the Greeks perished—or in the actual rebellion of our frustrated human nature. (Rank, 1941: 18)

Rank links social change and political change with education. Although somewhat a sceptic, he develops and emphasizes ideas which go 'beyond psychology', leading to what has become a 'Psychology of Difference'. This kind of psychology is not merely antagonism towards classical theory. It is the deconstruction of the grand narratives of freedom and progress made available by scientific means. Conflict resolution, as well as journalism with its critical social reporting, is a way of respecting differences.

A further option would be to please the academic highbrows and criticize the universal growth principle as overrated. Useful and adequate in biological explanations, it has a touch of absolutist dogmatism in a political context. The principle of natural growth regarding a nation is unacceptable if one bears in mind the role imperialism or fascism have played in history. The person-centred approach aims at enhancing and fostering freedom and one may be justifiably proud of a movement that played a role in the opening up of Eastern European countries to the West before the fall of the Iron Curtain. Rogers was always vitally interested in encounters with people living in difficult economic conditions. (For details refer to his work in Hungary and the Soviet Union.)

Transylvania seems to be a rather small piece of land. Probably nowhere else in the world is the following proverb so true: 'I will sing the song of the man whose bread I eat.' Over the centuries people were used to accepting and adapting to whatever their landlords demanded of them, consequently the idea of freedom and human rights is new and unfamiliar. The irony is that these very ideas were born here but they have yet to be truly lived here, or in any other country for that matter.

I hesitate to write with great pomp about freedom and commitment and justice. All are grand concepts and values we fight for in life, in therapies and in other applications of the PCA. Instead I am grateful to share this personal experience and I would like to end with a reference to the title of John Shlien's book *To Lead an Honorable Life* (2003). In this sense, let us be humble in every *transformation*. But we can study and learn to communicate clearly. Language, to be truly understood, must be spoken from the heart. This is politics enough.

REFERENCES

Bonatiu, M & Din, F (2004) Klientenzentrierte Psychotherapie in einer Strafvollzugsanstalt in Bukarest. In W Keil (ed) *Person: Internationale Zeitschrift für Personzentrierte und Experienzielle Psychotherapie und Beratung*, 1/2004 8. Jahrgang (55–9).

Frenzel, P & Przyborski, A (1993) On becoming a political person: a person-centered view. In E McIlduff & D Coghlan (eds) *The Person-Centered Approach and Cross Cultural Communication. An International Review*. Volume II (pp. 114–22). Linz: edition sandkorn.

Lago, C & MacMillan, M (eds) (1999) *Experiences in Relatedness: Groupwork and the person-centred approach*. Ross-on-Wye: PCCS Books.

Kinigadner, S (2004) Klientenzentrierte Therapie-Ausbildung in Rumänien. Bericht über ein Projekt der ÖGwG. *Person: Internationale Zeitschrift für Personzentrierte und Experienzielle Psychotherapie und Beratung*. Hg. Wolfgang Keil, facultas Verlag, Wien, 1/2004 8. Jahrgang, (69–73).

McIlduff, E & Coghlan, D (eds) (1993) *The Person-Centered Approach and Cross Cultural Communication. An International Review*. Volume II. Linz: edition sandkorn.

Rank, O (1941) *Beyond Psychology*. New York: Dover Publications Inc.

Rogers, CR (1986) The Rust Workshop. *Journal of Humanistic Psychology, 3* (3), 23–45.

Rogers, CR & Russell, DE (2002) *Carl Rogers: The quiet revolutionary. An oral history*. Roseville, CA: Penmarin Books.

Shlien, JM (2003) *To Lead an Honorable Life. Invitations to think about Client-Centered Therapy and the Person-Centered Approach. A collection of the work of John M Shlien*. Ross-on-Wye: PCCS Books.

Solomon, LN (1987) International tension reduction through the person-centered approach. *Journal of Humanistic Psychology, 27* (3), 337–47.

Swenson, G (1987) When personal and political processes meet. The Rust Workshop. *Journal of Humanistic Psychology, 27* (3), 309–33.

Wood, JK (1999) Toward an understanding of large group dialogue and its implication. In C Lago & M MacMillan (eds) *Experiences in Relatedness: Groupwork and the person-centred approach* (pp. 137–66). Ross-on-Wye: PCCS Books.

Chapter 24

THE CENTRE: A PERSON-CENTRED PROJECT IN EDUCATION

Fiona Hall

This chapter is about learning and how to learn despite education. It is about institutions, how to become proactive in a society made up of institutions and where there is a strong drive to create similar institutions. In short, it is about how to become political and remain sane.

I started my career in the UK as a person-centred counsellor working with families of children under 5 years old. I read Rogers' *On Becoming a Person* (1961) with its focus on the worth of the individual whilst working for an organization that actually had an agenda that was about the *organization* and not the clients. This struck me as untenable. For example, we were being trained as counsellors to empower the parents and at the same time other workers would be setting wheels in motion to have the same parents' children adopted or placed in care.

The impact of the training I received was life-changing. It soon became apparent that once parents have their voices heard, they start to become empowered. I became committed to the person-centred approach and was able to see my first attempts at practice as incredibly enabling and liberating—not just for my clients but for myself as well.

It was while I was devouring the work of Carl Rogers that I became aware of my own institutionalization. I had accepted without question that if you want to do a certain kind of work, say with families, you found the box where that activity happened. I had accepted, with some complaint but little questioning, the limitations of the agency and the atmosphere of fear of getting the work wrong. Now I started to question if it was good for me. It seemed to me that most of my energies were spent in endless meetings with an organizational agenda. The reason for the meeting would be family X, but I soon learned to mute my understanding of the dynamics and potential of that family in case I was seen as 'over-involved'. I began to realize that this only diminished my voice at these meetings.

The environment of a government-funded agency didn't offer much room to grow into new areas that I felt could contribute to social and political change. What could an organization that was stretched between public accountability and demands for error-free practice offer someone who was committed to preventative work? It could offer the door, but I found that for myself.

I left to set up a private practice where I worked with a mix of adults and children. I had three children of my own by this time and it was when two of my children were at school that the whole area of education became interesting to me.

I didn't see the parallel of my experience in social services with my children's experience of school until one of my children became so deeply unhappy at school that to send her for one more day would have felt abusive. I was still thinking in the box that goes something like—if your child is unhappy at school then the solution lies in the system. In this case, the solution apparently was communicating with the teachers. What I learned was that the system has to be rigid enough to cope with classes of about 30 children and one teacher who has a curriculum to deliver. It is an institution. There was no room for the personality of my child and so she was becoming alienated and demoralized. What her parents saw as gifts and blessings the teachers saw only as nuisance and distraction. The only healthy place for her to be was at home with us because we could provide an accepting environment. When I stepped (a child in either hand) out of the education system, I was grateful for my grounding in the person-centred approach.

Years as a therapist immersed in the core conditions gave me a familiar and trusted place to be with my child. My third child, at age three, retired from nursery after about two months of going two days a week. She was certain it was the wrong place for her and we agreed.

We made the shift from the school gates to a group of home educators. We found people who (more or less) thought like we did about parenting. We made the decision to live on a single academic salary. The income from my part-time private practice just about covered my professional expenses.

My partner is a scientist with a respect for the person-centred approach, especially in the teaching of science. I have a passion for enabling creativity, particularly children's creativity, to flourish. We increasingly had parents asking us quite anxiously about how we taught our children. You see, when you leave school you also leave any support and guidance of the state system. There may be regular inspections of your family, but the home educator cannot expect any help. So some excellent support groups have developed in various parts of the country.

The part of me that was committed to effecting social good was alive and bouncing. I had a dream about a resource centre where children could be and experience the core conditions and reconnect with early experiences of the joy of learning. This centre would also provide a meeting place for families. The informal home-educating groups mostly meet in each other's homes or community halls. These venues have their limitations on the projects children can do together. I was constantly part of conversations about the need for more resources; somewhere to meet that wasn't expensive. Finding neutral places for families to come together.

Talking to parents nationally it seemed that without structure or guidance, people sometimes floundered because of their lack of confidence. In the absence of an alternative they turned to theories that often left them feeling inadequate. These theories preached an apparently ideal way of parenting and educating children but left little space for the flawed people that most of us are.

The person-centred approach offers the home educator an affirmation of their desire to trust their child, and a relationship which allows for those feelings that most parents feel sometime: despair, anger and frustration, as well as all the positive feelings which are part of spending a lot of time with children. Rogers' *Freedom to Learn* offered reassurance: that to be who you are in the presence of another could teach the most important lesson. This offered affirmation of the approach which seemed so prevalent amongst the home educators I met, that when you trust the instincts of your child to know what she needs to know, then learning is a joy for everyone involved.

There was a small group of us who were excited about the possibility of starting a childcare place for families who wanted something different to the edu-care nurseries that were starting to spring up. We wrote the following description of our aspirations:

> This is a project that is beginning and will continue to take shape in stages.
>
> The overall aim will be to provide an environment for growth and learning that is person-centred. Carl Rogers pioneered the ethos, based on the core conditions of empathy, congruence and unconditional positive regard. This approach has been used most widely as a therapeutic model for counselling. It has also been applied to other settings, most notably education.
>
> The first resource will be a nursery for children under 6. All people working with the children will be trained in the person-centred approach. The children will experience care that will respect their individuality. Play, learning, socializing and all other aspects of their time in the centre will be child-led. The children will experience their creativity in a nurturing atmosphere and build their self-worth by attaining their own targets. Children will take control of their own learning. From learning to value themselves, children naturally learn to respect and value others.
>
> Carers will maintain the necessary structures to ensure the well-being and safety of the children. There will be space allocated to developing a resource centre for exploration and learning. This will be available to home-educated and schooled children.
>
> The next stage in the project would be to extend opportunity for learning and personal growth to families and adults. The Centre will operate as a cooperative and will take its shape and direction from those involved.
>
> Everyone matters!

There was a good deal of excitement for the project locally and there was a group of people who seemed to embody person-centeredness—or at least had an enthusiasm for learning about it. We all believed that through the person-centred approach we could offer a model for dealing with each other and the wider membership. There was already a certain carefulness to respect the difference between the families' styles and beliefs.

The idea met with strong support amongst home educators and professional educators. There was a core group who were keen to see the project become a reality and work started on shaping it and finding a home.

The following year was quite a heady time. We talked with home-educating parents and children, alternative education authors, discussed the idea at person-centred conferences, received support from the great and the good in the person-centred world, in local education authorities and in OFSTED: [1] people who felt that education had gone way too far in the direction of measuring all aspects of education into a desiccated heap. Others talked with local groups who were involved in non-mainstream education and with people who had a passion for passing on their knowledge or skills to children but who didn't want to become teachers. We talked with teachers who had lost faith in the system or who had left because they were close to burnout.

The idea of starting a nursery floundered. We had three people who all had wanted to start up this kind of childcare and all of them were unable to move it forward for very good reasons. This became a pattern for the project. The rest of the group, which was much larger, were the people keen to develop a resource for home-educated children. So we continued.

The next step was to find a person-centred way of moving the project forward. We had in our group a person who had worked happily for a large company that operated on Open Space principles. [2] I had also encountered this way of working at the Carl Rogers Centenary conference in San Diego and thought it was a system for creatively making decisions without being hierarchical. I was aware that although we were happy to use the Open Space format there might be others who would not be, just as in San Diego.

So in August 2002, the first public meeting happened. Out of it came a commitment to get the Centre started and work out the management structure as we went along. There was agreement that we would identify what needed doing and a hope that people would volunteer for the work. There was a great deal of enthusiasm to get projects up and running under the umbrella of what had now come to be called 'The Centre'.

We were offered the sole use of a large room in a rambling Victorian church

---

1. OFSTED (Office for Standards in Education) is the inspectorate for children and learners in England. They are a non-ministerial government department accountable to Parliament.

2. The Open Space meeting is conducted in a way that is designed to hold that moment when people come together with ideas and enthusiasm. Each idea is treated equally, and each person is free to choose where to channel his or her enthusiasm, see <www.openspaceworld.org>.

for a very low rent. Other users of the building were a homeless persons' hostel, a music school, toddler groups and a bicycle repair shop run for and by people who were unemployed. All of these groups had their own entrances and rarely met, but the promise was there for support and encouragement from the management groups of each.

The Centre opened in November 2002. The first group act was to get the children together to decide on a colour scheme for the room. We had an improbable group of colours chosen that worked wonderfully well, reds and blues. It was a long room, so we decided to divide it roughly into three: a creative/ play space; a booky, computer space; and a social space with sofas and kettle.

Resources seemed to flow in fast and soon the room was full of science equipment, instruments, paints, a computer …

Welcome to the Centre.

It exists to provide an environment where children and adults can come together to share the pleasure of learning in freedom from authority.

I invite you to step inside and visualize: a large sun-filled room, with the sound of traffic from the city centre in the distance. At the comfy end on the sofas are a group of girls choosing from the books each has read which they are going to read and discuss as part of their book club. Two boys have come on their own to finish a display of intricate plasticine figures, a project that emerged from an art group. A small child is playing chess on the computer. The older children are starting to arrive for the science club. They throw their bags down and start to get out the equipment. A parent is pinning up artworks around the room. The children are respectful of the needs of others and, although there is excitable conversation, it tends to be the children who remind each other of the need to keep noise levels down.

The science club is hosted by a parent of one of the children, who, like most children, has lots of questions about how the world works. The children are not given answers but are enabled to devise their own experiments with suggestions made from the parent facilitator about what materials they might use. I have taken part in these groups as an interested parent and watched the children interacting and growing in confidence as they realize that they don't have to be experts in order to make headway in science. They aren't told what the outcome of an experiment 'ought' to be. Instead an enthusiast who respects the efforts of each of them accompanies them on their experimental journeys. This is a pretty diverse group of young people and each week they turn up on time.

Another group started life as a drop-in session each week. The children were offered art and craft type activities while the parents chatted. Then the children decided they wanted the parents to help them with drama, a local church heard about this group and asked if they would put on a nativity play for them. The result was a pretty novel nativity play and the congregation were charmed.

So, the result was a success from the children's point of view. What we had created was a space where they could put their mark and each of them could use, confident in the knowledge that it was shared space. In that space they made their own decisions, they negotiated future sessions amongst themselves, they could start a project and come back whenever they liked to continue with it. Those who used it loved The Centre.

Fundraising too had been embraced and was fun. We ran a stall at large fairs offering reasonably priced healthy food for children. This raised us a comfortable sum as well as spreading the word about our existence.

That was what was happening on the main stage and it took most of the main players' time and effort to reach that point. It was glorious and good and I was ready to celebrate.

As with most emerging groups, however, all was not well. People were feeling sidelined or put upon or misunderstood. There was unhappiness and a struggle with ideology. There were rumours about the direction of The Centre, which had little to do with its philosophy.

An example of this happened at a point in the life of The Centre when its use seemed to be going well. Attendance and membership were good, the accounts were healthy and we were getting good feedback from the children about how they wanted their groups to develop.

The majority of the management group had asked for an agenda instead of using the Open Space format. I was happy for this change since it seemed to be an experiment in running this meeting that the others wanted to try.

I have parodied what happened because I want the feel of this phase to be here. This is how it felt (my own involvement is most closely represented by '*Ms Let's-get-on-and-do-something*') …

Mr Grump: *Where has all the money gone?*

Ms Let's-get-on-and-do-something: *It has been spent on setting up the Centre, here look at the receipts. The rest is in the bank. Here—look at the bank balance!*

Miss Particular: *There is unhappiness about the constitution, people didn't expect a hierarchy—it talks of 'executive members', people are unhappy about that.*

Ms Let's-get-on-and-do-something: *Yes, but it's not like 'executive toilets'—the domain of the privileged. The group who drew up the constitution were careful to share the responsibility. Executive roles will be shared out as needed and after all 'executive' means a person who executes something, we can't get around that. We can change the name to whatever feels comfortable.*

Mr Grump: *Why haven't you told us where the money is?*

Ms Let's-get-on-and-do-something: *Here are the statements, here are the chequebooks.*

Miss Put-upon: *There are complaints that the sessions held here are focused around a small number of children's interests, and some children have been coerced.*

Ms Let's-get-on-and-do-something: *That's really sad if someone has felt coerced. Is there anything we can do about that? As for the selection of activities, I offer what I can. There are more three-hour sessions each week for anyone to offer what they will …*

Miss Particular: *We will have to rewrite the constitution.*

Ms Let's-get-on-and-do-something: *Have you consulted the group who wrote this one?*

Miss Particular: *Oh, they clearly didn't spend much time on it. I'm sure they're not interested.*

Mr Grump: *We don't have enough money to pay the next quarter's rent, we will be in debt.*

Miss Put-upon: *There are Christian families who want nothing more to do with us.*

Ms Let's-get-on-and-do-something: *Why?*

Miss Put-upon: *Because of the yoga!*

Mr Grump: *Why are you being secretive about how much has been spent?*

Ms Let's-get-on-and-do-something: *An awful lot has happened over the last few months, I am sure all the information is here to share … we need to sit down and take time to understand what is going on.*

Miss Put-upon: *We need a figurehead; you should be our figurehead.*

Mr Grump: *But how can we trust her when she has got us so badly into debt?*

Miss Put-upon: *Yes, and I wanted us to get a thingamajig, and we didn't!*

Mr Grump: *Yes! And you got in the way of me running a whatsit session.*

Ms Let's-get-on-and-do-something: *Well Miss Put-upon you had a countersigned cheque to buy your thingamajig and Mr Grump you were given £50 as a starter grant to get your whatsit session going.*

Both Mr Grump and Miss Put-upon: *But you must be doing something wrong because we don't feel able to do anything.*

Suddenly there were huge and small issues which all needed resolving, but no time or energy to resolve them. Someone had to be at fault, the obvious people were those most active. So the people who needed most support were most demoralized.

The Centre continued, it attracted new members, but slowly. Part of the effect of the unhappy members was that new members were not recruited or were put off coming. What was created was something like two factions, but of course it was more complex than that.

The Centre had become controversial. If we pursued the idea of becoming an examination centre so that children didn't have to fit back into the education system in order to go on to tertiary education, we were trying to become a school, even worse maybe we were empire building. Because sessions were unstructured and children formed them out of their interests, we were anarchic and throwing our doors open to anyone passing, heaven forbid, even the homeless!

All we could do was to sit tight, carry on as usual and hope that it would blow over and that what had been good about the project would survive long enough to attract a second wave of activists.

Two years after it opened, my family was offered an opportunity to move abroad. By then I was sad about all that had happened. There was a group of person-centred therapists who were interested in taking over the project and developing it. This group was formed out of a support group of therapists that also used The Centre room. They had a good understanding of the issues and were supportive of the aims. They encountered many of the same difficulties as we did, however. The project has now been greatly reduced in scope and there is almost no involvement of the home educators.

I hope that all that is happening in alternative education, and the successful part of what was The Centre, may encourage the movement of using schools and libraries as creative resource centres, instead of pursuing the outdated notion that education is something that can be taught. I hope The Centre may one day grow again, or perhaps its brief flowering may have sent a seed or two out for the future.

Writing this has helped me get back in touch with all that was encouraging about the project. The enthusiasm I experienced in others was real, and the commitment I heard was real too. What we didn't realize was how much energy would dissipate when we moved from talking to acting. The boundaries we had in place were apparently firm: a constitution modelled on the Charities Commission template, a group of people all wanting a resource centre for children, a generous starter grant, a physical base, and a support network of 'elders' to provide support and guidance when needed. What we didn't have was the knowledge that this wouldn't be enough.

In a therapeutic session there is no doubt about the importance of speaking your own truth. However, in a social or political arena one person's truth may damage or kill something that is starting to grow. There must always be room for self-exploration and expression but there must also be value placed on social and political action.

So, here we had a good idea, the resource centre that from the childrens' point of view worked wonderfully well. However, we also had a need for grown-ups to manage issues such as finance, membership, advertising … making the decisions that enabled the resource centre to continue. Our chosen method was by consensus and for us all to be tuned in to the preferences of those involved. So the process was open to hearing the other, but the listening resulted in the number of issues around growing exponentially. We seemed to attract more and more powerless people who were experiencing being heard for the first time. Their anger and frustration destroyed The Centre.

> Most men lead lives of quiet desperation and go to the grave with the song still in them. (Thoreau, 1854)

An institution that placed such importance on the voices of the young and gave them a protected space within which they could truly express themselves creatively seemed unbearable to many of the adults. Our lives generally have been ruled by school, employers, and social pressure. Not only is it difficult to then see others being given the freedom to be, but I think it creates anxiety; what will become of the child who tastes autonomy? This is an expression of the fear that follows a glimpse of the power of the person-centred approach.

There is a dilemma. In politicizing the person-centred approach we need to look again at the way in which we value the expression of the individual. By politicizing the person-centred approach we are taking the values of the approach to a lot more people. The difficulty is that without the boundaries of the therapeutic context it becomes incredibly hard to deal with the effect this has on the person who encounters themselves in a new and liberating way. Even harder is dealing with the effect that person can have on all of those around them, as they learn to separate the strength of their feeling from the task in front of them. Everyone matters!

REFERENCES

Rogers, CR (1961) *On Becoming a Person: A therapist's view of psychotherapy*. Boston: Houghton Mifflin.

Rogers, CR (1983) *Freedom to Learn for the 80s*. Columbus, OH: Charles E Merrill.

Thoreau, HD (1854/2004) *Walden*. Princeton, NJ: Princeton University Press.

Chapter 25

POLITICIZING SCHOOL REFORM THROUGH THE PERSON-CENTERED APPROACH: MANDATE AND ADVOCACY

Jeffrey H. D. Cornelius-White

AND

Randel D. Brown

MANDATE: DISADVANTAGED CHILDREN LEFT BEHIND

The current zeitgeist in American educational reform is to test kids a lot and make them pass the test or get in special education to move to the next grade. Historically the British educational system separated students into different tracts based on high-stakes testing (Ransom et al., 1999). Regardless, the outcome is the same: too much pointless testing. This testing will allegedly 'leave no child behind'. However, in reality this practice is a 'big lie' because it accomplishes the opposite (Amrein & Berliner, 2003). It forces retention for many students. The mandate of 'No Child Left Behind' requires that low-achieving students must be retained to acquire the missing skills necessary to pass local and national assessments. First of all, no educational innovation has been unequivocally shown to be worse than retention. Being retained creates about twice the likelihood that the student will drop out of school and a second failing is 'almost guaranteed' (Hattie, 1999: 7). The effect size of retention with achievement is initially $d = -.15$, but grows to $d = -.83$ four or more years after retention (Hattie, 1999). This means that students learn almost 10% less in the following year if they are held back (failed) than if they were allowed to go on. This worsens to near 40% after four years.

More importantly, holding teachers and other educational professionals personally accountable for student achievement through high-stakes testing hurts students differentially and creates an environment disrespectful of children and teachers. Not only does this result in a disproportionate number of Black and Latino students in special education classes, the low-achieving students in regular classes get lower while the high get higher. Though studies are mixed, many people feel the tests are culturally biased in what and how they test. What is clear is that people of lower socio-economic class, Latinos and Blacks on average score lower. It is well established that on average all students' self-esteem drops as they progress through elementary school and into middle school, with larger drops seen in girls. However, low test scores can make this more dramatic as stigma from low achievement is added to the mix. Teachers are also blamed when students do not meet the government-imposed standards. Teachers and students are both disempowered.

The effects of this system parallel the effects of capitalistic practices. For the last few decades, the gap between the richest and poorest people in the UK and the US has grown. If students are minority, female, retained, low-achieving in school, or drop out, stigma can increase over time, making it more difficult for them to succeed by dominant societal standards.

Ironically, syntheses of meta-analyses have shown that one of the most robust principles in educational research is that the proximal is more effective than the distal (Fraser, Walberg, Welch & Hattie, 1987). A meta-analysis is a means of empirically combining the results from similar studies to show what an entire literature shows on a specific topic. Syntheses of meta-analyses then integrate these combinations and can involve millions of students and teachers. So what these syntheses show is that the closer you get with an educational innovation to what actually happens with the student, the stronger the impact will be upon the student. Intra-student variables like cognitive ability and disposition to learn are generally the most predictive of student outcomes. Interactive teacher–student variables as in student-centered education are also potent, but more distal variables like school aims, curriculum changes, and new legislation have relatively small effects upon individual student outcomes. In other words, the empowerment of students and teachers in interaction with students is empirically supported as the best way to improve student outcomes. Teacher–student interaction is amongst the most closely related to students and therefore is one of the best ways to improve student outcomes.

Another concern many have is the 'teaching to the test' phenomenon. When teachers are more concerned about test performance than student learning and development, they can emphasize memory and reproduction of the status quo rather than thinking behavior, which can critically evaluate and improve societal structures. Hence, teachers become more concerned with how students will do on the test than how much they learn to learn. Ironically, there is a strong reliable correlation ($r = .34$) of higher-order questioning with achievement (Fraser et al., 1987). What this shows is that students do about 34% better on achievement measures when asked to think, analyze, synthesize, and question rather than just memorize and reproduce 'correct' answers. Long-term memory is improved with more elaborate 'encoding' where students relate material to other material they know and like. If learning is personalized and authentic, it sticks better. While many people think holding teachers personally accountable for student achievement *is* a good idea, the public (71% of Americans) feels affective/behavioral education is more important than academic education, especially motivation variables like work habits and curiosity, and interpersonal variables like respect (Public Agenda Foundation, 1994). Character education has also become increasing supported by British citizens with 85% supporting 'education with character' (Arthur, 2003: 53).

We think that the mandate to improve schools is for everyone, not just those who are White and privileged. This improvement needs to involve affective/behavioral student outcomes, respect for teachers and students, and encouragement of critical thinking. The person-centered approach to education (PCAE) is an excellent and under-utilized answer. It is also empirically supported by at least 123 studies in seven countries with people of many ethnicities, ages, and abilities (Aspy, 1986; Cornelius-White, 2005; Cornelius-White, Hoey, Cornelius-White, Motschnig-Pitrik & Figl, 2004).

HISTORY: PCAE'S EVOLUTION AS A THEORETICAL AND RESEARCH TRADITION

From the late 1940s, researchers investigated an educational application of the then new, non-directive therapy paradigm. An early dissertation (Wieder, 1951) was conducted immediately following World War II and was concerned with the effects of non-directive education on two types of prejudice: ethnocentrism and fascist beliefs. Non-directive educational *technique* was compared with two control groups. While content retention was negligibly different among the groups, the study showed that both forms of prejudice were reduced in the non-directive group. Likewise, the non-directive class improved students' self-concepts, in terms of both self-acceptance and a lessening in the discrepancy between their ideal and real selves. From the early 1950s, Rogers emphasized democratic functioning resting on teacher empathy not just technique. By 1959, PCAE emphasized reciprocal *attitudes* of empathy, warmth and genuineness where both teachers and students respected each other. The heyday of PCEA research came from about 1965–1980, with research by Aspy and Roebuck (mostly in the United States) and Tausch, Tausch and colleagues (mostly in Germany), which was reviewed by Rogers (1983) and recently synthesized by the first author. This operationalized vision of PCAE included an emphasis on interpersonal *skills*, diversity, and critical thinking. Trained observers most commonly measured teacher variables. Diverse settings and researchers included significant numbers of Hispanics and Blacks. The research looked at tape recordings of teacher–student interaction to see how teachers really behaved (their demonstrated *skills*) not just whether they were unconditional, empathic, and real in *attitude*. Therefore, if a teacher demonstrated an understanding of what a student was saying on an audio recording, they demonstrated an interpersonal *skill*.

Currently, PCAE has evolved into the Learner-Centered Model (LCM), largely through the work of McCombs and colleagues (Lambert & McCombs, 1998; McCombs, 2004) and support from the American Psychological Association (1997). While McCombs acknowledges the influence of classical PCAE on the LCM, many authors do not (Lambert & McCombs, 1998). The LCM is also influenced by social constructivist ideas and is defined as an approach concerned with utilizing knowledge about both learners and learning. The operational definitions are close to definitions used in classical PCAE and are comprised of positive relationships, honoring students' voices, adapting to cultural and individual differences, and encouraging higher-order thinking. The LCM has also been explicitly and uniquely concerned with issues of diversity. The LCM is posed as a potentially potent reformer because of APA's (1997) endorsement of the Learner-Centered Principles. APA is the largest psychological association and exerts considerable worldwide influence with its policies and projects. If APA maintains its support of the LCM, and other systems, like governmental agencies, school districts, etc. take up the torch, educational outcomes may improve for many students, especially those disenfranchised by the current traditional practices.

In terms of the research, recent meta-analysis has shown, using a sample of over 355,000 students, that PCAE is more effective than the average educational innovation for overall cognitive outcomes, and substantially more effective for affective/behavioral outcomes (Cornelius-White, 2005). It does not appear to be more effective for one ethnicity, age group, or location. It is particularly strong in improving student variables that were discussed above as major problems in traditional education, such as student initiation, self-esteem, positive motivation, critical and creative thinking, and preventing drop-out (Cornelius-White, 2005; Cornelius-White & Cornelius-White, 2005; Cornelius-White & Godfrey, 2004). Looking at student initiation as an example, students participate more in classes, with talking and asking questions like 'why' and 'how' increased by 40–60%. In terms of positive motivation, they become more interested in subject matter, more curious, and are willing to work harder to learn the material.

ADVOCACY FOR PCAE AND LCM GOALS

A major thrust of the multicultural and community counseling literature, like that of this book, is the need to expand outside of the classroom and therapy office. Likewise, engaging multiple systems and working for social change to increase equality is important. The following are meant as a list of tips to help counselors, teachers, students, parents, administrators and others to advocate for PCAE and expand it from its traditional venue. It is not exhaustive or prescriptive, just a little starter set. We have drawn from Purkey and Stanley's (1994) list of 1024 ways to invite student success, which utilizes invitational education, a practice highly influenced by person-centered education with an active and growing international organization (see <www.invitationaleducation.net>).

TIPS FOR COUNSELORS

• Get involved with teachers, whether or not you are in schools.
• Conduct workshops on interpersonal attitudes and skills with teachers,

emphasizing role-play activities with students demonstrating person-centered attitudes and skills.

• Join political advocacy groups to reform education.
• Conduct encounter groups for parents and kids to discuss educational policy.
• Provide support to parent volunteers and parent-teacher groups.
• Create class activities where students learn to develop interpersonal relationships, believe in themselves and their ability to communicate with others.
• Create mini-workshops for students focusing on educational and community issues.

TIPS FOR TEACHERS

• Utilize your counselors. Urge them to teach kids person-centered attitudes and skills (following Carkhuff) as guidance activities. Peacemaking skills, non-violent communication, other peer mediation and total school conflict management programs are closely related to the person-centered approach and have excellent results.
• Greet each student as he/she comes into the classroom. Let them know you are glad they are in your class.
• Encourage critical thinking with your students about high-stakes tests, dropout, racism, and other factors that directly impact the quality of their education.
• Align yourself with kids and parents, remembering that you are all on the same team, regardless of the political message that you 'have to make' students perform on tests.
• Take a poll with your students about what they want to learn, feel and what they like and dislike. You may be limited in how much you can advocate for them, but just having a voice promotes social consciousness building.
• Develop positive expectations for all students, regardless of ability and past performance.
• Develop classroom activities that allow students to consider the feelings of other students.

TIPS FOR ADMINISTRATORS

• Coordinate rather than direct. Focus on warmth and understanding through accessibility and monitoring rather than distance, dictates, hierarchy and control.
• 'Visit the provinces' (Purkey & Stanley, 1994: 6). Be involved in all spaces in and around the school. Being in different spaces builds empathy for different people. Go to individual classrooms and interact with students. Spend enough time to generate meaningful conversation and student questions. Go to the kitchen and playground.
• Form brainstorming groups. As the old saying goes, 'None of us is smarter than all of us.' Include people from all subsystems of a school: parents, staff,

teachers, students, and community members. Seek consensus when making any significant changes.
• Encourage your teachers. Let them know you are interested in what happens in their classrooms.

TIPS FOR PARENTS

• Get involved in your parent-teacher organization.
• Build relationships with teachers, counselors and administrators.
• Call your political representatives and let them know how you want your tax dollars on schools spent.
• Engage in community outreach. Contact your school and local businesses and agencies to invite and/or offer an event, such as adopt-a-class, where families from a class get free stuff, coupons, visits, etc. This can be mutually beneficial economically and socially. Volunteer for classroom activities and field trips.

TIPS FOR STAFF

• 'Remember the Jello Principle' (Purkey & Stanley, 1994: 47). Schools are like bowls of Jello, where a touch one place can cause a jiggle throughout. This principle can help appreciation of seemingly small aspects and traditionally less important student and worker populations.
• Hold taste tests and cooking demonstrations and rename the school dining room to help everyone be involved and valued in the educational experience (i.e. cafeteria workers).
• Demonstrate school improvement projects to promote practical understanding and demonstrate appreciation of class differences and of other school personnel (i.e. custodians).

TIPS FOR KIDS AND TEENAGERS

• Form clubs. Student organizations help visibility and power amongst the most disenfranchised yet most important people in the educational system, students. Peer mediation, student government, and suggestion groups are often the most effective at correcting injustices in a particular educational system.
• With your teacher's permission, invite speakers you know from the community to your classroom.
• Talk with your teacher and fellow students about events that happen in your community.

REFERENCES

American Psychological Association (1997) *Learner-Centered Psychological Principles: A framework for school redesign and reform.* Washington, DC: APA.

Amrein, AL & Berliner, DC (2003, February) The effects of high-stakes testing on student motivation and learning. *Educational Leadership, 60* (5), 32–8.

Arthur, J (2003) Character education in British education policy. *Journal of Research in Character Education, 1,* 45–59.

Aspy, DN (1986) *This is School: Sit down and listen.* Amherst, MA: Human Resource Development Press.

Cornelius-White, JHD (2005) Learner-Centered Teacher–Student Relationships are Effective: A meta-analysis. Manuscript submitted for publication. Missouri State University.

Cornelius-White, JHD, & Cornelius-White, CF (2005) Trust builds learning: The context and effectiveness of non-directivity in education. In BE Levitt (ed) *Embracing Non-directivity* (pp. 314–23). Ross-on-Wye: PCCS Books.

Cornelius-White, JHD & Godfrey, P (2004) Pedagogical crossroads: Integrating feminist critical pedagogies and the person-centered approach to education. In G Proctor & MB Napier (eds) *Encountering Feminism: Intersections of feminism and the person-centred approach* (pp. 166–78). Ross-on-Wye: PCCS Books.

Cornelius-White, JHD, Hoey, A, Cornelius-White, CF, Motschnig-Pitrik, R & Figl, K (2004) Person-centered education: A meta-analysis of care in progress. *Journal of Border Educational Research, 3* (1), 86–91.

Fraser, BJ, Walberg, HJ, Welch, WW & Hattie, JA (1987) Syntheses of educational productivity research. *International Journal of Educational Research, 11,* 145–252.

Hattie, JA (1999) Influences on student learning. Inaugural Lecture at the University of Auckland, Australia August 2 1999.

Lambert, NM & McCombs, B (eds) (1998) *How Students Learn: Reforming schools through learner-centered education.* Washington DC: American Psychological Association.

McCombs, BL (2004) The case for learner-centered practices: Introduction and rationale for session. Paper presented at the American Educational Research Association Annual meeting, San Diego, April.

Phelps, R (1996) Are US students the most heavily tested on earth? *Educational Measurement, 15,* 19.

Public Agenda Foundation (1994) *First Things First: What Americans expect from public schools.* New York: Author.

Purkey, WW & Stanley, PH (1994) *The Inviting School Treasury: 1001 ways to invite student success.* New York: Scholastic.

Ransom, KA, Santa, CM, Williams, CK, Farstrup, AE, Au, KH, Baker, BM, Edwards, PA, Hoffman, JV, Klein, AF, Larson, DL, Logan, JW, Morrow, LM & Shanahan, T (1999) High-stakes assessments in reading: A position statement of the International Reading Association. *Journal of Adolescent and Adult Literacy, 43,* 305–12.

Rogers, CR (1983) *Freedom to Learn for the 80s.* Columbus: Charles E Merrill.

Wieder, GS (1951) A comparison study of the relative effectiveness of two methods of teaching a thirty hour course in psychology in modifying attitudes associated with racial, religious, and ethnic prejudice. (Doctoral Dissertation, New York University, 1951). *Dissertation Abstracts International, 12,* 02, 0163.

Chapter 26

EMOTIONAL LITERACY AND THE PERSON-CENTRED APPROACH

MIKE HOUGH

The concept of emotional literacy has some interesting parallels with person-centred notions of therapeutic change. This chapter introduces a discussion of these parallels and suggests that there is the possibility of a useful dialogue.

DEFINITION

Emotional literacy describes the ability to recognize emotions and use them for personal and social well-being. As a concept it has been popularized by Daniel Goleman (1996) but has its origins in the work of Salovey and Mayer (1990) and Gardner (1993). Goleman (1996) subdivides emotional intelligence into five domains:

- Self-awareness
- Self-regulation
- Motivation
- Empathy
- Social skill

He makes the claim that attention to emotional intelligence is an imperative for the twenty-first century if we are to survive and flourish economically and socially. Individuals and society as a whole will be better served by more emotional intelligence. In the seminal 'marshmallow test' those four-year-olds who were able to delay the impulse of eating marshmallows and thereby have some measure of control over their emotions were, by the time they were teenagers, more socially competent, personally effective, self-assertive, and better able to cope with the frustrations of life (Goleman, 1996: 81). This capacity—to impose a delay on impulse—he argues is symptomatic of greater emotional intelligence. It suggests a capacity to read a social situation and weigh up the personal and social benefits of giving in to impulse or delaying it for greater personal and social benefit.

Lance Armstrong, the now seven-times winner of the Tour de France, describes how during his battle to win the second Tour he became emotionally involved in an altercation with a fellow rider. On reflecting on the impact of this incident he concludes. 'Anger is not sustaining. You can't ride on it for long, and in this case it cost me my good judgement. First I gave in to sentiment, and then I let a quarrel distract me, and neither served me especially well' (Armstrong, 2003: 48). The process of becoming emotionally literate therefore requires an ability to recognize emotions both in yourself and others; then to apply to that recognition a process of review and reflection that allows the emotions to be harnessed for personal and social advantage. This is not the same as being cold and calculating nor indulging in naked self-interest. Giving vent to emotions, naming the emotional response, becoming aware of the complexity and often contradictory emotions raised by social situations are all important ways for individuals to navigate their way through human interactions. This capacity is so important that, Goleman argues, it should feature more prominently in our education systems.

One way of doing this is to see emotional literacy as the axis of the fourth 'R' of schooling. Thus, Relationship joins Reading, wRiting and aRithmetic as the fourth dimension of education. How we handle our relationships and harness our emotions can be taught and developed; they are essential components of the educated person and in fact they have survival value, particularly so at this moment in history. These are grand claims for a concept that is remarkably new. What gives these claims potency is that they appeal to a common-sense view of the world supported by the latest neurological research. This research suggests that there are portions of the brain, the hippocampus and amygdala in particular, which carry responsibility for processing and activating our emotional responses. Like our capacity to read, write and manage numbers, our capacity for self-awareness and for empathy (what Daniel Goleman (1996) calls our 'social radar') are to a certain extent prewired yet are amenable to growth and development depending on experiences and relationships in the world.

Howard Gardner (1983) constructed the concept of multiple intelligences and identified two of these as being 'personal intelligences' namely intrapersonal and interpersonal intelligence. He has been somewhat sceptical of the way his original thinking has been distorted in this area and in writing sixteen years later commented, 'Unfortunately, we don't know a lot about the personal intelligences. We do not understand their operations well, we do not know how to measure these intelligences and we are not skilled at training them' (Gardner, 1999: 201). However, he concluded, 'I am convinced that these [personal] intelligences will remain equally important, if not more so' (Gardner, 1999: 201).

Just because we can't measure a phenomenon doesn't mean it doesn't exist. What Gardner does acknowledge is that these personal intelligences may not be as discrete and separate from the other intelligences as he first formulated. In other words they may infiltrate our very being; they may be context specific; they may underpin our other competencies. In some ways this places emotional literacy even more at the core of our being but makes it less amenable to discrete definition. This has serious implications for those wishing to promote separate programmes of emotional literacy.

CRITIQUE

What is interesting is that schools are engaging in such programmes on the basis of very limited empirical evidence. Howard Gardner (1983), the founding father of multiple intelligences, revisited his original work in 1999 and was cautious about the claims subsequently made in the name of emotional intelligence. Calling some intelligences emotional implies that the others are devoid of emotion. This he was eager to refute. Emotions infuse all of our cognitive and intellectual life. He was also critical of the automatic incorporation of a positive morality within the definition of emotional intelligence, preferring to make a strong distinction between emotional sensitivity and being a good or moral person 'since someone who is sensitive to others' emotions may still manipulate, deceive or create hatred' (Gardner 1999: 206).

Matthews, Zeidner and Roberts have mounted the most systematic critique of the claims of the emotional intelligence advocates. 'Overall our conclusions concerning the prospect for a coherent theory of emotional intelligence supported by empirical evidence are pessimistic. The root problem is that EI is too generalized a concept to be useful' (2002: 539). They dispute the idea that general and transferable emotional literacy skills can be developed and argue that at best 'such skills are typically specific to the life issue concerned' (2002: 543).

Despite such vehement criticism and describing many of the claims of Goleman in particular as myths they do concede that myths do have their place and power as sources of inspiration and motivation. So, in that sense, the jury is out. A not-proven verdict (possible in Scots law) seems likely and more evidence is called for. Meantime the real world cannot wait. Schools and educationalists are eager to incorporate the affective domain into their repertoire of responses to promote the emotional development of young children but also to combat the growing perception of an unruly and difficult youth population. Here too we are in danger of falling for another myth, another 'folk devil and moral panic' (Cohen, 1972).

Although there is limited empirical evidence to validate the case for a discrete competence such as emotional literacy there are those, particularly in the educational world, who have latched onto the idea and built it into something of a cottage industry. They advocate, as does Goleman, that this represents a challenge to the accepted wisdom about intelligence and therefore the purpose of schooling. It legitimates the affective arena of human interaction as a valid focus for curricula and educational initiatives. They may be basing their views on a myth or playing a hunch but they operate in the real world as they see it.

EMOTIONAL LITERACY IN SCHOOLS

In order to find out more about this in practice, I spent some time in a number of primary and secondary schools in Glasgow interviewing teachers about their definition of emotional literacy and witnessing their programmes in action, based on these principles. What came across was a simple yet profound belief that happy pupils make effective learners. Rather than seeing emotional literacy as a remedial programme for those with emotional difficulties, it was viewed by these teachers and schools as a whole-school initiative impacting on all aspects of school life. It infiltrated relationships between all the adults and all the pupils in the school. It provided the cement on which the learning objectives of the school could be constructed. As one senior member of staff of a primary school commented;

> You can't learn well unless you feel secure. You should feel happy with your teacher. You should be able to feel secure with your friendships inside and outside the class, so the ethos of the school is totally at the centre of that.

The word 'ethos' appeared time and time again in the research. It is another notoriously difficult concept to evidence yet for those teachers and schools that actively sought to address issues of emotional literacy, it was axiomatic that school ethos was informed by care for self and others, including a deep awareness and harnessing of emotional responses built on genuine and accepting relationships. It is noteworthy that the language of the teachers when taking about emotional literacy readily drew on the key concepts of the person-centred approach.

In the secondary school sector, where attainment and the achievement of academic excellence as measured by exam results constitute more of the impetus, emotional literacy work was also recognized as having its place.

> In the bigger picture of school life, unless we spend the time on emotional literacy then as a school, we will not have the rise in attainment that we want to see. (Senior member of secondary school staff)

These are both senior members of staff involved actively in their professional lives taking forward concrete programmes and initiatives based on the principles of emotional literacy. They were motivated and involved in creating their own evidence even though the hard empirical data for the concepts on which the programmes were based was far from secure (as referred to above). In fact this is not that unusual in educational initiatives. Practice often precedes research.

Having briefly presented and critiqued some of the current thinking around emotional literacy, how might it resonate with the person-centred approach?

CONNECTIONS TO A PERSON-CENTRED APPROACH

INTER AND INTRA

As mentioned earlier, Goleman built his concept of emotional intelligence on the two pillars of interpersonal intelligence and intrapersonal intelligence previously identified by Gardner. Gardner goes to some effort to distinguish between them. Intrapersonal refers to the capacity to look inward and access one's 'own feeling life' and make distinctions and connections between internal emotional responses. Interpersonal capacities turn outward and refer to the ability to notice and make distinctions amongst the reactions, emotions and intentions of others. Whilst this effort to distinguish between the two is helpful, it has limitations. In relation to the person-centred approach there is a particular way in which the two can be conceived of as integrated. It is possible to describe a client's journey through therapy as being focused on developing and expressing competence and awareness in both domains. It is also possible to see how the action of the counsellor in offering an interpersonal relationship enables the client to experience and reflect on this relationship and begin to shift in terms of their internal (intra) self-perceptions. A client's internal dialogue for instance might be, 'I see myself as not worthy [intra] and have failed in all my relationships [inter]. This person, the counsellor, is relating to me as though they experience me as worthy [inter]. Perhaps I am OK [a shift in intra] and can begin to be different in the world (inter).' As Leijssen suggests 'Client-centred therapists have put a great deal of effort into offering an interpersonal relationship in which the client can recover and grow' (Leijssen, 1998: 131).

RELATIONSHIP

Relationship is at the heart of the person-centred world. In fact I believe it was a close call whether person-centred counselling emerged as such, rather that being termed, relationship-centred counselling. The latest work by Mearns and Cooper (2005) on relational depth continues this theme. Par excellence the person-centred tradition extols the value and potency of people in relationship. The quality of the relationship between people is the beginning, middle and end of the story. Whilst this can be particularly focused on the relationship between therapist and client, it remains true that the quality of all human relationships is the source of personal well-being. So, although as Wosket asserts 'There is a certain clarity and distillation that belong to the time limited and intimate nature of the therapeutic meeting' (Wosket, 1999: 38), this does not rule out the option, and in fact, desirability, of transferring our belief in the importance of the quality of the relationship to our lives in families, organizations, the workplace, etc. Congruence (openness) and empathy (appreciating the view of the other) not only provide the conditions for the counselling relationship, they also provide a reasonable basis for our survival and development in the home, school, neighbourhood, city and nation.

EMPATHY

Empathy is not only a pillar of the person-centred approach, it is acknowledged in all therapeutic approaches as being fundamental to the establishment of the therapeutic alliance. Furthermore some writers on empathy acknowledge its more fundamental place in human interaction. 'Although empathy works as a more or less constantly active system, found everywhere in daily life, clinicians look for special displays in "clinical" cases as if they were exceptional' (Shlien, 2003: 185).

It is this universal application of empathy that is taken up by Goleman (1996) when he locates empathy as one of the components of emotional intelligence (along with self-awareness, harnessing feelings, motivating oneself and handling relationships). He uses less clinical language to describe empathy as the ability to know how another feels and includes the ability to read nonverbal channels such as tone of voice and facial expression. He locates its origins in the hard wiring of young children who through motor mimicry react to a disturbance in those around them as though it were their own emotion. This mimicry becomes integrated as attunement if, he argues, the child receives attuned responses to their needs and emotions. The absence of this development of attunement can lead to disastrous consequences in the example of the psychopath who lacks the ability to respond with empathy to the feelings of others. This has some resonance with the idea of 'fragile process' as developed by Margaret Warner (2000).

This emotional literacy 'take' on empathy has potential to extend the therapeutically contextualized definitions of empathy more in evidence in the person-centred literature. It introduces the idea that empathy can be enhanced and developed. In primary schools, for instance, programmes of emotional literacy and the interactions of teachers with children are used to foster the development of this attuning response. Children are encouraged to find words for their emotional responses. They are confronted with the consequences of their actions of exclusion and bullying in relations with other children. In secondary schools, programmes of restorative justice confront bullies with the consequences of their actions and engage them in empathic awareness. This process is designed to redress shortcomings in their socialization, which may not have alerted them to the consequences of their action on others.

FINAL THOUGHTS—RELEVANCE TO
THE PERSON-CENTRED APPROACH

What is the relevance to person-centred thinking? One thought is to do with 'upstream work'. If the person-centred approach wants to develop from the confines of the one-on-one counselling relationship then emotional literacy feels like a useful starting place. If we want to lift our attention from not only assisting those individuals we meet at the river bank who are in some state of 'incongruence' but also explore at a broader level what caused them to be in the river in the first place, then our guide to exploring upstream could well be an understanding of emotional literacy. What capacities for caring for ourselves and others emotionally are being hindered or fostered upstream? That means taking a closer look at our society, our institutions, our schools and work places and asking how they foster emotional literacy. How far are they focused on a way of being rather than a way of doing? It also suggests some interesting alliances between counsellors and others, for instance educationalists, to foster not only such exploration but also undertake joint work. The recent initiative to appoint person-centred counsellors to work in schools across Scotland is one such opportunity context.

One danger, and there was some evidence of this in the research undertaken in schools, is that emotional literacy is readily hijacked by those interested more in social control than personal empowerment. New Labour politicians are increasingly seeing young people in a negative light and key policies on anti-social behaviour are witness to this. In *their* social construction of reality, young people are troublesome rather than troubled; they are troublemakers rather than victims, and their liberties are to be constrained rather than their diversity and potential celebrated. Programmes of emotional literacy can easily be hijacked to become programmes of social control teaching young people how to conform, how to divert legitimate anger into passive acceptance, how to accept the norms of polite adult society. At its worst, schools are buying into programmes of compliance that make the job of teachers easier but do little to assist young people to become assertive, articulate citizens of the future. Where there is scope to develop the literature of emotional literacy is in the arena of articulating values, beliefs and outcomes. Perhaps a dialogue with the person-centred approach would be fruitful for both?

REFERENCES

Armstrong, L (2003) *Every Second Counts*. London: Yellow Jersey Press.

Cohen, P (1972) *Folk Devils and Moral Panics*. London: McGibbon & Key.

Gardner, H (1983) *Frames of Mind: The theory of multiple intelligences*. New York: Basic Books.

Gardner, H (1999) *Intelligence Reframed*. New York: Basic Books.

Goleman, D (1996) *Emotional Intelligence*. London: Bloomsbury.

Leijssen, M (1998) Focusing: Interpersonal and intrapersonal conditions of growth. In B Thorne & E Lambers *Person-Centred Therapy: A European perspective* (pp. 131–58). London: Sage.

Matthews, G, Zeidner, M & Roberts, RD (2002) *Emotional Intelligence: Science and myth*. Cambridge MA: MIT Press.

Mearns, D & Cooper, M (2005) *Working at Relational Depth in Counselling and Psychotherapy*. London: Sage.

Salovey, P & Mayer, J (1990) Emotional Intelligence. *Imagination, Cognition and Personality, 9* (3), 185–211.

Shlien, JM (2003) *To Lead on Honorable Life*. Ross-on-Wye: PCCS Books.

Warner, MS (2000) Person-centred therapy at the difficult edge. In D Mearns & B Thorne *Person-Centred Therapy Today* (pp. 144–71). London: Sage.

Wosket, V (1999) *The Therapeutic Use of Self*. London: Brunner-Routledge.

Chapter 27

WHAT DOES IT HAVE TO DO WITH CLIENT-CENTERED THERAPY?

John Keith Wood

It is obvious that many significant endeavors have nothing whatever to do with client-centered therapy. There are also activities that are extremely valuable and cannot be called client-centered therapy but nevertheless contain the mark of the person-centered approach. One example is the connection between living well in a place and client-centered therapy. I will try to make this connection— that is, the similarities in values, attitudes, motives—apparent in this article.

The task is not new. Indeed, every occurrence of the person-centered approach has had to face this challenge. Before client-centered therapy had itself become the standard measure, people asked, what does this upstart non-directive therapy have to do with treating mental illness or helping children adjust? Now client-centered therapy has passed from reliable theory, solid practice and measurable results to conventional dogma. When Rogers began experimenting with encounter groups, out of a deep conviction in their ability to improve human relations, his own wife thought he was acting recklessly, jeopardizing his reputation and ruining his career. What did this adventure have to do with client-centered therapy? Now, group encounter is an irreplaceable part of group therapy, family therapy, and the countless self-help cults. When he began working with large groups, most of his psychologist colleagues from Chicago, who had barely managed to swallow encounter groups by thinking of them as a form of therapy, now jumped ship. What did convening large numbers of people to haggle over smoking rules or the parceling of time have to do with client-centered therapy? To those whose quest was learning and creativity, everything. Honest confrontation between good-willed—not necessarily like-minded—people, seeking truly participative consensus in governing, respecting cultural differences and the constructive power of positive intention are all consistent with client-centered therapy. Therapy and significant learning in groups each involve sincere people who are trying to understand each other's reality, accepting each other's human rights and valuing self-expression. Both seek to realize human potential in every dimension. Today, large group discussions of this ilk form the basis of 'town-hall meetings' in municipalities, business, and education. Appealing to the emotional attraction, they are even featured on afternoon television.

In other words, the same *attitude* and *values* (the same approach to human relations), the same roots that sprouted the theory and practice of client-centered therapy, also branched into these other endeavors. It is not that client-centered therapy is the parent of the encounter group child and the large group is the grandchild, community life being a great-grandchild. It is that all these activities are brothers and sisters whose parent is the person-centered approach. And they have the same intention: to realize human potential through personal relations, significant dialogue in large groups and active participation in real communities.

There is an intimate connection between realizing human potential and being a responsible and active member of a *real* community, in an actual place, contributing to preserving and improving the natural environment, natural and healthy food production, security, relevant education, the general quality of life. Indeed, the very first large group encounter that Rogers convened in 1974 had the intention 'to explore the social implications of the client-centered approach'.

Perhaps relating my own experience (although the reader may have his or her own to draw from), which spans many years of involvement with client-centered therapy, encounter groups, and large groups for sensible dialogue and creative learning, and now living and actively participating in a rural community, may help to illustrate one version of the pattern to which I am referring.

I began collaborating with Carl Rogers as he was beginning his interest in large group encounters. People constantly questioned the social relevance of client-centered therapy and small group encounter (which we had come to refer to as the client-centered approach): 'This is all very interesting, but how do you apply this approach in the real world?' I could see that essential learning way beyond therapy and social dialogue was being realized, then and there, in these groups. If one were patient, a firmer understanding of the relation to 'real life' might be found. I felt that the criticism was too early. Relax. Give it some more thought. Learn more. See what happens. At the same time I had to agree. In spite of our best efforts, what we were doing was, after all, rather pitiful in light of the enormous challenges we faced as a species. Couldn't the effective force of client-centered therapy be channeled more directly toward facilitating social justice and constructive growth?

Through the series of pioneer large group encounters during the 1970s we slowly began to realize that it could. Still, it was easier to experience than to articulate for widespread understanding. Rogers' 1979 book on personal power in which he tried to explain this phenomenon slipped into oblivion practically unnoticed. Perhaps because large group encounters, though often therapeutic, were clearly not effective as psychotherapy (Wood, 1997). Nevertheless, they had enormous value in fostering consensual governance, creative problem solving and dealing constructively with actual crises that arose in the group. It is not so much that the crisis contains its own solution. It is that a crisis is an enzyme for actualizing its solution by the group. The development of intuitive faculties was also a significant learning that was available in these large group experiences. The value of these encounters with very low structure was not in learning interventions that could be taken back home to change one's community or taken to Austria to bring peace to Central America. It was in experiencing how human potential is released in day-to-day real life situations. It was in learning about our basic human nature—for better or for worse—when we are grouped.

Why were these experiences so often called 'community'? For one thing, because people lived together, loved and fought, celebrated and grieved, worked out the values that governed their endeavors in sort of town meetings, overcame crises, invented appropriate rituals, and at times, reached what, for lack of greater clarity and articulation on my part, could be called an elevated state of wisdom. Perhaps a collective wisdom: a sensation of experiencing the unity of the group through the diversity of its particular members.

Does a group have an identity? Is it a thing in itself? The US Supreme Court said yes. Chief Justice John Marshall wrote in 1819 that corporations have properties of existence, 'Among the most important are immortality, and, if the expression may be allowed, individuality; properties, by which a perpetual succession of many persons are considered as the same, and may act as a single individual.' The court over the years has acted on this ruling by, for example, finding that a company (acting as a single individual as it were) was guilty of racial discrimination based on its history of hiring. Nevertheless, many people continue to insist that the group is nothing more than an assembly of individuals with no collective will.

Even if it is a thing in itself, does this make it a community? Many people do not think so. It lacks the resignation, the long-term commitments, the loyalties, the involvement, the day-in and day-out realities of real communities. Both opinions had some merit. These groups were and were not community. They were perhaps the cultivation of community. And they depended heavily on the place where they were convened. This is not a trivial observation. Rogers had always felt his facilitative conditions were essential and paid little attention to place. He felt he could do psychotherapy anywhere. Of course, he could conduct client-centered therapy in Tokyo or Amsterdam, even sitting on a park bench in a quiet wood. But not on the A-train at rush hour, or in the middle of the Rolling Stones' 'Goodbye Concert' in Yankee Stadium, or underwater in diving gear. The place must be 'receptive' to the activity. Ideally, it would itself be therapeutic. Rogers was able to ignore place because it was, in fact, always carefully *controlled*: a quiet, dimly lit room without distractions.

In studying large groups it is clear that though necessary none of the well-known personal conditions are sufficient. Much more influential in the group outcome is ambience: the place, the geographical, spatial location, and the composition or particularity of the people gathered together at a particular time. Time, location, people. More than anything else, I believe that ignoring these factors is what has made large groups gatherings in recent years, though stimulating to the uninitiated, not merely banal but largely irrelevant in terms of significant learning. Large groups have become an endangered natural resource.

Even when attention was paid to the environment, group composition, relevant discourse, the group may have become an effective learning experience, but it did not fully become a community. It was still somewhat of an abstraction. Where was the village, the town hall, schools, hospitals, commercial enterprises, the legal institutions? It was a community without a place.

My effort to learn to live well in a place began after having worked for several years in Brazil. In 1984, I accepted a post as full professor in the graduate school of clinical psychology at a major Brazilian university. At the same time I began living on a citrus farm not too far from the campus. Although teaching psychology could not hold my interest, becoming the *locum tenens*, the keeper of this place in rural Brazil, did.

At first, my wife and I concentrated on preserving the native vegetation and wildlife in our watershed, while slowly but deliberately changing our farming methods from conventional to natural agriculture. The work was straightforward, local, tiring and rewarding.

We began to see that *we* did not really take care of the land. We were a part of the land, the *conscious part of the ecosystem taking care of itself.* We extended the consciousness of *Jequitibá* and its rustling leaves, of the *lambari* in their scurrying schools, of the hawk in its tense glide, of *onça preta* in its silent stalking, of *feijão guandú* gathering nitrogen in its roots, of the lemon fattening in the sun, of the milk thistle concocting its bitter cure, of golden corn in bright green sheaths, of the restless muddied river, the crystal springs and the humid air. Most of all we championed the living earth, the *hum*us from which *hum*ans descended.

To seal the commitment to the natural environment this perception implied, we registered the 84 hectare watershed as an official ecological reserve—held in perpetuity for all future generations—to preserve and restore the biodiversity and beauty of a vestige of the great Brazilian coastal rainforest, the *Mata Atlântica.* As growing healthy food is not only noble but absolutely necessary for human survival, in the transition zones surrounding the protected forest, we practice natural agriculture, free from chemical insecticides, herbicides and fertilizers. We are certified organic growers and produce food for our own needs and for the region. We try to support the local economy, work to improve sanitation and schooling in our village, to promote social justice and to preserve the more constructive agrarian values: self-reliance, honesty, loyalty, fair employment, just social conditions, and good neighborliness.

No waste is exported from our property. Water is held in the land and cleansed by the forests. We aim for sustainable housing. Using *taipa*—that is earth walls—in new construction. Using natural and recycled building materials, solar energy, recycled waste water, preserving rain water. We are fostering environmental education, learning by doing, learning by direct experience as well as through carefully designed scientific experiments researching biodiversity, flora, fauna, soil preservation and restoration. This is almost completely opposite to industrial agriculture.

Industrial agriculture is capitalism's tool in globalization. What is wrong with globalization, after all it brought us the Internet? The farmer and poet

Wendell Berry, writing in the *New York Times* (9 February 2003) tells us: 'After World War II, we hoped the world might be united for the sake of peacemaking. Now the world is being "globalized" for the sake of trade and the so-called free market—for the sake, that is, of plundering the world for cheap labor, cheap energy, and cheap materials. How nations, let alone regions and communities, are to shape and protect themselves within this global economy is far from clear.' Our small regional effort is not merely a reaction to the worst in globalization, it is a viable alternative.

My wife, Lucila is an artist and art helps to guide our work—not so much in the production of things, but as a way of sensing and following the esthetic sense of a decent forest, decent agriculture and decent housing.

From our direct contact with the land, we have also become aware of the tremendous social implications in family-centered natural farming. In Latin America the trend toward misery is evident and well documented. The process goes like this: small families, trying to produce food using the methods of industrial agriculture cannot compete with the subsidized giant multinationals. They are therefore 'forced' off the land. Arriving in the densely populated urban centers they have difficulty finding work. Shelter is often just that, a corner under a bridge to keep dry. Since they must buy food, they are now 'food dependent'. Without money, this leads directly to misery and hunger. Producing more food (since there is already an abundance in the world) does not resolve hunger. Integrating natural farming methods for families to remain on the land, along with conservation of native vegetation and wetlands helps to resolve both social misery and protection of the environment for future generations. We are employing people and forming partnerships with those who are being dismissed by industrial farms. Thus, those who wish may stay on the land, applying their practical knowledge and not fall into the urban misery that characterizes countries exploited by the new industrial capitalism of globalization.

For me no further explanation is necessary. However, for those who might want to hear more about psychology, I can say a bit more. First of all, nature erases self-deception. Think about it: when you are alone in the woods there is no reason to be anything other than yourself. Also, one may note that accomplishing such social changes directly increases human potential, human dialogue between cultures and classes is fostered, individuals and groups become more consciously aware, perception is augmented and with it the phenomenon of the natural world grows. All of one's capacities are called on and, like muscles that are worked, grow with use. Not a day passes that I am not a scientist, resolving some technical problem in our watershed infrastructure or in the local municipality. I even consult on high-tech problems involved with using satellite images to map soil use and water conservation. Not a day passes that I am not a psychologist, working with neighbors on perceptions of our reserve, with the politicians in the municipality on domestic waste recycling programs, sanitation systems and conservation of pluvial waters. The technical solutions are simple.

Reaching consensus among merchants, realtors, politicians and citizen groups is a matter of psychology. Although I prefer to think of myself as a concerned citizen trying to do what is right, one could say that I have adopted a particular way of being a psychologist.

A final word. In this place at this time, our real work remains the preserving of the biological diversity of our small watershed. Reforesting with native trees areas of the ecosystem which have been degraded by failed agricultural projects and, where possible, allowing nature to do the important reforestation. In the transition areas where we practice natural agriculture we have cut runoff-retaining ditches following the curve of the land to prevent soil erosion.

Our citrus orchards are completely free of chemical fertilizers, synthetic pesticides and herbicides. Also, we rotate corn, oats, wheat and legumes. The corn and wheat are sold to a neighbor who has free-range chickens (that need organic feed). They lay fertilized eggs that are marketed regionally.

The social implications of farming may also be realized through cooperation between neighbors. For example, together with this neighbor and another organic farmer on the other side of the valley we are buying a cold press. We will plant sunflowers and extract the oil. Only what the droves of roving parrots pilfer is lost. The oil is sold for cooking (and can also be used to power our traction) and the residue is high in protein and ideal for supplementing the chicken feed.

We did not begin with the intention of forming a cooperative (which surely would have ended badly). My neighbor merely said he needed organic corn and could only find it a few hundred kilometers away in Paraná. I said, 'I have a field in which I could plant corn.' 'Fine, let's do it.' This neighbor grows tomatoes, lettuce, mushrooms, celery, carrots, potatoes, bananas, besides their specialty—eggs. We buy almost all of our food from them. We grow some ourselves, of course. And the other neighbor who also supplies our dairy products and sells our oranges and lemons in the local street markets said one day, 'Why don't we plant sunflowers and extract the oil from their seeds?'

Thus, it is possible to understand how realizing human potential—individually, in consort with others seeking to better themselves, or in living well in a place—when approached with a certain straightforwardness, consistency, honesty and integrity—is consistent with the expression of the person-centered approach.

REFERENCES

Berry, W (2003) *New York Times* (9 February).
Wood, JK (1984) Communities for learning: A person-centered approach to large groups. In RF Levant & JM Shlien (eds) *Client-Centered Therapy and the Person-Centered Approach: New directions in theory, research and practice* (pp. 297–316). NY: Praeger.
Wood, JK (1994a) The person-centered approach's greatest weakness: Not using its strength. *The Person-Centered Journal, 1* (3), 96–105.

Wood, JK (1994b) A rehearsal for understanding the phenomenon of group. *The Person-Centered Journal, 1* (3), 18–32.

Wood, JK (1995) The person-centered approach: Toward an understanding of its implications. *The Person-Centered Journal, 2* (2), 18–35.

Wood, JK (1997) Notes on studying large group workshops. *The Person-Centered Journal, 4* (Fall), 65–77.

Wood, JK (1999) Toward an understanding of large group dialogue and its implications. In C Lago & M MacMillan (eds) *Experiences in Relatedness: Groupwork and the person-centred approach* (pp. 137–66). Ross-on-Wye: PCCS Books.

Wood, JK (2002) The effect of group, sensible dialogue and innovative learning. Unpublished paper.

Chapter 28

TAKING SIDES—OR NOT?

ROSEMARY HOPKINS

Either you are with us, or you are with the terrorists.
(George Bush, 20 September 2001)

Treat people as if they were what they should be, and you help them become what they are capable of becoming.
(Johann Wolfgang von Goethe, 1749–1832)

Can I offer unconditional positive regard to people described as perpetrators of terror? And if so, how? What follows is an exploration of this challenge—weaving together political activism and the person-centred approach in my life. This is a personal journey, caught in time and continuing.

Early in my journey, I tried to apply unconditional positive regard as though it were a rule in the person-centred guidebook to life. I was puzzled by the degree of conflict I experienced in this position. I stayed with my unease and examined a wide range of responses both with people trained in the approach and with others unaware of the approach. I had no idea where I was going with this process, and yet felt sure I would become clearer if I trusted myself to remain open. Quite by chance, I discovered a paper by John K. Wood (1995) in which he describes what he believes the person-centred approach *is not* and what it *is*:

> Some people seem to like the idea that we might cultivate this way of being as a way of life, encountering every kind of day-to-day situation with this attitude and posture. It may be possible. However, I am suspicious of such utopian desires, especially when they are connected to such limited psychological systems. This posture does not need to be a way of life; it need only be capable of being applied effectively in situations that may improve life for many others. (p. 33)

I recognized that I can choose when to offer unconditional positive regard and still live by my principles. I am able to remain open to the obvious and the subtle, and to new discoveries as well as uncertainties and ambiguities. I also recognized how, in losing sight of these qualities, I was *taking sides*, believing there was a fixed right side, rather than coming freshly and openly to each situation and person, and responding to a range of possibilities—the bigger picture. John Wood distinguishes between client-centred *therapy* that derives from a method described by Carl Rogers and the person-centred *approach* in which methods evolve moment by moment according to the demands of the situation:

> [Carl Rogers] approached each situation with the same desire to understand, the same good humor, the same humility, the same honesty, the same non-judgmental acceptance of the individual or the group, the same curiosity and openness to learning, the same will to act constructively. He improvised from his knowledge and abilities in each specific case. (Wood, 1995: 26)

Wood's ideas opened up further possibilities for me, and I was able to continue journeying into my own definitions, my own stories, and my own discoveries.

WHAT IS TERROR?

How do I recognize, experience, or define terror? I hear terror in the cries of people running from the collapsing World Trade Centre in New York; I see terror in the face of a client ritually sexually abused as a child; I witness terror in the eyes of a father carrying a wounded child in Iraq; I imagine terror in the heart of a mother, seeing her child struggling for breath in the slums of Bhopal; I read of terror in the accounts of women raped by HIV positive men in the Democratic Republic of Congo; I smell terror in the images of house demolitions, of sewage polluted water-systems and of detonated car-bombs in Israel/Palestine.

I feel terror as intense fear in my gut, in my heart, in the tops of my arms and backs of my knees. I experience terror in my adrenal system warning me to fight or flee or freeze. I feel terror in an instant, and relief when the situation passes. I know terror that comes in the night or when I dare to imagine violent situations shown on television screens. What I can barely imagine is the enduring terror—endurance that continues with no apparent end except death. I have never felt the terror of people who live with injustice and oppression, with poverty, disease, and hunger, with constant risk of violence, whether face-to-face or from a remote missile, where the perpetrator is known or unknown.

Around 3,000 people died hideous deaths in the terrorist attacks in New York on 11 September 2001; more were injured, and many others experienced terror and grief. I was due to fly out of New York that afternoon and I recall my terror of separation from my family, and my terror of the unknown. The names, images, and stories were well documented, caught on camera and video, the terror shared worldwide through the media. The perpetrators were identified. Mourning, blame, retaliation, and retribution followed.

On another continent, on 3 December 1984, in the sleeping city of Bhopal in central India, at least 8,000 people died with their eyes and lungs on fire, drowned in their own fluids, and crushed in narrow alleys trying to escape a cloud of poison gas from the Union Carbide pesticide factory. I have read accounts of that night and they fill my heart with horror, with terror. Twenty years on, more than 120,000 people in Bhopal are still ill, one a day dying of gas-related causes, thousands living in extreme poverty unable to work or provide food for their families. The perpetrators of that ongoing terror refuse to accept the charges of 'culpable homicide' for a death toll that has officially exceeded 20,000, [1] described by Greenpeace as 'an ongoing environmental and health catastrophe'. [2]

What I know is that I need to be able to dig deep in my empathy and not allow myself to become numb to the atrocities of both immediate and ongoing terror. I need to dare to imagine the horror of a situation, and to recognize the trail of causes leading to the terrible consequences. The terror experienced in Bhopal did not start the night the silent plume of gas drifted over the slum dwellings. Its origins were in the corporate world that placed a chemical plant in that location and then failed to meet safety regulations or clean up the site after the chemical leak. The terror experienced in New York did not start the morning two hijacked planes flew into the World Trade Centre. Its origins lay in the political and economic worlds of a superpower and in the world of conflict between fundamentalist Christians and Muslims (Vidal, 2002).

Terror exists closer to home for me at Scotland's Trident nuclear base at Faslane. In the beautiful Gareloch are four submarines with enough nuclear firepower to destroy half the world. These submarines are part of the British Navy—my country, my side. I know that they are deemed inappropriate, disproportionate, and illegal under the Geneva Conventions. [3] However, my government tells me these nuclear weapons are a deterrent and in safe hands. I need to be willing to recognize terror as terror, actual or potential, whoever the perpetrator. Terror is not determined by which side is being threatened or doing the threatening.

WHO ARE THE PERPETRATORS OF TERROR?

On 20 September 2001, when President Bush stated to the US Joint Session of Congress and the American people 'Either you are with us or you are with the terrorists', he invited an international audience to join him 'in answering force with counter-force and terror with counter-terror' (Bell, 2004: 65).

In another part of President Bush's address to Congress he repeated the

1. <www.bhopal.net> showing extracts from 777, the newsletter of the Bhopal Medical Appeal, Autumn 2004.
2. <www.greenpeace.org/international/news/bhopal-disaster-has-no-paralle>, the world's worst industrial disaster.
3. Scottish Campaign for Nuclear Disarmament, <www.banthebomb.org>.

much-asked question: 'Why do they hate us?' The word *they* became synonymous not only with the terrorists but also with anyone of Islamic, indeed Middle Eastern or Asian, appearance. The word *us* became synonymous not only with victims but also with the good, the free, and the righteous. How quickly those in power can label the perpetrators of terror by appearance, colour of skin, cultural dress, and religion. How quickly those in power can use national security and patriotism to deprive everyone of human rights and freedoms. How quickly those in power can blame someone else.

I grew up in South Africa on a diet of fear, apartheid, and *separate development*—a culture of *them* and *us*. I still find myself easily *taking sides*, and aligning myself with the *good people*. For *good people* you may read powerful, right, and with God on their side (Sardar & Davies, 2002). For me now, *good people*, ironically, are more likely to be the liberal minority, activists for peace and justice, and people suffering oppression and deprivation.

Perpetrators of terror are not confined to one side or another, to the presence or absence of military uniform, to the use of regular weapons, suicide bombs, torture or a sword. I am part of a system that supports the design, development, manufacture, and trade of arms and armaments. My taxes go towards funding this military action in Iraq where thousands of civilians [4] have died and many more have been injured and are without regular supplies of water, fuel, and electricity, or adequate medical supplies. I accept my responsibility for acts of terror in the world, perpetrated in my name.

We are now living in a world of international terrorism, a world in which 'terrorism is the war of the weak and war is the terrorism of the strong' (Bell, 2004: 59). One hundred years ago, only 15 per cent of the deaths in conflict areas were civilians; since the end of the Cold War, 90 per cent of those killed in conflict areas have been civilians. [5]

Sometimes I can acknowledge and understand the actions of brutality and violence, of self-gratification and destruction, *and* remember that the people who commit these atrocities and perpetrate terror are human beings. At other times I face an impenetrable wall where the situation and the perpetrators appear to be beyond my capacity to understand. Then I feel overwhelmed by my feelings of rage, sorrow, and compassion for the victims, and I resort to judgement, blame and dismissal of the perpetrators.

I have an image of concentric circles. In the inner circle are those I tolerate and in the outer circle are those I do not tolerate. In the in-between circle are those about whom I vacillate. The inner circle of tolerance contains people whose circumstances I can understand, whose stories I can imagine. The inner circle contains people who, although sometimes powerful, are usually powerless; people who are victims of terror themselves, people who are brutalized by the system in

---

4. <www.iraqbodycount.net>.
5. New Internationalist 367, May 2004.

which they live. The outer circle of intolerance contains people whose circumstances and stories I may also understand. But I see them as people motivated by privilege and power, greed and fear, people who believe in hubris, apparently ignorant of impending downfall, apparently dismissive of the suffering they will cause—the 'Chosen People' (Longley, 2002).

UNCONDITIONAL POSITIVE REGARD

I have returned to my earliest sources on the complexities of unconditional positive regard and reminded myself of its key features. It is an attitude of consistent acceptance (Mearns & Thorne, 1988). Both inside and outside the counselling relationship, unconditional positive regard can clash with my values, whether introjected by earlier influences or gathered in the process of personal growth and development.

Integrating unconditional positive regard into my daily life has widespread consequences, in family relationships, community diversity, national equal opportunities, and international human rights. How, when, and to whom I choose to express unconditional positive regard is a reflection of how I choose to live my life; it is my relationship to and with people and planet, from litter in the street to global warming. In making that choice, I accept my responsibility to respond with wide vision, willingness, and generosity of spirit. How I think affects how I live my life, as Lama Surya Das (1997: 153) writes with the words of the Buddha from *The Dhammapada*:

> The thought manifests as the word;
> The word manifests as the deed;
> The deed develops into habit;
> And habit hardens into character;
> So watch the thought and its ways with care,
> And let it spring from love
> Born out of concern for all beings ...
> As the shadow follows the body,
> as we think, so we become.

I need to be willing to suspend judgement, giving myself time to explore and understand my fears, and to reach beyond my fear to acknowledge and understand the threat I am experiencing. I need to be prepared to live my values and express my attitudes through my actions and words in a way that is sustaining for me and for others. Suzanne Spector (1999: 188), writing on the person-centred approach, describes how 'when the mind-set of the past is confronted with the wealth of possibilities and options, the culture may become overwhelmed and take refuge in old patterns of fortress tribalism and division of the world into us and them.' I value her view of starting 'with the concept of the "we" ' (1999: 189) as a way of resisting the pull of taking sides.

The key to unconditional positive regard lies for me in interrelatedness, and my willingness to dare to explore the bigger picture, and to imagine the bigger story. I am inspired by the words of Martin Luther King:

> In a real sense all life is interrelated. We are caught in an inescapable network of mutuality, tied in a single garment of destiny. Whatever affects one directly affects all indirectly. (Letter from Birmingham Jail, 1963: 85)

HOW DO I OFFER UNCONDITIONAL POSITIVE REGARD TO PERPETRATORS OF TERROR?

All that you have read so far is the back-story to my response to that question: definitions of the terms and discoveries in my journey towards answering the question. What follows is a gathering of stories that demonstrate qualities familiar to people committed to the person-centred approach and familiar to those committed to the practice of non-violence. In these stories you will meet people who have inspired me with their courage and determination, their imagination and honesty, and above all their belief in possibilities and their faith in hope. Each of these qualities weaves the cloth of unconditional positive regard I can draw around me in my relationship with perpetrators of terror. That cloth reminds me of my choices; that cloth folds easily around me at times; that cloth falls heavily to the ground at others.

I need to be honest with myself, to be congruent, to be open to all my feelings and thoughts, to be able to hold them all, to be able to hold the *both–and*, to be willing to ask myself *and what else?*

Carl Rogers recognized 'the complexity of one's changing self in each significant moment' (1967: 172), believing we are capable of change, as individuals, as groups or as nations. He emphasized the values of being open and transparent, and believed that this is what makes the difference in relationships between individuals as well as between nations—that every human being is capable of moving towards being constructive and trustworthy.

I have no experience of violence to myself, and I was not in South Africa when my cousin's teenage son and daughter were murdered on New Year's morning in 1999. However, my feelings about this violent act are of horror, of fear, of pain, and of deep sorrow. I don't know what led the killer to take those young people to a deserted place, strip them naked, and shoot them. I feel almost overwhelmed by nausea and revulsion remembering what happened, and yet when I allow myself to think of their killer, I feel not only horror but also deep sadness. I don't hate the person (believed to be a man) who killed them. I don't know his story, the story of another human being.

Nor have the killers of my childhood best friend's husband in South Africa some 10 years earlier. This killing was political, and I feel rage and hatred for a regime that was so brutal in its policies and attitudes that human beings became perpetrators of terror, humiliation, violence and death. To feel hatred and blame and hold onto those feelings uses up energy that can be better expressed in thoughts and actions which sustain me and those around me. To feel anger and use that energy constructively and creatively serves me well.

For me, the story I hear or the story I tell myself is what makes the difference—the circumstances of the story, and how much of the story I am willing to hear, imagine, and then feel. It is the words I hear, and the thoughts and images I create in my mind that make the difference—the labelling, generalizing, blaming and *taking sides—or not.*

So many stories break and unfold as the media describe the process; often, so little context is given. How do I know which side to take, whether to support one side or another? The Glasgow University Media Group (Philo & Berry, 2004) describes lack of context as one of the main findings in research of television coverage of the current conflict between the Israelis and Palestinians. They point out that information is presented differently for Palestinians and Israelis on casualties and motives, and superficial coverage demonstrates how easily ignorance and misunderstanding develop. I am beginning to realize how much easier it is to demonize, to take sides, to succumb to a culture of polarity. I am realizing how much information I need to understand the circumstances, the process, the story; how much willingness I need to be open to the bigger picture and to allow myself to feel compassion and express empathy.

I have been encouraged and inspired by the stories of men and women in many parts of the world who have been able to feel their pain and rage, and also to reach out and make contact with perpetrators of terror. For some, this means being in physical contact with the person or people who caused them harm. For others, this means finding a way to make contact with *others* across the divides of race, religion, gender or *difference.* For still others, their passion for peace, justice, truth and reconciliation has taken them on a lifetime journey of seeking for and finding ways of meeting violence with non-violence, meeting intense fear with patience and courage, meeting rage with empathic understanding and forgiveness. I am learning much from people who have come together in projects like the Forgiveness Project [6] and Peace Direct [7] and are finding a language in which to express their feelings of pain and of hope.

In the summer of 2004, I heard of Jo Berry, whose father, Sir Anthony Berry, died in the IRA Brighton bomb in 1984. I was deeply moved by her

---

6. An organization working with grassroots projects in the fields of conflict resolution, reconciliation and victim support <www.theforgivenessproject.com>.

7. A movement of people challenging violent responses to international, regional, national and local conflicts through peaceful resolution of conflict <www.peacedirect.org>.

journey through grief and blame, pain and anger in search of healing. To make sense of her traumatic loss, Jo began listening to the stories of ex-prisoners in Ireland, and as she did so, she discovered new feelings of disloyalty and experienced accusations of betrayal.

As part of her healing process, Jo wanted to contact Patrick Magee, then serving eight life sentences for the Brighton bombing. She wanted to meet him 'as a human being and to hear his story' (Peace Direct, 2004: 16). In 1999, under the Good Friday Agreement, Patrick was released from prison. They met for the first time in 2000, and talked for three hours. Both of them needed to tell their story; both wanted to be understood; both were looking for personal transformation. They have met many times since. Patrick is clear that he does not seek forgiveness, and Jo expresses unease with the word itself, saying:

> [I]f I forgive Patrick I will never again be able to feel challenging emotions such as rage and anger. And yet, I've had an experience of such empathy with him that I've felt there is nothing to forgive. I have walked in Patrick's footsteps for a long time and a part of me has finally reached a place of understanding and acceptance ... The judgements fall away as I realize that if I had lived his life I may have made the same decisions. This experience stays with me and gives me the freedom to feel all of my emotions. (Peace Direct, 2004: 17–18)

Patrick speaks of his personal obligation to meet Jo, believing that through understanding and respect there is a way forward. He has been able to express his experience of injustice and the oppression of the Republican Catholic community in Northern Ireland—not for a brief period, but for generations. He describes the process of meeting with Jo as 'an experiment', both of them being willing to risk the unknown.

The stories of both Patrick and Jo have helped me to make sense of some of my dilemmas and difficulties, to explain the process of being able to retain feelings which at the time feel overwhelming, and also to empathize with the perpetrator, or not. I have learned from them about patience and commitment, resilience and perseverance. And in meeting them face to face, I have witnessed the deep respect they have for each other. As they continue their personal work separately and together, they also contribute to the peace process nationally and internationally,[8] taking their experiences out to others who are struggling with issues of retaliation, restitution, and reconciliation. While Jo is clear she no longer feels a victim, and is more focused on shared experience than division, Patrick is clear 'no one side is blameless' and is convinced of the need to address 'our own culpability' as well as the 'hierarchy of culpability' (Peace Direct, 2004: 29). Both are realistic about the difficulties of peace work; both are strengthened by hope.

---

8. Projects they have started include Causeway and Building Bridges for Peace, <www.buildingbridgesforpeace.org>.

My meeting with Jo and Patrick, on the 20th anniversary of the Brighton bomb and of the violent death of Jo's father, was not how I imagined it would be. I have spoken of feeling inspired by their stories, but that evening in London, I discovered a confusing disquiet in me that took several weeks to unravel. Jo spoke eloquently and with deep feeling, and I became aware of her quiet presence at the centre of the gathering. I felt myself watching and waiting for Patrick to speak; and as he continued to defer to Jo, I experienced a growing unease.

I now understand that I had unconsciously ascribed victim status to Jo, as an innocent *individual* caught up in an attack on the Conservative Party, symbol of oppression in Northern Ireland. I had unconsciously ascribed victim status to Patrick, as one of an oppressed *group* in Northern Ireland. Up to that moment, I felt drawn to them both as individuals, and yet during the meeting I felt myself wanting to champion Patrick—I was *taking sides*. As members of a *group*, rather than individuals, I saw Jo as the privileged one, and Patrick as the oppressed one, and I felt very uncomfortable with the conflict in my head and my heart. From my own privileged position, I was siding with the oppressed one, unable to hold perpetrator and victim in my head and heart simultaneously, unable to accept the victim in the perpetrator and the perpetrator in the victim, as well as my own capacity to be both victim and perpetrator.

Making sense of this process has released me from a confused place I had reached in my journey to discover how I offer unconditional positive regard to perpetrators of terror. With Jo and Patrick, I was able to free myself from prejudice and approval, from *taking sides* and to accept both of them. I am learning to pay attention to how and when and why I shift my position, no matter what the story. The language I use in my inner dialogue has a direct bearing on my thoughts, how I perceive both perpetrators and victims has a direct bearing on my attitude, and how I feel as a result of this process has a direct bearing on how I express myself.

Holding perpetrators of terror in positive regard is not simply being altruistic; I experience it as a matter of self-interest, an essential part of my ability to care for myself. If I fill my life with blame and hatred, with anger and pain, and if the stories that I tell are only the stories of blame and hatred, anger and pain, then I am not only demonizing the *enemy*, but I am also limiting myself. In doing so, like the perpetrator, I become focused on terror.

I have choices. I can choose to concentrate on blame and hate. I can choose to turn towards understanding and compassion. I can choose to stay in my outrage, my incomprehension, or my confusion. I am clear that getting stuck in anger, or consumed by hatred, can be harmful to me and to others. I need to be as open to the possibility of compassion for the perpetrator as I am to compassion for the victim. Archbishop Desmond Tutu, chair of South Africa's Truth and Reconciliation Commission, says of forgiveness, 'If you can find it in yourself to forgive then you are no longer chained to the perpetrator.' [9]

---

9. <www.theforgivenessproject.com/stories>.

I need to be able to hold onto my humanity, in its fullness, and to make choices as to how best to live and to be effective. To do this I have identified a set of principles. I believe that people:

- are worthy of respect as fellow human beings
- have no monopoly of truth—diverse truths can exist together
- share responsibility for the past and are responsible for the future
- have the capacity to be both victim and perpetrator
- are capable of change

The tools I am finding helpful and encouraging in holding to my principles are:

- curiosity
- information
- listening
- empathic understanding
- imagination
- compassion
- willingness to live with not-knowing
- patience
- hope
- inspiration

I believe that the teachings of Carl Rogers about talking and listening, about empathic understanding, and about openness to acceptance do hold true in the world as well as in the counselling room. I also recognize that in a culture of fear and blame, of litigation and judgement, of retribution and retaliation, I need to seek out others who share my principles and my ways of being. I do believe that there is nourishment in being together and sharing common purpose. I need to pay attention to the possibilities of collective compassion and understanding in a world led and dominated by fear-driven politicians, corporate greed, and media sensationalism—a culture of collective blame and collective punishment.

In *Encountering Feminism* (Hopkins, 2004) I wrote of the terrorist part of me being an inhuman part of me. I now wholeheartedly revise that statement. The *perpetrator of terror* in me is as human as the *victim* in me. I need to be aware of, and to take responsibility for all of me and to recognize the consequences of my attitudes and actions, for me and for others. I continue to challenge myself to condemn an action *and* accept a perpetrator of terror without compromising my principles, to avoid the pull to take sides, and to remain open to each situation with hope and generosity of spirit. I stand with the words of Martin Luther King (1964), as he accepted the Nobel Peace Prize:

I refuse to accept the idea that man is mere flotsam and jetsam in the river of life which surrounds him. I refuse to accept the view that mankind is so tragically bound to the starless midnight of racism and war that the bright daybreak of peace and brotherhood can never become a reality. I refuse to accept the cynical notion that nation after nation must spiral down a militaristic stairway into a hell of thermonuclear destruction. I believe that unarmed truth and unconditional love will have the final word in reality. (p. 110)

REFERENCES

Bell, M (2004) *Through Gates of Fire*. London: Phoenix.

Hopkins, R (2004) On becoming an activist. In G Proctor and MB Napier (eds) *Encountering Feminism* (pp. 70–9). Ross-on-Wye: PCCS Books.

King, ML (1963) Letter from Birmingham Jail. In JM Washington (ed) *I Have a Dream— Writings and speeches that changed the world* (p. 85). San Francisco: HarperCollins.

King, ML (1964) Nobel Prize acceptance speech. In JM Washington (ed) *I Have a Dream— Writings and Speeches that Changed the World* (p. 110). San Francisco: HarperCollins.

Lama Surya Das (1997) *Awakening the Buddha Within*. London: Bantam Books.

Longley, C (2002) *Chosen People*. London: Hodder & Stoughton.

Mearns, D & Thorne, B (1988) *Person-Centred Counselling in Action*. London: Sage.

Peace Direct (2004) *Unarmed Heroes*. Forest Row: Clairview Books.

Philo, G & Berry, M (2004) *Bad News from Israel*. London: Pluto Press.

Rogers, CR (1967) *On Becoming a Person*. London: Constable.

Rogers, CR (1942/1987) In H Kirschenbaum & VL Henderson (eds) *The Carl Rogers Reader*. London: Constable.

Sardar, Z & Davies, MW (2002) *Why do People Hate America?* London: Faber & Faber.

Spector, SM (1999) Exploring the 'We': Global, relational and personal perspectives on being in relationships. In I Fairhurst (ed) *Women Writing in the Person-Centred Approach* (pp. 187–92). Ross-on-Wye: PCCS Books.

Vidal, G (2002) *Perpetual War for Perpetual Peace*. Forest Row: Clairview Books.

Wood, JK (1995) The Person-Centered Approach: Toward an understanding of its implications. *The Person-Centered Journal, 2* (2), 18–34.

Chapter 29

A PERSONAL VIEW OF HOW ACTIVISM IS RELEVANT TO THE PERSON-CENTRED APPROACH

Mae Boyd

WHY POLITICS IS RELEVANT

Like many others, I am outraged: a child dies every 15 seconds from lack of safe water; most of the 30,000 daily human deaths are preventable; half of the people living in sub-Saharan Africa are living on less than a dollar a day—half the level of subsidy given to European cows; a sixth of all humanity live in slums; and at least a billion people subsist on the equivalent of a dollar a day or less whilst the concentration of wealth among a handful of people at the top has set new records (Hubbard & Miller, 2005: 2). Person-centred counsellors along with others in the helping professions witness the emotional and psychological impact of this ill-divided world. We see the individual despair and existential crisis faced by many. We see the more visible exploitation and oppression experienced by women and children sometimes violently and sexually abused; by asylum seekers from war-torn and impoverished countries; and we see the emotional pain of many other marginalized groups. How we explain this pain to ourselves and how we locate ourselves in a system that creates this pain matters hugely for our development as counsellors and the development of better theories which can help us prepare ourselves to work, not as experts on daily living, but as human beings engaged in the same struggle as our clients. A quote from an Australian Aborigine sums this relationship up beautifully:

> If you have come to help me, you are wasting your time. But if you come because your liberation is bound up with mine, then let us work together. (cited in *The Just Word*, 2002: 1)

It has been a great liberation to me to find a way of working and a theoretical understanding in the person-centred approach that so respects and values individual human beings. Empowerment and liberation are central to the approach and this is what drew me, and I suspect many others, to it. It is revolutionary in that it eschews the expertise many therapists give to themselves through their powerful professions, intellectual theories, claims of a scientific evidence-base for their practice, and diagnostic categories. But what happens in a counselling relationship is only a very small part of the world a counsellor and a client find themselves in. We need to look outward to other explanations of social as well as personal change. Our shared world does not end at the counselling room door.

A crucial question for me is not just why social change is relevant to the person-centred approach but how we counsellors make connections with movements for global justice and social change. For it is these connections that bring light and vibrancy to the issues and debates within the person-centred approach. Political involvement is not just an optional extra or the eccentricity of a few. We can choose to be active or passive in that involvement—we cannot help but be involved. In the absence of strong political movements for human rights, the active process of bearing witness that we do as counsellors inevitably gives way to the active process of forgetting. As Corporate Watch put it regarding environmental concerns, 'the earth is not dying, it is being killed and the people who are doing it have names and addresses' (Hubbard & Miller, 2005: 222). Standing aloof is in itself conformist and conventional. We counsellors need a social context that 'affirms and protects the victim and that joins victim and witness in a common alliance' (Herman, 1992: 9). I want to be part of such a common alliance between the person-centred approach and movements for social change, other helping professionals with similar concerns, and the mental health users' movements.

COMMON STRUGGLE

In a world increasingly dominated and laid waste by global capitalism, it is the common struggle which continues to offer the best hope for the creation of a society based on the recognition of both universal and particular needs. In collectively struggling to change and improve the world we change ourselves. As person-centred therapists we aim to bring our complete selves to contact with our clients, and experience as a political activist is part of that encounter. Because it is a social relation, therapy has a real political content. It can touch the human heart and promote freedom but it can also undermine clients by accepting as normal and unchangeable, their lived social experience. We need to develop a political critique of our person-centred approach to reveal 'the hidden inner assumptions, [which] grounds it in its history and does not pretend that the observer stands separate from the observed' (Kovel, 1976: 13). In this regard, Peter Schmid makes some tentative suggestions including this need for social criticism which must have a critical eye on 'power and control, on interests and expertism; and they have to be emancipatory in nature' (Schmid, 2004: 48). As Rogers and Pilgrim point out (2003: 175) even our person-centred form of professional knowledge entails the professional having a general theory of human functioning and change that forms the frame of possibilities which each client unknowingly enters. We may decide to be non-directive or even process-directive, but it is we who decide. We may negotiate all things but we do so from a position of power. Expertise in all its forms is a source of disempowerment and we would do well to look to those who develop anti-professional critiques—and to know why some can argue that people may be better advised to struggle on without the 'help' of any professional (Masson, 1988; Furedi, 2003).

AN ENGAGED PERSON-CENTRED PRACTICE

In *Globalisation, Global Justice and Social Work* (Ferguson et al., 2005) the editors argue that involvement with social movements for justice can play a role in what they call the rediscovery of a 'new engaged social work practice'. Maybe this involvement can help us develop an 'engaged person-centred therapy practice' which could provide us with the powerful context for looking at the human problems we share with our clients and help us understand their very roots. We need further analysis of power in the counselling relationship of the kind already begun (Proctor, 2002) particularly in relation to current theories of oppression. But we can go further. Marx's theory of alienation is a theory of potentially enormous value to those of us working within welfare and social institutions. It helps us see the need to change the conditions that give rise to mental distress and estrangement whilst at the same time offering the relationship to clients that we see as so powerful within the person-centred approach. We need to explore the many different ideas, movements and theories that could add to the person-centred approach. Powerful as I believe the person-centred approach to be, there are no grounds for privileging our insights as person-centred therapists. That is why in any project for social justice we need to look to others concerned with social justice, whether they are other therapists from different traditions, other professionals, service users or political and social movements. We person-centred people cannot be relied upon to be trustworthy experts in living or 'credible secular priests'. We have to understand that the mental distress we seek to alleviate is over-determined by the social forces of poverty, warfare, ageism, sexism, racism, violence, trauma and loss (Pilgrim, 1997: 149) and that others have valuable lessons to teach us. Otherwise we could be accused of professional arrogance and a kind of psychological reductionism that usually has profoundly conservative social consequences. Like social workers, psychologists, teachers, psychiatrists and many others, we see in individual clients the effects of an alienated world. It is what we do with that insight that matters. To help prevent person-centred counsellors becoming another set of competing professionals, we need to look to the users' movements and their critiques of the content and delivery of services.

COUNSELLORS, PESSIMISM, CAPITALISM AND
THE NEO-LIBERAL AGENDA

I suspect there are at least a few amongst the person-centred tribes in Britain who were more politically involved in the 60s, 70s and early 80s but who became disillusioned with political life and retreated into more satisfying therapeutic work. It was indeed a difficult time after the miners were crushed and the Tory government looked as though they were there forever. The collapse of communism confirmed its nature—as oppressive and corrupt as its Western counterparts. In the USA the Vietnam protesters were beginning to show up in government and supported neo-liberal economic policies and agendas. Despite the radicalism of their generation, they had been persuaded that the only way to create wealth was to allow a free, entrepreneurial class to forge ahead. A trickle-down effect would then lift those in poverty in the Third World to better living and ensure, if not an egalitarian society, a reasonably prosperous one. This continues to be the argument of Tony Blair and Gordon Brown today and it is presented as if there is no alternative. No wonder many, including some person-centred counsellors, have fallen into a kind of fatalism and pessimism about ideas of social justice and social change. But hopefully we have not totally forgotten the exhilaration of being with students and workers fighting back, nor forgotten how miners transformed themselves in their struggle against Thatcher, nor forgotten the confidence and enthusiasm gained in the mass upsurge against the poll tax. The great movements of the 60s and 70s—the women's movement, the civil rights movement, the gay movement as well as struggles of organized workers—gave a context to the work of Carl Rogers. It was a radical world to inhabit for those therapists who chose it as their preferred location. Some drew parallels with other activists and theorists like Paulo Freire whose *Pedagogy of the Oppressed* (1972) laid the foundation of popular education and social transformation in Latin America. He was also a socialist who wanted to see revolutionary change and stirred up in people 'the capacity to dream of a reality which would be much more human, less ugly and more just' (Kane, 2001: 56). He is of interest to us in the person-centred world because of his similar beliefs in the intrinsic worth of human beings, their vocation to become fully human in communion with others—a project thwarted 'by injustice, exploitation, oppression and the violence of the oppressors' (Kane, 2001: 36). Between the 60s and 70s and the present day, it has not been easy to find such a dynamic and comfortable political world. But all that is changing!

ANOTHER WORLD IS POSSIBLE

A developing worldwide social movement with its cry that 'Another world is possible' burst onto the world stage in the protests in Seattle against the World Trade Organization (WTO) in 1999.

The anti-globalisation movement is the first movement that represents a break with the 20th century and its truths and myths. At present it is the main source of politics for an alternative to the global right. When on February 15 [2002], 100 million people took to the streets, the *New York Times* referred to it as a second 'world power', a power that in the name of peace opposed those who wanted war. (Bertinotti, in Ferguson et al., 2005: 222)

There is a new mood of radicalism fuelled by this movement often referred to by different names—'movement for social justice', 'anti-capitalist' or 'anti-globalization' movement. But as activist and writer, Susan George puts it: 'We are "pro-globalisation" for we are in favour of sharing friendship, culture, cooking solidarity, wealth and resources' (Callinicos, 2003: 13). As these different labels suggest, there are real debates within but, as a movement, it has moved beyond single-issue campaigns and there is a sense that as we march forward together, as we did in Prague, Seattle, Washington and Genoa and then at Gleneagles, in this project for social justice, we debate and discuss. We develop the movement and we change ourselves in the process. This movement is characterized by its enormous diversity on the one hand and its universalism on the other. In Seattle when we stopped the conference of the World Trade Organization (WTO) at the beginning of December 1999, we saw 'incredible sights of Teamster President James Hoffa sharing a stage with student anti-sweatshop activists, of Earth Firsters marching with Sierra Clubbers, and a chain of bare-breasted BGH (Bovine Growth Hormone)-free Lesbian Avengers weaving through a crowd of machinists' (Charlton, 2000: 2). This diversity has been replicated in the World and European Social Forums (WSF and ESF) culminating in 200,000 people from 135 countries at the WSF (<forumsocialmundial.org.br/>) in Porto Alegre, Brazil in 2005 and 20,000 delegates from many leftist organizations, non-governmental organizations and campaigning groups at the ESF in London in 2004 (<fse-esf.org/>). Worldwide links are being made between anti-war protests, trade union rights, fair trade, concerns about pollution, economic exploitation and other pressing social issues. Can person-centred therapists find a place in this list? It should not be too difficult for there are many ways to be involved.

YA BASTA!

As well as the massive demonstrations across the world against the war in Iraq, smaller actions have had an effect despite the mainstream media's reluctance to tell us about them. In January 2003 Scottish train drivers refused to move munitions; in Italy people have been blocking trains carrying American weapons and personnel; US military bases have been blockaded in Germany; thousands have demonstrated at Shannon airport which is being used by the US military to refuel its planes en route to Iraq; and disquiet is growing over the CIA torture planes, some of which landed at Prestwick, which have been moving 'terrorists' to countries which are good at interrogation (Miller, 2004: 27). As people become involved in one, often local, struggle, they are seeing the links with others and are making contact. The Zapatistas in Mexico, sparked by the attempts of both the Americans and their own government to extend neo-liberal trade policies to the poorest regions of Mexico, organized an uprising and told the world 'Ya basta!' (Enough!). Their slogan has been picked as a symbol of resistance all over the world. In the aftermath of the tsunami, many are asking how governments can provide for armies to occupy, bomb and maim, but cannot allow developing countries sovereignty over their own resources, or help in such a humanitarian crisis.

Whether you involve yourself in a struggle for trade union rights in Colombia, for land for the landless in Brazil, to bring the troops in Iraq home to Britain and America or to 'Make Poverty History', you gain an invaluable sense of empowerment and a lasting commitment to social change. Domingos, a former shoemaker who joined the MST (Movimento dos Trabalhadores Rurais Sem Terra—Brazil's landless rural workers' movement) puts it this way: 'From the moment in which you involve yourself in the struggle, you begin to acquire a bit of consciousness and you begin to fight not just for your rights but for the rights of all the exploited in Brazil and the world' <www.mstbrazil.org/>.

RESISTANCE IS FERTILE—THE POLITICS OF HOPE

What a good time to be thinking about the person-centred approach and social change! In July 2005 the G8, the leaders of the most industrialized nations in the world—the nearest thing we have to a world government, albeit self-appointed and unaccountable—met in the luxury of Gleneagles Hotel. No democratically elected international or national assembly has given them any mandate. No international law authorizes the G8 members to make decisions for the world. Yet over the past 25 years this is precisely what they have done. Their neo-liberal free-market policies have produced unprecedented global inequality, an impending global environmental crisis and the prospect of unending war (Hubbard & Miller, 2005). 'G8 Alternatives' along with a number of organizations from across Europe and beyond, together with unaligned individuals, took part in a stunning range of protests in Scotland in July 2005. Despite the many differences it united us in the belief that another world is possible. A quarter of a million people took part in the 'Make Poverty History' demonstration. Old and young, Black and White, children in prams and clowns with nothing more offensive than banners, songs and speeches, surrounded by police in full riot gear with dogs and on horses, protested outside an empty Dungavel Detention Centre. Permanently empty of their usual occupants of women, men and children seeking asylum and refuge is how we want to see Dungavel. Faslane nuclear base was closed and the carnival-like atmosphere was replicated in smaller actions around Scotland. Nearly 5,000 people attended a G8 Alternatives Summit discussing and debating *Ideas to Change the World.* On the opening day of the G8 Summit there were peaceful blockades of the roads. Despite misinformation, the redirection of coaches of protesters and intimidatory searches, 12,000 marched in a cacophony of chants, bagpipes and African drums up to the fence surrounding Gleneagles. Rose Gentle, anti-war campaigner, touched the fence almost to the hour of the year before when she buried her 19-year-old son Gordon. It is the nearest she has got to those world leaders who sent her son, ill-equipped and with only six weeks' basic training, to the illegal war in Iraq. That she is not alone in her grief is a powerful expression of the therapeutic nature of social movements. To be part of these social movements can only make person-centred counselling more moral, relevant and humane.

Then came the London bombings. This atrocity arose from the swamp of an aggressive foreign policy: it took Britain to war with Iraq; it has killed over 100,000 Iraqis; it has tortured innocent people in Guantanamo and Abu Ghraib; and it destroys hope and creates misery and despair. We as counsellors know a great deal about how individual human beings experience that misery and despair. I am glad to have been part of 'G8 Alternatives' and will now continue to be part of whatever grows out of it, knowing our movement is stronger. We operated on the basis of consensus and my person-centred values have been challenged to the extreme. But it is absolutely worth it. It seems clear to me that this person-centred approach that so respects and values human beings must ally itself with social movements seeking human emancipation. 'An Invitation to Explore the Person-Centred Approach and Political Processes', organized by person-centred counsellors in Scotland in September 2005 has been a step in this alignment. It was advertised by the following quote with its wonderful message of hope that each individual together with others can indeed make another world possible. It is as good a place to end as any:

> I heard Paulo Freire, late in his life, describe the conversations he repeatedly had with friends. This is my memory of his words. He said, 'They say to me, "Paulo, you know the corruption in the government, you've been exiled, why are you so naïve as to think you can do anything?"' He replied, 'To me, it is a matter of fact. It is an ontological reality that the next moment has yet to occur. I am in the present. I have the possibility of co-creating that next moment. Hope is not foolish; it is foolish not to use my subjectivity to shape events.' (Carol Wolter-Gustafson, 2005, personal communication)

REFERENCES

Callinicos, A (2003) *An Anti-Capitalist Manifesto.* London: Polity.

Charlton, J (2000) Talking Seattle. *International Socialist Journal, 86* (available from <http://pubs.socialistreviewindex.org.uk/isj86/contents.htm>)

Cheney, D, Rumsfeld, D, Wolfowitz, P, Bush, J & Libby, L (2000) *Rebuilding America's Defences: Strategies, forces and resources for a new century.* Washington, DC: Project for the New American Century (PNAC).

Ferguson, I, Lavalette, M & Whitmore, E (2005) *Globalisation, Global Justice and Social Work.* London: Routledge.

Freire, P (1972) *Pedagogy of the Oppressed.* London: Penguin.

Furedi, F (2003) *Therapy Culture: Cultivating vulnerability in an uncertain age.* London: Routledge.

Herman, JL (1998) *Trauma and Recovery.* London: Pandora.

Hubbard, G & Miller, D (eds) (2005) *Arguments Against the G8.* London: Pluto.

Just Word, The (Fall, 2002) (newsletter of The Ignacio Martin-Baro Fund for Mental Health and Human Rights) <www.martinbarofund.org/newsletter>.

Kane, L (2001) *Popular Education and Social Change in Latin America.* London: Latin American Bureau (LAB).

Kovel, J (1976) *A Complete Guide to Therapy.* London: Penguin.

Masson, J (1988) *Against Therapy.* New York: Atheneum.

Miller, D (ed) (2004) *Tell Me Lies: Propaganda and media distortion in the attack on Iraq.* London: Pluto Press.

Neale, J (2004) *What's Wrong with America?* London: Vision.

Pilgrim, D (1997) *Psychotherapy and Society.* London: Sage.

Proctor, G (2002) *The Dynamics of Power in Counselling and Psychotherapy.* Ross-on-Wye: PCCS Books.

Rogers, A & Pilgrim, D (2003) *Mental Health and Inequality.* London: Macmillan.

Sanders, P (ed) (2004) *The Tribes of the Person-Centred Nation.* Ross-on-Wye: PCCS Books.

Schmid, PF (2004) Back to the client: A phenomenological approach to the process of understanding and diagnosis. *Person-Centered & Experiential Psychotherapies 3* (1), 36–51.

Chapter 30

TOWARD A PERSON-CENTERED POLITICS

John Vasconcellos

BACKGROUND

Every one of us human beings ought be profoundly grateful to those bold visionary pioneers of humanistic (including person-centered) psychology— Carl Rogers and Abraham Maslow and Rollo May, together with their leading cohorts Viktor Frankl and Virginia Satir and James Bugental and Sidney Jourard, and many more. For they brought us human beings into the age of discovery of the person—searching for our selves and for meaning, moving toward becoming a person, growing in authenticity and transparency, and becoming whole persons whose intellects and emotions and bodies are each fully liberated and altogether integrate.

All that leads each of us toward becoming possessed of what Maslow characterized as a *'democratic character structure'*—which really existentially equips and prepares us to live, individually and altogether, engaged in constituting and operating a truly democratic society.

With that opportunity so grandly presented to us, each of us humans owes it to both ourselves and to our society at large to search out and explore and adopt and experience at least some of the various therapeutic modalities which have arisen from our discovery of our personhood, altogether enabling each of us to aspire to and realize our innate potential for becoming a whole healthy human being. Only that will enable each and all of us, individually and altogether to grow and rise to the enormous historic opportunity and challenge now so profoundly confronting us all.

For our traditional society—especially our politics and our governments, most all of our institutions and our policies, our programs and our practices— are today failing us miserably, often entirely. They are failing both (in their capacity) to inspire us, and (in their capacity) to enable us to solve our problems. And in my estimation they are beyond fixing, they cannot be improved so as to become able to deliver what it takes to meet our growing human visions and needs and aspirations.

That is because, even as we humans have developed and boast of our 'New Economy', (including entrepreneurship, information and knowledge, the Internet and its going global) and cherish our 'New Demography' (including women as equals with men, all races and nationalities appreciated and welcomed, gays and lesbians out of their closets and senior citizens out of their nursing homes, and everybody valued and welcomed—however dis/abled), and revel in our 'New Consciousness' (including self-esteem and authenticity, embodiment and integration, partnership and collaboration—altogether holistic and humanistic)— we yet find ourselves stuck with 'The same old politics'.

Here and now we owe it to ourselves and to our larger society to recognize, and to commit ourselves, again individually and altogether, to undertake the next great era of discovery—how to translate the tenets of our person-centered psychology into the entirety of our social and political realms and how to transform the entirety of our social and political realms according to the faithful tenets of our person-centered psychology.

It is not hyperbole to state that the very future of our human race depends upon our successfully making this revolutionary transformative journey altogether—beginning right now!

This socio-political frontier is immediate and daunting, as well as essential and vital to our hopes and future—because our own individual capacity for fully realizing ourselves as persons depends upon the totality of our respective life experiences, which come at the hands of those who operate our culture and institutions and their various processes and policies and programs.

Fully appreciating the promise and application of person-centered psychology, we cannot afford to any longer tolerate or perpetuate our traditional culture's cynical assumptions regarding our human nature and potential, and its resulting programs and practices, with their crippling (even paralyzing) effects upon our capacity for fully recognizing and then realizing our full humanness.

We owe it to ourselves and to each other right now to faithfully and boldly and enduringly carry our enhanced selves wholeheartedly into a comprehensive effort to create instead a new person-centered politics—serving to transform our politics and our governments at every level, as well as the entirety of our social realms.

Our calling is therefore altogether radical and subversive—because it goes to the very root of our society and culture and institutions, and deeply challenges and subverts the entirety of our old culture's basic formative assumptions regarding our human nature and potential. We must enlist and mobilize ourselves right now in nothing less than 'The new human revolution!'

Futurist Willis Harman in his 1969 essay, *The New Copernican Revolution*, first called our attention to this emerging revolution when he compared it to that initiated by Copernicus and Galileo regarding the centrality of the earth versus the sun—which served to subvert all of science and religion and culture, and propelled us into the next stage of human aspiration and exploration, discovery and realization.

Harman went on to point out our subsequent additive revolutions spawned by the discoveries of Charles Darwin (evolution) and Sigmund Freud (the discovery of our interior dimension and landscape)—each again challenging our most basic assumptions about our selves and our worlds, and thereby subverting all the old ways even as each laid new foundations for the new world of discovery and mastery that are still continuing today.

Harman then appropriately identified and named our today's revolution as *The New Copernican Revolution*—shifting the entirety of our faith and expectations and experiences from the traditional cynical vision of our human nature as negative and sinful, evil and dangerous—to the emerging positive faithful vision of our human nature and potential—that is good and gracious and healing.

And of course our adoption of that faithful vision of ourselves, our human nature and potential, strikes right at the tectonic plates that under-gird our traditional negative culture. Our new vision serves to subvert all our old ways— of guilt and shame, fear and repression, disownment and alienation—for addressing our evil selves. Instead we find ourselves committed to nurturance and liberation, healing and self-actualization of the entirety of our good-natured selves!

What a revolution our humanistic pioneers began, what a revolution we are now becoming and advancing, what an essential revolution this is for all of us persons to recognize and enlist in and mobilize for, so as to fully realize all of our innately good human capacities and save our terribly threatened world!

Two decades later Carl Rogers, in an informal talk in the mid 1980s at the University of California, Irvine, expanded upon Harman's insight, saying, 'I've been doing psychology for 60 years, and I've come to believe that we humans are innately inclined toward becoming life-affirming, constructive, responsible and trustworthy.'

Therein we find our charter for a new sense of our selves, and of our human needs and rights, and a foundation for growing and expecting, wanting and even demanding, a whole new society, a whole new politics and government, altogether befitting who we are becoming as whole healthy self-actualizing persons.

The women's movement then went further and taught us that '*The personal and the political are one!*' My friend Stanley Commons once recognized and proclaimed, 'The politics we do is who we are!'

Let me tell you now my own personal story, living and mirroring the great historical movement of our times, pursuing my own dual odyssey, both for becoming a person and for becoming a political force for the people (36,000,000) and State of California.

For 38 years I represented 'The Heart of Silicon Valley' in the California Legislature (retiring in November, 2004 after becoming Emeritus Dean of the Californian Legislature). For those same 38 years I was in pursuit of becoming a whole healthy human being, a person who could survive and even thrive with/ in, rather than being done in by, the politics of our times. And I publicly lived my own search, even as I grew in stature and influence within the Legislature and throughout our state.

I initiated my search for personhood at the age of 34, in the hands of a person-centered psychologist, Jesuit Leo Rock, a protégé of Carl Rogers, who held me in positive regard as I totally came apart from my longstanding studiously constructed top-down guilt/shame/fear-ridden non-personhood.

My reinvention processes took me (during a 14-month period in 1968–70) through nine Esalen-type weekend workshops (including with Carl Rogers, Rollo May, Abraham Maslow, James Bugental, Sidney Jourard and John Heider).

Then I engaged in a decade of bioenergetics (with Stanley Keleman, then Lou Pambianco), which reintroduced me to my embodiment, profoundly changed my sense of comfort and possibility, as well as my capacity to live with wholeness and integrity, seeing into and beyond the big picture, able to provide leadership of vision and action, passion and patience, idealism and pragmatics, altogether a much more whole person leading a much more holistic life, effectively on both fronts, personal and political.

Perhaps you want to reflect upon your own personal odyssey, recognizing whether, and whether and how, it is preparing you for taking a much more inspired and visionary and public and pragmatic role in our effort to create and advance a whole new faithful politics.

For it is now time for each and all of us to carry our enhanced healthier selves into a crusade to create such a new politics—befitting who we are becoming as self-esteeming self-actualizing persons. And in fact, we have begun to envision and design, create and generate such a whole new politics. We have named it *The Politics of Trust.*

And so it is that each and all of us growing human beings must commit and engage ourselves, enlist and mobilize ourselves altogether in carrying forward our *New Fully Human Revolution.* Nothing else can satisfy us and our heightening aspirations and deepening capacities, nothing less can transform and save our culture and society and institutions, and our human race itself.

So in addition to our gratitude to our person-centered pioneers, we must face our challenge and whole-heartedly accept and live out our resultant responsibility. My educator father's lesson to me was 'From those to whom privilege and opportunity are given, we have the right to expect much'—and I would add—including their full engagement in our human struggle/s to improve our human condition/s.

So we must now, each and all of us, enlist ourselves in an historic effort, broad and deep, smart and strategic, wise and comprehensive—to assure that every institution and practice, policy and program, is entirely transformed according to our faithful person-centered vision of our selves, our human nature and potential.

It's time we recognize the social and political character of who we are becoming as persons, it's time we engage ourselves altogether in realizing the promise of this New Copernican Revolution.

That pathway necessarily includes each and both of two bold radical whole agendas—a process agenda and a content (subject matter) agenda—each and both befitting our enhanced sense of our selves, who we are becoming as persons, as we grow toward recognizing and then realizing our innate capacity for becoming life-affirming, constructive, responsible and trustworthy.

The resultant process agenda certainly must include all of our politics and government (as well as all of our society and culture) becoming increasingly open and transparent, democratic and egalitarian, appreciating and nurturing, inclusive and participatory, with resultant healthy individual persons and healthy communities, each encouraging the other.

THE EXPANDING HUMAN AGENDA

Already we have begun to recognize the import of our faithful vision in our personal lives—from natural childbirth all the way to the more natural dying of the hospice movement—including our own self-esteem, our parenting, our learning, our healing, our sustainable economic development, our conserving our environment, our preserving public safety and our aging, and including truly person-centered visions of truly healthy human leadership.

We have identified 16 of these public policy arenas, altogether constituting what we have named, 'The Expanding Human Agenda'. Each of these embodies our person-centered approach to public policy, transforming our entire culture and institutions, policies and programs, into person-centered operations. And we have already developed in almost every one of these arenas, model person-centered policy initiatives.

PRINCIPLE 1 SELF-ESTEEM AND RESPONSIBILITY

Each of us human beings arrives inclined toward goodness, full of potential, altogether deserving of self-esteem.

PRINCIPLE 2 FAMILIES AND PARENTING

Every child deserves and benefits from parents who have developed their capacity to nurture healthy growth and development.

PRINCIPLE 3 KINDERGARTEN – GRADE 12 TEACHING AND LEARNING

Each child arrives wired for learning, with a powerful instinctual drive for learning that must be recognized, liberated and encouraged to become life-long self-sustaining learners.

PRINCIPLE 4 HOLISTIC HIGHER EDUCATION

Every adult learner deserves and benefits from an advanced education that is whole-person-centered, which empowers her/him to become passionate self-initiating learners for life.

PRINCIPLE 5 HOLISTIC HEALTH AND HEALING

Each human arrives with an inherent capacity for wellness, is responsible for choosing a healthy lifestyle, augmenting that with holistic and allopathic modalities as needed.

PRINCIPLE 6 DIVERSITY AND INCLUSION

Each of us humans arrives as a unique worthy person, deserving of acceptance and dignity, equality of opportunity, full inclusion and participation. We must outgrow any learned prejudice.

PRINCIPLE 7 INDIVIDUALITY AND COMMUNITY

Each of us individuals is innately inclined toward community, and a healthy caring community naturally supports the healthy human development and self-realization of each and every one of its members.

PRINCIPLE 8 CONSERVING OUR ENVIRONMENT

Insofar as each of us realizes our own good nature, we will recognize that all of nature is precious, deserving of our faithful stewardship.

PRINCIPLE 9 SUSTAINABLE ECONOMICS

Our new economy will prosper by recognizing that our human development and our economic development are interdependent and must be/come sustainable.

PRINCIPLE 10 HEALTHY ORGANIZATIONAL DEVELOPMENT

Every organization will benefit by appreciating and empowering each of its members to realize her/his innate capacities for growth and self-realization, trust and partnership and team-building.

PRINCIPLE 11 COLLABORATION AND PRODUCTIVITY

As we deepen our (experience of our own) trustworthiness, we'll more readily trust other persons, find ourselves more inclined toward partnership and collaboration, altogether increasing productivity.

PRINCIPLE 12 PROMOTING PUBLIC SAFETY

We humans are not born innately inclined toward violence—violence is learned behavior. We ought to seek always to prevent violence and, where need be, to treat and cure it. And our systems must in fact promote rather than lessen our public safety.

PRINCIPLE 13 PEACE AND NON-VIOLENCE

We humans are not innately warlike, rather we are inclined toward peace. War results from a breakdown of trust between persons and/or nations. The more of our trustworthiness we develop and practice, the less we will pose any threat to any other person.

PRINCIPLE 14 AGING AND DYING

Instead of only growing old, each of us humans must commit ourselves to be/come 'older and still growing', with continuing rights to lives of inclusion and dignity, opportunity and productivity.

PRINCIPLE 15 GOVERNANCE AND ELECTIONS

All persons have the right to open transparent honest representative government and elections, all grounded in our innate capacity for healthy self-governance, and always dedicated to serving our public interest/s.

PRINCIPLE 16 TRANSFORMATIONAL LEADERSHIP

Instead of needing followers, the finest leader inspires other persons to realize their innate capacity for becoming their own leaders.

In summation, we owe it to ourselves and to our grand/children to enlist ourselves in these respective efforts to transform each of those social and political dimensions of our lives. We must come together now, and grow and enlist ourselves further into a comprehensive crusade to realize the promise of our increasingly multicultural democracies, with gender equity, in this age of technology, in this global economy.

A PERSON-CENTERED POLITICS—'THE POLITICS OF TRUST'

Even as we individually transform each and all of these 16 social and programmatic realms, we must, individually and altogether, take the next crucial step. We must enlist ourselves altogether in a comprehensive effort to challenge and change the entirety of our social and political realms, toward a person-centered theory and practice, altogether toward a whole person-centered politics.

Such a person-centered politics must inform and transform the entirety of each and every level of operation of our government (from repression to nurturance), all our politics (from 'cynical' to 'faithful') and all leadership itself (from 'transactional' to 'transformational').

And we have very good news: such a person-centered politics is already under way, having already gained enough shape and movement that it is ready for your enlistment, our mobilization, altogether toward moving it into becoming the mainstream of our politics. It is, in fact, becoming recognizable as the most plausible and promising (both profound and pragmatic) pathway to that alternative politics of healing and hope we've all been so long yearning and searching for.

We've named our new person-centered politics 'The Politics of Trust'. I invite you to check out our website, <www.politicsoftrust.net>, for a working model of what is now available for you and to you as we seek to create a new faithful person-centered politics.

In these perilous times, it is up to each and all of us to live and act boldly, shrewdly and strategically—so that we can make what seems to be impossible, in fact operational. And that really sets up our challenge in all its enormity—it is ambitious, and it is crucial!

Our success in advancing person-centered politics depends upon the whole-hearted partnership of all the persons who have embarked upon y/our own person-centered journeys.

Hugely ambitious? Sure! And every bit as hugely essential! For our current politics and government no longer serve either to inspire us or to solve our problems. For as Einstein pointed out, 'We cannot solve problems operating out of the same assumptions that led to their creation in the first place!'

And 'The Politics of Trust'—proposing its utterly contrary faithful vision of our selves, our human nature and potential—strikes directly at the root of just about all of the problems that beset our politics and governments today—'cynicism'.

So let us commit and constitute ourselves to being the pathway toward a more healthy human future. Let us become the modern day equivalent of American revolutionary heroic journalist Thomas Paine, and so give words to what we are advancing that we make the seemingly impossible instead seemingly inevitable.

The future belongs to those who recognize emergent patterns and become and create vehicles for converging and unifying them into whole new basic operational systems. A person-centered politics leads the way into our future by discovering a formula for triangulating our *New Economy* + our *New Demography* + our *New Consciousness* into a whole new operational system, our person-centered politics, *The Politics of Trust.*

How timely! Our person-centered politics locates itself somewhere out front, beyond left and right, providing a place for all of us coming together into a faithful committed pragmatic coalition for effective problem-solving, to improve our human condition/s and to make better our entire world.

And our person-centered politics situates itself right at the intersection of the ever deepening disillusionment with traditional politics, and the ever more elevating aspirations of our many kindred-spirited human fellows. We must become hospice workers for our traditional culture of cynicism, and midwives to help usher in this new person-centered politics befitting our emerging culture of faithfulness in us humans.

Our enormous challenge is to smartly and strategically enlist and prepare and empower enough of ourselves and our fellow humans to coalesce into a critical mass for social person-centered change. And when we figure out how to converge and fuse the technological approach to empowerment developed through the Internet by the Howard Dean 2004 US Presidential campaign with this psychological approach to empowerment proposed by 'The Politics of Trust', we will have found the new fire that will sweep our respective societies and bring us altogether into a far more peaceful, hopeful healing human politics and world.

Little did we dream when, back in the year 2000, we initiated this endeavor, that within five years we would grow it into becoming the most plausible and promising (both profound and pragmatic) pathway toward that alternative politics of healing and hope we've all been yearning and searching for.

I am buoyed by the declaration of noted American political journalist Lou Cannon (not given to hyperbole), 'It surely will fill a void, and I know you can do it!' and by 85-year-old noted Los Angeles civic leader Fred Nicholas (one of my precious mentors), 'If anybody can do this, it's you!'

Finally, much as I am inspired by their confidence, I know my capacities for success are utterly dependent upon the whole-hearted partnership of you and many other leaders of our society.

The scepticism we encountered when we first proposed this person-centered politics has been replaced by rampant curiosity, hopefulness and encouragement— by more caring committed talented diverse persons. They are recognizing our promise, enlisting and taking ownership with a real desire to help us discover effective strategies for moving our person-centered politics into becoming the mainstream of our politics.

We have in fact proceeded to discover a realistic working formula for that new politics.

As Lao Tzu wisely taught, 'The longest journey begins with a single step'. We have taken that first step toward developing our person-centered politics into an inspiring model, reawakening grass roots democracy, really empowering the people, renewing government of and by and for the people.

The future is ours to choose. The time is ripe; enough persons are inspired and awakened, self-esteeming and self-actualized, centered and ready. I hope you find yourself resonating with this proposal for a person-centered politics—that you will make our vision your own, igniting your passion to participate wholeheartedly in bringing our person-centered politics to life throughout the world in our times.

Will you join us right now as a full-fledged partner in advancing 'The Politics of Trust'?

REFERENCES

Harman, L (1969) The New Copernican Revolution. *Stanford Today*, Winter, 1969.

Chapter 31

CONCLUDING REMARKS

PETE SANDERS

Gillian Proctor drew her opening remarks to this book to an end with the sentence,

> This is a gathering of many different voices; a range of contributions from academic theorizing and critical analysis through personal testimony, and description of radical projects to practical suggestions for change. (p. 4)

Regardless of whether you have dipped in and out of the book or read it from cover to cover, the truth of Gillian's statement will have become apparent. The variety of contributions in style and content is, and I don't use this word lightly, amazing. The book exercises those parts not usually reached by person-centred publications. Readers have been taken from pure theory through personal reflection to community action. After excursions into personality development, centuries-old ethnic conflict and many projects to improve social conditions and interpersonal relations, we end up with the *realpolitik* of a political speech.

This volume repeatedly visits the tension between the individual and the community in thought, word and deed, and like a puppy worrying a favourite slipper, it will not let go. And with so many voices, the effect is, thankfully, disconcerting. Just when the reader gets a comfortable confirmation of their views, they meet something challenging, unpalatable even, and so the exercise continues.

After reading and re-reading these writings in the editorial process, I was struck by the number of themes that kept recurring, independent and unbidden, from a variety of contributions. So, to conclude the book, and by way of reflection, I offer a few of these themes that seem to be arising when politics and the person-centred approach come together. I hope it is not too obvious to suggest that each of these themes could have arisen in many books with a political bent. There is something of the soundbite about them. However, I find it uncomfortable to contemplate why they don't figure more widely, other than piecemeal, when person-centred practitioners convene. I hope I can live up to at least some of the improved expectations of myself that I have after contact with this work.

POWER

Power is possibly the least surprising theme to emerge, since critics and advocates alike believe that the PCA has something to offer in the debate on power in relationships. However, it is clear that person-centred practitioners are no longer (indeed if they ever were) naïve as to its importance or the fact that *regardless* of non-directive intent, structural and role power is implicit in all helping relationships. We find person-centred practitioners wrestling with the implications of Proctor's (2002) analysis of power and person-centered therapy. In addition to analysis, several authors in this book bring their personal struggles with, and tentative solutions to, the issue.

ALIENATION

Notwithstanding its having been being mentioned in a chapter title, alienation is referred to in a number of chapters. Although it is not a term used by Rogers—he used the term 'estrangement' to describe the disjunction between self and experience (Rogers, 1959: 226)—the concept is clearly equivalent. In various places throughout the book, contributors allude to and directly discuss alienation from experience, from our 'real selves', from each other, from the world. It is noteworthy that, in recent years, the concept has enjoyed something of a mini-renaissance and is being more widely examined. This should not be surprising when we consider the person-centred interest in 'connection', 'community', encounter and dialogic approaches. What, after all, are connection and encounter the antidotes to?

INDIVIDUALISM/COMMUNALISM

Here we find another ubiquitous tension, this time one that seems to give human relations the tautness required to play the tune of life. It may well be a good thing that we can never resolve the dilemma of 'individual' versus 'society', since it contributes so much energy not only to the debate but to our everyday actions. It is the stuff of which politics is made and keeps re-presenting itself in many chapters. The person-centred approach has traditionally been located (some would say has *located itself*) at the individualist pole of this dimension and some contributors defend this position whilst others question it. The very fact that it keeps creeping in to personal accounts and theoretical analyses is testimony to its ubiquity. That it continues to be 'outed' and discussed in a person-centred forum can only be a good sign.

CULTURAL ISSUES

A clutch of chapters go to the uncomfortable centre of a rarely uttered question— can there really be a shortcoming in the theory or practice of person-centred approaches to therapy and wider applications? Is the PCA ethnocentric; rooted in Western culture and largely unfit or inappropriate without modification to other cultures? The frequency with which practitioners with non-White ethnic origins persist in asking this question demands proper consideration and a respectful answer. For obvious reasons their experiences must not be dismissed, but also because we are not seeking to establish person-centred theory as a universal totalizing discourse in therapy. We are trying to give voice to all participants in the debate about how we live with ourselves and each other. To that extent at least, the person-centred approach has a unique political contribution to make.

EMPATHY

It is interesting that, of the so-called person-centred 'core' conditions, empathy is the one that recurs more frequently as a theme. It would seem that, for this collection of writers at least, the mindful effort genuinely to understand the other person is the beginning of person-centred politics. Careful research would be required to separate issues of communication from empathy, since both figure strongly in this book, however, Reinhold Stipsits appears to embrace both the need for clarity and the open, undefensive cordial intent that might just make such empathic communication 'politics enough' (Stipsits, this volume, p. 253).

ACTION

Finally, weaving through the theory, value statements and personal reflection is the almost omnipresent call to action. Person-centred practitioners contemplating political presence speak with practically one voice: thinking and feeling, whilst necessary, are not sufficient, it would appear. *Being* is not enough—*doing* completes the picture. When separated, not only are being and doing both the poorer, but so is the whole human race, connected as we are.

To be whole political entities, we each need to act, whether in our individual domain of influence or in community with others. Interestingly it doesn't seem to matter what we do, as long as our doing remains true to our values, but *doing*, it would seem, is one of the ways we can reconnect with our experience, each other and the world.

REFERENCES

Proctor, G (2002) *The Dynamics of Power in Counselling and Psychotherapy: Ethics, politics and practice.* Ross-on-Wye: PCCS Books.

CONTRIBUTORS

Jane Balmforth   After studying English Literature at Durham University I taught English as a Foreign Language in Madrid and Rome. I later worked in Indonesia for Voluntary Service Overseas as a teacher trainer and Programme Officer, and then moved to Glasgow, where I trained as a person-centred counsellor. I currently work as a counsellor at the Royal Scottish Academy of Music and Drama and am learning about person-centred research while studying for an MSc in Counselling at the University of Strathclyde.

Gay Barfield, PhD, LicMFT, was a member of the Center for Studies of the Person (CSP) based in La Jolla, California, for nearly 30 years, where she helped create one of the first Women's Centers in San Diego and the 'Living Now Institute', among other national and international events. In 1984, she and her long-time colleague, Carl R. Rogers, became Co-Directors at CSP of the Carl Rogers Institute for Peace, a project to apply person-centered principles to real and potential crisis situations. She has received numerous honors from organizations recognizing outstanding women, and in 1992 received an award from the County of San Diego for 'improving human relations', particularly for a series of cross-cultural 'Living Room Dialogues' on inflammatory US/Mexican border issues.

Mae Boyd   I am a political activist because it allows me to keep human in this ill-divided world. It helps me understand the human distress I see in my work as a social worker and counsellor—and most importantly, how it can be transformed in the struggle for social justice. I work for The Children and Young Persons' Counselling Service in South Lanarkshire Council. My partner Dave and daughter Rachel are the loves of my life.

Jude Boyles has worked as a counsellor for 14 years. Prior to her training Jude worked in feminist organizations supporting women who had experienced male violence. For the last five years she has worked at the Medical Foundation for the Care of Victims of Torture. In March 2002 Jude set up and now manages the Medical Foundation North West, the first centre to be established outside of the central office in London. Jude remains an active feminist, and is a member of three feminist campaigns working around male violence against women.

Randel D. Brown, PhD, is Associate Professor of Special Education and Director of Special Education Programs at Texas A&M International University, and Editor of the *Journal for Border Educational Research*. His interest in the person-centered approach comes from interaction and mentoring of colleagues and friends. His professional focus is facilitating the development of special education teachers, educational diagnosticians and people with disabilities. Randel enjoys painting, photography, golfing, bowling, deep belly laughs and spending time with family and friends.

Khatidja Chantler is a person-centred counsellor and supervisor with a critical approach to practice. 'Race', gender and class are of personal and political interest, as are the ways in which these are erased in dominant theory and practice. Publications include: British, European and international journal articles; book chapters and co-authored books: *Attempted Suicide and Self-harm: South Asian Women* and *Domestic Violence and Minoritisation*. Khatidja currently teaches and researches in social work at the University of Manchester.

Mick Cooper is Professor of Counselling at the University of Strathclyde and a UKCP-registered psychotherapist, whose work is informed by person-centred, existential, interpersonal and postmodern ideas. Mick has co-authored, with Dave Mearns, *Working at Relational Depth in Counselling and Psychotherapy* (Sage, 2005), is author of *Existential Therapies* (Sage, 2003) and has written several papers and chapters on person-centred, existential and self-pluralistic approaches to therapy. Mick lives in Glasgow with his partner and three daughters.

Jeffrey H. D. Cornelius-White, PsyD, LPC, is Assistant Professor of Counseling at Missouri State University, Editor of *The Person-Centered Journal*, Associate Editor of the *Journal for Border Educational Research*, and a family member. He learned the person-centered approach in Chicago and in life. He is a social justice advocate and the author of several works in person-centered education, including a meta-analysis. Jeff likes to bike, swim, play, read, write, listen, talk, and interact with nature.

Renata Beatriz da Silva is Brazilian, a clinical psychologist, person-centred therapist and play therapist. She is completing a MSc in clinical psychology at Pontificia Universidade Católica do Rio Grande do Sul (PUC-RS) with a grant from CAPES. She has been working as supervisor in the program that provides person-centred therapy to impoverished and maltreated children and adolescents described in Chapter 14.

Elizabeth S. Freire is a Brazilian psychologist, person-centered therapist and supervisor at the Institute Delphos. She has an M.Sc. in Clinical Psychology and she is completing a Ph.D. in Developmental Psychology at Universidade Federal do Rio Grande do Sul (PUC-RS) with a grant from CAPES. She had been the co-ordinator of the Person-Centred training program of the Institute Delphos and currently she is residing in Scotland where she works as tutor and researcher at the University of Strathclyde.

Deborah Giacomelli is Brazilian, a psychologist, person-centred therapist and play therapist. She has worked as supervisor in the program that provides person-centred therapy to impoverished and maltreated children and adolescents described in the Chapter 14.

Fiona Hall   I was a practising person-centred therapist for over 20 years in Britain. I now teach counselling at the University of Canberra and provide supervision to community counselling organizations. My journey towards an authentic existence began with three years spent studying philosophy, from which I learned that the way to health and happiness is a humanistic one. I live that commitment which includes struggling with the difficulties of being person-centredly present, but enjoying the depth of relating it offers.

Sheila Haugh is Convenor for the British Association for the Person-Centred Approach and a Senior Lecturer at Leeds Metropolitan University, where she is Course Leader for the MA in Client-Centred Psychotherapy. She has been involved for many years with the person-centred approach in various capacities; counsellor/therapist, supervisor, facilitator and trainer. She is a BACP accredited counsellor and a UKCP recognized psychotherapist.

Rosemary Hopkins   Born and educated in South Africa, I've lived and loved on three continents—Africa, North America and Europe. Now, as a wife, a mother and a grandmother, a counsellor and a peace and justice activist, I am exploring and discovering ways to integrate my values and principles in my practice, and also finding ways to express them in the political world, both local and global—or not.

Mike Hough is Senior Lecturer in the Counselling Unit at the University of Strathclyde. He helped establish and direct a postgraduate Certificate in Counselling Skills course and delivers counselling skills training to professional groups and voluntary organizations. He currently directs a school-based counselling project in 13 schools across the West of Scotland. He has conducted research on school-based guidance and pastoral care systems and his current enthusiasms include emotional literacy and school-based counselling.

Suzanne Keys works as a psychotherapist, supervisor and facilitator in London, France and Martinique. She edited *Idiosyncratic Person-Centred Therapy: From the personal to the universal* (PCCS Books, 2003) and has written about human rights, ethics, politics, love, prayer and therapy. She is currently interested in the interconnections between the political, spiritual, sexual and therapeutic. She is also curious about how becoming a mother for the first time affects it all.

Indu Khurana has been practising as a person-centred therapist since 1992, formally qualifying in 1999. She currently works as a therapist, a supervisor and a writer. Indu has contributed to *Trauma, the Body and Transformation—A narrative inquiry*, edited by Kim Etherington, as well as writing a regular monthly column in the *East London Advertiser* on social and political issues. Helping others to realize their fullest potential is Indu's passion and is a model of making your dreams come true by following the signposts of inner knowledge. She can be contacted at <indu@sunai.co.uk>.

Sílvia H. Koller is Brazilian, Professor at the Federal University of RS, Brazil, Chair of the Center for Studies on At Risk Children, President of the Brazilian Association for Research and Graduate Studies in Psychology, ad hoc representative of Latin America at International Society for Studies in Behavioral Development, and Member of the Scientific Committee of ISSBD Biennial Meetings. Her research focuses on developmental and positive psychology. Currently, she is the Editor of the Interamerican Journal of Psychology, and was recently invited as Associate Editor of the IJBB (ISSBD).

Colin Lago was Director of the Counselling Service at the University of Sheffield from 1987–2003. He now works as an independent counsellor, trainer, supervisor and consultant. Trained initially as an engineer, Colin went on to become a full-time youth worker in London and then a teacher in Jamaica. He is a Fellow of BACP, an accredited counsellor and trainer and UKRC registered practitioner. Deeply committed to 'transcultural concerns' he has had articles, videos and books published on the subject.

Pauline MacDonald has worked as a full-time Primary Care counsellor for the past five years in various locations in West Yorkshire, and currently Lancashire, since completion of a BA (Hons) in Counselling and Psychology. She works as a feminist client-centred counsellor hoping to empower individuals experiencing mild to moderate mental health distress. She has an interest in how organizations work and their political use.

Beryl Malcolm   I work in a Child/Adolescent Mental Health Team. I also supervise trainee Play Therapists. My background and training are in teaching, counselling and Play Therapy. I am particularly interested in ethnicity issues in counselling/therapy. My Play Therapy MA research focused on race and culture in child therapy. I have worked in various settings in the voluntary and statutory sectors. I grew up in London, but have lived in the North of England for 19 years.

Dave Mearns is Professor of Counselling recently retired from directing the Counselling Unit of the University of Strathclyde in Glasgow, Scotland. He is author of seven books including, with Professor Brian Thorne, *Person-Centred Counselling in Action* and *Person-Centred Therapy Today*. He also has authored *Developing Person-Centred Counselling* and *Person-Centred Counselling Training*. His most recent book, with Professor Mick Cooper, was published by Sage (UK) in September 2005 and is entitled *Working at Relational Depth in Counselling and Psychotherapy.*

Seamus Nash I work at Kirkwood Hospice in Huddersfield, West Yorkshire leading the Family Care team. I am a psychotherapist with a background in both social work and community education. I am currently researching practitioners' understandings of the term 'person-centred' for my PhD at the University of Strathclyde. Amongst other things, I am passionate about advancing the PCA in both research and practice. I also love small children, music, guitars, talking, listening and being with people.

Maureen O'Hara, PhD, President Emerita, Saybrook Graduate School has trained therapists worldwide, worked with Carl Rogers and others in developing large group person-centered processes. Maureen is a futurist and 'big picture' observer. Her current preoccupations include the impact of cultural shifts on the evolution of consciousness, the emergence of a new post-enlightenment global world-view, and what psychotherapists can contribute. Maureen is a Fellow of the World Academy of Arts and Sciences, and Fellow of the American Psychological Association.

Lois Peachey I qualified with a Diploma in Humanistic Person-Centred Counselling in 2003 at the age of 42. Since then I have been slowly gaining some counselling experience and working as an advocate in mental health, in which my counselling training has been invaluable. My learning at the sharp end of mental health informs my counselling work in a mental health support agency. I have become very interested in the political issues surrounding society's mental well-being and would like to study further in this area. I am getting involved in developing a gay and lesbian support group for mental health service users. I live in Ipswich, Suffolk, a diverse town in a rural county.

Clive Perrett Born 1948. Blissful childhood on country council estate. Rebellious adolescence in suburbia. 1965 inspired by CSV, then scholarship to Oxford and 3 years' confusion ; 1970s breakdown and drop-out years—beautiful chaos and radical left politics. Road sweeper, hospital porter, factory worker, gardener, playleader, support worker, university lecturer, FE teacher, now Dyslexia Support Co-ordinator in FE college. Married to a PC counsellor; one son and two step-sons. Unpublished PhD entitled 'Magic, science, and modernity'.

Aline Piason is Brazilian, a clinical psychologist, person-centred therapist, play therapist and supervisor. She is one of the Directors of Delphos Institute and also works as tutor in its training program in person-centred therapy. She has been working as supervisor in the program that provides person-centred therapy to impoverished and maltreated children and adolescents described in Chapter 14.

Gillian Proctor, DClinPsych, is a Clinical Psychologist with North Bradford PCT mental health team and an honorary research fellow at the Centre for Citizenship and Community Mental Health at the University of Bradford. Ethics, politics and power are her special interests and publications include: author of *The Dynamics of Power in Counselling and Psychotherapy* (2002, PCCS books) and co-editor of *Encountering Feminism* (2004, PCCS Books). She is currently exploring dynamics of power in a new relationship with her puppy!

Pete Sanders retired from practice after more than 25 years as a counsellor, trainer and supervisor. He is now a director of PCCS Books. He continues to have an interest in the politics of mental health and following the developing theory and practice of client-centred therapy.

Rundeep Sembi I am a volunteer counsellor at Leicester University and an advocate for People's Voices, an independent charity based in Buckinghamshire, supporting adults with physical disabilities and sensory impairment. I have a diploma in Humanistic counselling and a postgraduate diploma in Interdisciplinary Women and Gender studies from Warwick University. In short, I am passionately concerned with identifying and making visible the barriers that exist to hinder marginalized groups from achieving their potential.

Kamer Shoaib is a specialist Asian counsellor, hypno-psychotherapist and supervisor in the NHS. She works freelance and has a consultancy service in Oldham. Her psychotherapeutic practice is informed by 24 years of personal and professional experience and exposure to issues relating to South Asian communities in both statutory and voluntary sectors. She has researched South Asian women for her Masters degree. Her special interests include race, (socio) culture, diversity, identity gender, transcultural work.

Reinhold Stipsits, PhD, Professor in Pedagogics, University of Vienna, Austria, and Guest Professor in Cluj-Napoca, Romania. Licensed Person-Centered Psychotherapist in Austria, co-founder of various Austrian training institutions in Person-Centered Psychotherapy. I also served as a staff member in Cross-Cultural Workshops across Europe, worked with Carl R. Rogers, and also in learning programs in England, France and Italy. My work focuses on diversity and plurality. Through my experiences from working in the East and West I have gained a balanced understanding of the PCA.

John Vasconcellos recently retired after 38 years representing the heart of Silicon Valley in the California legislature. His tenure was especially unique because of his having engaged himself throughout those 38 years in an intensive personal growth and self-realization odyssey, which enabled him to reinvent himself as a person, which informed his 'expanding human agenda' and politics. Known as 'the conscience of the legislature', he is the co-founder of 'the politics of trust'.

Bea White is a person-centred counsellor and accredited by BACP. She has worked at a low-cost centre in Portslade since 2001 and is currently involved in setting up the As You Are Centre in Brighton aiming to offer affordable counselling, groupwork and training. She is interested in power, oppression and ethics, the impact of traumatic experiences and groupwork as a means of healing and reducing isolation. She believes in affordable, accessible and ethical services.

John Keith Wood (1934–2004), joined Carl Rogers as a graduate student in 1971 after a first degree in mathematics and engineering and career as an aerospace engineer. He collaborated with Rogers in writing chapters and papers, and on several projects where his particular interest was the application of client-centered principles to large groups. He married and moved to Brazil with his wife, the Brazilian artist Lucila Machado Assumpção and together they worked a citrus farm near Campinas where they initiated organic sustainable agriculture.

INDEX

PCCS Books

www.pccs-books.co.uk

• positive, radical, critical psychology •

• person-centred therapies •

• the person-centred approach •

Series

Steps in Counselling

Primers in Counselling

Rogers' Therapeutic Conditions

Client-Centred Therapy and the Person-Centred Approach Essential Readers

Critical Psychology Division